THE PARABLE OF THE TRIBES

The Problem of Power in Social Evolution

THE PARABLE

THE PROBLEM OF POWER

Andrew Bard Schmookler

UNIVERSITY OF CALIFORNIA PRESS

OF THE TRIBES

IN SOCIAL EVOLUTION

BERKELEY • LOS ANGELES • LONDON

University of California Press
Berkeley and Los Angeles, California

University of California Press, Ltd.
London, England

Library of Congress Cataloging in Publication Data

Schmookler, Andrew Bard.
    The parable of the tribes.

    Bibliography: p. 339
    Includes index.
    1. Social evolution.   2. Civilization.   3. Man.
4.   Power (Social sciences)   5. International relations.
6.   Social conflict   7. Choice (psychology)   I. Title.
HM106.S43   1983   909   83-9213
ISBN 0-520-04874-1

Printed in the United States of America

1   2   3   4   5   6   7   8   9

To my mother and my father
who gave me a great deal
to bring together

CONTENTS

BOOK II. THE NATURAL AND THE UNNATURAL

PART II. Power and the Loss of Wholeness

BOOK I

THE PARABLE
OF THE TRIBES

Chapter One

The Parable of the Tribes

1   Introduction

For Western man, the progress of understanding has been a humbling experience. At the dawn of the modern era, the heliocentric revolution in astronomy evicted man[1] from his privileged home at the center of the universe, consigning him instead to a tiny planet of what turns out to be a minor star. That left man nonetheless a special being among the creatures of the earth, a quintessence of dust fashioned specially by the Lord of the Universe in His own image. But this gratifying self-image was forever altered in the nineteenth century by the theory of biological evolution that revealed man's fundamental kinship and continuity with other living things. Still, man in his pride could point to his unique nature, to the spark of divine reason which ordered his life, elevated him from his own animality, and entitled him to dominion over the world. Then, at the beginning of this century, the brilliant insights of psychoanalysis showed how thin is the veil of consciousness and rationality, how dominated man is by an unconscious animal self, how man is not master even in his own house.

---

1. The word "man" here refers to the human species generally. It is used because our language makes it convenient, and is not intended to imply that women have played a lesser role in human life.

One fortress of our pride has remained. Whatever man's shortcomings as a creature, there can be no doubting man's powers as a Creator. In the globe-spanning structures of civilization, behold his works!

Now comes the parable of the tribes, a theory to illuminate the nature and determinants of civilization. It shows that even in those structures where man's power and ability are most tangibly embodied—even in the evolution of civilization—man is as much the victim as the master.

2. Understanding Change

There *is* something special about the human animal. Of all the earth's creatures, we are the creators of change. After ten thousand years of steadily accelerating transformations, virtually all the life on this planet is now caught up in the destiny of the creature with the unique ability to invent his way of life.

That mankind has the power to transform the conditions of life for ourselves and other creatures does not mean we understand the powers we exercise. Just as human hearts beat for aeons before the circulation of the blood was understood, so the forces that drive the stream of change in human social life could come from us yet escape our comprehension.

People often do not recognize, much less grasp, the effects of their actions. Four thousand years ago (as Geoffrey Bibby describes in a book of that title) change in civilized societies was so gradual that people thought that life had always been as it was then. The question of explaining change hardly arose in their minds. Yet they were actively (if inadvertently) effecting one of the great revolutions in the history of life—the evolution of civilization. Change that was cataclysmic by the standards of life's previous development was nonetheless too slow to be visible in the perspective of a single lifetime.

Now, change has so quickened that one cannot help but witness dramatic metamorphoses in civilized societies. Before our eyes, ancient tribal groups are being welded into nations. Whole societies adopt new forms of social and economic organization. Intellectual revolutions and technological innovations constantly alter people's methods of production, transportation, housing. Traditional values and ideologies all over the world are altered or overthrown as they encounter new and unexpected conditions.

History's acceleration has made manifest what has been true from the beginning of civilization: the structure of life for civilized peoples has been constantly subject to profound changes as new cultural ways are developed and replace the old. We can see now that civilization is an evolving system.

4

The question is: what determines the direction in which civilization evolves? It is a vital question, for if we are shaping our destiny without comprehension, how likely is it we will shape it well? For our powers to exceed our understanding is dangerous. What is remarkable about this question besides its fundamental importance is the paucity of attention it receives. There seem to be two principal reasons for this neglect: (1) some do not search for an answer because they believe none can exist; and (2) some do not search for an answer because they assume they already know it.

(1) In an age of specialized analysis, there is a prejudice against general questions and general answers: the study of forests is considered best pursued as the study of particular trees. Even as pictures from satellites open our eyes to sweeping vistas, our world view tends to be myopically mired in the magnifying-glass stage. The parts are delineated in excruciating detail, whereas the whole is left for some invisible hand to assemble or is regarded as no more than the sum of its parts.

Admittedly, it may be that no general explanation can illuminate the transformations of human life over the ten thousand years of civilization. The reasons for change might be wholly different from one time and place to another. Perhaps history must remain the museum of the unique that most present historians claim it to be.

If we nonetheless persist in seeking to explain the overall thrust of history, it may profit us to ask: what kind of idea might conceivably be able to encompass so vast and diverse a panorama as the history of the development of civilization? An admirable precedent lies before us: the Darwinian theory of biological evolution. In an era growing newly aware that living systems are changing and not fixed, Charles Darwin created a most satisfying theory for explaining an evolutionary process. His idea is elegant and comprehensive. All it requires are two things: a *diversity* of alternative forms and a systematic process of *selection* among those alternatives according to some consistent criteria. Once genetic theory could account for the generation of alternative forms, Darwin's concept of natural selection could, in a single brilliant stroke, illuminate one of the deepest mysteries of the universe. By constant operation over innumerable generations, natural selection could mold the indescribable complexity of the phenomena of life; the generality of its application did not violate the uniqueness of the particular living structure.

The concept of selection—combining great simplicity and extraordinary explanatory power—is doubtless one of the magnificent intellectual creations of the human mind. Moreover, such a concept offers the best hope of giving us an elegant and parsimonious explanation of far-reaching changes in complex systems. Although the past one and a half centuries have produced various theories of what has been called "social

5

evolution," very few have been evolutionary theories in that most essential Darwinian sense of postulating a process of selection among alternatives to account for the overall trends in the evolution of civilized societies. The goal of this work is to find such a clarifying evolutionary theory for the development of civilization.

(2) An evolutionary theory of sorts is already present in the minds of many. Therein lies the second reason why the pursuit of a general theory of civilization's evolution is not more energetic: why search for what one already has? To many people, change seems explicable by a commonsense theory, one so obvious in fact that it generally remains implicit rather than stated outright. I now present briefly this commonsense explanation. Understanding the drama of our social evolution is too important a matter to be left in the dim light of unstated assumptions.

3. The Common Sense: Selection by Human Choice

This commonsense theory of social evolution offers a benign and reasonable view of human affairs. According to this image, people are continually hunting for ways to better their condition. (One immediately recognizes the Economic Man of capitalist theory.) The alternatives are readily generated by this pursuit of improvement. The longer the hunt goes on, the more alternatives are discovered. And, since man is an inventive as well as exploratory creature, what is discovered in the world is increasingly supplemented by what people have created. With the passage of time, therefore, more and more cultural alternatives become available for all aspects of our cultural business—how and what to produce, how to govern ourselves, what to think, how to travel, play, make music, and so on. The process of selection is done by people. The criterion for selection? People choose what they believe will best meet their needs, replacing old cultural forms when new and better ones become available. Again, the resonance with economic theory is striking: social evolution is the product of choices made in the marketplace of cultural possibilities.

This theory can be aptly illustrated by the development of a cuisine. In the beginning, people are surrounded by plants and animals of unknown nutritive value and taste. Over the course of time, everything gets tried. People learn from their experience. They remember what tasted good, what was poisonous, even what diet made them feel healthy. They experiment with new combinations, new ways of preparing, storing, and curing foods. Constantly, they select for the most satisfying cuisine. As people from one region contact people from another, they exchange ideas and ingredients. Each group now benefits from the other's recipes, and altogether new recipes come into being as new combinations of foods become possible—one group's nuts are traded for another's herbs, citrus comes to the New World as the tomato is taken to the Old. Selection continually generates improvement.

Despite all the buffeting the modern Western notion of progress has received since 1914, the assumption remains strongly embedded in our world view that history is about progress. This commonsense evolutionary theory is part of that assumption. Each generation has more options to choose among, and more collective experience upon which to base its choices. Each can improve upon the heritage it receives. The story of civilization can be seen as The Great Ascent.

The reader no doubt suspects that I have set up this theory of social evolution by human choice only as a straw man to be struck down. Of course this is true—but only in part. Like most commonsense ideas it captures an important truth.

This model of selection can account for much of the development and spread of new components of civilized culture. In part, culture is indeed a kind of market in which new possibilities—in making pottery, in telephone service, in musical expressions, in vaccinations—replace or supplement old because people want them. Without making any pre-judgment about the nature and complexity of human wants, we may grant that choices based on those wants are important in determining the way our cultural systems evolve.

But this benign model of social evolution suffers from a fundamental problem. If such a process has governed the evolution of civilization, how are we to explain why human life under civilization has not been better?

4. The Rube Goldberg Problem: A Critique of the Commonsense Theory

The commonsense theory of selection by human choice leads one to expect a continuous betterment of the human condition. For a story of improvement, however, the history of civilization makes rather dismal reading, and as the culmination of ten thousand years of progress the twentieth century is deeply disappointing. It is not simply that history is strewn with regrettable events, with accidents leaving carnage and wreck-age on the thoroughfare bound for Progress. The road itself has been treacherous. If the stupendous historical transformation in the structure of human life has been the result of people choosing what they believe will best satisfy their needs, why have not human needs been better met?

The idea of history as progress is itself of relatively recent origin. And those who endorse that idea are usually looking only at relatively recent history for support. Compare premodern Europe with contemporary Western societies, the argument goes. Have we not come a long way from those dingy and bloody days of superstition, plague, despotism, and poverty? But even the advances of modern civilization have their nightmarish side, escalating as they have the destructive capacities of civilization. We look with mounting apprehension at the weapons of thermonuclear warfare, at the repressive apparatus of the totalitarian state, and at the disruptions of the ecological flows upon which life on earth depends. And even if we embrace modernization as progress, this stretch of history is but a small fraction of the total span of civilization. Looking at history as a whole, it is far from clear that the main "advances" of civilized societies have consistently improved the human condition. In earlier eras of history, the cutting edge of civilization's progress led from freedom into bondage for the common person. The great monuments of the ancient world were built with the sweat of slaves whose civilized ancestors had not known the oppressor's whip. After four thousand years the pyramids of Egypt can still stand as an emblem of the problem of civilization, that its achievements are more reliably impressive than benign.

If the same forces have driven social evolution throughout history, and if the way has been downhill at some times and uphill at others, we should not be sanguine that any recent trends toward progress point to the meaning of our destiny.

The idea of progress has relied in another way on the lack of a clear vision of the distant past. The life of primitive peoples is widely assumed to have been nasty, brutish, and short. The step from the "savage" state to the "civilized" is consequently assumed to have been straight up. Increasingly, however, as anthropologists have taken a closer and less ethnocentric look at hunter-gatherers, the evidence has shown that primitive life was not so bad. Primitive societies, a category confined in this book to simple hunting-and-gathering peoples, provide an important point of reference for two reasons: they give a perspective on civilization by showing the human condition that civilization has transformed; and they help to illuminate our nature as a species, for they show the kind of life we are biologically evolved to lead.

Without romanticizing the primitive condition into a paradise without ills, we must nonetheless appreciate that modern primitives (and, by an inferential leap, our primitive ancestors) led a surprisingly humane existence. Among hunting-and-gathering bands, the burden of labor is comparatively small, leaving more time than most civilized peoples have known for play, music, dance. The politics of these small societies are largely free of coercion and inequality. Relationships are close and enduring. Primitives enjoy a wholeness and freedom in their lives which many civilized peoples may well envy.[2]

This new view of our starting point demands a new look at the entire course. If we lift our vision of primitive life out of the degradation to which civilized mythology has consigned it, the commonsense view of social evolution becomes more difficult to sustain. Even if we grant that ten thousand years have improved the human condition, there seems something disturbingly disproportionate between the immensity of the changes that ten millennia of social evolution have wrought upon human societies, and the small (even debatable) advances in human well-being. If we were to persist in viewing the great edifice of civilization as structured for the purpose of meeting human needs, civilization would seem to be a gigantic Rube Goldberg contraption. Rube Goldberg's machines were comic because of the grotesque mismatch between means and ends— like a structure the size of a house to light a cigarette, or a twenty-eight– step process for waking someone up in the morning. If we view social evolution as the result of people continually choosing better ways to meet their needs, civilization becomes a kind of joke.

But before we are reconciled to this vision of history as ludicrous, we should see whether the commonsense theory of social evolution can somehow survive the evidence that the progress of human well-being has been both inconsistent and disappointing.

One possible way of meeting the challenge is to argue that when people choose they do not necessarily choose wisely. Whether one attributes the limits of human judgment to folly or to sin, people evidently often make choices hurtful to themselves. Smokers keep smoking, fat people keep overeating, procrastinators avoid necessary tasks, and few of us are as good to those we love as we would like to be. Saint Paul saw it as central to the human condition that we cannot follow even our own best judgment. And, of course, even our best judgment may not be very good:

---

2. The idea that the life of hunter-gatherers may be a particularly satisfying one for human beings is explored further in chap. 2, "Unfree Choices," and again in chap. 4, "The Question of Human Nature" and "Eden." The freedom of hunting-and-gathering peoples from warfare of the sort that has plagued civilized history is a focal point in chap. 3, "Red Sky at Morning," and is dealt with also in chap. 2, "The Mother of Invention," and chap. 5, "Fighting Mad." In chap. 3, in the three "Evolution" sections, the original size and structure of primitive societies are juxtaposed with the subsequent metamorphoses effected by civilization. Part of that picture ("Evolution toward More Effective Central Control") portrays the egalitarian nature of primitive political relations, a subject treated again in chap. 7, "Men Are Not Ants." That the economic life of primitives is not so beset by drudgery and the feeling of privation as many have imagined is discussed in chap. 5, "Under the Yoke." In several places in chap. 5, ways are described in which hunter-gatherers enjoy a wholeness and peacefulness of mind often subverted by civilized life. (The anthropological sources for the arguments are noted in the text.) The reason for this way of drawing the boundary between primitive and civilized is touched upon again in chap. 3, "Red Sky at Morning."

we build high rises on hurricane coasts and on earthquake faults, we trust deceptive and hypocritical politicians, we exhaust our soils, we ingest pathogenic chemicals. . . . So it should not be surprising if the course of civilization is full of blunders—political arrangements that become oppressive, economic systems that lead to famine, social organizations that produce anomie.

One can add to the shortcomings of the human decision maker the extraordinary difficulty of these decisions. For the progress of civilization has been a continuous advance into uncharted territory. Even the wisest judge needs precedents, and civilized peoples have repeatedly been compelled to deal with unprecedented problems. Even intelligent people, under those circumstances, will adopt solutions which do not work or which work today but sow the seeds of tomorrow's problems. Irrigation brings a miracle of greenness in the short run but leads eventually to the disastrous spread of deserts over salted soils. People are attracted to the manifest abundance economic modernization can provide but may not realize the costs in social disruption and fragmentation that development may entail. In the marketplace of social evolutionary possibilities, the payment due is not always calculable until long after the contract for "progress" has been made.

Both these ideas are valuable for understanding the problematic aspect of human destiny. People do indeed sometimes choose foolishly. And at the frontiers of social evolution people are faced with the difficult challenge of finding their way through uncharted, unexplored territory. These answers, however, do not seem sufficient to solve the problem posed by civilization's ills. The intelligence and industry of our ancestors is simply too impressive to allow us to load the failures of civilization to meet human needs onto their supposedly blundering choices. When we scrutinize what our ancestors in any given time and place were able to do with their situation, what generally stands out is not their folly but their soundness and their resourcefulness.

Something important is missing from the picture. It is like some problems that have arisen in the history of astronomy. What is visible fails to explain how the heavenly bodies are moving, so astronomers search for an invisible source of the disturbing force. Another body is presumed to exist even if it has not yet been seen, for its gravitational pull is manifest. Such is the gravity of the pull of civilization's evolution from the course of human welfare that we must posit a kind of social evolutionary black hole to account for the wide disparity between the expected and the actual movement of our systems.

It is time now to begin moving toward a new theory. We must go beyond the visible force of human actors making choices to discover a force more hidden yet powerful enough to warp the course of social evolution. Although the commonsense theory would lead us to expect history to bring the fulfillment of human dreams, one can as aptly call history a nightmare from which we are trying to awaken. Why?

5. Toward a Bigger Vision

The problem in comprehending the destiny of civilized man is that our vision does not readily encompass the magnitude of the drama.

The experience of a lifetime gives an inadequate perspective. Unlike Bibby's ancients of four thousand years ago, we can see change. But we have difficulty seeing what is constant amid the change. We were born into a vehicle already far along on an extended trajectory so that our present experience is intelligible only in terms of forces that acted in the past.

Of course, we have historical knowledge to supplement our contemporary experience. For the most part, however, the perspective of history has tended to reinforce rather than to correct a vital blind spot. That blind spot is our tendency to take civilization as a given, that is, to view our species' story as if we were somehow born to the civilized state, as if like Athena we had sprung fully armed into being. For many centuries, the study of our history meant the study of previous civilized societies. To look at where we began has been to look at ancient civilizations.

Starting with the wrong assumptions as given, we end with asking the wrong questions. Human beings, born into life, have always tended to regard death as the big mystery. But in an overwhelmingly lifeless universe, the dead is the given and the life we take for granted is the deep mystery. Being born into the conditions of civilization leads people into a similar error about what is the given and what in need of explanation.

History, then, has traditionally not allowed our vision to transcend the civilized condition that needs explaining. But in the last century or so, the perspective of "natural history" has revealed to us how extremely truncated is that old view of time. Our infancy was not in the cradle of civilization, but far, far back before then. Our human ancestors go back hundreds of thousands, perhaps several millions of years. But our ancestry is still more ancient. Our story, as much as that of any creatures on earth, goes back to the beginning of life, more than three billion years ago. Walking a time line of the earth's history overwhelms our provincial sense of time. From the earth's beginning to the point where life emerges is a number of paces. It is a long walk before mammals have appeared, but only a few steps from there to the appearance of the human animal.

11

The time of recorded history is scarcely visible. What we call history is like a period at the end of the long story of life on earth.

All this is now "common knowledge," but in most of us that knowledge remains only superficially integrated into our vision of ourselves. Old preconceptions die slowly. It is no longer intellectually respectable to believe the human story began six thousand years ago in some garden in the Middle East. But even a century and a half after Darwin's voyage, this cataclysmic change in our knowledge has hardly influenced most of our thinking about human destiny. Although many fine minds work at this process of intellectual integration, we have not yet grasped the full implications of the more grounded and complete perspective. This task remains central in the human search for self-understanding.

The larger vision is, in particular, indispensable to solving the problem we are investigating here. This work shows how the key to the mystery of civilization's problematic course lies in the extraordinary fact of the emergence of our species from biological evolution into a new kind of evolution.

To understand the world as we find it, we must go back to the world as it began. In the beginning . . .

6. The Way of Life

Out of matter and energy obeying natural laws, there emerged life. Whence came the stuff of the universe and the laws to govern its behavior are matters for speculation beyond the scope of my inquiry. Given them, the emergence of life seems to have required simply the proper conditions, and time. By chance, certain aggregations of matter emerged which had the ability to persist and to replicate themselves. The implications of this reproductive capacity for selection over time are obvious. Those aggregations with the ability to increase will begin as an infinitesimal proportion of the total system but will grow steadily compared with the static (inanimate) configurations of matter. Life gets a foothold in the early stages because the living is selected over the nonliving.

For living things to persist, or survive, their environment must provide them with the substances and energy they need to maintain and to reproduce themselves. As life grows denser, the environment on which each organism depends consists increasingly of other living things. The survival of each, therefore, comes to depend upon how well all the others maintain crucial flows of materials and energy throughout the system. Life requires environmental reliability. The implications for natural selection are clear. Selection molds not just individual species but entire ecological communities, favoring those combinations of creatures that most reliably act synergistically to maintain the flows on which all the creatures depend. As life developed on this planet, the networks of interdependence and cooperation expanded until some of the major flows became global in scope. The earth's atmosphere as we know it is a product of the living ecosystem.

Biological evolution is, of course, the story of change, but stability is one of its most important products. The regularity of events supports the health of life, whereas the unpredictable and unprecedented threaten it. The living emerged out of the nonliving and remain vulnerable to changes inflicted by the inanimate processes of the universe. Thus, the regular rising and setting of the sun and the regular succession of the seasons form part of the pattern of life for earth's creatures. But the unpredictable variations in sunspot activity can injure the ecosystem. Life has not yet managed to make earth's climate completely reliable, and inanimately caused disturbances (such as ice ages, or atmospheric disruptions) may be the reasons for prehistoric waves of extinctions of species.

Genetic changes in living creatures have often been the consequence of the unexpected intrusion of inanimate forces, for example, cosmic radiation causing mutations. Because mutations have been an essential ingredient of biological evolution, it is sometimes forgotten that the overwhelming majority of mutations are injurious. The very few that are advantageous, however, are selected for and perpetuated while the many, many others disappear. Although living systems change, therefore, they resist change more than they incorporate it. The new forms spread very gradually, and only if time proves them consistent with the long-run survival not only of the individual but of the ecological balance on which his descendants will depend.

We can better understand biological evolution if we see it less as a process of change than as a creation of order. Natural selection has molded an order of indescribable complexity from the molecular level to the global. Each piece of the intricate pattern of life must play its specific and narrow role in the whole. This order is rigid but not coercive, for there is no governing power in the system. Each creature follows its own law, but that law itself has been written by an evolutionary process that secures the orderliness of the overarching system of life. Each creature is free in the sense that none of its impulses are prohibited. But it is a freedom without choice.

During the course of biological evolution, the behavioral rigidity of living things has become steadily less complete. An animal that can respond to different situations differently has adaptive advantages. It is not that biological evolution has rejected the rigid in favor of the flexible, since the more mechanical life forms have remained abundant. Rather, certain niches in the ecosystem favor flexibility. The more complex and heterogeneous the environment an animal lives in, the better served it is by a wide behavioral repertoire and the ability to perceive what behavior is called for. That more flexible creatures like mammals have arisen late in the evolutionary process compared with the more rigid reptiles (not to mention still more primitive forms) is evidence not so much of superiority as of complexity and of the fact that greater complexity takes longer to evolve. Conceivably, such flexibility could be entirely programmed into the genes. Indeed, in insects some fairly elaborate discriminations are completely, or almost completely, genetically "wired." But after a certain level of complexity is reached, such an approach would be terribly cumbersome—worse than computers that play chess by considering every imaginable move at every point. Selection has therefore favored a more efficient route to behavioral flexibility—learning.

With the emergence of learning, the control of organismic behavior by genetic blueprints ceased to be absolute. A creature's own experience—not just the aeons of ancestral experience carved by selection into its genes—could now play some part in shaping how it acts in the world. The capacity to learn creates a new discontinuity between the living and the inanimate worlds. First came matter and energy obeying physical laws, then came organisms mechanically following laws inscribed by ages of evolution. The animal that can learn is something new in that the determinants of its behavior are not wholly created outside of itself. As long as genetic control remains absolute, the living present is wholly bound by the evolutionary past. With the emergence of learning, the present gains a degree of latitude to shape itself.

The emergence of learning many many millions of years ago, however, did not change the nature of the order that biological evolution had created. In retrospect we can see it as only a hairline crack in the tight structure of the living system. For one thing, the hereditary structure of the learning animal would itself greatly determine what was learned, channeling perceptions and predisposing the animal to certain lessons. A baby duck, for example, will imprint on the first object of the right size it sees moving in the right way after it is hatched. This example suggests one more reason why learning in animals did not really alter the basic reliability of animal behavior: the experiences in which learning would take place were in themselves quite predictable. A baby duck is virtually certain—in the absence of some experimenter's manipulations—

14

to imprint upon and subsequently follow its own mother. Harlow's experiments in depriving baby rhesus monkeys of their mothers has shown how significant for the monkey is the social learning it gets in its relationship with its mother. But in the monkey's natural environment, that learning will occur in very predictable ways in a reliable maternal relationship. What is learned, therefore, remained for millions of years an extension of what is genetically given. The two elements combined to form an essentially predictable animal nature that left intact the reliability of behavior on which the integrity of the natural order depends.

A hairline crack can always get wider. The escape from complete genetic programming, however slight at first, could always grow. However magnificent the Creation of biological evolution, without a Creator it cannot look forward. What is selected for is what has worked. The selective process does not "know" where a given evolutionary experiment will ultimately lead. For millions of years, the experiment with learning did not disrupt the essential continuity of biological evolution, the stability of the living order. But then the experiment created the great learning animal, man. Then learning created something new—the cultural animal.

7. The Emergence of Culture

Human learning has changed the world in a way the learning of other animals did not. This is not primarily because we are individually more intelligent than other individual animals, though we are. Rather it is because our intelligence has crossed that threshold where it becomes possible for us to pool our learning collectively and to transmit its fruits down through the generations. At that point, the capacity to learn became transmuted into the far more potent ability to create culture.

In the history of the theory of biological evolution, the most intense controversy was over the inheritance of acquired characteristics. Did the experience of one generation inform the genetic heritage of the next? Of course, this Lamarckian view was eventually rejected. With that rejection, the gains of experience became like a biological Sisyphean task— Sisyphus being the mythical figure whose task it was to roll a big rock up a hill only to have it roll back down and have his task begin anew. When a smart elephant dies, its knowledge dies with it, and its descendants must begin their learning from the beginning at the bottom of the hill. If we had no way to accumulate our learning, our intelligence would not significantly differentiate us from other animals. The human invention of culture at last allows learning to become cumulative. Some acquired characteristics can at last be inherited, not genetically but through the transmission of information from one learning animal to another. The cumulative learning of a group of human beings is its culture.[3]

Culture opened a gap in the rigid regime of the living order. Gradually, over the last one or several million years, our ancestors widened the range within which human creativity, rather than human genetics, determined the way human life was lived. Tools were invented, manufactured, and used in the basic processes of life. Language and other symbolic forms were created for the communication and representation of experience. Like the beginnings of learning in the distant evolutionary past, the beginnings of culture were no doubt modest and unobtrusive. And as with learning, the success of the new experiment quickened its development. Over hundreds of thousands of years, culture and genetics acted together to reinforce this acceleration of cultural development. The selection for individuals whose hands were good at tool use led, over the generations, to the evolution of hands better suited to tool use. The advantages of those who could use language well led to brains and mouths better equipped for working with language. More and more the human animal enjoyed an unprecedented freedom. It could create its own way of life.

To some, the emergence of culture is the crucial point in the discontinuity between man and the other creatures. According to this view, if the first volume of our Natural History is to be called The Physical World, and the second The Evolution of Life, the third should be entitled The Rise of Culture. Culture introduced the capacity for freedom of choice onto the earth, and in this freedom lies the special destiny of mankind.

This focus on the importance of culture therefore harmonizes with the view of human destiny as governed by human choice. If we wish to solve the riddle of the special evils that seem to plague our efforts, it proposes, we must look to our special freedom to choose how we act in the world. The wolf may be cruel, but when it kills the lamb, the death of the lamb is not an injury to lambkind. It is part of the pattern of survival not only for wolves but for the sheep as well. But man the hunter, with the ungoverned creativity to employ fire and spear, was able to hunt its prey to extinction. After three billion years of life, the gap created by culture allowed into the world for the first time an unpredictable animal. As life had always depended upon a well-governed order to protect the

---

3. The findings of primatologists have revealed that in our capacity to create culture, as in so much else, our uniqueness is less than absolute. Macaque societies have proved themselves able to absorb into their collective culture the innovations of particular individuals; similarly, some chimpanzee groups have developed tool-using techniques to get into termite nests. Clearly, however, the differences in degree between these instances and the human use of culture amount to a difference in kind.

health of living systems, the emergence of an ungoverned creature can destabilize the regime. The creature with the freedom to choose can be dangerous—to himself, to others of his kind, to all life. A relatively recent experiment, this gift of freedom represented by culture may yet be rejected by biological evolution, selected against perhaps in a thermonuclear cloud inflicted upon the world by a few creatures using their freedom of choice insanely.

Mankind's problems still look like problems of freedom. If the evils of civilization pose a riddle, the solution would seem to be found in the myth in Genesis. There only the human animals, of all the earth's creatures, can sunder paradise because only they confront the choice between good and evil, between obedience to the surrounding order and disobedience.

But we have not finished with our story of the evolution from the dead stuff of the universe to the living systems of civilization.

8. The Breakthrough to Civilization

I have said that with culture human beings gained the freedom to create their own way of life. Before civilization, this was true only in a very limited sense. Among hunter-gatherers, culture might be seen more as an adornment on a structure of life reaching back to precultural times than as a radical departure from the biologically governed past. These primitive bands, in their size and structure and in their means of subsistence, maintained a fundamental kinship with the primate groups from which they emerged. In other words, despite the notion that the beginnings of culture represent the point of radical discontinuity between man and the rest of nature, our ancestors developed culture over hundreds of thousands of years without greatly disrupting the continuity in the relationships among individual, society, and the natural order. As long as human societies sustained their lives with the food that nature spontaneously provided, they could develop culturally only within strict limits.

Then came a major cultural innovation in the technology of subsistence. When plants and animals were domesticated, mankind began truly to depart from the place in the living order given it by nature. At first, some ten thousand years ago, the economy of domestication was merely an appendage to the ongoing hunting-and-gathering economy. Gradually, the new way of life supplanted the old. It took several millennia before the power of this breakthrough to usher in a new age became manifest. It was not just that man's role in the ecosystem was forever altered by his unprecedented power to rearrange the living system for his own purposes. Beyond that, the new abundance brought about by developing agriculture made possible open-ended changes in the previously fixed size and structure of human society. Except in a few extraordinary locations, a hunting-and-gathering society was by necessity a small, fairly mobile group. The rise of agriculture made possible a more settled life with far larger populations living in the same territory under a single social organization. Since the labor of a few could now feed many, an extensive division of labor became possible. The breakthrough in food production cleared the way for the rise of civilization. From the narrowly circumscribed conditions of primitive social life, suddenly all things seem to become possible for the cultural animal.

It is therefore not culture per se which marks the point of discontinuity evident in the unfolding of human destiny, but a particular stage of cultural development—civilization. Civilization is here defined as that stage or subset of cultural evolution which begins with the innovations of domestication, that is, with the shift from food gathering to food production. The rise of culture was, of course, a prerequisite for the rise of civilization, but the development of culture in itself did not imply a radical change in human life. Just as the emergence of learning opened a crack through which culture could ultimately stream through, so did culture open a small gap through which could eventually gush the remarkable transformations of the evolution of civilization.

The possibilities for change became open-ended. The biologically evolved constraints suddenly were removed, and the mushrooming forth of new civilized social structures could and did occur.

With all things apparently possible, it is disturbing to see what actually developed. In the five thousand years following the first steps out of the hunter-gatherer way of life, full-scale civilization arose and showed a frightening face. The social equality of primitives gave way to rigid stratification, with the many compelled to serve the few. Warfare became far more important, more chronic, and more bloody and destructive. And the new dominion of man over nature had already begun to turn the green mantle that covered the birthplace of civilization into a rough and rocky desert.

Once again we confront the ills of civilization, and again the drama looks like one of freedom abused. If culture is freedom, civilization seems to be the same freedom greatly magnified. To this point, our search for the bigger vision has not challenged the commonsense theory in which human choice reigns, but appears rather to have deepened it. With the coming of civilization, with the sudden explosion of possibilities, animals bursting out of nature's grasp were sure to get into trouble, like rampant sailors in port on leave. Animals ill-equipped for sudden freedom were bound to seek the protection of new cages, like the human herds the

Grand Inquisitor served. If anything, it seems, we are now in a better position to appreciate just how extraordinary and dangerous human freedom is.

But as cultural evolution erupted into civilization, something strange happened to human freedom. As man became freer of the controls of nature, he became subject to new, perhaps harsher necessities. Paradoxically, the very open-endedness of human possibilities created forces that drove human destiny in a direction that people did not and would not choose. Civilization represented not the old cultural process coming to fuller fruit but a new phenomenon governed by *a wholly new evolutionary principle*. The emergence of this new principle marks the vital point of discontinuity in the history of life and explains civilization's problematic course.

In two steps, I now show how this is so.

9. The Struggle for Power

In his classic, *Leviathan,* Thomas Hobbes describes what he calls "the state of nature" as an anarchic situation in which all are compelled, for their very survival, to engage in a ceaseless struggle for power. About this "war of all against all," two important points should be made: that Hobbes's vision of the dangers of anarchy captured an important dimension of the human condition, and that to call that condition "the state of nature" is a remarkable misnomer.

In nature, all pursue survival for themselves and their kind. But they can do so only within biologically evolved limits. The living order of nature, though it has no ruler, is not in the least anarchic. Each pursues a kind of self-interest, each is a law unto itself, but the separate interests and laws have been formed over aeons of selection to form part of a tightly ordered harmonious system. Although the state of nature involves struggle, the struggle is part of an order. Each component of the living system has a defined place out of which no ambition can extricate it. Hunting-gathering societies were to a very great extent likewise contained by natural limits.

With the rise of civilization, the limits fall away. The natural self-interest and pursuit of survival remain, but they are no longer governed by any order. The new civilized forms of society, with more complex social and political structures, created the new possibility of indefinite social expansion: more and more people organized over more and more territory. All other forms of life had always found inevitable limits placed upon their growth by scarcity and consequent death. But civilized society

19

was developing the unprecedented capacity for unlimited growth as an entity. (The limitlessness of this possibility does not emerge fully at the outset, but rather becomes progressively more realized over the course of history as people invent methods of transportation, communication, and governance which extend the range within which coherence and order can be maintained.) Out of the living order there emerged a living entity with no defined place.

In a finite world, societies all seeking to escape death-dealing scarcity through expansion will inevitably come to confront each other. Civilized societies, therefore, though lacking inherent limitations to their growth, do encounter new external limits—in the form of one another. Because human beings (like other living creatures) have "excess reproductive capacity," meaning that human numbers tend to increase indefinitely unless a high proportion of the population dies prematurely, each civilized society faces an unpleasant choice. If an expanding society willingly stops where its growth would infringe upon neighboring societies, it allows death to catch up and overtake its population. If it goes beyond those limits, it commits aggression. With no natural order or overarching power to prevent it, some will surely choose to take what belongs to their neighbors rather than to accept the limits that are compulsory for every other form of life.

In such circumstances, a Hobbesian struggle for power among societies becomes inevitable. We see that *what is freedom from the point of view of each single unit is anarchy in an ungoverned system of those units*. A freedom unknown in nature is cruelly transmuted into an equally unnatural state of anarchy, with its terrors and its destructive war of all against all.

As people stepped across the threshold into civilization, they inadvertently stumbled into a chaos that had never before existed. The relations among societies were uncontrolled and virtually uncontrollable. Such an ungoverned system imposes unchosen necessities: civilized people were compelled to enter a struggle for power.

The meaning of "power," a concept central to this entire work, needs to be explored. Power may be defined as the capacity to achieve one's will against the will of another. The exercise of power thus infringes upon the exercise of choice, for to be the object of another's power is to have his choice substituted for one's own.[4] Power becomes important where

4. As used here, power is a coercive capacity. Power may also be defined as the ability to restrict the range of another's choices. It is thus differentiated from the kind of persuasive power that changes how others decide to exercise choice (except to the extent that, as, for example, in brainwashing, and less obviously in many other forms of indoctrination, coercive power creates the situation in which persuasion becomes possible).

In the discussion in chap. 7, "The Market as a Power System," a noncoercive (option-expanding) form of power is incorporated into the overall picture of the problem of power in the evolution of civilized systems.

two actors (or more) would choose the same thing but cannot both have it; power becomes important when the obstacles to the achievement of one's will come from the will of others. Thus, as the expanding capacities of human societies created an overlap in the range of their grasp and desire, the intersocietal struggle for power arose.

But the new unavoidability of this struggle is but the first and smaller step in the transmutation of the apparent freedom of civilized peoples into bondage to the necessities of power.

10. The Selection for Power: The Parable of the Tribes

The new human freedom made striving for expansion and power possible. Such freedom, when multiplied, creates anarchy. The anarchy among civilized societies meant that the play of power in the system was uncontrollable. In an anarchic situation like that, no one can choose that the struggle for power shall cease. But there is one more element in the picture: *no one is free to choose peace, but anyone can impose upon all the necessity for power.* This is the lesson of the parable of the tribes.

Imagine a group of tribes living within reach of one another. If all choose the way of peace, then all may live in peace. But what if all but one choose peace, and that one is ambitious for expansion and conquest? What can happen to the others when confronted by an ambitious and potent neighbor? Perhaps one tribe is attacked and defeated, its people destroyed and its lands seized for the use of the victors. Another is defeated, but this one is not exterminated; rather, it is subjugated and transformed to serve the conqueror. A third seeking to avoid such disaster flees from the area into some inaccessible (and undesirable) place, and its former homeland becomes part of the growing empire of the power-seeking tribe. Let us suppose that others observing these developments decide to defend themselves in order to preserve themselves and their autonomy. But the irony is that successful defense against a power-maximizing aggressor requires a society to become more like the society that threatens it. Power can be stopped only by power, and if the threatening society has discovered ways to magnify its power through innovations in organization or technology (or whatever), the defensive society will have to transform itself into something more like its foe in order to resist the external force.

I have just outlined four possible outcomes for the threatened tribes: destruction, absorption and transformation, withdrawal, and imitation.

21

In every one of these outcomes the ways of power are spread throughout the system. This is the parable of the tribes.[5]

The parable of the tribes is a theory of social evolution which shows that power is like a contaminant, a disease, which once introduced will gradually yet inexorably become universal in the system of competing societies. More important than the inevitability of the struggle for power is the profound social evolutionary consequence of that struggle once it begins. *A selection for power among civilized societies is inevitable.* If anarchy assured that power among civilized societies could not be governed, the selection for power signified that increasingly the ways of power would govern the destiny of mankind. This is the new evolutionary principle that came into the world with civilization. Here is the social evolutionary black hole that we have sought as an explanation of the harmful warp in the course of civilization's development.

The idea is simple; its logic, I believe, compelling. In scant and partial form, this idea appears in a variety of places.[6] Nowhere, however, has it been developed beyond the most germinal stage. And nowhere has it been shown to provide an essential key to the strange destiny of our species, as I intend to do in this work.

11. The Reign of Power

The rise of civilization enormously escalated conflict among human societies. This escalation alone would have magnified the importance of power in human life. But the reign of power derives far less from the struggle for power in itself than from the selective process that struggle generates. Even if intersocietal competition had always been as intense as it became with the rise of civilization, it could not have had an equally dramatic and swift social evolutionary impact. For selection can only operate to the extent that there is a diversity of types among which to choose. Even though primitive societies are surely not absolutely identical to one another, their differences can exist only within fairly narrow limits. The potential importance of selection among them is correspondingly limited. With the emergence of civilization, however, these limits fell away and considerable diversity became possible. The greater the diversity among societies, the more important selection among them becomes, for the civilized societies that survive or die can represent very different approaches to human social life. The social evolutionary trap that snared

5. These four possible outcomes are examined in greater depth in chap. 2, "Heads I Win, Tails You Lose."

6. E.g., Tylor (quoted in Harris, 1965, p. 212); Bagehot, 1956, p. 32; Keller, 1916, pp. 62–63; Mosca, 1939, p. 29; McNeill, 1963, p. 806; Carneiro, 1972, pp. 733–738, Lenski, 1970, p. 91.

mankind thus had two jaws—the new open-ended cultural possibilities and the escalating struggle for power. The first made significant selection possible, and the second determined that adequate competitive power would be a primary criterion for social survival. Selection sorts through the wide variety of cultural possibilities, inexorably spreading the ways of power.

The competitive power of a society is a function of many components of its culture. The way it is organized—politically, socially, and economically—is important. Vital, too, is its technology. Ideology and the psychological structure of the people are also essential determinants of a society's power. The consistent selection for power, therefore, can shape the whole cultural life of civilized peoples in its many dimensions.

Among all the cultural possibilities, only some will be viable. The selection for power can discard those who revere nature in favor of those willing and able to exploit it.[7] The warlike may eliminate the pacifistic; the ambitious, the content. Civilized societies will displace the remaining primitives, modern industrial powers will sweep away archaic cultures.[8] The iron makers will be favored over those with copper or no metallurgy at all, and the horsemen will have sway over the unmounted. Societies that are coherently organized and have strong leadership will make unviable others with more casual power structures and more local autonomy.[9] As the parable of the tribes spreads the ways of power, what looked like open-ended cultural possibilities are channeled in a particular, unchosen direction.

What is viable in a world beset by the struggle for power is what can prevail. What prevails may not be what best meets the needs of mankind. The continuous selection for power has thus continually closed off many humane cultural options that people might otherwise have preferred. Power therfore rules human destiny.

If the ambition of societies for power grew originally out of Malthusian necessities,[10] it did not need to remain so. As the selection for power continued, it ultimately would favor those whose hunger for power exceeded their material need. In the beginning, people struggled because they truly needed room to live. As civilization developed, the struggle became more one for the kind of *Lebensraum* that represents a love of power for its own sake. The struggle for power developed a life of its own that would feed an unnatural growth in the "necessities" imposed

7. On how the parable of the tribes illuminates the evolution of man's relationship with nature, see chap. 7, "Man's Dominion."

8. See chap. 2, "Two Great Waves of Change."

9. The implications of the selection for power on the structure of civilized societies are explored in chap. 3, especially the sections on the evolution toward larger, more complex, and more centrally controlled societies.

10. For more on this, see chap. 2, "The Mother of Invention."

by power upon humankind. The selective process insured that it would most definitely not be the meek who inherited the earth.

Just as the freedom from the regime of nature brought upon mankind a new bondage to power, so also did the open-endedness of possibilities prove not a release from but a part of the trap. Because the process of cultural innovation is open-ended, there can be no end point in the maximization of power. (The awesome power of ancient Rome could not survive today even in weaker regions of the world.) The evolution of civilization is therefore marked by a perpetual (though sometimes interrupted) escalation in the level of power a society must possess to survive intersocietal competition.[11] The reign of power thus has no limit.

Yet this reign—and this point must be stressed—is a subtle one. When the determining force is a selective process, the force can have an overwhelming impact without being blatant in operation.

First, a selective process gains its potency from being cumulative over time. It is a mill that grinds slowly but exceedingly fine. At any given time, the ways of comparative weakness may coexist with those of power, surviving for generations and even centuries. The relations among societies are not like an ongoing tournament programmed to eliminate the losers as efficiently as possible. Eventually, however, the bill from the parable of the tribes becomes due; the deficit in power leads to social evolutionary default. Perhaps the powerful nation finally turns and swallows its weaker neighbors, like the Romans in Italy, the Soviets in Lithuania, the Chinese in Tibet. Or perhaps, the more powerful culture extends its reach to threaten more distant peoples, like the projection of Roman power into ancient Britain or the coming of the Europeans to North America. Selection is a patient process. Sifting gradually, almost casually, through the cultural possibilities over many millennia, it can exert a decisive influence over the emerging shape of civilization without having to be central to the drama at any given time. Given enough time, a force that is consistent and enduring becomes decisive. The selection for power is such a force.

This leads to a second point about a theory of social evolution like the parable of the tribes: it is not reductionistic. To claim that power has had primacy in shaping the destiny of civilization does not imply that the striving for power is at the heart of human social existence and that everything else is merely a function of power. In this respect, the parable of the tribes is wholly different structurally from a theory like Marx's. Marx asserted that certain aspects of a society's economic life were most

11. On the perpetual escalation of the level of power needed, see chap. 3, "The Adrenalin Society." On the interruptions and temporary reverses of this escalation, see chap. 7, "The Death of the Unnatural."

24

fundamental and that the rest of the culture (e.g., politics and ideology) was essentially "superstructure" determined by the economic substructure. It was, he said, in the economic dimension of social life that the real engine of historical change was to be found, leading civilization from one stage to another. The parable of the tribes proposes no such causal relationships among the aspects of culture. The reign of power does not mean that power determines what social life is about.

The selective process stands outside the immediate arena of human existence. An analogy may be drawn from biological selection. When coal began to coat everything in Britain with dust, a species of moth that had been white began over the generations to darken. The light-colored individuals were too easily spotted by predators against the coal dust and were selected against. Yet, that selection directed a change toward darkness in no way implies that darkness became central to the butterfly's life processes, determining how it flew, what it ate, how it reproduced, and so on. By the same token, the parable of the tribes can claim that the selection for the ways of power has dominated the profound transformations of the evolution of civilization without claiming that power has been the central preoccupation of civilized peoples or that power maximization has been their principal goal.

People, of course, have an awareness that moths do not. So while the moths may have unwittingly been transformed by the power of their predators, people have known that power is a problem in human affairs. If those moths had human intelligence, they would have sought ways of darkening themselves without waiting for accident to do the job. And, in fact, civilized peoples, seeing themselves caught up in a struggle they could not avoid, have sought to cloak themselves in the protective covering of adequate power. (No one should know this better than we who for more than a generation have been engaged, with horrified self-awareness, in an ever-escalating arms race.) Therefore, power has played a role, and an important one, in the very arena of human affairs even as it played a cumulatively decisive one through an external process of selection. Power has been but one human concern among many, however, and the parable of the tribes neither does nor needs to claim otherwise.

The parable of the tribes thus does not require that history be rewritten. At any given time and place people were doing what they appeared to be doing with or without this new, social evolutionary perspective. The action of history looks the same through this vision, but suddenly visible is a subtle by-product of this action with long-term significance. The parable of the tribes illuminates not the pieces of history so much as the entire sweep of history. For it is in the overall trajectory of civilization that power has its reign.

12.   Power versus Choice in Social Evolution

The parable of the tribes provides a perspective on social evolution quite different from the commonsense view. Even without rewriting history, the parable of the tribes puts it in a wholly new light.

The Question of Choice.—The commonsense model emphasizes the role of free human choice: social evolution is directed by a benign process of selection in which people choose what they want from among the cultural alternatives. Viewed from the perspective of the parable of the tribes, human destiny is no longer governed by free human choice. At the heart of the loss of choice is not that some could impose their will upon others, but that the whole reign of power came unbidden by anyone to dominate human life. People inadvertently stumbled into a struggle for power beyond their ability to avoid or to stop. This struggle generated a selective process, also beyond human control, which molded change in a direction that was inevitable—toward power maximization in human societies.

The parable of the tribes is not, however, rigidly deterministic. It does not maintain that specific events are preordained. Even major developments can arise owing to relatively fortuitous circumstances. The history of a continent may be altered by a burst of human creativity, a people's destiny may hinge on the wisdom or folly of its leaders, the texture of a culture may bear for ages the imprint of some charismatic visionary. What the parable of the tribes does assert is that once mankind had begun the process of developing civilization, the *overall direction* of its evolution was inevitable. This is suggested by the way civilization developed in those regions of the Old and New worlds where it arose more or less independently: their courses show significant parallels (see Steward, 1955). People can act freely and intelligently, but uncontrolled circumstances determine the situation in which they must act and mold the evolution of their systems.[12]

Thus we find that the major trends in the transformation of human society have had the effect of increasing competitive power. This effect in itself does not prove that the selection for power has been the cause of these trends, especially since many of these transformations also increase a society's ability to achieve goals outside the realm of competition. A major purpose of what follows is to make compelling the case for the contention of the parable of the tribes that the reign of power has been a significant factor in dictating the principal trends of the social evolution.

History-makers.—People do make history. Historical "forces" can be expressed only in the doings of flesh-and-blood human beings. In the

---

12. For more about the limitations on human choice in history, see the next chapter, "The Theft of Human Choice."

commonsense view of social evolution, history is shaped by "the people" in general. To recognize that some people play a large historical role and that others play almost no role at all still falls within the realm of common sense. This inequality does not challenge the essentially democratic view of history as governed by human choices if the history makers are seen as representative of humanity. They can be representative if, like George Washington, they are first in the hearts of their countrymen, or if, like Bach or Edison, they have an extraordinary ability to create what the people want.

The parable of the tribes, however, sees the history makers as an unrepresentative lot. To the extent that social evolution is governed by the selection for power, it is the power maximizers who play the important role in the drama of history. This group is selected for its starring role not by the human cast as a whole but by impersonal and ungoverned forces. They are therefore not representative in the democratic sense. Nor in the Gallup Poll sense, for they are selected because of how they are different from the other actors. They are different in their capacity to get and to wield power. Finally, they are not representative in the sense of the hero who carries his community's banner and fulfills his community's aspirations, for the power wielders of history have often been the conquerors, the destroyers, the oppressors of their fellow human beings. Though we must see history as a drama in which the main actors are the powerful and aggressive, we should not slip into seeing them as the villains, for it is not the actors who set the stage or who govern the thrust of the plot.[13]

The category of "power maximizers" embraces a couple of different kinds of actors in the human drama. Most especially, it includes entire sovereign social entities (like the imperialistic tribes of the parable) who impinge upon other, previously autonomous societies. The parable of the tribes focuses primarily on the intersocietal system because that system forms the comprehensive context for human action,[14] but more importantly because in that system anarchy has been most complete and least curable. Anarchy is at the core of the problem of power, making struggle inevitable and allowing the ways of power to spread uncontrolled throughout the whole like a contaminant. Thus, nowhere has power had so free and decisive a reign as in that arena of sovereign actors where, by definition, there is no power to hold all in awe.

Yet the problem of power exists in some form also within societies; for even though in one sense societies are governed, in another more

13. The role of the history makers and, in particular, the extent that the will even of the powerful can be said to have determined the direction of history are explored in chap. 2, "Choosing the Choosers."

14. For more on this point, see chap. 7, "Men Are Not Ants" ("Wheels within Wheels").

profound sense they are usually subject to anarchy. The formation of government and the establishment of the rule of law can be—and usually have been in large measure—the embodiment of the rule of raw power rather than a restraint upon it. The search for a fuller understanding of the problem of power in social evolution leads therefore to an *intrasocietal analogue* of the parable of the tribes. And the category of history's power maximizers includes those groups (like the feudal class) and individuals (like Stalin) who are successful in competing for power within a society's boundaries.[15] Again, it is those distinguished by their capacity to grasp and wield power who gain the means to shape the whole (social) system according to their ways and their vision. And again, the history makers are cast in their roles not by the people affected but by an unchosen selective process; and generally, they are not those whom mankind would choose to guide its destiny.

Government may frequently be the agency of the rule of power, but only government can restrain power in the interests of other values. If people, rather than the impersonal selection for power, are to control their destiny, it will be through the design of systems to control power.[16]

The Spread of Cultural Innovations.—Both the commonsense view and the parable of the tribes would predict that innovations tend to spread from their place of origin. Both would predict an erosion of cultural diversity among societies, but the two theories view this process of cultural homogenization differently. If innovations are seen as "improvements," naturally they will spread. When people in more "backward" areas learn of better ways of meeting their needs, they will adopt them. Cultural diversity is thus diminished by a process of diffusion. In the perspective of the parable of the tribes, the historic trend toward cultural homogeneity is decreed by the reign of power. Whether or not a cultural innovation spreads throughout the system of interacting societies depends not so much on its ability to enhance the quality of human life as on its capacity to increase the competitive power of those who adopt it. The ways of power inevitably become universal. While the diffusion model represents cultural homogenization as the result of free human choice, the parable of the tribes stresses the role of compulsion: the conqueror spreads his ways either directly or by compelling others to imitate him in self-defense.[17]

15. The parable of the tribes usually regards a society as a single entity, society being defined as "a group manifesting sufficient cooperation internally and sufficient opposition externally to be recognizable as a unit" (Quincy Wright, 1965, p. 145). But it is nonetheless also true that a society is an arena within which smaller entities contend.
16. These issues are explored in chap. 7, "Men Are Not Ants."
17. The question of cultural homogenization is explored in chap. 3, "The Common Denominator."

Civilization and Human Needs.—If civilization were governed by human choice, we would expect it to be fairly well designed for the fulfillment of human needs. This expectation led us earlier to the Rube Goldberg problem, the ludicrous disproportion between the gargantuan apparatus of civilization and the disappointing benefit in human terms. The parable of the tribes sweeps aside this dilemma. If the selection for power, and not choice, has governed the evolving shape of civilized society, there is no reason to expect the design to correspond with the needs of human beings. According to the parable of the tribes, civilized peoples have been compelled to live in societies organized for the maximization of competitive power. People become the servants of their evolving systems, rather than civilized society being the instrument of its members.

Not that the selection for power systematically selects what is injurious to people. The process is not hostile to human welfare, simply indifferent. Many things that serve power serve people as well, such as a degree of social order and the provision of adequate nutrition to keep people functioning. (As this implies, there are a great many roads to hell that the need for social power helps close off.) But the parable of the tribes suggests that the service to people of such power-enhancing attributes of society may be entirely incidental to their raison d'etre. Those of us who now enjoy affluence and freedom as well as power[18] are predisposed to believe that benign forces shape our destiny. But to the extent that our blessings are incidental by-products of the strategy for power at this point in the evolution of civilization, our optimism may be ill-founded. If the forces that now favor us are the same as those that earlier condemned masses of people to tyranny and bondage, the future requirements of power maximization may compel mankind not toward the heavenly utopia to which we aspire but toward the hellish dystopias that some like Orwell and Huxley have envisioned. Our well-being may prove to be less like that of the squire who feeds himself well off the land that he rules than like that of the dairy cow who, though pampered and well fed, is not served but exploited by the system in which she lives. The bottom line that governs her fate is not her own calculation; when she is worth more for meat than for milk, off she goes to the slaughterhouse.

Power and Choice.—Wisdom is often less a matter of choosing a particular view as the truth than of combining different truths in a balanced way. So it is with the parable of the tribes and the commonsense view of social evolution. The selection for power does govern a good deal of the

---

18. It is an irony that those in a position to be able to read a critique of civilization like this work will with very few exceptions be drawn from the tiny minority of earth's population who are the greatest beneficiaries of contemporary civilization.

evolution of civilization, but people also shape their destiny by their choices. The power wielders are, to be sure, prominent in the human drama, but there are creative and charismatic figures (Shakespeare, Buddha) whom we choose to give a very different kind of power to shape our experience. The ways of power may spread by compulsion, but antibiotics, fine silks, and the idea of liberty can diffuse throughout the world by human choice. Thus, while human well-being may be incidental to one major social-evolutionary force, there is room for human aspiration to dictate a part of the story. I therefore argue not that the parable of the tribes has been the sole force directing the evolution of civilization but only that it has been an extremely important one.

The vastness of human history allows room for many valid theories. The parable of the tribes is one of them. When its broom has swept across the litter-strewn path of the evolution of civilization, a good deal of debris will remain. But where is a broom that can clear up more of history's path?

The selection for power has set important limits upon the cultural possibilities available to civilized peoples. Nevertheless, within whatever range the necessities of power have allowed, human beings have striven, and striven successfully, to create cultural ways to express and nourish their humanity. Wherever possible, people have tried to increase the beauty and decency and meaning in their lives. One aspect of the striving for a humane world can be imaged as the flowering up of life-serving forms through the cracks in the concrete of power: even in the most inhuman systems (like concentration camps) people often create cultures to fulfill their needs.[19] Besides the attempts to find gaps in the rule of power, mankind has often worked to overcome power itself, adopting values and laws and customs that diminish the free play of power in the world. These efforts have been only partly successful, but they are important. The evolution of civilization can be seen as a dialectic between the systematic selection for power and the human striving for a humane world, between the necessities imposed upon man regardless of his wishes and the efforts of man to be able to choose the cultural environment in which he will live.

This work focuses on the problem of power rather than on the beauties civilized man has brought forth, not because the positive aspects of civilization are considered trivial but because the problematic aspects urgently demand our understanding.

---

19. Irving Goffman's *Asylums* shows how in the most power-dominated of social environments, (such as prisons, hospitals, military bases), people develop enormously complex networks of secret life to drive a wedge between themselves and the roles imposed by the dominant powers. For all their power, the surrounding systems cannot eradicate what people do to "flesh out their lives" (Berman, 1972, p. 2).

13.   A Tragic View of Human Destiny

Since the rise of civilization, there has been a strong note of torment in the human condition. The problem has been not only that the circumstances of civilized life entailed suffering but also that the sufferings themselves brought guilt. Those who are afflicted often believe they are being punished. All the more reason for a sense of collective guilt when so many of the world's ills seem to come from the hands of man. A theme therefore recurs in the reflections of civilized peoples that man is a flawed and sinful creature, and that his sinfulness is responsible for the agonies of humankind. Indeed, that view is very current today, even among people with no theology of sin and retribution. Those who see in our species a threat to the survival of the entire ecosystem, who look upon the carnage we inflict upon our own kind, and who regard the ever-growing mountains of armaments as a manifestation of insanity also seem to suffer guilt for belonging to so dangerous a species. Using a very commonsense view of human action, they regard the unquestionable destructiveness of our works as indisputable proof of the monstrosity of human nature.

The parable of the tribes does not hold that view. That theory offers no indictment of human nature. The irresistible social evolutionary forces that have swept us along since the breakthrough to civilization have depended very little on human nature for their origin and their direction. All that was required was that we be creative enough to develop culture to a certain point of freedom from natural limits, and that we be capable of (not necessarily inclined toward) aggressive behavior. Almost any animal can be aggressive under the right conditions. A cultural animal is by definition both social and flexible, and so presumably could learn to meet the demands of very different social environments. If a society needs for its members to be primed for collective aggressiveness, that inherent capacity for aggressiveness will be brought out, encouraged to hyper-develop. We have no need of Ardreyesque images of bloodthirsty primate hunters to explain the bloodiness of civilized history.[20] Thus, any creature who met those two requirements would have been condemned to a similar fate. Its nascent civilized culture would, like ours, have become caught up in the parable of the tribes, its social evolution compelled toward power maximization with all its destructiveness. Similarly, wherever else in this immense universe life may have evolved, and evolved to the point where a cultural creature has broken free of biological constraints, we may suppose that the same problem of power has arisen. Unless special

20. The distortions of human nature demanded by our evolving civilized systems are investigated in chap. 5, "Power and the Psychological Evolution of Civilized Man."

31

circumstances of terrain prevented the simultaneous contact and anarchy among societies, the parable of the tribes would plague these extraterrestrial civilizations as well. The eruption of such cultural freedom out of the tight biological order inevitably leads to the problem of power.

To be alarmed about the destructiveness of our civilized systems is more than appropriate. It is fitting that we each take responsibility to do what we can to avert catastrophe. But there is no good reason for tormenting ourselves for guilt as a species. The path of our misdeeds was, in essence, laid down before us like a streambed where the rainwaters inevitably flow. It is true that our problems stem from our not staying in the place given us by nature, but this was due not to any especial hubris or ambition on our part, but to our creativity. We are like the hero who cannot escape the fate described before his birth by an oracle. As the old and chastened Oedipus says of himself in *Oedipus at Colonus,* we have suffered our deeds more than we have acted them, have been more the victim than the criminal.

The parable of the tribes presents a tragic picture of human destiny. The parallel with tragedy goes beyond that knell of inevitability surrounding the action. We discover also the tragic paradox that first confounds one's common sense and then leads one to a deeper awareness. The hero of tragedy is trapped in a world where everything seems paradoxically twisted into its opposite. His very blessings become his curses. His strengths become his weaknesses. His freedom of action the means of his entrapment. So, also, according to the parable of the tribes, is man in relation to the evolving systems of his own creation. A tragic paradox changed man's liberation from the regime of nature into bondage to the ways of power. Because all things seemed possible, one thing—power—became necessary. The very fact of open-ended development sealed the trap shut.

The insight of tragedy is that while man is able to do much, he is not able to control the consequences of his heroic doings. Like Heracles, man has gained great strength and, maddened by forces beyond his ken, he uses this strength to murder his own family. Like Oedipus, man explores the mysteries of the origin of his kingship and discovers blood upon his hands. The tragic hero propels the action, but is not master of his destiny. In the same way the parable of the tribes shows that with the rise of civilization human creativity ceased to drive the mill of cultural evolution but rather became its grist.

Yet the fall of the tragic hero is paradoxical, the very loss becoming a kind of gift. Humiliation is transformed by a deeper awareness into a saving humility. Only when the tragic hero recognizes his limits in the face of forces beyond his control can he cease to be a helpless victim, the prey of a destructive destiny of his own unintended creation. And so with civilized peoples. Only when we attain a tragic wisdom about our story can we hope to lead history beyond tragedy.

14. Hope

The parable of the tribes may seem to be an irredeemably pessimistic view of the dilemma of civilized peoples. It seems to say that civilized man is forever condemned to live in a condition in which some of his worst sins will be selected and magnified into laws of his cultural existence. But this is only partly true. There is indeed no way to return the dangerous djinni of human powers to the bottle. Even if we could, the parable of the tribes says we would only retrace the original, often nightmarish course of our history. Even if there is no turning back, there may be a way of moving forward.

If we are lucky, the evolution of civilization to this point may prove to have been a transitional period in the history of life. It may be a period of anarchy and destruction between two eras of synergistic order. In the beginning, there was the biologically evolved order that gave and protected life. Then the break of a single species from that order brought into the world the reign of power which now threatens life with destruction. But perhaps before power has a chance to fulfill its worst threats, mankind will be able to use its growing opportunities to shape a new order which, like the old, will control the actions of all to the degree needed to protect the well-being of the whole.

The creation of a new order requires an end to the intersocietal anarchy that has been the overarching context of civilized life. Anarchy is the inevitable outcome of the fragmentation of mankind, and it was inevitable that civilized societies would emerge in a fragmented state. As long as the human cultural system was fragmented into a multiplicity of separate units, the problem of power remained insoluble. Even if any region of the world managed to solve the problem by extending unity and by living in peace, those people were still vulnerable to the reintroduction of the contaminant of power from outside its regional system. In our times, however, the possibility of an escape from this fragmented system is beginning to emerge. For the first time, the world is becoming a single interdependent system in which all the world's peoples are in contact. Meanwhile, the age-old struggle for power goes on and may annihilate us before we can create an order that controls power. But the centuries ahead give us the opportunity to place all human action within a structure that for the first time makes truly free human choice possible.

33

Even so, it is far from clear how to get from here to there, or even what kind of world order "there" should be.

Having eaten the fruit of the tree of knowledge, we became as gods in power—and now must do so in wisdom. Having escaped the control of nature, mankind must create controls for itself, replacing the wholeness of nature with an artificial wholeness, substituting for the law of nature a human law.[21] Here is another paradox: the laws of man require power, for power can be controlled only with power. The challenge, therefore, is to design systems that use power to disarm power. Only in such an order can mankind be free.

The next two chapters explore in some depth and detail two of the main ideas of chapter 1. At the heart of chapter 2 is the idea:

> *Choices have been stolen from mankind; we should therefore understand that civilization has evolved in directions people did not choose.*

The central idea of chapter 3 can be stated:

> *The selection for power well explains many of the main transformations in the structure of civilized societies.*

Or:

> *Civilized societies have been shaped according to the requirements of power maximization.*

Readers who want to proceed to fundamentally new dimensions of the parable of the tribes—as opposed to these elaborations of points already made—are directed to Book II, "The Natural and the Unnatural," which begins on p. 131.

---

21. The concepts of natural and artificial wholeness are discussed in chap. 6.

Chapter Two

The Theft of Human Choice

1. Unfree Choices

The essence of freedom is the ability to choose that which one wants.
When people can act on the basis of such freedom, what they do and
what they make are true expressions of themselves.

The parable of the tribes argues that throughout the evolution of
civilization, human beings have been robbed of that freedom. And it
maintains, consequently, that civilization as we see it in history is neither
the fruit of human choice nor a reflection of human nature.

For some it seems logically necessary that civilization is a mirror of
man, the product of human choices. Is not history made by people acting
deliberately? Therefore, must we not conclude that deliberate human
choices must rule the course of social evolution? Excluding such extra-
human forces as earthquakes and climatic shifts, is it not inescapable that
history reveals the nature of our species writ large?

Such logic, which to many seems mere common sense, underlies what
in the preceding chapter we called the commonsense theory of social
evolution. This logic is so common because it is an outgrowth of the bias
of much of our Western scientific tradition according to which the whole
is merely the sum of its parts. Employing the logic of such reductionism,
it has been asserted at various times that chemistry is only physics, that

biology is only chemistry, that psychology is only biology, and (as in this instance) that aggregate human phenomena are only psychology. By this reasoning, the ultimately satisfactory explanation of so aggregate a phenomenon as "the evolution of civilization" would be expressed not in terms of human choices and actions but in terms of physics. (After all, is anything in history *not* matter and energy acting in time and space?) Indeed, as great a theoretician as Sigmund Freud, when he was on the verge of creating psychoanalysis, announced his hopes for a psychology reduced to the terms of physics. While his genius fortunately transcended his philosophic bias, his intentions reveal our cultural assumptions about how the world is put together—in pieces. If you understand the pieces, you will understand the whole.

What is wrong with this approach? What *is* the whole besides the sum of its parts?

The whole is the way the parts are put together. The higher level of organization is the structure in which the parts act. By determining the environment of the constituent elements, the structure shapes how the elements act. The behavior of the parts is therefore fully explicable only in terms of the surrounding whole.

The various levels of organization—physics, chemistry, biology, and so on—are irreducible. Each governs its own dimension of reality. As a new level of organization arises, new laws arise with it. The laws of the lower level are never violated, but neither are they sufficient to explain the higher level. The new laws are superimposed upon the old, or emergent from them (Thorpe, in Roslansky, 1969, p. 76). The whole is more than the sum of its parts because it brings those parts into a structured system governed by principles that do not apply to the parts themselves. Writing generally of the nonreducible nature of living systems, Paul Weiss explains: "Each sub-system dominates its own subordinate small parts within its own orbit or domain, as it were, restraining their degrees of freedom according to its own integral portion of the overall pattern, much as its own degrees of freedom have been restrained by the pattern of activities of the higher system of which it is a part and participant" (in Koestler and Smythies, 1970, pp. 14–15).

This passage clears the path for us to intuit the limits to the role of human choice in social evolution. Although the phrase "restraint of freedom" seems somewhat metaphorical in describing the possibilities for molecules (chemistry) within the structure of a cell (biology), or for a cell within a body, it captures well the predicament of individual human actors (psychology) in the systems of civilization (human aggregate—social evolution). We can, in this context, describe the parable of the tribes as an effort to show how with the rise of civilization a new level of organization emerged, governed by new laws that "restrained the freedom" of human beings to shape their own destiny. While people continued to make choices and to act on them, the new laws that emerged in the system of competing civilized societies greatly reduced people's range of choice. The concept of emergence opens a trapdoor in the cage of the commonsense but fallacious logic that must attribute all the evils of civilization to its human members.[1]

Let us look more closely at the concept of "free choice." The issue here has nothing to do with the ancient philosophic problem of free will and determinism. For present purposes, we can accept at face value our own experience that we do indeed make choices, and we can dismiss as irrelevant whether the way we choose among our options is causally determined or somehow placed outside the bounds of causality. Our issue concerns not how we choose among options, but what options we have to choose among.

Imagine a man walking down a street. He suddenly feels a gun pressed against his back and hears a voice saying, "Your money or your life!" He is being offered a choice, but it is not a choice he would choose. He would probably state his real preferences: "To tell you the truth, I'd rather keep my money and continue on my way uninjured as I was doing before you appeared." Because of the coercive circumstances in which he finds himself, this option is foreclosed.

Anarchic situations generally present people with just such limited and unattractive choices. Imagine a fire breaking out in a crowded theater. If someone provides leadership quickly enough, and people respond cooperatively, the anarchy of panic can be averted and an orderly exit attempted. If no order is introduced, the dangerous anarchy of "every man for himself" can swiftly develop even though no one wants it or benefits from it. A system suddenly emerges which, while itself not designed by human choice, limits the range of choices available to its constituent human members. Each person may find himself faced with the options: "I can stay here and burn to death or I can try to get out at the expense, probably, of trampling others." Individuals who are neither murderous nor suicidal may be forced to choose between murderous and suicidal courses of action.

When unchosen overarching circumstances foreclose all acceptable options, the subsequent choice cannot be regarded as a free one.

The parable of the tribes shows how civilized peoples have been compelled over millennia to make such unfree choices. The anarchic system of civilized societies has indeed been like a crowded theater on fire. Perhaps worse, for there has been no real chance of introducing a beneficial

---

1. E.g., the logic of the statement: "As with all thinkers who begin with the assumption of the essential goodness of man and nature, Mumford suffers from an inability to explain the existence of evil" (Starr, 1976, p. 60).

order (at least until now). The historical scramble for survival among inevitably competing societies has been like a panic in slow motion. And peoples who under more benign circumstances might have opted for a gentle and vital approach to human life have been forced by the emergent order of civilized societies to choose between murder and suicide.

Thus can the whole "restrain the freedom" of the part.

2. Two Great Waves of Change

The evolution of civilized societies has been a many-faceted process on-going over thousands of years. For the sake of simplicity, however, we can identify two comprehensive transformations of human society. The first was the steady replacement of primitive, hunting-and-gathering cultures by civilization. The second, which continues even in our time, is the transformation of what might be called archaic civilized societies into modern ones. Sometimes these changes are called (at least at their origins) the Agricultural Revolution and the Industrial Revolution, reflecting perhaps the preoccupation in our age with technology. But it is not the technological component alone that is important here. In each case, social, political, and economic reorganization makes essential contributions to the social evolutionary importance of these transformations. (Indeed, in the rise of modern society it can be argued that the important technological change was fostered by previous institutional changes.) It may be useful to give these changes names reflecting their comprehensive nature—first the civilizing, and second the modernizing of the world.

With both these transformations, once the new type had emerged in one part of the world it steadily spread throughout the human cultural system eliminating its predecessor. The question arises: did the new cultural way spread because the world's peoples chose it over the old or because they were compelled to abandon the old? The parable of the tribes, of course, focuses on the element of compulsion in social evolution, on the irresistible spread of the ways of power. We must regard at least as suggestive the fact that both these transformations tremendously magnified the power of societies, conferring strong competitive advantages over societies maintaining the older ways. But this in itself does not prove that people were forced to abandon the cultural practices of the earlier era. What actually happened?

A. *The Spread of Civilization*

Over thousands of years, lands that had been peopled by small hunting-and-gathering bands became the territory of civilized societies which practiced food production and which were organized in increasingly complex ways. How did this change occur? Did the example of civilized societies inspire neighboring groups to emulate them in search of a better life? Or did the more powerful new type—more populous, more aggressive, better organized for struggle—force the disappearance of primitive societies? The record of what transpired millennia ago is far from clear, but the testimony of anthropologists who have studied this transformation casts doubt on the plausibility of the more benign image of primitives happily choosing the path of civilization. If, as Leslie White suggests, primitive society "was unquestionably the most satisfying kind of social environment man has ever lived in" (1959, p. 107), it hardly seems likely that people would willingly leave it. Indeed, Morton Fried argues that "the emergence of new forms of society" was the reason hunting-and-gathering societies did not remain viable (1967, p. 107). If the means by which the original civilizations spread remain largely a matter of speculation, the way primitive societies have been displaced in recent times is clear. Around the world, the advance of potent civilized societies has shattered and destroyed the primitive cultures in their path. A leading scholar of this process, Stanley Diamond, calls these primitives "conscripts to civilization, not volunteers." And he concludes with the far-reaching generalization: "No primitive society has gone to civilization as to a greater good" (1964, p. vii).

B. The Modernization of Archaic Civilizations

A second leap forward has been the fruit of European civilization and its transplants. Over several centuries, a new kind of culture emerged employing industrialization in technology, the nation state in government, the market system of economic organization, the scientific approach to knowledge, and an antitraditionalist receptivity to change in the ideological sphere and in social life generally. All across the globe, we see non-European cultures now changing in such overall directions. Surely, the superabundance of data available on this process of modernization should allow us to say unequivocally whether this change has been forced upon or chosen by the peoples of these recently archaic, traditional societies. And surely, the evident eagerness of these nations to modernize makes inescapable the conclusion that this transformation at least is the product of free choice.

Unfortunately, the truth is not so crystal clear. To judge the nature of the choices these people face we must bear in mind the nature of the dramatic encounter between traditional societies around the world and the potent new kind of culture developed in the West. It is hardly the case that the nations of Europe stood upon the hill as a beacon of progress inviting others to come to witness and follow their lead. However convinced were the Europeans of their *mission civilisatrice*, or their white man's burden, they hardly chanced the transformation of non-European societies to the choice of the natives. Rather, in the most systematic and comprehensive exercise of raw power in the history of the world, the nations of Europe ruthlessly employed their modern potency in the imperialist domination of most of this planet. This colonial intrusion by force puts a new light on the apparent "choice" of modernization.

First, the cultural transformation was already begun by force. The imperialist powers intruded upon archaic societies to wreak changes the conquerors desired regardless of the will of or costs to the conquered. When these peoples shook off their imperialist masters after fifty or two hundred and fifty years of colonial subjugation, their options may already have been limited. Despite the resiliency of cultures, the option of resuming those old cultural ways that preceded the arrival of the gunboats may have been foreclosed by the imperialist's destruction of the old culture. (To take an easily visible aspect of this, the present map of Africa reveals nations whose borders are the legacy of the colonial regime and often correspond little to the cultural boundaries of the peoples themselves.) W. W. Rostow asks how the revolutionary modernization process got "detonated," and he answers: "The general answer is, of course, that traditional societies were fractured . . . by their contact with more advanced societies" (1971, p. 58). To the extent that the way back has been blocked by the rubble of power's impact, we may question how much the choice of going forward is indeed a free one.

Second, the experience of colonial conquest demonstrated quite vividly to the world's peoples the dangers of being weak in a world where power is uncontrolled. There can be no doubt that the trauma of colonialism has profoundly shaped the world view of the now-liberated peoples of the world. It is quite manifest that this experience still dominates the attitudes of these nations on contemporary international issues. So we can readily imagine that this same trauma could dictate their choice to modernize. At the psychological level, it is likely that the conquest would discredit the traditional culture that proved impotent to prevent the humiliations and injuries of subjugation. At the same time, there is an inevitable tendency to identify with the aggressor, to admire and value the very power one hates and fears. On the more practical plane is the realistic perception that one must achieve power simply to survive nationally and culturally. Decades or centuries of exploitation surely would suffice to demonstrate that the ways of weakness, whatever their intrinsic attractions, must be abandoned. In the preceding century, Japan scrambled to modernize itself, a choice that was manifestly unfree. The Japanese, writes David Kaplan, "had stood to one side and carefully observed the rest of Asia being carved up and apportioned by the various European powers. Japan really had very little choice in the matter; it was industrialize or be gobbled up like the rest. She therefore industrialized" (in Sahlins and Service, 1960, p. 90). Even for countries that have freed themselves from imperialist domination, as Denis Goulet notes in *The Cruel Choice*, there remains a defensive motivation behind modernization: "Ex-colonies seek equal status with politically mature nations and know that demands must be backed up by economic muscle" (1977, p. 327). Right now, China's present leadership is embarked on a similar effort of crash modernization whose purpose—like Japan's before—is at least partly defensive. Among its explicit motives is the realization that with an expansionist Soviet Union threatening from the north, China must transform itself in the ways of power if it is to escape Soviet domination or destruction. Said the Shah of Iran in 1978: "Backward countries will have no place in this world. A third-class country will be crushed. The world is not a place of charity. To be among the ranks of first-class nations, the whole people of Iran must produce and give of themselves"(*Newsweek*, July 24, 1978, p. 36). The "rising expectations" of peoples wanting the material advantages of modern productivity is no doubt part of the motivational force behind modernization. But how much of this global transformation must be explained rather by the necessities of self-defense in a world ruled by power?

Third, the policies of these new nations may reflect more the aspirations of their ruling elites than those of the people generally. These elites, it is often observed, are usually the most westernized elements of their societies. This is no coincidence, for the struggles to cast off the colonial powers often required, as the parable of the tribes would predict, the emulation of the European foes: power can be overthrown only with power. It may be, therefore, that the drive to modernize is in this respect as well a legacy of the rule of power. As the Shah of Iran learned too late, the leader's passion for modernization at the cost of traditional values is not always shared by the people.

The constriction of human choice by power is not, of course, the whole picture. It is also the case that modernization's enhancement of human powers extends the conceivable range of human options, and reflects peoples' desire for a life freer of disease, drudgery, and privation. Still, just as some regard primitive life as more satisfying than the civilized life that followed it, there are those who maintain that "it is far from certain that achieving [modern] development's benefits makes men happier or freer" (Goulet, 1977, p. 326).

The question of the relative role of power and choice in impelling the global thrust toward modernization must remain open. But it is at least arguable that this historic change is not best (and certainly not solely) to be understood as a process governed by the free choice of the world's peoples.

Even if we conclude that power, not choice, has determined history's two great waves of change, it does not necessarily imply that the changes were detrimental. The two questions are separable. On one hand, people might freely make a disastrous choice. On the other hand, people might be forced to march into the promised land. People may prefer to cling to the old even when offered a new, superior way of life simply out of a conservative attachment to the stable and familiar. It may be that people are fortunate to have been compelled to accept the spread of the modern advanced cultural forms. Nevertheless, it remains important whether freedom or compulsion governs the transformation. For to the extent that power sweeps people unwillingly along the social evolutionary currents, we cannot trust that the course of social evolution serves human interests.

3.   Heads I Win, Tails You Lose:
The Nonalternatives of the Parable of the Tribes

The parable of the tribes begins: "Imagine a group of tribes living within reach of one another." It leads to the question: "What are the possible outcomes for those tribes threatened by a potent and ambitious neighbor?" We discover that the possibilities are quite limited. But more important, they all amount fundamentally to the same thing: the inescapable permeation of the entire system by the ways of power. It is, therefore, a parable about the theft of free human choice.

Let us look more closely at the four possibilities to which the threatened societies are confined. They are: (A) withdrawal, (B) destruction, (C) transformation, and (D) imitation.

A. Withdrawal

The only way to escape the compelling pressures of the intersocietal system is to escape from that system, that is, to remove one's social group beyond the reach of other societies. It is thus only in the least accessible regions of the earth that the most primitive of human societies have been able to survive into our times. They have survived in the dense jungles

42

of Africa, the desert wastes of Australia, the lands of the Arctic, and, as recently discovered, in the tropical forests of the Philippines. The correlation between remoteness and "backwardness" is, of course, subject to a different interpretation: those on the fringes do not benefit from the flow of new cultural ideas. But history does not show that if left unmolested the "backward" will leap at the opportunity to move forward.

In some cases, the surviving hunting and gathering peoples were never threatened by more powerful societies. Rather, it just happened that of the hundreds or thousands of primitive societies that once existed, they were among the last to be reached and challenged by civilization. Sometimes, though, these societies have indeed retreated from impinging neighbors, withdrawing into the more inaccessible areas for refuge. This appears to be true of the peoples of the Amazon, and perhaps of the Tassaday of the Philippines. It is also true of the Quintana Roo of the Yucatan, described by Robert Redfield in his classic *The Primitive World and Its Transformations*. Beyond the reach of more powerful societies, they can remain free to choose a way of life that is intrinsically viable but competitively disadvantageous.

Escape, however, can only buy time for the ways of weakness. For the ever-growing power of civilized societies elsewhere continuously extends the reach of the more advanced social types. Transportation and communication develop, bringing the inaccessible within reach. New methods of resource exploitation are invented, making previously useless territory more attractive. Populations rise, requiring new areas for dense human settlement. And the selection for power creates states and ruling elites for whom the extension of their domination is an end in itself, a habit pursued for its own sake. Thus, in time, the British Empire brought remote Australia within its grasp, virtually destroying the native cultures. Right now, the ambitious rulers of Brazil steadily extend their systems of exploitation into the domains of the Amazonian tribes. There is no longer anywhere to hide.

In any case, for societies already civilized the option of withdrawal is less open because of the logistics involved. A small group can run off into the mountains or the jungles. Even a tribe can retreat, as in the westward migration of some American Indian tribes as the Euro-American civilization threatened them from the east. But more settled and dense civilized societies are not so portable. They must stand and face the threat when it arrives.

Again, remoteness buys time. If it is distant enough, a comparatively archaic civilized society can be safe from more powerful contemporaries. So, while the crucible of competition was producing the powerful nation-states of Europe, the civilized societies of Asia could continue as before until, during the past three centuries, the power of the European societies grew to reach and threaten them.

The relentless growth of power dictates that the confrontation can only be postponed, not canceled. When it comes, the old option of going on as before will be foreclosed.

B. Destruction

When the encounter comes, the weak are often at the mercy of the strong. And sometimes the strong show no mercy. Cultures have been obliterated, peoples exterminated.

It was from a people suffering for generations under the aggressor's sword that the idea emerged that the meek shall inherit the earth. The advance of more modern Caesars has also frequently led to millenarian expectations of salvation (e.g., in the cargo cults of some Pacific Islanders). Yet too often the dream of rescue is shattered by the reality of destruction, the earth that is inherited being just enough to cover the bodies. (Quoth the West Indian, René Maran: "Civilization, civilization—the European's pride and their charnelhouse of innocents. The Hindu poet Rabindranath Tagore, one day in Tokyo, said what you are. You build your kingdom on corpses." [quoted in Hodgkin, in Owen and Sutcliffe, pp. 103–104].)

If the alien invaders want what their victims have, but have no use for the victims themselves, the temptation for annihilation is there. Extermination is especially possible when the discrepancy in power between the two societies is wide. Thus it is in the contact between the most advanced and the most primitive that, in our times at least, thorough cultural destruction most often occurs. What the primitives have is land, and their use of it is so inefficient in terms of productivity that it serves the imperialists' ambitions little to merely establish themselves as rulers, to place themselves at the top of the ongoing system and collect the revenue. They will wish, rather, to establish their own system, transplanting their own people and methods to the new land. The natives are seen as superfluous. Writing for the U.S. Department of State in the early 1920s, Alpheus Snow wrote that when the relationship between the colonists and the aborigine peoples is competitive, "the settlement of the land question is always difficult. . . . Economic competition leads to war between the colonists and the aborigines, which invariably results in the more or less complete extinction of the aborigines" (1921, p. 134). Difficult indeed. The famous American historian, Francis Parkman, wrote of the American Indian: "He will not learn the arts of civilization, and he and his forest must perish together" (quoted in Rogin, 1976, p. 115).

Since the modern era dawned, the potent European civilization has spread through such destruction in many places where the native peoples

44

were sufficiently backward and sparse to give the conquerors good opportunity. It has occurred in Australia, in parts of Africa and South America, and in North America. They came to such places less as masters than as replacements. Mismatched wars led quickly or eventually to death for the invaded. Those who survived became the outcasts of the new society, their cultures destroyed in the advance of the more powerful type. From a social evolutionary standpoint, what is significant is not that the genetic heritage may survive imperialistic genocide but that the cultural heritage is destroyed simply because it confers weakness upon its carriers.

The advance of modern imperialism left the more densely populated areas peopled by the natives, the conquerors lacking either the ruthlessness, the motive, or the means to carry out systematic genocide on such large groups. Ancient conquerors, however, were often fully prepared to slaughter whole peoples to make room for their own. We who live in the historical shadow of Auschwitz cannot rest secure in the belief that mass exterminations cannot accompany any future conquests, especially if, in the coming decades, a worsening imbalance between food and population leads to widespread famine. Even in the past few years, some have worried that the Vietnamese might use their recent conquest of Cambodia to replace the (remnant) native Khmer population with their own people.

Digression: The Moral Check?—But what of "rights" and "justice"? This is a question that inevitably recurs with the parable of the tribes. How can power have free reign when people are by nature concerned with the moral dimension of their conduct? The discussion of genocide and cultural destruction is an apt introduction to that issue.

People are moral creatures. Unfortunately, although moral scruples can act as an obstacle to the unbridled pursuit of interest, they prove too often an easily surmountable barrier. For one thing people often use rationalization and hypocrisy to make moral principle a tool of rather than a check upon self-interest (as Marx so rightly pointed out). Beyond that, the jurisdiction of moral injunctions is often confined to relations within one's own group. The out-group is typically entitled to no such consideration. "Thou shalt not kill" was hardly intended as God's commandment to the Hebrews to be pacifists. The chronically dangerous "state of nature" among societies inevitably feeds intersocietal amorality. Also, the selection for power may select against moral sensitivity: nice guys are finished first.[2]

---

2. So fiercely does the incessant struggle for power shape human moral possibilities that even the teachings of Jesus ("Resist not evil") can be transformed to serve the hunger for power in this world. Thus went the rites of the Hospitalers, a Christian military religious order of the time of the Crusades: "Take this sword; its brightness stands for faith, its point for hope, its guard for charity. Use it well . . ." (in Seward, 1972, p. 21).

Justice has rarely saved the rights of those whose societies have lacked the might. It was the founder of American justice, John Marshall, who wrote (in Johnson v. McIntosh, 8 Wheaton 543) that "all the nations of Europe who have acquired territories on this continent have asserted in themselves, and have recognized in others, the exclusive right of the discoverer to appropriate the lands occupied by the Indians" (quoted in A. Snow, 1921, p. 117). When the Hebrews went into Canaan, to claim the land God had promised them, they slew those whom they found there and counted it not among their sins. God says this to Moses about Og, the king of Bashan: "I have delivered him into thy hand, and all his people and his land. . . . So they smote him, and his sons, and all his people, until there was none left alive: and they possessed his land" (Numbers 21:34, 35). Just as the right can be construed to fit one's own sense of mission and manifest destiny, so can it be disregarded. In one of those classics which founded the science of history, Thucydides describes the encounter between the ambitious Athenians and the Melians who resisted them. The Athenians' speech to the Melians, in Thucydides' account, is frighteningly forthright in its portrayal of the rule of power in their own conduct and in human affairs generally:

> For ourselves, we shall not trouble you with specious pretenses—either of how we have a right to our empire because we overthrew the Mede, or are now attacking you because of wrong that you have done us—and make a long speech which would not be believed. . . . You know as well as we do that right, as the world goes, is only in question between equals in power, while the strong do what they can and the weak suffer what they must. (*The Peloponnesian War*, Book V)

It is in such a world that genocide and the destruction of conquered cultures can occur. Thucydides goes on to tell us: "The siege was not pressed vigorously; and some treachery taking place inside, the Melians surrendered at discretion to the Athenians, who put to death all the grown men whom they took, and sold the women and children for slaves, and subsequently sent out five hundred colonists and inhabited the place themselves."

The rule of power, the destruction of the innocent, are most ancient problems. Our vision of our own times will be clouded if we fail to recognize that. Some believe modern imperialism manifests the eruption of some new disease into human affairs. They are thus led to disparage Western civilization as uniquely corrupt and degraded. Some are aghast at the amorality of the Soviet Union which relentlessly presses forward its expansionist drive. They are led to regard that totalitarian regime as a nation unlike all others in its irremediable viciousness. But the disease lies not in any civilization, or race, or economic, or governmental system.

The world has seen it all before, since history began. It is more than two thousand years since Thucydides wrote or recorded the Athenians' speech whose overstatement, regrettably, is not grotesquely extreme:

> Of the gods we believe, and of men we know, that by a necessary law of their nature they rule wherever they can. And it is not as if we were the first to make this law, or to act upon it when made: we found it existing before us, and shall leave it to exist forever after us; all we do is make use of it, knowing that you and everybody else, having the same power as we have, would do the same as we do. (Ibid.)

The parable of the tribes attempts to explain whence comes this "necessary law" of the nature of civilized societies, and why the efforts to substitute a more moral and benign law to protect the weak have not succeeded better.

C. Transformation

Even if a people and their culture survive conquest by a more powerful society, the option of continuing life as before may be stolen from them. They may be compelled to adopt the ways of their masters. The extent to which conquest results in cultural transformation can vary across a wide spectrum. Destruction might be seen as one extreme on this continuum, where the powerful replace the original people and their ways with their own. At the other extreme, the conqueror may simply seek to extract regular tribute or revenue from a society which otherwise is left unmolested. The freedom of the conquered to continue their own way of life depends on a variety of factors. A review of these factors will help illuminate the workings of the parable of the tribes.

Sometimes the fate of the conquered culture depends simply on the attitude of the invaders. How tolerant are they, or how vindictive? In her interesting study, *Politics and Culture in International History*, Adda Bozeman describes some differences in attitude among the conquerors of the ancient world. The Assyrians were typical of the early empire builders in their urge to sweep away alien customs and place their stamp upon local cultures. Under Assyrian domination, temples were destroyed, peoples were deported from their homelands, and so on. The Persian Empire (of about 600 B.C.) took a more tolerant approach, not only permitting but even supporting local institutions and customs. After them, the Romans also refrained from wanton intrusion against the cultural integrity of subordinate peoples. They instituted whatever was necessary for maintaining their dominance. Beyond that point, they discovered, tolerance paid off.

Among recent empire builders, such a diversity of approaches has persisted. When conquerors from Europe and (later) America invaded other societies, they were armed not only with unprecedented power but also with what they saw as the one true religion. Enjoined by their faith to save the godless from eternal perdition, some of the imperialists set out to uproot native religions and to stamp out customs they regarded as superstitious or immoral. Persuasion was often aided by the force at the ruler's command, and in some parts of the world the destructive impact on native cultures was considerable. The path of Islam's rapid spread across Asia was likewise cleared in some areas by the sword. The infidels were given the nonchoice of conversion or death. Today, the dogmatically atheistic imperialists of the Soviet Union seek to impose not only their domination but also their world view on those peoples whom their empire encompasses, suppressing traditional Christian, Jewish, and Islamic religious practices and training, and other non-Communist ideologies. And the ancient culture of the Tibetans has, for several recent decades, suffered a systematic campaign of cultural suppression and transformation undertaken by their Chinese conquerors.[3]

The vindictiveness and intolerance displayed by many conquerors often seems irrational. There can, however, also be practical reasons for rooting out the cultures of subject peoples. Contemporary totalitarian empires clearly have the political goal of eliminating potentially competing centers of power. The Western imperialists of the nineteenth century often systematically changed the political, demographic, and economic structure of their colonial possessions in order best to serve the interests of the mother country. Sometimes these changes were far-reaching. As an example, we may take the British transformation of Ceylon (now Sri Lanka). Writing earlier in this century in *Imperialism and Civilization*, Leonard Woolf described the change:

> When the British came to Ceylon little more than a century ago, the hills and mountains in the center of that island were wild places, the inhabitants Sinhalese living in scattered villages. The hills and mountains are now over large areas cleared of forest and jungle; the land is owned by Englishmen in the employ of [English] companies; the labour on the states consists of Tamils imported from India, belonging to a different race and religion and speaking a different language from the Sinhalese. The area is administered by an English Civil Servant responsible to an English Governor, himself responsible to the Colonial Office and Parliament in London. The laws and ordinances of this administration, made and applied by Englishmen, regulate minutely the everyday lives of the inhabitants not only in matters of public order, but also of the ownership of land, agriculture, trade, industry, labour, religion and education. In other words, the whole life of this area has been completely revolutionized in the space of a hundred years. (1928, p. 55.)

3. That such campaigns do not succeed easily or quickly is discussed later in this chapter, "Qualifications: Limits on the Transformative Effects of Conquest."

Finding the original culture of Ceylon inappropriate for their purposes, the British treated the island as so much raw material to be rearranged to achieve British ends. One senses here not so much hostility as indifference toward the natives and their ways.

Some have contrasted modern imperialism with the conquests of archaic times. The conquerors of old, Woolf says, were not inclined to wreak great changes on the societies they conquered, as the modern British did in Ceylon. They were more likely to be content simply to place themselves atop the ongoing system as rulers. A good illustration of this continuity of the native society, even while archaic conquerors came and went, is found in the history of Peru. This history is described by Julian Steward in *Theory of Culture Change*. When the Incas welded an empire out of the various societies in the region, "The Inca institutions affected the states and communities to the extent that it was necessary to make the empire function, but this did not mean that everything at the lower levels had to be changed. Much was left alone" (1971 p. 59). The Spanish conquest of Incan Peru was in some respects one of the most dramatic cultural extensions of history. It was no palace coup, not even a conquest within a given cultural system as when the Spanish controlled the Netherlands. It was rather a sudden leap of a civilization nourished in one region of the world onto a new continent with an altogether alien tradition. Even so, the integrity of native cultural life was not shattered. Again Steward: "Under the conquest, Spanish national institutions replaced those of the Incas, but the lower levels of native cultures were not so drastically altered. . . . (M)any native rulers were retained in lower positions and a large portion of village activities went on as in native times" (ibid.). The people who had been paying tribute to the Incas now were forced to pay tribute to the Spanish. Of course, the Spanish colonial domination left a profound imprint upon the continent, else "Latin" America would not be a meaningful grouping of societies. Nonetheless, in contrast with the modern European imperialism of the nineteenth century, archaic empires like those of the Spanish and of the Romans before them wrought less deep and systematic transformation of the societies they conquered. The question arises: Why?

We encounter once again the idea that modern imperialism is something new and unprecedented. Woolf, for example, sees the difference as rooted in a change in the imperialists' motives—mere rule is no longer enough. The new methods and motives of the modern conquerors are attributed by many to something special in the dynamic of capitalism. Whereas those hungering solely for glory might be content just to rule, the capitalist conqueror hungers for profits and therefore he rearranges all social life to maximize productive efficiency. With the new kind of economy, the ruling part reaches deeper into society. George Lukacs, in his essay "Class Consciousness," stresses how, before capitalism, the state "remains insecurely anchored in the real life of the society. One sector simply lives out its 'natural' existence in what amounts to a total independence of the fate of the state" (1971, p. 55). Thus the Incas and the Spanish conquistadors can come and go, while the peasant society lives on. But then comes capitalism, which continually forces deeper interrelationships, drawing the daily lives of the people within its orbit. Steward's account of cultural continuity and discontinuity in Peru proceeds to describe the impact of the eventual intrusion of modern economic forces. Such factors as the production of cash crops and the institution of wage labor ultimately "struck deeply at the heart of community culture . . . destroying the basis of the native communities and converting the mass of Indians into a national laboring class" (1955, p. 60). According to one view, then, modern imperialism brought great cultural changes because it was the carrier of a special economic system that uniquely permeates and transforms everything it touches. The bourgeoisie, wrote Marx and Engels in *The Communist Manifesto,* "compels all nations, on pain of extinction, to adopt the bourgeois model of production; it compels them to introduce what it calls civilization into their midst, i.e., to become bourgeois themselves" (in Feuer, 1959, p. 11).

This view may have some validity, but it misses, I believe, the most important point. Here we come to the crux of the issue. When the victor and the vanquished are on comparable levels of political and economic development, the change of rulers may have little impact on the society as a whole. If, however, the more powerful society has tapped wholly new springs of power, the most advantageous use of the new imperial acquisition may require transplanting the new more potent methods. In the first instance, the ruler's purposes are served simply by taking his "cut" of the action and letting the game go on as before. But when the new ruler knows a game that could yield a much bigger cut from the same underlying resources, he has practical reasons to impose his new game onto the old culture.

It is therefore during those "two great waves" that imperial expansion has most reliably entailed the imposition upon conquered peoples of profound cultural transformations. Modern imperialism is not unique, therefore, but a recurrence of a quite ancient phenomenon. Old imperialists as well as new changed whatever was necessary to integrate fully the conquered lands into their own power-maximizing systems. When a sophisticated agrarian and urban civilization brought far more backward areas under its control, it too remade its acquisitions into its own image. David Kaplan describes the spread of the Chinese empire: "Fanning out from the Yellow River Valley, Chinese culture moved relentlessly southward . . . engulfing lands, peoples and cultures and putting a permanent stamp of 'Chinese' on them. Those people that could not be assimilated were either driven into less desirable areas of exploitation or exterminated" (1960, p. 84). The degree of change is a function less of the nature of the conqueror or of his systems than of the size of the gap between conqueror and conquered. It is worth noting where the imprint of Roman civilization went deepest. It was not in those areas, like the Middle East, which had already known and practiced a level of organization and technology comparable to that which gave the Romans their ascendancy. Rather it was in those regions, like France and Spain (which now speak Romance languages), whose less advanced social order required for efficient management the more far-reaching introduction of Roman methods and institutions (see Morgenthau, 1972, pp. 353–354). When archaic civilizations were the cutting edge of power, their imperialists also reached into the heart of conquered societies and wrought changes. Once a conquered people had been fully integrated into those power systems—when they had been yoked into settled life, agricultural productivity, and subservience to a distant ruler—the state could afford to be "insecurely anchored" in the daily life of the people. Changes of rule could then occur without revolutionizing the native culture.

The same is true of modern civilization: conquest means transformation when the gap is widest. "Modern" power is not just capitalist. Although capitalism may have been instrumental in forging the tools of modern power, these tools can be wielded by other kinds of social systems. We see, for example, that a modern communist industrial state also permeates and transforms archaic structures that fall to its imperialist domination, as the Russian-dominated Soviet system is doing in the Asian parts of its realm. Where the apparatus of modern power is already established—industrial production, modern state bureaucracy, the various elements of "human capital"—a new conquering ruler is not likely to change significantly the subjugated culture. Past wars among the industrial powers of Europe and the present Soviet domination of its European satellites suggest that conquests among modern societies (like those before among the archaic) result in rather limited transformations in the culture of the conquered.

Therefore, while cultural transformation is not an inevitable fruit of intersocietal competition, it is most likely to occur on precisely those occasions where the victory of one society over another is attributable to major cultural differences germane to the generation of power. In other words, where the selection for power would make the heaviest impact, just as there is a conquering society most likely to transform the conquered into something more closely resembling itself.

This correlation between the size of the gap and the extent of the transformation is reinforced by another factor: the duration of domination. The longer people with one culture maintain domination over those with another, the more deeply will the conquering culture stamp its imprint upon that of the conquered. Changing a people's culture takes time. The more enduring conquests are most likely to occur not when nations of similar power alternate in ascendancy but when the differences in power are sufficient to give one group more permanent advantage. Napoleon's brief domination of Europe, therefore, had a relatively limited impact on the cultures of the conquered, but the American Indian cultures are still being changed into offshoots of Anglo-American culture. (One may speculate that had European ascendancy not collapsed so soon after the colonization of Africa, African culture might have been as shattered and transformed as American Indian culture has been.) A wide gap in power, then, is most likely to give the conqueror the time to transform the native culture.

If by virtue of its comparative weakness a society is conquered, but it remains unchanged, it will remain vulnerable to reconquest by some other power at a later time. Eventually the ways of weakness will be changed. To repeat, the selection for power is not certain at any given time, but over the long haul it is irresistible.[4]

D. Imitation

In the first three outcomes, the ways of power spread when the mighty expand into areas where the weak have been. Resistance by the weak has been either absent or inconsequential in this picture. In actuality, resistance has counted for little when the advantage of the mighty has been overwhelming and when the threat has come so suddenly (in historic terms) that the weak have had little time to prepare to meet it. Thus,

---

4. There is one more way that conquest spreads the ways of power: the mere fact of being conquered can change the consciousness of the subjugated people. As some early ideologists of modern democracy argued, people are not born with a saddle on their backs for some ruler to ride upon. We began as members of egalitarian bands, not by nature given to subservience. When peoples still enjoying such natural liberty and dignity come under the conqueror's yoke, they are changed. Redfield describes that transformation: "as the civilizations moved outward to meet peoples still tribal and folklike, they slowly transformed the country people nearest at hand into peasantry" (1953, p. 51). For instance: "The Latin American Indian begins as a member of a morally independent folk society whose people look across at the invader and conqueror; he becomes a peasant, looking up—and down—toward a ruling class" (p. 42). This yoke of subordination is a particularly important part of the domestication of the civilized human animal which prepares him to serve in the systems of power.

Even when a people have known rulers, the experience of alien conquest can so distress and enrage them that they become obsessed with the value of power. The Romans, for example, emerged with their lust for world conquest after recuperating from their own earlier devastation (Toynbee, quoted in Rostow, 1971, p. 43). In the contemporary world, some of those who seek to explain Soviet militarism and expansionism see them as the fruit of an insecurity rooted in a recurrent national trauma of invasion.

when an advanced civilization abruptly appears in gunboats offshore, the native peoples have been compelled to retreat, to suffer their own destruction, or to allow their cultural system to be significantly absorbed or transformed by the conqueror. More meaningful resistance, however, is frequently possible for peoples who can watch the threat grow, as it were, from seed right in their own backyard. Societies in the same cultural system will often have roughly comparable capacities, and can observe each other closely enough not to be taken by surprise by power of an unforeseen magnitude. But if the ability to observe the growth of a neighbor's power gives one the chance to preserve the capacity to resist him, it does not otherwise increase one's freedom of choice. If one society in the system develops an important competitive advantage, its neighbors lose the option of continuing their way of living as before. The course of resistance also requires transformation in the ways of power. It requires the imitation of one's more potent foes.

The word "civilization" speaks of cities, and the first urban cultures arose many millennia ago in Mesopotamia. These first cities could coordinate networks of production and power exceeding what had preceded them. This new power imposed upon neighboring areas the imperative to imitate the new organization. McGuire Gibson writes that "As the primal cities grew stronger and more aggressive in both trade and warfare, the populations in other areas were forced to aggregate to meet the threat. . . . The only workable adjustment was the elaboration of similar complex organizations" (in Renfrew, 1973, p. 208). Just as with the rise of urban political organization in Mesopotamia, so later with the rise of the nation state in Europe.[5] According to C. N. Parkinson: "Formidable were the first consolidate states, of which England was among the earliest. Rival kings endeavored to follow suit, creating national realms, each from fear of the other. France arose from fear of England, Great Britain was formed from fear of Spain, Germany from fear of France, Austria from fear of Germany, and Italy from fear of Austria" (quoted in Service, 1971, p. 58n). Later strides by conquerors like Napoleon and Hitler in harnessing the resources of society for military power would compel those nations who arose to resist them to transform themselves in similar directions. Despite their swift defeat, they left an enduring social evolutionary impact. They helped bring the evolution of political-military structures toward that stage in power maximization we call "total war."[6]

5. See also Edward Luttwak on how the prolonged confrontation with the Roman Empire of the many peoples on the Rhine and upper Danube led these peoples to form "the larger federation of the Franks and Alamanni, who could concentrate much more manpower in attacking the frontiers" (1976, p. 128).
6. On this point, see chap. 3, "Evolution toward More Effective Central Control."

Aside from the political and military bases of modern power, there is the economic-industrial. Once the potent new technology emerged in the competitive European system, the need to imitate was irresistible. After a case-by-case overview of the actual conditions under which industrialization was undertaken in Europe (and elsewhere), W. W. Rostow summarizes: "In all cases, reaction to foreign intrusion, actual or threatened, is relevant to the domestic thrust towards modernization" (1971, p. 95).

Power can be resisted only with power. Potent breakthroughs thus require emulation. This is true not only within Europe, where modern power emerged in an intensively competitive international environment, but thence around the world as the omnivorous Western powers invaded other continents. The defensive imitation by the Japanese was mentioned earlier—"industrialize or be gobbled up like the rest." (See also Landes, in Rostow, 1971, p. 72.) Also mentioned has been the imitation of the West by those seeking to free their societies from imperialist domination. Rupert Emerson describes this ironic link: "The anticolonial forces have derived their inspiration and ideas primarily from the teachings of the colonial powers themselves, have for the most part adopted Western forms of organization and action, and have been led by men intimately acquainted with the West" (1968, p. 5; see also D. Kaplan, 1960, p. 88).

Imitation in the struggle for power continues to distort cultural development, as two superpowers thousands of miles apart eye each other, fearful that the other will gain a competitive advantage. An American observer of the cold war wrote in 1960: "All things Communist remain anathema, but the slightest word of some new development in Russia is sufficient to set in motion investigations by several congressional committees and private foundations to find out why we are not doing the same thing" (H. Wheeler, 1960, p. 181).

The tyranny of power is such that even self-defense becomes a kind of surrender. Not to resist is to be transformed at the hands of the mighty. To resist requires that one transform oneself into their likeness. Either way, free human choice is prevented. *All ways but the ways of power are blocked.*

4. Qualifications:
Limits on the Transformative Effects of Conquest

The selection for power does not operate as mechanically as the parable of the tribes, in its simple form, may seem to imply. The civilized world is not an arena of incessant contest in which the losers automatically are compelled to surrender their cultural identities in favor of those of the winners. It is time to modify this overly simplistic image.

(a) I said earlier that as conquerors the Romans learned that tolerance pays off. This lesson points to one of the saving graces of the rule of power: that domination is not a function merely of coercive force. A given people will resist subjugation more or less vigorously depending (among other things) on the perceived costs of submission. The intolerant and destructive conqueror will be opposed most vigorously. Alexander the Great, with a reputation for fairness and mercy toward those who did not resist him or break their agreements with him, was sometimes welcomed as a conquering ruler. By contrast, Hitler, who relied for his domination of other peoples more completely on pure coercion, provoked resistance all over Europe. In the second book of *Discourses*, Machiavelli describes how the Romans extended their rule by being invited by others to come in and settle their disputes. In this manner, "not only the arms of the Romans, but Roman law began now to prevail" (II.21). By contrast, his native Florence sought to bully others into subordination. Of this, Machiavelli says: "Had the Florentines, whether by means of confederation or by helping them, been easy-going with their neighbors instead of treating them roughly, they would unquestionably be the lords of Tuscany today. I do not mean to say that armed forces should never be used, but they should be used only as a last resort, when other means prove inadequate" (ibid.). Machiavelli clearly is questioning not the ends in striving for power but solely the choice of means: brutality has its costs. The ruler who relies on brute force needs more power to conquer and hold the same territory. Therefore, the value of consent must be part of the calculus of power.

A power that is accepted has, fortunately, an advantage over one that is resisted. Since acceptance requires that the subordinated people be given something they value, this fact has significantly moderated the destructive impact of the ruler of power.[7] Among the consequences, as the Romans saw, is that a ruler is unwise unnecessarily to attack the culture of those he rules. Our era has given us proof that peoples will fight and die to preserve the dignity and integrity of their cultures. A conqueror who insufficiently respects the autonomy and ways of life of those he dominates—Basques, Kurds, or whomever—ultimately increases the threat to his domination. Force, said Edmund Burke, "may subdue for a moment; but it does not remove the necessity for subduing again; and a

---

7. The reign of power has been made less violent, though not less efficacious, by a related factor. To "give" subordinated peoples something they value (in order to gain "acceptance" of one's rule) may mean simply to refrain from taking it away. As a means of extending one's power, the threat of force may be superior to its use. To use force may be to spend the bases of one's power, and thus the best players in the struggle for power recognize, with the Romans of the imperial period, that it is "much better to *conserve* force, and use military power as the instrument of political warfare." Armed with that recognition, the Romans "conquered the entire Hellenistic world with few battles and much coercive diplomacy" (Luttwak, 1976, p. 2, italics in original). The essence of power is domination, not destruction.

nation is not governed which is perpetually to be conquered" (quoted in Lenski, 1966, p. 51). The very weak are not saved by this, for their resistance counts for little. And even the potentially strong can be intimidated into submission by a ruthless regime of terror. But the flame in the human spirit never dies altogether. Orwell's vision of *1984* underestimated this resilience. That year is coming fast upon us, and recently we have seen striking Polish workers kneeling in Gdansk in prayer.

(b) The praying of the Polish workers suggests a second factor that tends to preserve the cultures of conquered peoples: people hold tenaciously to their traditional culture. Cultures are therefore not easily transformed. Cultures reside in people and are transmitted from generation to generation through the socialization process, a process that is extremely conservative. The older generation communicates to the younger much of what it received from the generation before. Usually they do so out of devotion to what they have internalized. Inevitably they do so because they cannot help teaching what they are, and they cannot help embodying what they have seen modeled before them. In China, for example, the revolutionary Mao strove with his Western Marxist-Leninist ideology to root out and cast away the old tradition but, in spite of himself, he ended up giving the revolution a profoundly Confucian flavor. For a conqueror to transform the culture of the conquered, he must intrude upon the socialization process over an extended period. Modern totalitarian states have developed powerful ways of undermining traditional socializing institutions like the family in order to strengthen their power to shape the young. But change comes slowly, and not inevitably. While workers on strike pray in Poland, the Chinese reportedly have contemplated allowing the Dalai Lama to return to Tibet as a symbol of more cultural autonomy for the un-Sinicized Tibetans. The conqueror indeed leaves his mark on the native culture, but cultural change is not automatic or total. The English colonization of India surely Anglicized Indian culture, but just as surely the ancient stream of Indian culture persists in modern India. The force for change through the selection for power must overcome formidable forces for continuity.[8]

8. Then there is the intriguing example of the Jews. Deprived by conquerors of their homeland for two thousand years, the Jewish people were able to preserve (though not without external influences) a distinctive cultural identity in Diaspora. They achieved this despite bloody campaigns of persecution and annihilation waged by dominant cultural groups. The modern part of the story contains a great irony, however. When the Jews were homeless, power seemed unable to work its way, unable to banish Jewish culture from the earth as it had obliterated the cultures of so many vanquished peoples. But after a mere generation of existence, the Jewish state—perpetually threatened by hostile neighbors—has been transformed from the Israel of Chaim Weizmann and David Ben Gurion to that of Menachem Begin and Ariel Sharon. The ways of power, alas, seem again to have prevailed—though at this writing, in the wake of the massacre in Beirut, one can hope that Jewish ethics may soon again guide the policy of the Jewish state.

(c) Another set of challenges to the theory is raised by the repeated Mongol conquests of China. In the first place, these victories of nomadic tribes over a sophisticated settled civilization appear to represent the triumph of the backward over the advanced. The parable of the tribes tells us that a principal characteristic of "advanced" culture is its stronger competitive power. In the second place, in the aftermath of these conquests we do not find the civilization of the Chinese transformed into the likeness of its conqueror; rather it was the conqueror who was absorbed into the cultural stream of the China he had conquered. This, too, appears to contradict the parable of the tribes. Let us consider each of these points.

(1) The recurrent Mongol invasions of China represent a widespread and general phenomenon in civilized history: the predations of nomadic "barbarians" upon the settled agrarian civilizations. That these tribes are frequently called barbarian is indicative of the common assumption that culturally these groups were comparatively backward. Of course, by many criteria they were; not being settled, they could accumulate less than their agrarian counterparts, and this "traveling light" set limits upon some dimensions of cultural development; and, living under extremely strenuous conditions, they did not develop the exquisite cultural refinements that many consider synonymous with "civilization" (in the Kenneth Clark sense of the word). But if one looks at civilization from the standpoint of this work—and not with an emphasis on fine porcelain and embroidered silks—the nomadic hordes represent not a "backward" social type but a particular branch of civilized development. The armies of Genghiz Khan were hardly "primitives," however crude or "savage" we may find some of their conduct. (Indeed, where is the story of civilization without its crudity and savagery?) Civilization begins with the domestication of plants and animals. If the agrarian life of settled civilization was one path by which people left the primitive state, the life of pastoral nomads was another. The two types were generally better suited for different ecological environments, and so for the most part they coexisted—albeit not always peacefully (as the story of Cain and Abel may symbolize).

The nomads, therefore, represent a particular type of civilized development. These pastoral peoples had their own problems with power, and as with the settled societies we more frequently call civilized their struggles helped to mold them in the direction of power maximization. The struggles among the small nations of the Mongols were chronic, and when Genghiz Khan emerged into history as the scourge of civilization, he and his organization had already been "selected" (and shaped) through a prolonged series of wars by which the societies of Mongolia had been unified under his command (Grousset, 1970, pp. 193, 226).

57

Moreover, in the business of warfare, the peoples led by Genghiz Khan, however backward they may have been in the niceties valued in the courts of China, were as "advanced" as anyone in the world. Their way of life had fashioned a society of tight discipline and organization. "This nation of nomads, a people on the march, was organized like an army"; the people were "ever ready for the word of command" (ibid., pp. 21, ix). In weaponry, horsemanship, ferocity, and tactics, these tribes posed a military threat quite formidable by the standards of archaic civilization. René Grousset writes, in his classic work, *The Empire of the Steppes:*

> The nomad, retarded though he was in material culture, always possessed a tremendous military ascendancy. He was the mounted archer. . . . Chinese, Iranian, Russian, Pole or Hungarian could never equal the Mongol in this field. Trained from childhood to drive deer at a gallop over the vast expanses of the steppes, accustomed to patient stalking and to all the ruses of the hunter on which his food—that is, his life—depended, he was unbeatable. (p. x)

Certainly, a civilized society like China had certain advantages in power over the nomads. For example, their sheer superiority in numbers gave them a significant edge.[9] But none of these advantages could keep the barbarians from threatening the empire at its edges. Indeed, the threat went both ways: a strong China would frequently make successful military forays into the steppes to crush the nomads. However we judge the contest in archaic times, eventually the branch of civilized societies that led to settled life proved to possess the stronger potential for the development of power, for the settled societies were better able to develop and utilize sophisticated and massive forms of technology. Thus, the coming of artillery made of Genghiz Khan and his followers the last of a great line of nomadic conquerors. Writes Grousset: "The cannonades with which Ivan the Terrible scattered the last heirs of the Golden Hordes, and with which the K'ang-hsi emperor of China frightened the Kalmucks, marked the end of a period of world history. For the first time, and for ever, military technique had changed camps and civilization became stronger than barbarian" (ibid., p. xi). (It is largely because the settled life of civilized development ultimately proved the more potent—as well as because members of settled societies have almost always written the histories of the world—that our view of the nomads is colored by a mixture of fear and condescension.)

It is less than clear that the nomadic tribes were basically more powerful than the settled civilizations even before the decisive appearance of modern weapons technology. The actual conquests with which we are concerned here came at particular junctures in Chinese history. China

9. On the value of greater numbers, see chap. 3, "The Evolution toward Larger Societies."

could be conquered when it squandered its latent power in corruption and disunity.[10] When the sedentary empire was in a "ruinous state," the nomads could gather in the empire piece by piece. Thus Grousset describes Genghiz Khan as "testing the quality of his army against the weakest of the three states among which the lands of old China were divided" (ibid., p. 226). And when the great Khan's armies spread out westward, they found a Muslim world also rendered "divided and helpless" before a Mongol invasion by the "mortal enmity between sultan and caliph" (ibid., p. 230). When it is in a fragmented and demoralized state, the intrinsically more powerful society does not always win.

For these reasons, the Mongol conquests of China do not contradict the parable of the tribes.

(2) To explain how the Mongols could triumph, however, does not explain their "Sinicization" once their conquest was achieved. The beginning of a response to this challenge to the parable of the tribes lies in the recognition that true conquest and domination are matters less of winning the war than of controlling the peace.

Once China, or some part of it, had been conquered, what were the Mongols to do with it? The option of turning Chinese society into an image of that of the pastoral nomads was hardly feasible (militarily, demographically, or geographically). Once the prize was won, the conquerors were frequently confused about what to do with it. Coming from a military tradition of raid and retreat, the invaders often withdrew with their booty after destroying everything else. But so numerous were the Chinese that there were always others to take the place of those slain. "Under such conditions, Mongol generals were compelled to recapture certain fortresses two or three times over" (ibid., pp. 228–229). The Mongol confusion about what to do with their conquest emerges out of Grousset's description of the sacking of Peking:

> The Mongols captured the city, massacred its inhabitants, pillaged the houses, and then set the whole place on fire [in 1215]. It is clear that the nomads had no notion of what could be done with a great city, nor how they might use it for the consolidation and expansion of their power. . . . They burn and slay not so much from cruelty as from perplexity, and because they know of nothing else to do. (p. 230)

Since the Mongols could make very limited use of China in the context of their own way of life, their conquest could only mean pillage and senseless destruction so long as the Mongols did not adapt.

If the invaders were to make use of the considerable resources of Chinese civilization to expand their own power, it was necessary both that

10. On the tendency of power systems to fall as well as to rise, see chap. 7, "The Death of the Unnatural."

Chinese culture be left essentially intact and that the Mongols adjust themselves to the requirements of running a complexly organized, highly productive society. The Mongols bore no system, transplantable into China, which could increase (or even match) the yield in productivity of the ongoing Chinese system. (Their situation thus contrasts with the example cited earlier of the British in Ceylon.) If the conquerors wanted to reap the most benefit from their acquisition, therefore, they were better off harnessing the power of the conquered society than destroying or changing it. China as it was, however, could not be run by the Mongols as they were. There is a famous line to the effect that China can be conquered from horseback, but it cannot be ruled from horseback. To exploit China most effectively, Marshall Sahlins and Elman Service write, the nomads "had to abandon the very organization which had made conquest possible in the first place" (1960, p. 85). Indeed, to rule China at all the nomads were forced to transform themselves and to perpetuate the native system: "Since in administrative matters they lacked all experience, and their own tribal institutions were not adapted to the complicated task of ruling a large agrarian society, they had to make use of traditional Chinese ways of government. . . . The landed gentry again became the backbone of society, and the primitive rules of nomadic origin had to conform to their way of life" (Zürcher, 1975, p. 317).[11]

The repeated Sinicization of the Mongols thus does not so much contradict the parable of the tribes as it indicates the need for a subtle understanding of power: that controlling the peace is the ultimate victory of a conquering culture. The cultural resources of the nomadic invaders were inadequate to control China, much less to supplant the Chinese culture. Yet later invaders from the West—using military power, but short of complete conquest—would undermine the ancient structures of Chinese civilization more fundamentally. Unlike the Mongols, they bore not only arms but also a material culture capable of supplanting the old ways.

5. Choosing the Choosers: The Historymakers

The parable of the tribes shows how the choice of continuing the ways of weakness is taken from mankind by the workings of power. Sooner

---

11. An additional factor, no doubt, is the attractiveness of the "high culture" of China. The rigors of life on the steppes, after all, may be better for toughening a person than for giving him pleasure. Alexander and his conquering Macedonians were similarly attracted to the beauties and pleasures of the culture of the sophisticated Persians whom they conquered. In such instances, cultural influence can be said to be governed by choice, against the direction of power's flow. But power plays a role here as well: as conquerors, the Mongols (or Macedonians) were well positioned (at the top) to enjoy the finest fruits of the "superior" culture. What the Mongols chose, therefore, was not Chinese culture as a whole, but a very small and special piece of it made possible by power's regime.

or later, by one means or another, the ways of the powerful will supplant the ways of the weak. In a world where power is uncontrolled—where it is a contaminant—a powerful few can compel the many who are weak to follow their lead.

History is shaped by the powerful. I have reviewed how this is true in the intersocietal system, yet it is true also within societies where steps of crucial social evolutionary importance have been taken. Without the control by a powerful elite, the many might never have submitted to the discipline of urban civilization. The political structures of the archaic states, according to S. N. Eisenstadt in *The Political Systems of Empires,* were brought about by the initiative of the ruling elites, with the peasantry empowered to take no active role in the process. "The largest and economically fundamental stratum within the bureaucratic societies was thus both politically inarticulate and basically neutral or indifferent to the key premises of these polities" (1963, pp. 13, 210). The powerful few again compelled the many in the original establishment of industrialization. Britain was the birthplace both of the Industrial Revolution and of modern democracy, but it was hardly by democratic choice that the industrial process began. The sacrifices of the many were severe and involuntary. Forced to leave the land and become a proletariat, the many in industrializing Britain presented a "picture of unrelieved hardships and misery, a picture of a population barely literate, ignorant of affairs, geographically immobile in the main, grossly underpaid, poorly housed and fed— above all a population with almost no effective access to Government" (Sprout and Sprout, in Boulding and Murkerjee, 1972, pp. 220–221).

Perhaps the idea that history is shaped by the powerful requires us to take a different view of the role of choice in the evolution of civilization. Rather than say that mankind has been robbed of free choice, ought we instead simply to say that it is the powerful who choose while the weak are compelled to follow? Karl Deutsch, in his *Nerves of Government,* offers a useful definition of power: "In simple language, to have power means not to have to give in, and to force the environment to do so. Power in this narrow sense is the priority of output over input, the ability to talk instead of listen" (1963, p. 111). Perhaps the parable of the tribes overemphasizes the silenced choices of those who must listen, and does not sufficiently attend to the heroic choices of those powerful few who make history. From this point of view, the idea that "power rules" is meaninglessly abstract. It is the powerful who rule. Human beings of flesh and blood make choices and sweep aside the human and other obstacles in their environment to achieve their ends. They compel others to "listen" to their grand ideas. Admittedly, it is not mankind as a whole that shapes its destiny. But, the argument goes, some people play that decision-making role for us all. The earlier section "Heads I Win, Tails You Lose" rather arbitrarily looks at history from the standpoint of the weak. Threatened tribes may indeed have few options, but what of that potent and ambitious tribe that starts the process?

A heroic or elitist view of history looks at the problem of power this way. It is the powerful few, armed with a vigorous spirit and a plan for the future, who force mankind along the road of progress. The many lack the vision and the moral discipline to make the sacrifices necessary to take us forward. It is these few of courage and action—not impersonal "forces"—who shape our destiny.

This heroic vision of history is not as fashionable as it was in other times when power was more openly celebrated. Nonetheless, in the many places around the world where progress and development are being pushed by those in power, such a view continues to mold and justify the way power is wielded. An admiration for power may predispose one to see history in elitist terms, but one's attitude toward the historymakers is entirely separable from the question: should the direction of history be understood ultimately as chosen by the powerful few, or as imposed by unchosen forces?

The parable of the tribes and the "heroic" view concur at least on the point that in history it is the few who have talked while the many have been compelled to listen. To conclude from this that the choices of the few therefore necessarily govern history is to commit again the reductionist fallacy that sees the whole as only the sum of its parts. From the reductionist standpoint, the idea that "power rules" is meaninglessly abstract because the properties of the surrounding whole have been disregarded. Forces created by the whole can determine the course of the parts. The parable of the tribes shows how such forces do in fact arise. Crucial here, again, is the process of selection. The powerful get to speak because the unchosen structure of the system determines which messages will be heard. The powerful few appear to choose, but the selective process generated by the ungoverned system confers upon them that role. At one level, a kind of heroic creativity can make history. But at a more fundamental (not merely abstract) level, as I said in the first chapter, human creativity has not driven the mill of cultural evolution but has become its grist. *That which chooses the chooser determines the choice.*

This points to one more implication of the parable of the tribes concerning the significance of inequalities of power among people. To the elitist of the right, on one hand, this theory has said that in an ultimate sense his heroes have not governed history as he has believed. To the champion of the downtrodden on the left, on the other hand, the parable of the tribes says that the role of the powerful is more important than he may suspect. The power of A over B has usually been decried because it represents an injustice. What gives A the "right" to talk and force B to listen? Why should A have things his own way at B's expense? Certainly, injustice is a problem of utmost importance. Yet to these costs of power inequalities, which are paid in the present, the evolutionary perspective of the parable of the tribes adds another, ultimately more important cost, which must be paid by the future.

In the first chapter, I said of the historymakers that they were an unrepresentative lot. Who gets to speak and who must listen is a function of the overarching system. The ruler of a democracy, for example, is selected according to different criteria from those governing the selection of a dictator. Ideally, in a democracy those with the power to speak are chosen by the people generally as representing what they want said. In most human affairs, however, it is the power to compel that differentiates the "speakers" of history from the "listeners." They are not chosen as democratically representative. Nor are they a "representative" sample, for differences in power are the fruit of other profound differences— in ways of being, of valuing, of acting, of organizing. If A and B were identical, then once A and B were dead there would be no reason for history to care that A imposed his will on B. But the As of history are different from the Bs. Thus *those who get to talk have something different to say from those who must listen.*[12]

The nonrandom (nonrepresentative) nature of the selective process adds a dynamic social evolutionary consequence to the static problem of injustice. The fact that the powerful few can impose their choices means that not only do they as people dominate the present but also what they represent as a way of living will dominate the future.

6.   The Mother of Invention

A. *Introduction: Beyond Selection*

Uncontrolled circumstance, I have argued, has proclaimed the powerful to be kings of our destiny. In the realm of power, therefore, the human drama only appears to be shaped by heroes. Nonetheless, it is among

---

12. Relevant here are the roles of the sexes in history. Among the historymakers of almost all civilized systems, women have been markedly underrepresented. To some extent, biology (i.e., child-bearing and child nurturing) is destiny here; but to some extent, also, it is a function of women's lesser power. At any event, if as civilization has evolved women have been compelled to "listen," and if the two sexes are sufficiently different in nature to embody different messages, it would be no wonder if, as some suggest, civilization has distorted the conditions of human life by accentuating masculine principles to the neglect of the feminine. (For a suggestive intimation of how the struggle for social survival may play a vital role in fostering cultures where men are dominant over, and hostile to, women, see Sanday, 1981, pp. 23, 25.)

those pioneering few who have striven at the cutting edge of history that, if anywhere, human choice plays a meaningful role in the evolutionary process described by the parable of the tribes. Let us look more closely, then, at the creative element in the evolution of civilization, at those points where human beings have chosen the innovative ways that selection then imposes upon mankind generally.

As an evolutionary theory, the parable of the tribes functions as a model for a selective process, as does Darwin's idea of natural selection for biological evolution. In the theory of biological evolution, the emergence of the diverse forms among which selection can take place is explained by the process of mutation. Mutation is an essentially random process which contributes to the creation of biological order only because it combines with a nonrandom selective process. Biological evolution, one may say, employs no author but only an extremely patient and effective editor. The evolution of civilization is different. The cultural "mutations" do not just happen, they are created. Human beings are something new in the history of life: a species that purposefully creates its own possibilities. As the product of purpose, the emergence of cultural variation is a reflection not of randomness but of order. Cultural evolution is therefore the product of two nonrandom processes: human purpose governing the origin of cultural alternatives and a selective process determining the spread of some of these alternatives at the expense of others. If the parable of the tribes reveals the limits of human control over the selective process, perhaps the image of man as the chooser of his own destiny can be restored by a closer look at the process of cultural innovation.

B. Leaving the Primitive State

Let us begin with the apparent choice to leave the primitive state and begin on the path of civilization. Roughly ten thousand years ago, some groups evidently chose to take the crucial first steps that began civilization by domesticating plants and animals. Why? The parable of the tribes can evidently offer no explanation. That theory suggests that the struggle for power arose out of those first steps toward ecological control and therefore cannot explain those steps. The significance of the question is amplified by a more or less subtle primitivist undercurrent in my discussion of civilization. The natural order, I have said, nourishes all the life within it, and when people lived in their natural condition they were in fuller harmony with their environment and with themselves. Leslie White was quoted as saying that primitive society "was unquestionably the most satisfying kind of social environment man has ever lived in."

The obvious vulnerability of so primitivist a notion of this original Garden of Eden is: if people loved it so, why did they leave it?

In part, one can reply that these innovators would not have had the faintest idea of how profound would be the actual impact of the changes they initiated. The process went on for many, many generations before the new technology was more than a supplement to the old, hunting-and-gathering way of subsistence. The travelers would hardly have known they were leaving home. By small degrees they opened the lid on a new age, not having any way to know what a Pandora's box it would turn out to be. But still the question remains: why change at all? What can be known about this Prime Mover of the whole civilizational process?

An obvious possible answer is that people began to control their environment as soon as they knew how to. The human being, some claim, is a restless creature thirsting for mastery. It is part of the nature of our species to come upon a phenomenon, to see how it works, and to conquer that part of the world for our own benefit. So we can assume that if plant domestication began in the hills of Central Asia some ten millennia ago, it was there and then that the insight flashed in some human brain that seed + earth = new plants. That image seems compelling in an age like ours where technological capability seems to imply (in some circles of the powerful) a policy imperative. Such a view also harmonizes with the commonsense notion of cultural evolution which regards change as positive and which portrays mankind as plunging forward through any opening to a preferable option.

Unfortunately for that popular view, anthropologists have discovered that explanation to be untenable. Primitives all over the world, it has been found, have possessed the understanding necessary for domestication without choosing to implement it. We can infer from that observation that homo sapiens knew how to produce food long before certain groups chose to do so. This inference is not subject to challenge on the basis that our species lacked the intelligence before prehistoric times to grasp the essentials of food production, for all evidence is that the intellectual capacity of human beings has not changed appreciably since many millennia before the first departure from the hunting-gathering way of life.

Another approach to the problem has been to attribute to the time and place of innovation some special and unprecedented climatic conditions conducive to domestication. The recession of the Ice Age, the changing shore lines, and varying quantities of fish, fowl, or herd animals are factors that have been adduced to account for the breakthrough to food production. Without going into an elaborate review of the evidence, we may note simply that it appears that these climatic factors, while they

65

probably were involved, are quite insufficient to solve our problem. The circumstances were simply not exceptional enough to account for so unprecedented a development.

As I pondered this problem in the early 1970s, I was struck by an interesting coincidence. I had read that mankind had entered virtually all the regions of the earth as a hunter-gatherer. The prehistoric record showed, moreover, that many of these primitive migrations had occurred during the last ten thousand years or so before the crucial innovation of food production—across the Bering Straits into America,[13] southward from Asia into Australia, eastward into Polynesia. In biological terms, ten thousand years is a short time. One is struck by the swift and dramatic expansion of human territory and by the relative simultaneity of this expansion with the beginnings of food production. This coincidence seemed highly suggestive of the possibility that these two important prehistoric developments were different responses to the same circumstance. And the circumstance that might explain both was growing population pressure.

The line of Homo is of comparatively recent origin. Our ancestors began in one part of the world, perhaps Africa, and very gradually spread. A given hunting-and-gathering society is limited in the territory it can occupy and in its population density. Population growth in the prehistoric period, therefore, could mean neither the territorial expansion of individual societies nor the increasing density of settlement by a society in a given terrain (except to a limited degree). It required, rather, the "budding off" of new groups from old groups, with migration into previously unoccupied terrain to allow each primitive society access to the necessary resources. This kind of expansion can continue only while there is available territory to move into. The dramatic movement of primitive peoples across oceans and Arctic wastes suggested that the original landmass was becoming saturated, and some groups were getting squeezed out. The covering of the earth with primitive societies implies the human species was reaching a crucial juncture: territorial expansion could no longer accommodate the growth of Homo sapiens. In the absence of new land, the old land would have to be used more efficiently. It was in this context, I speculated, that the breakthrough to food production might be illuminated.

For an early draft of *The Parable of the Tribes* that speculation had to suffice. Since then, however, I have discovered the work of Mark N. Cohen, an anthropologist who has thought along similar lines and has,

13. It may be that the earliest crossings into the New World came before this time.

moreover, substantiated the thesis with considerable archaeological data from the various regions where food production may have independently originated. The material evidence of prehistory, he argues in *The Food Crisis in Prehistory* (1977), demonstrates that increasing population pressure required people to find successively more intense ways of exploiting the same environments. While some groups were migrating to new continents, others were moving into less desirable areas of the older continents, or were broadening the range of wild resources used for food. Eventually, "they were forced to become even more eclectic in their food gathering, to eat more and unpalatable foods, and in particular to concentrate on foods of low trophic level and high density" (ibid., p. 15). The origins of agriculture then comes "as simply one more in a series of adjustive strategies" (Cohen, 1975, p. 475) to deal with the problem of population pressure. Seeing this vital technological transition in the context of global demographic stress, he suggests, helps explain the emergence of agriculture in different parts of the world at roughly the same time.

The same kinds of forces stimulated subsequent innovations in agricultural technology as cultural evolution proceeded toward full-scale civilization. This is the thesis of Esther Boserup in *The Conditions of Agricultural Growth* (1965). As with the first steps, so with the later: people took the creative leap as death gained on them from behind.

The thesis that population pressures drove people to innovate in food production does not bear directly on the parable of the tribes, but the two points of view together help create an overall perspective on the human condition. In both, the impinging pressure of other societies creates problems. Indeed, just as "economic intensification" arose as an alternative to territorial migration, conversely, so did the intersocietal struggle for power emerge as territorial expansion through conquest became a possible substitute for more intensive use of the same land. The necessities of power originally grew out of Malthusian necessities.

This common element of necessity is pertinent to our present concern: the role of free human choice in molding human destiny. Earlier, Diamond was quoted as saying that "No primitive society has gone to civilization as to a greater good." This statement reflected upon the powerlessness of primitive groups to protect themselves against the onslaughts of more potent social types. But it now appears Diamond's generalization may apply even for those human groups who took the first steps toward creating the new social types. Their choice was not a free one between continuing to live in the old way and adopting a new way of life, for the old option was being steadily taken from them. As in the ancient biblical myth, the human beings did not choose to leave the Garden of Eden. Rather, in both instances, they are evicted because their eating undermines the basis of the original order.

As with the necessities of the parable of the tribes, so with the Malthusian necessities, we discover the tragic paradox: mankind's success as a species combined with his creative power to make him that singularly troubled animal who cannot live "at home." Because man was resourceful, he made his environment resourceless. Only the flexible and inventive animal was not compelled to come to balance with the natural environment, so only he was compelled to career on an unbalanced evolutionary course.

Cohen makes clear how the way of "progress," though it (temporarily) solved the problem of life and death, did not represent an improvement of the human condition.

> Agriculture is not easier than hunting and gathering and does not provide a higher quality, more palatable, or more secure food base. Agriculture has in fact only one advantage over hunting and gathering: that of providing more calories per unit of land per unit of time and thus of supporting denser populations. (1977, p. 15)

A choice, yes, but not a free one as to a greater good. The diet of hunter-gatherers, he says, is at once more nutritious, more various, and more enjoyable than that of agriculturists. Moreover, the ethnographic data suggest that the activities required of the hunter-gatherer are preferred to those of food producers (p. 27). People will choose the less preferred only when they have no choice. Agriculture, he concluded, will be practiced "only when necessitated by population pressure" (p. 15).

Thus, at this great divide in cultural evolution, before the parable of the tribes has begun to drive the evolution of civilization, we find innovation as much the child of human necessity as of human freedom.

C. The Escalator of Civilization

The change to food production opened the gates to a profound restructuring of human social life. As the new technology emerged, new kinds of society became possible. Innovation in all spheres accelerated: new forms of society, new divisions of labor, new ways of making things. To repeat, the very open-endedness of the possibilities created new necessities. At the core of the emerging problem was this: that human societies had a new possibility for social expansion and significant new motives for it. Even if, as we have discovered, primitives eventually became subject to Malthusian population pressures, their circumstance largely precluded

68

their using conquest as a solution: the political capabilities of the band precluded territorial expansion by a given group; the economic practices of hunters and gatherers made slavery or other forms of domination both unworkable and unprofitable; the demands of a mobile life-style made plunder both impossible (since one's neighbors had no large stores of wealth) and useless (as one could not accumulate wealth oneself) (see Service, 1966, p. 60). All these constraints on the motives for intersocietal conflict changed with the evolving civilized social systems. The new technology of food production sowed the seeds for an inevitable and ever-escalating struggle for power among societies.

In trying to solve one problem, mankind inadvertently created another. Malthusian economic pressures which shaped human choices in the earliest stages of the evolution of civilization were increasingly overshadowed by the necessities of intersocietal competition. It may be, for example, that the early political differentiation in civilized societies was instituted primarily for more economic security and diversity. The undifferentiated egalitarian band gave way to a larger organization with a central authority, some believe, because of the benefits of a redistributive network embracing heterogeneous regions. In subsequent stages of political evolution, however, it appears that the intersocietal struggle for power increasingly provided the impetus for creating the new political structures. Confronted by chronic threats to their social survival, people invented new structures to make their societies competitively more powerful. The escalation of conflict, the evolving structure of civilized society, and the mutually reinforcing relationship between the two are discussed further in the next chapter.

To the extent that innovative energies have been channeled by the necessities of social survival, the choice has hardly been a free one. "Innovate or die" has often been the option that civilized peoples have confronted. Those who have created the "new springs of power" favored in the selective process of the parable of the tribes are ultimately perhaps as unfree in their choices as those whom they threaten. When a tribe is threatened by a hostile neighbor, I said, there are four possible outcomes. A fifth, perhaps, should now be added: Escalation.

In the chronic struggle for power among societies, the differentiation between offense and defense becomes blurred. No doubt, a good deal of hypocrisy beclouds the motives of those who struggle to maximize power. Yet, there is a sense in which even aggressive uses of force are frequently motivated by defensive needs. States that have lost their appetite for power, Machiavelli believed, are doomed to be destroyed by their more vigorous neighbors (Berlin, 1972, p. 26). The Russian czars believed that "that which stops growing begins to rot" (Jervis, 1976,

p. 63). The idea that a good offense is the best defense is expressed by Alciabades in his speech in favor of the Athenian expedition to Sicily, as rendered by Thucydides:

> Men do not rest content with parrying the attacks of a superior, but often strike the first blow to prevent the attack being made. And we cannot fix the exact point at which our empire shall stop; we have reached a position in which we must not be content with retaining but must scheme to extend it, for, if we cease to rule others, we are in danger of being ruled ourselves. (6.19)

Even offensive wars, Rousseau has similarly declared, are essentially "unjust precautions" for self-protection (quoted in Waltz, 1959, p. 180).

If aggression is one defensive way of escalating the struggle for power, power-relevant innovations can be another. As with the previously mentioned early stages of political evolution, so with some of the modern ones: Cyril Parkinson says that the originators of the nation-state, whose advance compelled their competitors to emulate them, were themselves motivated by defensive anxieties caused by the strife-torn intersocietal system. Similarly with the first industrial revolution. Rostow suggests that England's "takeoff," which spread across the continent like a contagion because of its significance for competitive power, was stimulated in part by the English perception of a threat from France. Another example comes readily to mind from the experience of the generations now living. It was the United States that inaugurated the era of nuclear weaponry—an escalation in destructive power of epic proportions. But this extraordinary innovation was not made boldly with a sense of freedom. Rather it was made in fear, as a response to Nazi aggression and in particular to the fear that Hitler's war machine would make and use the bomb first.[14] (And if the Nazis had been first, would it be much less valid to suggest that the devastating impact of the intersocietal struggle had driven men to make the bomb, and had indeed formed their whole warped power-worshiping view of the world?) The innovators who labor at the cutting edge of power maximization seem as driven by the unchosen struggle for power as the others.

Since each escalation is quickly matched by emulation, every advantage is a temporary one. Thus, the innovators are doubly unfree: at the outset

---

14. From C. P. Snow's Journal of 1939: "Yet the bomb must be made if it really is a physical possibility. If it is not made in America this year it may be next year in Germany. There is no ethical problem. . . . It is better, at any rate, that America should have a six months start" (cited in Snow, 1981). A decade later, an aid to Secretary of State Acheson recorded from the meeting where the decision to make the H-Bomb was made: "[President Truman] asked, 'Can the Russians do it?' All heads nodded, yes they can. 'In that case,' Truman said, 'we have no choice. We'll go ahead.'" The Joint Chiefs had written to the President: "Possession of a thermonuclear weapon by the U.S.S.R. without such possession by the United States would be intolerable" (Bundy, 1982).

they are pressed by the inescapable insecurities of intersocietal anarchy, and in the end they have merely designed a trap of which they too become victims. The bold few who escalate the level of power maximization are ensnared by a poetic justice—or injustice—as in those tales where the evildoer is tricked into passing cruel sentence upon himself.

D. Conclusion: Innovation as Directed by Human Purpose

This picture of dire necessity as the mother of invention is, of course, only part of the total picture of cultural innovation. People do not constantly have their backs against the wall, and certainly the breathing room that civilized life has often provided people has facilitated human creativity as much as the struggle for survival has channeled it. My concern in this section, however, has been not with innovations generally but with those "bold and pioneering" few who have created those cultural forms which have spread because of the parable of the tribes. For these power-relevant innovations, the universal insecurities and necessities of the struggle for power are indeed often central to understanding the nature of the creative process. And even if the nonchoice of "innovate or die" is atypical of cultural innovations in general, this discussion of major cultural advances made under Malthusian and competitive threats to survival does point to a general truth about human innovation: people create new cultural alternatives to meet perceived human needs.

In much sociological and economic thought on the subject, invention and technological change have been regarded as comprising a self-contained system unfolding according to its own logic. The sequence and direction of innovations supposedly proceeds independently of human needs and choices. Technology becomes, in this view, a kind of Franken-stein monster, a wantonly destructive self-impelled system of human creation but not under human guidance. This image seems reminiscent of the parable of the tribes, but later I argue that it must be rejected for its isolation of technology as the source of human helplessness.[15] In the present context, I begin by rejecting its theory of innovation. In his study, *Invention and Economic Growth*, my late father demonstrated that invention in the economic sphere is directed by human needs as reflected in the marketplace. Innovation, he showed, is a dependent variable, an instrument of human purposes. (What is true of economic innovations should perhaps be presumed true of cultural innovations generally.) Against the argument that inventive activity occurs in those areas where technology had yet to unfold, he demonstrated that wherever there remains demand

15. See chap. 7, "Man's Dominion."

for a particular good, innovations will continue to improve it. Even so venerable and simple a device as the horseshoe continued to be the object of considerable innovation until the new invention of the automobile redirected the way human needs expressed themselves in the market. His work, an exhaustive empirical examination of data in patent activity and investment, would thus seem to free human creativity from the grip of the Frankenstein monster to become the servant of human choice.

But, again, not all human choices are free. If innovative activity is directed by human needs, those needs may be determined by forces altogether unchosen. Mankind has indeed created a Frankenstein monster—not our technological machinery but the system of civilization as a whole with its inevitable struggles for power. As we who participate in the arms race of the second half of the twentieth century know only too well, a system can be so structured that the pursuit by each actor in it of his own quite genuine needs can serve ultimately to threaten or destroy the well-being of all. Our moment in history merely dramatizes more vividly what has been true throughout the evolution of civilization: that the innovations made in the struggle for survival may prove in the end to be in the interests of no one.

Thus, we reach a rather striking and important irony: that the responsiveness of innovation to human need compounds rather than ameliorates the impact of the parable of the tribes. The parable of the tribes begins as a model for selection which we at first assumed needed passively to await the emergence of power-enhancing alternatives. But in cultural evolution these alternatives are not random mutations but innovations that are directed by human purpose. Here we hoped to find human choice restored to center stage in the social evolutionary drama, but the restoration turns out to be ambiguous. There are, of course, innovators like Pasteur who responded to medical crises (in anthrax, cholera, or rabies) with bursts of creative genius, and inventors like Edison whose ingenuity created devices people could use to enhance their comfort and enjoyment. But even if many cultural innovations are made free of the grim competitive pressures of the parable of the tribes—that disease which mankind unwittingly has inflicted upon itself—nonetheless it is true that the same intersocietal struggles that bring about the selection for power simultaneously generate intense human needs that direct the course of cultural innovation.

People are not moths passively allowing selection to transform them. They are armed with a creative intelligence to discover threats to their survival and to invent the means for overcoming those threats. We find, therefore, that in the history of civilization, important innovations in technology, in political structure, in economic organization, in ideology, were created quite consciously by people striving to armor themselves to survive a hostile intersocietal environment. Thus it is that, in the domain where necessity impinges, the ability of human beings to create new cultural forms to achieve their purposes, far from restoring to people the choice of their destiny, magnifies the impact of the selective process and speeds the evolution of civilization still further in the unchosen direction of power maximization. In this realm, it is as though the wind is still directed by the parable of the tribes, and human choice can only act to make still larger the sails of our vessels.

Chapter Three

Shaped by Power

Introduction

In ten thousand years, the morphology of human societies has changed drastically. If we stand back to watch this dramatic unfolding of civilization as if we were watching time-elapsed photography, our attention is captured by certain overall trends in the structural transformation of human society. This chapter identifies some of these salient trends and seeks to explain them with the parable of the tribes. I have already touched upon some of the transformations dictated by the selection for power through intersocietal competition, particularly in technology and in sociopolitical organization. Here I examine some of the dimensions of the evolving shape of power more closely and systematically.

1. Red Sky at Morning: The Dawn of Civilization and the Rise of Warfare

Let us look first at a change not in structure but in spirit—the rise of belligerency among human societies. This, after all, is the engine that drives the evolutionary process described by the parable of the tribes. Before the selection for power could disfigure the face of human existence, it was necessary first for the struggle for power to erupt. I have argued essentially on a logical basis that the beginnings of civilization made inevitable a continual struggle for power among societies. Compelling argument about how things must have been, however, is no substitute for actual testimony about how things in fact were.

To be valid, the parable of the tribes requires that civilized societies have chronically struggled against one another. It does not require, however, that warfare among human societies began only with civilization. Some (e.g., Robert Bigelow) assert that fierce intersocietal conflict has always characterized our species. Even if that were true, even if civilized societies only continued a previous pattern of intersocietal struggle, the rise of civilization would have given such struggles a new social evolutionary impact.

According to the parable of the tribes, the struggle for power has directed social evolution primarily by generating a selective process among social types and, secondarily, as seen in the preceding chapter, by channeling human creativity into the development of power-maximizing innovations. Only with the rise of civilization could either of these fruits of the struggle for power significantly transform human societies. This is because the ecological constraints on primitive societies so narrowly limited their possible range of development. Selection requires diversity, and conflict among societies that were of necessity much alike can generate only limited selection. By the same token, the range of innovations that might be introduced was also quite narrow among primitive societies compared with the possibilities opened up by the advent of food production and, thereby, of civilization. Therefore, even if chronic conflict was old, its social evolutionary consequences would have been new. The range of social possibilities became so much greater in degree that the fruit of intersocietal struggle would be different in kind. Whether pre-civilized societies were peaceful or warlike, the beginnings of civilization would still mark the essential point of discontinuity in human social evolution.

It nonetheless remains important whether chronic intersocietal strife represented a change in the human condition, for it influences in what light we perceive the fate of the human animal imprisoned by the rule of power. The parable of the tribes requires no especial bellicosity of nature in the civilization-making creature. The structure of the overarching system mandates that some of the worst sins of such a creature would inevitably be magnified into laws of its social existence. If we should adopt an Ardreyesque picture of natural man with human blood dripping from tooth and club, our sympathy for our species' plight would be diminished. We want to know, then, whether or not the rise of new social

75

evolutionary forces compelled human beings to take on bellicosity as an alien garment.

Violence is no doubt part of the human repertoire. The fact that we are hunters and carnivores means that spilling blood is one of the things that "natural man" does. But is the shedding of human blood as central to our nature as a species as civilized warfare has been to the nature of recorded history? Is the destructive predation of human groups upon one another written as deeply into our genes as it is into the story of civilization?

In his work, *The Hunters*, Elman Service writes that "warfare is exceptional at the band level of society and it is not prolonged nor is the death toll great" (1966, p. 60). Most students of primitive war suggest that it is so different in character, let alone in scale, from civilized warfare that it is misleading to use the same term to refer to them both (see, e.g., Lesser, in Fried et al., 1968). H. Speier writes of primitive war that "Measured in terms of destruction such a fight is highly inefficient and ludicrously ceremonious" (quoted in Suttles, 1966, p. 161). Similarly, Lionel Tiger and Robin Fox tell us that at the "primitive level there is not—nor was there ever—much of what we would recognize as 'war.' The history of our international violence has been, for more than ninety percent of the time, a history of raid and skirmish" (1971, p. 214). The picture that emerges from these conflicts between primitive human groups is of a ritualized, almost ceremonial display of hostility which produces a minimum of injury or damage.

What, then, is signified by these displays of sound and fury? It is perilous to explain human behavior in too mechanical or simple a fashion. The difficulty in explaining intersocietal conduct among hunter-gatherers is compounded by the diversity one finds in their customs, in their sense of territoriality (see Sahlins, in Quiatt, 1972), and in the proximity of neighboring groups. Nonetheless, it may illuminate more than it obscures to note the apparent kinship between these ceremonious displays we call primitive war and some intergroup behavior among nonhuman primates.

In many species of animals, displays of hostility and conflict (usually of nondestructive kind) are utilized to maintain an ecologically desirable distance among the units of population. Where the units are individual animals, the mock combat is one-to-one, as in the territory-defending dive-bombing practiced by many birds. Primates, however, are social animals, and the units among which some distance may best be kept are primate societies. The howler monkeys, whose name derives from their raucous intergroup displays of hostility, vividly illustrate the use of sound and fury. The film *The Evolution of Good and Evil* shows that among

76

Japanese macaques, when one group is about to enter a feeding ground presently occupied by another, its alpha (dominant) male will climb a high tree and rattle it furiously to announce their approach to the second group and give it time to depart. According to Adolph Schultz in *The Life of Primates:* "The relations between different groups of a population of wild primates will rarely degenerate into actual fighting, being mostly settled by means of long-range threatening or mere warning signals" (1969, p. 239). Not all primates are equally territorial, or equally rigid in dividing the membership of different groups: the great apes, for example, demonstrate some fluidity in each of those dimensions. Nonetheless, it may be as the anthropologist Wayne Suttles has suggested (1969, p. 161) that where intergroup hostility has been displayed by primitive societies it has been to serve an ecologically adaptive function.

Human societies in their natural condition, therefore, do not seem especially violent or bloodthirsty: their wars are few and brief and minimally destructive. Primitive war, I suggest, may better be understood not as a foreshadowing of the destructive civilized combat to come but as a legacy of man's evolutionary origins, a variety of primate social behavior that served a useful purpose.

Even with the first steps toward civilization, the picture begins to change. In Gerhard Lenski's scheme of the steps in social-evolutionary development, hunting-and-gathering bands are followed by "simple horticultural societies," relatively more settled social groups supplementing the food nature spontaneously provides with some active human food production. Lenski compares the patterns of intersocietal relations on either side of this line demarking the advent of food production:

> This is not to say that warfare is unknown in hunting and gathering societies, but rather that it tends to be a very occasional activity. In simple horticultural societies, however, warfare is elevated to the point where it becomes a way of life, with food production and other industrial pursuits relegated to a secondary place at least in the lives of the men. (1966, p. 122)

Archaeological evidence suggests that during the Neolithic period, when some societies first crossed the great social-evolutionary divide, conflict escalated. The remains from the early Neolithic, William McNeill writes, "suggest remarkably peaceful societies" (1963, p. 22). Later in the Neolithic, according to V. Gordon Childe, we infer that warfare increased from the fact that "battle-axes, daggers and other arms appear in the grave of every adult male" (quoted in Lenski, pp. 197–198). Warfare rises with the rise of civilization.

This notable escalation at so early a stage of civilization brings into focus a source of ambiguity in many discussions of primitive war. These "simple horticultural" societies appear "primitive" from a modern point of view. And, indeed, many describe as primitive warfare the combat of such societies, and even of other more advanced social types (such as African kingdoms). The exalted level called "civilization" is reserved, in such discussions, for societies that built cities, developed written language, and perhaps achieved other sophisticated advances. Of course, as Humpty Dumpty has argued persuasively, words can mean whatever we choose for them to mean. The question is: what distinctions are most useful? If we are to draw a single line to mark the most significant break in the development of human societies, I have suggested it should be where human beings left the place that had been given them in the natural order. That it should not be earlier, at the beginning of culture, I argue on the basis of the essential continuity of human life that followed that point for hundreds of thousands of years. I also maintain that it would not be later, with the full blossoming of large-scale civilization: the breakthrough that opened up the range of possibilities clearly planted the seed that would inexorably grow to that full blossoming. The case for that cleavage in the story of human development is now strengthened by the discovery that a discontinuity occurred in the history of intersocietal relations which became visible well before the first appearance of full-scale civilization. Therefore, the term "primitive" is here reserved for hunting-and-gathering bands, and the history of warfare supports that narrow definition.

Although the very beginnings of civilization brought crucial changes in warfare, the subsequent development of civilization nonetheless brought further escalations in the level and significance of intersocietal conflict. To follow this escalation further, we can turn to Julian Steward's generalizations about the course of development of the five apparently pristine civilizations: Mesopotamia, Egypt, China, Meso-America, and Peru. In his *Theory of Culture Change,* Steward notes striking parallels of development among these civilizations.[1] He outlines five stages bridging the course of development from hunting-and-gathering societies to the emergence of full-scale civilization. Compare his description of the third (Formative Era) with the fifth (Cyclical Conquest) of these stages:

> In the Formative Era, state warfare was probably of minor importance. There is little archaeological evidence of militarism, and it is likely the warfare was limited to raids. (1955, p. 202)

1. Such parallelisms suggest, of course, that similar forces worked to shape these civilizations. While this in itself does not validate the parable of the tribes, the absence of a common pattern—by implying the absence of common social evolutionary forces—might lessen the plausibility of that theory.

78

The diagnostic features of [the Cyclical Conquest period] are the emergence of large-scale militarism, the extension of political and economic domination over large areas or empires, a strong tendency toward urbanization, and the construction of fortifications. (p. 196)

Intersocietal competition molded evolving civilizations into power-maximizing systems and, conversely, these systems geared for conquest kept the kettle of strife boiling among human groups.

This brief review of the findings of anthropologists and archaeologists shows that the escalating struggle for power among societies, which I say became inevitable with the beginning of civilization, did indeed occur. The theoretical perspective of the parable of the tribes helps explain these findings of rising belligerency among human societies.

If Mars rose with the dawn of civilization it is because, as civilization developed, the reasons for conflict changed. Truly primitive war may have been a nondestructive device to achieve ecological spacing among groups. It may be that among the first food-producing societies, the rise of conflict was a reflection of the same problem of population density that apparently prompted primitive peoples to begin the process of domesticating the sources of their food. Crowded together with an unprecedented inability to space further apart by retreating into other lands, those societies may have fallen into a pattern of feud and revenge. This may apply, for example, to the chronic warfare among horticultural peoples in the jungles of New Guinea and the Amazon.[2] As population pressures intensified, as societies became better organized to control new lands, and as horticulture was replaced by larger-scale agriculture, intersocietal conflict changed further. Carneiro writes that as agricultural societies impinged upon each other, "the major incentive for war changed from a desire for revenge to a need to acquire land. And as the causes of war became predominantly economic, the frequency, intensity, and importance of war increased" (1970, p. 735). And W. W. Newcomb writes: "In a very real sense 'true' warfare may be viewed as one of the more important social consequences of the agricultural revolution" (in Dole and Carneiro, 1960, p. 329). "True war" is defined by Newcomb as "competition for anything that is valued by the group involved."

From ceremonious display to revenge feuds to wars of competition and conquest. That escalation of conflict which itself changed the human condition is the fruit of that previous change whereby unlimited growth became a new potential of human societies. In a finite world, entities able to grow indefinitely will quickly come up against each other. Intersocietal

2. For some evidence connecting spacing and warfare in the Amazon, see Chagnon, in Fried et al., 1968.

competition inevitably becomes a drama of life and death, and war moves to center stage in civilized life. Before conflict created change, as in the parable of the tribes, change first created conflict.

As civilization emerged, the human environment was, therefore, drastically altered. In the beginning, human society was embedded in nature. The interactions upon which people focused in their life processes involved natural elements and nonhuman living things. One thinks of the deer and buffalo drawn by prehistoric hunters on the cave walls of Lascaux. The salience of the natural world in the environment of primitive peoples is evident also in Colin Turnbull's *The Forest People*. The pygmies of the Ituri forest experience themselves as enveloped in a magical relationship with "the Forest." In the primitive world, other human groups are peripheral. In early civilized societies, the focus remained on natural processes of fertility and seasonal change upon which survival depended. But as civilization developed further, and as intersocietal conflict intensified, other human groups became increasingly important parts of the environment. As survival in the struggle for power became more and more a central challenge for human societies, their perspective on the world shifted. We can find evidence, both touching and terrifying, of this transmutation of the world and of the spirit of human life in the changing religious imagery of emerging civilizations. Lewis Mumford describes a change of symbols in the development of Mesopotamian civilization:

> While the sacral copulation of Babylonian king and priestess in the divine Bedchamber that crowned the ziggurat recalled an earlier fertility cult, dedicated to life, the new myths were mainly expressions of relentless opposition, struggle, aggression, unqualified power. (1961, p. 51)

And Robert Adams relates a transformation in the religion of Meso-American Indian civilization at a similar stage of development:

> The priest-representative of older gods personifying natural forces was ultimately replaced in Tula after a period of more or less open struggle by a figure whose identification with a cult of human sacrifice found favor with newly formed groups of warriors bent on predatory expansion. (1966, p. 162)

As the requirements for survival changed, the focus on the life processes of nature yielded to a preoccupation with the death processes of intersocietal strife.

War is a problem of civilization. Our language obscures from view the true nature of the step our species took into the civilized state. "If only people would behave in a more civilized fashion," we say, "we would all be better off. Our security is threatened by outbreaks of savagery." Perhaps we civilized folk are projecting our own savagery onto the comparative innocents of the primitive state. Perhaps the apparently inappropriate connotations of terms like "civilized" and "savage" reflect the ethnocentric bias of those whose legacy has shaped our language. Or perhaps this distortion should be seen as part of the means by which our systems seduce us into giving them our allegiance and unquestioning service. But really it is with civilization that human "savagery" becomes an agonizing part of the human condition. As civilization dawns, the ground of human existence turns an unearthly shade of red.

I have established, then, that the engine to drive the selection for power existed and that it started up only with the rise of civilization. This reinforces the image of man as a creature more tormented by forces outside himself than rent by his own inherent viciousness. Human societies, inescapably imperiled by one another, were rapidly transformed by innovation and selection to meet the requirements of power. The cancerous growth of power thus disfigured the face of human society.

A few thousand years have sufficed to alter the edifice of society into something barely akin to the natural nest of human life. Shaped by power, civilized societies have grown ever *larger,* ever *more complex,* and ever *more effectively controlled by a central ruling part.* Let us investigate these trends in social metamorphosis.

2. The Evolution toward Larger Societies

Two points need to be established: (*a*) that there is an overall historical trend toward larger societies and (*b*) that the selection for power largely accounts for this trend.

(*a*) On the first point little room exists for controversy: whether we consider size in terms of population or of land area, societies have grown. In the beginning, human beings lived in bands of a few dozen members. Scholars have offered a variety of typologies for the sequence of social types that marked the early development of civilization, but regardless of which one chooses, the later types are larger than the earlier. Lenski, for example, provides the following table which, though derived from recent and contemporary societies, probably gives a rough picture of the trends of the early evolution of civilization (1970, p. 104):

Type of society	Median size of communities	Median size of societies	Number of societies
Hunting and gathering	40	40	93–62
Simple Horticultural	95	95	48–45
Advanced Horticultural	280	5,800	107–84
Agrarian		Over 100,000	58–48

Not only do the communities grow larger, but beginning with the Advanced Horticultural societies, the immediate community ceases to be synonymous with the whole society. This indicates a redrawing of the society's boundaries around a growing radius of territory. The emergence of agrarian societies did not, of course, mark an end to the mushrooming growth of the civilized society. Steadily, though not without reverses, over the last five thousand years the process of growth has continued until today societies have populations in the hundreds of millions and boundaries surrounding millions of square miles.

(*b*) On the second point, power relates in two ways to this unquestionable fact of social expansion: (1) size confers power and (2) power facilitates expansion.

(1) The importance of large population for competitive power is a point stressed by the most astute students of power in earlier ages. Machiavelli, for example, wrote in *Discourses:* "Those who desire a city to achieve great empire must endeavor by all possible means to make her populous; for without an abundance of inhabitants, it is impossible ever to make a city powerful" (II. 3). And Clausewitz, still the starting point for discussions of the science of war, likewise stressed the importance of numbers. Writing less than two centuries ago, Clausewitz said that while leadership and military ardor are also necessary, there were very few examples in "modern" times of outnumbered forces winning. Superiority of numbers, he said, is "the most general principle of victory" (1943, p. 63).

It may be, as some suggest, that the growing reliance of military forces upon sophisticated technology is reducing the importance of population for national power. Intersocietal competition, in this view, is becoming capital intensive rather than labor intensive. Nonetheless Katherine and A. F. K. Organski argue in *Population and World Power* that even in an age of nuclear weapons national military power is a function of population: population, in their view, largely determines production, and the level of production determines the potential for military power. Similarly, Hans Morgenthau writes that

> Without a large population it is impossible to establish and keep going the industrial plant necessary for the successful conduct of modern war; to put into the field the large number of combat troops to fight on the land, on the sea, and in the air; and finally to fill the cadres of the troops, considerably more numerous than the combat troops, which must supply the latter with food, means of transportation and communication, ammunition, and weapons. (1972, pp. 113-114)

There are crucial qualitative differences among populations, however, so that a tiny (and admittedly externally supported) nation like Israel can survive successive assaults by her far more populous neighbors; and for many contemporary nations the growth of population is a major obstacle to national development. Nonetheless, the planet's two superpowers—out of the more than one hundred and fifty sovereign entities in the world today—are the third and fourth most populous countries. Furthermore, the presumption that the largest nation (China) is destined to become a superpower—if its development is not preemptively cut short by the power to its north—seems based primarily on the belief that so populous a nation must become a major actor on the world stage.

It appears that power remains sufficiently a function of population as to leave largely intact the ancient wisdom that in numbers is strength. And since in strength is the means of social survival, we are probably justified in concluding that selection through intersocietal competition has been a factor in fostering the historical trend toward more populous societies.

As with population, so with territorial size. All else being equal, more land means more power. For one thing, territory is necessary to support population, so that if high population is advantageous it follows that large territory is also. For another, more land means more resources besides those needed for the food production needed to support a large population. Control of resources confers power for economic competition and for direct military conflict. Looking again at the superpowers, note that both are very large and resource rich. And as China's future power is presumed because of her population, so is the expectation of Brazil's eventual ascendancy in world power based largely on the wealth of resources it controls by virtue of its immense size.

A large territory not only magnifies the productive potential of a society but also increases the chances of resource self-sufficiency, for encompassing more land generally means possessing not only more, but more various resources. Greater self-sufficiency yields greater power. In earlier eras, when intersocietal commerce carried a negligible proportion of a society's total consumption, virtual self-sufficiency in necessities was not only indispensable, it was unavoidable. In the contemporary world, the volume and range of trade are so large that many of the more prosperous nations depend upon global flows of materials for their biological and industrial survival. It may seem at first that the need for control of resources has been supplanted by the need for mere access, thus diminishing the importance of territorial size. Japan, for example, produces as much as the Soviet Union with half its population and a small fraction of its territorial resources. Japan's dependence on external sources for food, energy, and other raw materials does not impede its productive power as long as the lines of trade remain open. But commerce depends

83

upon peace, whereas national power is ultimately tested in war. Access to materials one does not control is always uncertain. Although trade makes self-sufficiency superfluous when amicable relations obtain among nations, a nation's dependency on others for necessities makes it vulnerable to extortion or deprivation when intersocietal competition pushes aside the cooperative relations of commerce. The dependency of the United States on energy resources others control has already demonstrably diminished American power, and many now believe that the security of the United States is threatened by its need for strategic minerals found in abundance only in the territory of its chief rival (the USSR) and in a part of the world beset by instability (southern Africa). A nation not self-sufficient in materials crucial to its daily life and/or to the conduct of war must stockpile in peacetime what it would need for war. Still more burdensome, it must include among the areas over which it is prepared to go to war the sources of those essential supplies. The more extensive one's areas of dependency, therefore, the more precarious the defense of one's security. This contributes to the tendency for continent-sized nations to be today's superpowers.

Controlling land, therefore, remains a vital component of power, and selection is likely to continue to favor, as it has throughout history, those societies which control more territory. That trend may in fact be accelerating in the modern era, for though too far-flung an empire was difficult to rule in the past, revolutionary advances in communication and transportation have greatly reduced such obstacles to the growth of giant states.

(2) If the big tend to win, it is also true that the winners get bigger. Among the four outcomes of the parable of the tribes, all but "Imitation" entail the expansion by force of a single society swallowing up the domain of other previously autonomous societies. The "growth" of civilized societies is not, therefore, an organic process analogous to the way mighty oaks from little acorns grow. In a finite amount of land already presumably well sprinkled with human societies, such free growth into open space is barely possible. Growth, of necessity, means conquest. In an article whose thrust is strikingly akin to the parable of the tribes, the anthropologist Robert Carneiro seeks to explain the emergence of those gigantic full-scale civilized societies which arose indigenously and not through transplantation from the outside. He begins with the important observation that a common element among these areas—areas such as the Nile, Tigris-Euphrates, and Indus valleys in the Old World and the Valley of Mexico and the mountain and coastal valleys of Peru in the New—is that *"they are all areas of circumscribed agricultural land"* (1970, p. 69, italics in original). The significance is that in so circumscribed an environment, societies can expand only at the expense of one another. These regions

84

began, Carneiro says, with a multiplicity of "small, dispersed and auton-omous farming communities." When population growth brought these little societies up against each other, warfare for land ensued and the defeated village might be incorporated "into the political unit dominated by the victor." Using Peru as an illustration, Carneiro writes that "Through the recurrence of warfare of this type, we see arising in coastal Peru integrated territorial units transcending the village in size and degree of organization" (p. 135). Of course, the rise of these larger entities changed nothing, for there remained a number of independent societies and the region in which they coexisted remained confined. In regions of this kind the only way such a process of war and territorial consolidation can end is for the entire area to come under the control of a single dominant power. This, Carneiro argues, is what happened. In Peru, for example, "The culmination of this process was the conquest of all Peru by its most powerful state, and the formation of a single great empire" (p. 136). Power thus impels the evolution toward ever larger civilized societies.[3]

The role of power in creating larger societies hardly ceased with the first great empires. Ortega y Gasset once wrote: "A nation is an invitation extended by some men to others to join them in a common undertaking" (quoted in Service, 1971, p. 57). But history shows this view to be unduly sanguine. The invitations were often extended at knife point. The uni-fication of the Chinese empire several centuries B.C. was the fruit of the Warring States period, and most immediately of the military conquest of the other states by Ch'in. Most of the "nations" of contemporary Europe were first empires at whose creation force played a central role. For example, the United Kingdom was united by the ability of England to subjugate the Scots, the Welsh, and the Irish. The role of force was considerable also in the unification of Spain, France, Prussia. Less than five hundred years ago, according to Charles Tilly, Europe had five hundred formally autonomous governments, whereas today there are fewer than fifty (cited in R. N. Adams, 1975, p. 266). So it has been throughout history. The Soviets (and their Czarist predecessors) have continued to demonstrate how superior power can be used by ambitious rulers to diminish the number of autonomous societies and to construct enormous systems of power—in their case covering now more than 8 million square miles.

The unification of previously autonomous states is not always imposed by force. The American colonies, for example, chose shortly after their successful anticolonial revolt to form a more perfect union. Yet one of

---

3. On the Indian subcontinent during the Vedic period, there was an ongoing process of fusion whereby the conquest of one tribe by another molded tribes into peoples and nations (Bashan, 1954, p. 34). Later, aspects of Indian political and military culture arrested the movement toward con-solidation (see p. 109 n. 10).

the chief arguments for unification found in *The Federalist* is the recognition that size confers power, thus, that a United States of America would be better able to defend itself. In Western Europe today, some first steps have been taken toward creating a United States of Europe. Societies might choose to form a cooperative union for a variety of reasons besides the maximization of competitive power, as the economic union of the Common Market indicates. Still, it is interesting to note the argument put forward a few years ago by the French scholar Michel Tatu (1975) that the principal impediment to the progress of European unity is the enjoyment by the Europeans of the American nuclear umbrella. In other words, with security needs guaranteed from the outside, there is insufficient impulse to sacrifice autonomy for wider union. It appears that even where peoples have voluntarily joined in creating a larger society, the workings of power have played a role in shaping their choices.

Between the facts that size confers power and that power leads to expansion, people have had little free choice about the trend toward ever-larger societies. Even if people might prefer the closer intimacy and human scale of small social groupings, the parable of the tribes has fated them to live in larger ones. As Tocqueville laments with characteristic eloquence and clarity:

> If more but smaller nations existed, I do not doubt that mankind would be more happy and more free; but the existence of great nations is unavoidable. . . . It profits a state little to be affluent and free if it is perpetually exposed to be pillaged or subjugated. . . . Small nations are often miserable, not because they are small, but because they are weak; and great empires prosper less because they are great than because they are strong. . . . Hence it occurs that, unless very peculiar circumstances intervene, small nations are always united to larger empires in the end, either by force or by their own consent. (quoted in Aron, 1965*b*, pp. 250–251)

To what extent it is appropriate to lament the foreclosure of the option of small societies is not entirely clear. For one thing, the precariousness of very small societies is not attributable solely to the uncontrolled play of power. As many of today's tiny entities discover, smallness carries with it a risk like that of an investor who neglects to diversify his portfolio: one mishap—like a blight on the main crop—can spell disaster. For another, although it is undoubtedly valuable for a society not to be so large that its members lose all sense of identification and participation, it is not clear that an entity of a billion people is appreciably more alienating than one of a million. The evidence of psychological anthropology suggests that groups of band size (a few dozen) or even of tribal size (a few hundred) are especially congenial social homes for our species. But once one leaves face-to-face familiarity far behind, how much difference do successive orders of magnitude make? Moreover, the technology of mass communications now allows a certain intimacy of national life, so that, for example, the connection between the American electorate and their leaders is probably closer now than in the Age of Jefferson, despite the considerable increase in numbers and area since then. Plato argued that the optimal size of a republic ought not to exceed the several thousand that could assemble to hear a single orator at the same time, yet in an age of global satellite communications, we can all hear a single speaker and even watch the perspiration form upon his face. We have entered in some important respects an era of a "global village." These intimacies, however, are one way and therefore fundamentally different from the give-and-take of a village-sized community. We can wonder whether leaders of such inhumanly large groupings can maintain their contact with the people for whom they are responsible, whether, indeed, we are equipped by nature to fully recognize human realities that lie outside our immediate experience.

A final point concerns a paradox in the relationship between the struggle for power and the increasing size of civilized societies. The consolidation of societies by force illustrates the problem of power, but, just as important, it represents a solution to that problem. The problem arises from interaction under conditions of anarchy. Unification helps end the anarchy. What is achieved often only through war can also be regarded as an extension of the peace. This, too, was well understood by the writers of *The Federalist*: disunited, the states would be prey not only to outsiders but to one another. Carneiro's model of circumscribed lands "culminates" in a single empire because unity allows the process of struggle and consolidation to stop. Of course, it does not really stop, since "circumscribed land" is a relative concept, as we who can speak now of Spaceship Earth well realize. As societies continue to extend their reach, what once seemed like unification of some whole becomes diminished in the new perspective into the creation of a single competitor in a larger whole. The process of conflict and consolidation thus continues, with no very plausible culmination possible besides either an ultimate conflict that ends in mutual annihilation or an ultimate consolidation that extends the peace in some form of unified global order.

3. The Evolution toward More Complex Societies

A "complex" whole contrasts with one that is "all of a piece." The more complex the whole, the more its functioning must be understood in terms of a multiplicity of parts. The complex differs from the simple in having more identifiable parts which are more different from one another and more separated from one another into autonomous domains of operation.

By all these related criteria, the trend of history has been for societies to become more complex. David Kaplan summarizes the trend thus: "Each successive culture type exhibiting general dominance has become increasingly heterogeneous; it is organizationally more complex, with more parts and subparts, and with greater functional differentiation between them" (in Sahlins and Service, 1960, p. 73). Talcott Parsons, in his *Societies: Evolutionary and Comparative Perspectives*, stresses the increasing differentiation within societies, as does Lenski. Durkheim's famous *The Division of Labor in Society* contrasts the "mechanical solidarity" of primitive society, in which each part is like the others, with the "organic solidarity" of modern societies, in which different parts have different functions. The increasing division of labor among society's members corresponds also with an increasing division of functions among social institutions. Eisenstadt, in his study of the bureaucratic structures of imperial societies, sees a historic trend toward increasingly autonomous institutional spheres within societies. Clearly, *the evolutionary trend toward increasing social complexity in various respects has been a central observation in anthropological and sociological thought*. The trend, then, is clear. Does the parable of the tribes help explain it?

It can be demonstrated that complexity increases power. This does not in itself confirm the argument that the selection for power explains the trend toward increasing social complexity, but it does make that argument more plausible. Social complexity facilitates social power in two ways: (1) The larger the society the more complex the organization it requires. If it is necessary to be big, it is consequently necessary to be complex. (2) Social complexity in the form of the division of labor enhances a society's power by enabling it to perform feats impossible for an equally large collectivity of unspecialized parts.

(1) The connection between size and complexity is easily seen. A one-celled creature does not need a complex and differentiated circulatory system as does its multicelled evolutionary descendant. When all the cells of an animal are directly exposed to the sources of nutriment, as with a simple segmented chain, it need not develop a separate digestive system. Norbert Wiener illustrates how increased size requires greater structural complexity:

> Let us compare two artificial structures—the cottage and the skyscraper. The ventilation of a cottage is quite adequately taken care of by the leak of air around the window frames, not to mention the draft of the chimney. No special ventilation system is necessary. On the other hand, in a skyscraper with rooms within rooms, a shutdown of the system of forced ventilation

would be followed in a very few minutes by an intolerable foulness of air in the work spaces. Diffusion and even convection are no longer enough to ventilate such a structure. (1954, p. 56)

The expansion of human societies during the evolution of civilization has similarly required that complex systems be designed to perform tasks that happen as a matter of course in small societies. Redistribution of food can be as simple as handing out meat around the fire. As civilization advanced, special buildings and a special priesthood might be employed to achieve the same purpose on a larger scale. The task of social integration imposes a similar problem. This need is easily met in a small-band society the solidarity of whose members is continually reinforced by immediate dealings, by kinship, by proximity, and by shared experience. These means can hardly suffice for a society whose members are too numerous to know one another, and are divided into many separate communities. In order to grow larger without falling apart, societies have had to develop structural mechanisms to hold the whole together and allow it to function. These mechanisms include increasingly complex systems of transportation and communication: the invention of writing may in part represent a means of accommodating expanding networks of intercommunication, and Robert Heilbroner (1971) has suggested that without complex computer technology today's corporate economic systems could not function on a global scale.

We can also look to the development of legal institutions as a key to the ever-greater challenge of regulating social interactions in a harmonious and effective way. The following table (prepared by Lenski from George Murdock's ethnographic data) shows how complexity of legal systems increased in the succession of social types (1970, table 6/10, p. 138).

Degree of Development of Legal System by Societal Type
(in percentages)

Type of society	Substantial	Moderate	Slight	Total	Number of societies
Hunting and gathering	0	36	64	100	11
Simple horticultural	38	50	13	101	8
Advanced horticultural	63	25	13	101	16

Since the more "advanced" is also the larger society, it would be a mistake to assume that this legal development represents the triumph of order over chaos, that it indicates progress in civilizing the savage human animal. E. Hoebel, in *The Law of Primitive Man,* argues persuasively that it is otherwise:

89

> As for law, simple societies need little of it. If the more primitive societies are more lawless than the more civilized, it is not in the sense that they are *ipso facto* more disorderly; quite the contrary. It is because they are more homogeneous; relations are more direct and intimate; interests are shared by all in a solid communality; and there are fewer things to quarrel about. Because relations are more direct and intimate, the primary, informal mechanisms of social control are more generally effective. Precisely as a society acquires a more complex culture and moves into civilizations, opposite conditions come into play. Homogeneity gives way to Heterogeneity. Common interests shrink in relation to special interests. Face-to-face relations exist not among all the members of the society, but only among a progressively smaller proportion of them. . . . Access to material goods becomes more and more indirect, with greater possibilities for uneven allocation, and the struggle among members of a given society for access to the available goods becomes intensified. Everything moves to increase the potentialities for conflict within the society. The need for explicit controls becomes increasingly greater. The paradox (albeit only a paradox for those who unwittingly *assume* that civilized people are more moral than uncivilized) is that the more civilized man becomes, the greater is man's need for law, and the more law he creates. Law is but a response to social needs. (1964, p. 293, italics in original)

As with the ventilation of a skyscraper, so with achieving social order in a larger and more advanced society. As with the evolution of bigger animals, so with civilization's development. (In Mumford's organic metaphor, "little communal cells, undifferentiated and uncomplicated, every part performing equally every function, turned into complex structures organized on an axiate principle, with differentiated tissues and special organs" [1961, p. 34].)

(2) If complexity is a by-product of growth, it is also directly instrumental in the maximization of power. A society's power is a function not only of the magnitude of the human and natural resources it commands but also of the efficiency with which they are used. Nothing so contributes to efficiency as that central aspect of complexity, the division of labor. This insight was, for Adam Smith, the foundation of the science of economics. At the outset of *The Wealth of Nations,* he wrote: "The greatest improvement in the productive powers of labour and the greater part of the skill, dexterity, and the judgment with which it is any where directed, or applied, seem to have been the effects of the division of labour" (1937, p. 3). He explains how this magnification of productivity occurs:

> This great increase of the quantity of work, which in consequence of the division of labour, the same number of people are capable of performing, is owing to three different circumstances; first, to the increase of dexterity in every particular workman; secondly, to the saving of time which is commonly lost in passing from one species of work to another; and lastly, to the invention of a great number of machines which facilitate and abridge labour, and enable one man to do the work of many. (p. 7)

The first two circumstances relate to production within a static framework; the third concerns advantageous changes, which of course are the most important in the long perspective of social evolution. The expertise that comes from specialization is indispensable for many kinds of advance, particularly after the complexity of knowledge in each domain of human endeavor goes beyond a certain level. Four hundred years ago it was easier to be a Renaissance man than it is today. Ever since the agricultural revolution first empowered the labor of some to free others to channel their energies into other pursuits, specialization has enabled societies to undertake and achieve tasks that would otherwise have been impossible. The advantages of the division of labor are manifest not only in economic but also in all other areas of endeavor, including the military and the political. Thus, by maximizing what a society can achieve with what it has, the division of labor has enhanced social power and therefore has been favored by the selective process described by the parable of the tribes. Moreover, since the division of labor is limited, as Adam Smith noted, by the size of the system, size and complexity have a mutually reinforcing relationship.

Even if it were true that social complexity has been imposed on civilized peoples as a necessity, people might want to choose it anyway. It is not self-evident, therefore, that the trend toward social complexity should be regarded as part of the tragedy of civilized man. The benefits of the division of labor are clear and many. The costs, by contrast, are less calculable and far less tangible than the "comparative advantages" on the basis of which Adam Smith argued we should let the shoemaker make our shoes and the baker bake our bread. What is lost is a kind of wholeness or integrity in the individual human life. In the nineteenth century, as the market system greatly accelerated the progress of specialization and the subordination of man to the productive apparatus, some of the more perceptive and sensitive observers lamented the costs. "For the younger Marx, the division of labor is *the* repressive institution" (Weisskopf, 1971, p. 67). Adam Smith has illustrated his paean to the division of labor with the case of pin production, but Tocqueville responded: "What can be expected of a man who has spent twenty years of his life in making heads for pins?" (1945, II, 168). A human being is more than a cog in the productive apparatus. Again Tocqueville: "(I)t may be said that in proportion as the workman improves, the man is degraded" (ibid.). Division may lead to power, but wholeness is inseparable (as the etymology suggests) from health. Ralph Waldo Emerson decried the fragmentation of the human condition by the division into specialized roles:

> Man is not a farmer, or a professor, or an engineer, but he is all. Man is priest and scholar, and statesman, and producer, and soldier. In the *divided* or social state these functions are parcelled out to individuals, each of whom aims to do his stint of the joint work, whilst each other performs his. . . . Unfortunately, this original unit, this fountain of power, has been so distributed to

the multitudes, has been so minutely subdivided and peddled out, that it is spilled into drops, and cannot be gathered. The state of society is one in which the members have suffered amputation from the trunk, and strut about so many walking monsters—a good finger, a neck, a stomach, but never a man. (1933, pp. 56–57, italics in original)

The complex society tends to fragment the human condition in still another way. In the more primitive society, the various roles in a person's life are all of a piece: work and play, kinship relations and work relations, religious and economic functions are not strictly divided but are bound together in a single fabric of social life. The division of life into discrete institutional spheres brings with it, as Redfield shows (1953), a shattering of this unity with costs in confusion, alienation and disorientation.

Thus, there are costs and benefits. Our systems teach us preoccupation with the material benefits and disable us from feeling the spiritual costs. It behooves us to give pause before we give allegiance to systems shaped by power. A deaf man can pass through a room filled with music and say, "There was nothing there at all."

4. Evolution toward More Effective Central Control

One very important aspect of the division of labor among society's parts has been the differentiation of a centrally governing part from the society as a whole or, to use an apt and familiar organic metaphor, of the head from the body politic.

A system has effective central control to the extent that there exists within it a part that can direct and coordinate all the parts of the system. The evolution of civilization has manifested a broad trend toward the creation of such control. This has entailed first a differentiation of power among the members of society and second an elaboration of the organizational means by which the powerful parts can control the society as a whole.

In the beginning, in hunting-and-gathering bands, human beings lived in a condition of equality (except for some differences based on age and sex) where no one had the power to command another. Service wrote of such societies in *The Hunters:* "There is no pecking order based on physical dominance at all, nor is there any superiority-inferiority ordering based on other sources of power such as wealth, hereditary classes, military or political offices" (p. 88). Similarly, the first stage of Fried's scheme of *The Evolution of Political Society* is named "Egalitarian." The successive stages on Fried's evolutionary account are marked by increasing social inequalities. In the second, "Rank Society," some members of society have better access to social goods and more authority than others; in the third, "Stratified Society," such differences have intensified and become hereditary. With the fourth and last stage of this process, "State Society," full-scale civilization has emerged and with it a highly centralized power system in which the very few control the lives of very many. This progressive differentiation of an increasingly powerful part of the social body is a salient characteristic also of the evolutionary schemas of Service *(Origins of the State and Civilization)* and Lenski *(Power and Privilege: A Theory of Social Stratification)*. Before civilization, authority is limited to persuasion occasionally and without compulsion by people respected for their wisdom. Once civilization has blossomed fully, some individuals have the power of life and death over their fellows.

In the several thousand years since state societies appeared, the strengthening of central control has continued, but not through the further differentiation between powerful and weak elements within society. Indeed, it is difficult to imagine how polarization could ever extend beyond gulfs created in the ancient world such as those between a deified ruler like the ancient Pharoah and the masses toiling in involuntary servitude. Rather, the central power grew by the progressive elaboration of the means for exercising power, such as the bureaucracies described by Eisenstadt *(The Political Systems of Empires)*. The power represented by the Roman caesar and the Chinese emperor far transcended that in a king of a less advanced polity. But the difference did not lie in a still higher ratio of power between ruler and subject, for many a petty king could on a whim behead those below him. The difference lay in the elaborate hierarchical system through which power could be exercised. The ruler became the apex of a command pyramid.

The growth in the size and complexity of civilized societies changed the essence of central control. The polarization between weak and powerful individuals became less important, the creation of systems of social governance more so.

It may seem at first that the modern trend away from the absolutist ruler signifies a reversal of the alleged social evolutionary movement toward centralized power. It represents, on the contrary, an advance of central control to a new level. In a simpler society, the power of the few over the many might have sufficed to put the whole under effective central control. In the more complex systems that have evolved, control requires a good deal more than having power in principle. Today, a brutal tyrant like Idi Amin can terrorize his people, but without an effective organization of control he cannot truly govern them. The priority of systems of control over inequalities of power is shown in the political evolution of modern Europe. Centralization first entailed the steady erosion of feudal autonomy under the pressure of the growing central monarchs. In order to rule effectively, the absolutist regimes introduced bureaucratic administrations during the sixteenth through the eighteenth centuries (Gerth and Mills, 1953, p. 210). This institutionalization of power, though required, necessarily also rendered the basis of central control impersonal. As M. Beloff observes in *The Age of Absolutism,* for the monarchs

> to create efficiency meant to organize and institutionalize their royal power, to build up an impersonal bureaucracy, to complete the process by which the Court shed responsibility for the practical as distinct from the ceremonial functions of kingship, to develop a financial system by which the revenues necessary for public purposes should no longer be inseparable from the private income of the king, considered simply as a landowner—in other words to assist in the birth of the modern State. And the modern State has no need of the hereditary absolute monarch. (1954, p. 23)

The king becomes in retrospect a stepping-stone for the forward march of central power. "In the long perspectives of Versailles or St. Petersburg," writes Mumford in an apt architectural metaphor, "the central human figure, King or Czar, became ever smaller and soon reached his political vanishing point. . . . Versailles, beheld at a great distance, is no more formidable than a horizontal factory unit, built for the straight line assembly of puppets" (1961, p. 391). The disappearance of the human embodiment of power by no means implies that the grip of hierarchical dominance upon the social whole has been relaxed. "The modern state," says Paul Viollet, "is just the king of other days bringing to a triumphal end his unremitting work" (quoted in Jouvenel, 1949). About which Jouvenel adds: "All that has happened is that the royal power house has been improved on: its controls, moral and material, have been made progressively more efficient so as to drive ever deeper into society and to take from it an ever tighter clutch of its goods and men" (1949, p. 9).

The proliferating tentacles of the governing part reach deeper and deeper. Even modern democracy does not contradict this evolutionary tendency. The theoretical equality of power among modern democracy's citizens exists only on election day. In between is in place an enormous apparatus of control with growing power, as conservatives and libertarians bewail, over many facets of social life. Democracy does, however, check central control to the extent that those at the top of the governing hierarchies feel restrained by their eventual accountability to the electorate. Still more important, to the extent that government is constitutionally limited in what it can do, democracy truly reduces central control. Nonetheless, modern democracies have shown during periods of recognized national emergency that their central part can exert quite substantial control.

Thus, the democratization of modern state power, like its institutionalization, does not really contradict the overall social evolutionary trend. As Deutsch writes of the culmination of the process of centralization of power within society: "Modern governments, compared to those of past centuries, have greatly increased the weight of their power over their own populations" (1968, p. 25).

The development of civilization, therefore, manifests the progressive differentiation of a head and a central nervous system to govern the social body. In what ways is this historic trend the fruit of the selection for power in the competitive intersocietal system?

For one thing, the process of territorial consolidation described earlier itself implies a form of increasing centralization: if a system previously comprised of autonomous entities is brought under one control, power has been centralized within that system. Since power has frequently been the means of such unification, it can be said that power leads to an increase in central control. Although consolidation entails the ingestion of other societies rather than the restructuring of a given social system, it should be noted that the difference between the two is not absolute: autonomy and sovereignty are often matters of degree. It is ambiguous, for example, to what extent the flow of power in premodern Europe from a multiplicity of feudal strongholds to a single national capital is to be seen as an intrasocietal restructuring and to what extent a protracted conquest of many societies by a single power. It has often been observed that the centralization of power by European monarchs at the expense of the once autonomous nobles was made possible by changes in the technology of warfare that enabled an attacker to violate the once impregnable security of fortified castles. Armed with gunpowder, the conquering royal power could centralize control. As Andrzejewski observes generally: "The predominance of attack over defense promotes the territorial concentration of political power (centralization), while if defense becomes the stronger form of warfare, a trend towards the territorial dispersion of political power (decentralization) is likely to ensue" (1954, p. 75). Conquest, across or within boundaries, leads to central control.

It is more important, however, to note the reverse relationship: that more effective central control increases a society's power. Central control enhances the competitive power of a society in three ways: by providing or enforcing *unity of purpose;* by directing the *coordination* of the parts' activities; and by inducing the parts to *sacrifice* for the sake of the whole.

A. Unity of Purpose

Without sufficient control at the center, a political unit may disintegrate into factions and dissipate its potential power in internal conflict. So warned the authors of *The Federalist:* divisiveness being inevitable among peoples, it behooves a nation trying to survive in a hostile world to create at the center a power strong enough to weld the parts together. The same applies to those unities formed by force from the extreme disunity of conflict: an empire requires at its core a strong central power. Says Machiavelli in *The Discourses:*

> Since all our actions resemble those of nature, it is neither possible nor natural that a slender trunk should support a heavy branch. Hence a small republic cannot take possession of cities and kingdoms which are stronger and larger than itself; and, should it do so, it will happen as it does in the case of a tree which has a branch bigger than the trunk: it will support the branch with difficulty, and with the least wind it will be destroyed. This is just what happened to Sparta. It occupied all the cities of Greece. Then, when Thebes rebelled, all the other cities rebelled and the trunk was left without branches. In Rome's case, this could not happen, for it had so large a trunk that it could easily support any branch. (II. 3. 1–3)

The size of a power system is correlated with its power only to the extent that the system's parts are unified by will or by force behind a common purpose. Unification by will being unreliable, history has favored centralized organization. Today on this planet two huge power systems confront each other—the North Atlantic Treaty Organization and the Warsaw Pact. The former, NATO, is an alliance of genuinely sovereign nations, whereas the Warsaw Pact is essentially an empire held together by an army of occupation. In the long run, the resentments provoked by coercion may destroy the Soviet empire. The disunity resulting from NATO's decentralized structure, however, has rendered the West—despite its enormous latent power—considerably more vulnerable to its more single-minded rival. The peoples of East Germany, Hungary, Czechoslovakia, and evidently now Poland, have been driven back into the Soviet fold during the past generation. But there is no one to prevent the French from going their own way, or the Danes from seeking a free ride, or the West Germans from giving to their *Ostpolitik* whatever weight they wish in relation to their security alliance with the West. Jacques Bousset, teaching the value of centralized power to his charge, the Dauphin under Louis XIV, wrote: ". . . 'all Israel obeyed as one man. They were forty thousand men, and all this multitude was as one.' This is what is meant by the unity of a people, when each man renouncing his own will takes it and joins it to that of the prince and the magistrate. Otherwise there is no union; the people wander as vagabonds like a dispersed flock" (in Tierney et al. 1972, p. 77).

B. Coordination

Unity of purpose is not enough. An army may be unanimous in its desire for victory, but if its actions are disorganized it will not prevail. Shared intentions are impotent without coordination of efforts. Writes Jay in *The*

Federalist: "What would the militia of Britain be, if the English militia obeyed the Government of England, if the Scotish militia obeyed the Government of Scotland, and if the Welch militia obeyed the Government of Wales! Suppose an invasion—would those three governments (if they agreed at all) be able with all their respective forces, to operate against the enemy so effectually as the single Government of Great Britain would?" (p. 21).

Not all forms of coordination require central control. An ecosystem, for example, has a most intricate coordination of synergistic actions with no central power. A market economy can likewise rely upon Adam Smith's "invisible hand" to weave together the pursuits of atomistic economic actors into a coherent fabric of exchange.[4] But in the direct contests of power among civilized societies, the requisite coordination demands a directing authority at the center. The different demands of these different systems can be illuminated by an analogy with the mathematical concept of the vector. A vector has both magnitude and direction. The synergy of an ecosystem or a market economy produces a maximal magnitude (in biomass or GNP) with no unifying direction. When a system must act in concert to achieve a single defined purpose, as to maximize power in intersocietal competition, its energies must be not only great in sum but unified in direction. Competitive power is like a vector, and a central authority is needed to wield it like a spear. The need for the many to act as one requires some "one" to control the many. The struggle for power is like a game of chess, and the side that prevails will not be that whose pawns conduct their wars individually but that whose pieces are deployed in a coherent strategy.

This analysis shows why the epitome of central control is the military organization, which is a hierarchical pyramid based on the premise of unquestioned obedience to those above. In his work, *The Rise of the West,* McNeill makes mention of "the elements of warlike organization from which political institutions without exception descend" p. 22. This may be overstated, but it is likely that the intersocietal struggle for power, necessitating central direction, has been a major force behind the centralizing trend in the evolution of political structures. Service, for example, has conjectured that "It is possible that intense competition and frequent warfare among tribes was an important condition for the rise of chiefdoms in the first place, inasmuch as planning and coordination have obvious advantages in war" (1962, p. 151). Talcott Parsons's scheme for early political evolution likewise mentions as a major source of political centralization "the development of a centralized military apparatus for conducting wars against outside societies" (1966, p. 49). The rise of the

---

4. On the limitations of that kind of cohesion, see chap. 7, "The Market as a Power System."

kingship in the ancient civilization of Sumer, in McNeill's account, is also the fruit of chronic competitive pressures:

> In proportion as war became chronic, kingship became necessary. Concentration of political authority in the hands of a single man seems to have become the rule in Sumerian cities by 3000 B.C. . . . (T)he institution of kingship stabilized itself in Sumer by superimposing military relationships upon an older religio-political system. The authority of a field commander over his army served as prototype for the king's authority over the city. (1963, p. 43)

Just as centralizing innovations were pivotal in the erection of the first great civilizations, so have they been in the course of modernization; and as with the early political institutions, so with the modern nation-state has the flow of power toward the center been impelled in large measure by the demands of intersocietal competition. It was, writes James L. Davis, "in the crucible of international conflict that modern state-building occurred. . . . The struggle of the great powers for hegemony was the greatest force impelling rulers to develop armies, to crush rebellious aristocracies, to create loyal bureaucracies, and to collect taxes" (1971, p. 29). Similarly, Jouvenel, whose main purpose in *On Power* is to trace the growth of state control in European society, says: "The development of absolute monarchy in both England and France is linked with the efforts of their respective dynasties to resist the dangers from Spain. James I owed his wide powers to the Armada. Richelieu and Mazarin could raise high the prerogatives of the state because they could invoke unceasingly the peril from abroad" (1949, p. 144). And it was war, according to Aron, which "accelerated the final triumph of the [centralized] Prussian state" (1954, p. 87).

We should note again that this centralization has two chief components. One—to which we have been attending—is the concentration of political power within the system in a central authority. The second is the extension of the reach of that political power, enabling it more effectively and more completely to command all the resources of the system to maximize competitive power. Although the monarchs of Europe may have had "the determination to make all their citizens work and sacrifice for established state purposes" (Davis, 1971, p. 29), they were limited in their abilities to do so. The French Revolution extended the penetration of the central power into society. The English contemporary of the Revolution, Edmund Burke, lamented that in France "The state is all. Everything is referred to the production of force. . . . Were France but half of what it is in population, in compactness, in applicability of its force, it would be too strong for most of the states of Europe, constituted as they are . . ." (quoted in Jouvenel, 1949, p. 140). This leap in effective central control also springs from the arena of competition for, according to

Leopold Ranke, "it cannot be denied that the French state [with its "new centralization of power" was] formed in the midst of a struggle with Europe and designed to cope with it" (quoted in Von Laue, 1950, p. 213). In our own times, this mobilization of the resources of society for a coordinated effort to maximize power has ascended to a new level. In the words of Hans Gerth and C. Wright Mills, writing in the shadow of World War II:

> The mobilization of the modern nation's resources for war has reached a total state—in scope, intensity, and efficiency. . . . The coordination of all institutional orders involved in war leads to totalitarian measures of planning. All large-scale organizations in all institutional orders are coordinated to further the supreme end of victory. Art and science, religion and education are committed to the cause. The media of mass communications help to concentrate fears and aggressions, maximizing their intensity and directing them against the enemy as the "total threat." Accordingly, economic, psychological, political and military warfare are some of the many special aspects of total war. (1953, p. 225)

The apparent eagerness of the totalitarian rulers of our times to extend their power around the world and the still-growing apparatus for the total domination of society by the state suggest that we have not yet seen the end of the trend toward the power-enhancing centralization of control.

As the necessities of power have influenced the origins of these centralized structures, it will come as no surprise that the selection for power has mandated their spread. Service, for example, writes that "once a chiefdom (even if slightly developed) is pitted against mere tribes it will prevail, other things being equal" (1962, p. 151). Structural transformation is mandated by the rule of power. The emergence of the modern nation-state in Europe compelled emulation by others in the region. At the time of Louis XIV in France, or soon thereafter, Mosca says: "The strengthening of central authority and the absorption of local sovereignties became more or less completely generalized throughout Europe. The few states, such as Poland or Venice, that would not, or could not, move with the times and transform their constitutions, lost power and cohesion and disappeared before the end of the eighteenth century" (1939, p. 376). Upon the rubble of the ancien regime, Napoleon constructed a still more potent edifice of power whose instruments included the mass army and the new psychology of nationalism, both of which channeled more human energies into the service of national might. The military historian Alfred Vagts says in *The History of Militarism* that Napoleon's enemies "recognized that he must be conquered by his own instruments of victory" (p. 128). After Napoleon's defeat, the victors compelled France to abandon the system by which it had conquered Europe. Of these nations, according to Jouvenel, only the Prussians retained something of that system themselves. Then, the Prussians revealed the superiority of their power in their victory over France in 1870: "Their success frightened Europe so much that every continental country followed Germany's example and introduced military conscription. The splendid result of this was that in 1888 Europe's armies on a peace footing were the same in numbers as at the height of the Napoleonic Wars—3,000,000 men" (Jouvenel, 1949, pp. 149-150).

Germany, in its imperialist ambition, carried forward the imperative toward total war. According to Hindenburg's program of 1916: "the richer means at the disposal of our enemies [must be balanced] by applying everything that our land contains in the line of resources, and what industry and the farm can produce, exclusively to the demands of war" (quoted in Vagts, 1937, p. 426). And then came Hitler. Hitler, according to Jouvenel, compelled Britain and the United States to emulate the German method of war. Even in the bastions of liberty, the leaders were compelled to look upon their fellow citizens as resources for the prosecution of the war (pp. 151–152). The effects of these escalations may not be evanescent. "We are accustomed," writes Paul Goodman, "to write Hitler off as an aberration, who was of little political significance. . . . But in fact the military emergency that he and his Japanese allies created confirmed the worst tendencies of the giant states, till now they are probably irreversible by ordinary political means" (1970, p. 3).

The West still agonizes, in the shadow of totalitarian imperialism, over how many of its values must be sacrificed to maximize power.[5] Societies not wishing to reduce themselves to military machines nonetheless must contemplate the limits to their choices suggested by Herbert Spencer's general observation, over a century ago, that "Societies in which there is little subordination disappear, leaving outstanding those in which subordination is great" (quoted in Service, 1971, p. 21).

C. Sacrifice

A third way that centralization can enhance a society's power is closely related to the first two: the ability of the controlling part to sacrifice other parts for the sake of the whole. Altruistic forms of loyalty such as patriotism can move people to sacrifice themselves in the service of their country, but the power to compel that sacrifice is more reliable. In a sense, this sacrificial power is a special case of the ability to enforce unity of purpose: the purpose of maximizing the power of the whole can be made to supersede any goals that the subordinate parts may have to maximize

5. See Epilogue to Book I, "Power and Choice in Our Times."

100

their own individual welfare. Such sacrifice can also be regarded as an element in the ability of the ruling part to coordinate the activities of all the parts in an overarching strategy: the commander deploying his resources wants to be sure that the parts will obey without each needing to be persuaded that the plan is in its own self-interest. Yet, as there is more involved than agreement about ends and coherence in action, this capacity to transform subordinate human beings into mere means of the system's ends deserves separate discussion.

Again, it is helpful to draw a comparison with chess, where a single decision maker controls each side. In chess, one wins by protecting one's king and capturing the king of one's opponent. All other pieces are entirely expendable. It is true that in the real world, unlike in chess, there is such a thing as a Pyrrhic victory. Nonetheless, a society has a competitive advantage if it can use its members like chess pieces whose own welfare can be disregarded for the sake of the goals of the central power, especially in war.[6] Even in democratic societies where the central power must account to the people, warfare leads to compulsory induction into hierarchical organizations that are authorized to severely punish desertion from the organization or refusal to obey even suicidal orders.

In societies where the few can control the many over indefinite periods, enforced sacrifice can strengthen the economic bases of power as well. Generating and managing an economic surplus have been a vital part of the growth of power for thousands of years. Civilized societies have been able to generate a surplus, despite the miserable conditions in which the majority of people have lived, because those who have controlled the resources have been powerful enough to disregard the welfare of their fellows. People become tools, and concern for their welfare becomes reduced to a calculation of the costs and benefits of their main-

---

6. For an illustration of how the intersocietal struggle for power can both stimulate and select for the people-sacrificing central ruler, consider R. W. Tucker's analysis of Russian history from his aptly titled article "Swollen State, Spent Society": "In using [the state-directed 'revolution from above'], Stalin forbore to mention a fact of which he was well aware, that coercive revolution from above in a long-range state-building process was no new phenomenon in Russia's history. A previous such process had its background and origin in national adversity: the conquest in 1240 and 200-year subjugation of the Russian lands by the Tatars. The tsarist state, centered in Muscovy, developed from the fourteenth to the seventeenth centuries in a protracted struggle for the reconstitution of the national territory, a 'gathering of Russian lands,' in a hostile environment that comprised not only the declining but still strong Tatar khanates but also powerful neighbors on three sides: Ottoman Turkey in the southwest, Poland-Lithuania in the west, and Sweden in the northwest. Through war and diplomacy, Muscovy expanded from an area of about 15,000 square miles in 1462 to that of the transcontinental Eurasian state that it finally became.

"The expansionist drive placed a great premium upon military strength. *Because of the country's economic backwardness and technological inferiority to its Western neighbors, the government sought to mobilize the resources for war by enlisting the population directly in its service. The exploitative relation of the state to society brought an extension of coercive controls and the growth of the centralized governmental systems*" (1981–82, p. 416, italics mine).

101

tenance: on the one hand, one could keep a skilled slave healthy not for his sake but for one's own, just as one changes the oil in a car to protect the investment and not out of empathy for the car; on the other hand, one could depreciate in full a slave in a Roman galley ship after a few months of hard use, as one might throw out the old oil from a car. Resources that might have been used to meet the real needs of many of a society's members are freed for other purposes. Frequently, of course, the elites who have controlled such resources have squandered them on superfluous luxury and ostentation. Sometimes, however, the dominant groups have invested in economic or military development which increase the competitive power of their societies.

This potentiality of the economics of sacrifice to magnify a society's power, combined with the operation of the parable of the tribes, may have been a factor in the social evolutionary trend toward that increasing social inequality which, in premodern eras, was a primary dimension of the centralization of power. (At each step in that progression from egalitarian bands through rank and stratified societies to state societies a larger proportion of human needs could be sacrificed to empower the system as a whole.) The economics of sacrifice has a modern history as well. Modern power requires a modern economy, which in turn seems to require massive front-end investment. Investment, of course, entails the diversion of resources from meeting current human needs. Since people in most societies about to embark on economic modernization have lived under poor conditions, such investment demands substantial sacrifice. Barbara Ward writes of this:

> A developing society must at some point begin to save, even though it is still poor. This is the tough early stage of growth which Marx encountered in Victorian England and unfortunately took to be permanent. It is a difficult phase in any economy—so difficult that most societies got through it by *force majeure*. . . . No one asked the British laborers moving into the Manchester slums if they wanted to save. . . . The Soviet workers who came to Sverdlovsk and Magnitogorsk from the primitive steppes had no say in the condition of their work. Nor have the Chinese in their communes today. (quoted in Heilbroner, 1970, p. 91)

The ability to enforce economic sacrifice on a people who would not choose it remains a component in the generation of competitive power, and this ability requires the centralization of political power within society.

The forces of social evolution, then, have driven mankind out of the simple egalitarian societies of our origins into massive centrally controlled organizations.

The selection for power in intersocietal competition may not have been the only impetus behind this movement, but it has been a major one. The human costs of this journey are too obvious to need elaborate exposition. Liberty, equality, and fraternity have all been scarce among civilized societies. Although democratic revolutions in the West have enabled some peoples to ameliorate some of the most flagrant abuses of inequalities of power within societies, even the peoples of democracies are compelled to choose centralized structures: any large complex social system needs a hierarchy of control to function effectively, and any civilized society faced with external threats must use central control to maximize its competitive power. Even if the ruling parts used their powers only for the well-being of the whole society—which of course is usually far from the case[7]—the compression of human social life into the hierarchical mold would cramp the full flowering of our humanity. There is a mature dignity in the primitive—the noble savage—or in the yeoman farmer of Jeffersonian democracy which survives with great difficulty in a world where most must function as adults in situations where others govern them by command. In a complex world to stand erect like a human being ceases to be a simple thing.

5.   Reflections on the Disadvantages of Centralization

The dependence of social power on central control presents a more complicated case than the other two morphological characteristics we have considered (size and complexity). The indisputable advantages of centralization are counteracted, to a degree, by other factors. Let us consider three possible ways in which the concentration of power within a system can detract from the system's power.

A. *Ignorance*

"All decisions should be made as low as possible in the organization. The Charge of the Light Brigade was ordered by an officer who wasn't there looking at the territory" (Robert Townsend, quoted in *Whole Earth Catalogue*). It is all fine and good for Israel to obey as one man, but how is the commander to know what to tell them to do? Here, increasing complexity is the foe of increasing central control. What if the game of chess involved several thousand pieces moving simultaneously and individually on a $1,000 \times 1,000 \times 1,000$ three-dimensional board? What would hap-

---

7. This aspect of the problem of civilized power structures is discussed in chap. 7, "Men Are Not Ants."

pen then to the advantages of a coherent strategy in the absence of a mind capable of composing one? Napoleon can sit on his horse to observe the battle of Borodino and to direct the major movements of troops and cavalry, but he cannot tell each man where to place his foot for the next step or where to point his gun for the next shot. When war became a more complex engagement, as in World War II, generals were forced to rely more upon the initiative and judgments of lieutenants and sergeants.

Central authority attempts to deal with the problem of ignorance through bureaucratic organization. Bureaucracy is still hierarchy. Those at the top control as much as the complexity of the organization's task will permit, and they delegate to those below them authority within narrow limits. A sergeant in platoon warfare may compose a strategy of attack or defense of a particular position, but his responsibilities for that position have been given him down the chain of command. Overall goals and strategies are still decided at the top. Through a hierarchic organization, those at the top attempt to deal with what would be overwhelming complexity without relinquishing any of their real power.

The limits of this approach have become most evident in the sphere of economic activity. Some large-scale economic enterprises are simple enough to be easily overseen. Like Napoleon directing large troop movements, the Pharoah's overseer could effectively coordinate thousands of slaves constructing vast public works.[8] The demands of a modern economy, however, are different. A modern economy is an extraordinarily complex system requiring intricate coordination. To orchestrate its movements is a task of a wholly different order. In communist countries, ideology has combined with the determination of the elite to monopolize power to dictate a centralized planning of the economy. To cope with their enormous task, planned economies have created vast bureaucracies. But bureaucracy is not a tool for all purposes. Bureaucracy may solve the problem of having someone on the scene able to prevent the Light Brigade from committing suicide. Because of its essentially analytic structure, however, bureaucracy cannot well perform a task of synthesis, for example, coordinating the innumerable flows of a modern economy. The presumed blessing of Adam Smith's "invisible hand" is that no one has to bring the pieces together, for the interactive system does it by itself. The visible hand of the Central Planner has trouble sorting things out. The Yugoslav economist Borivoje Jelic writes:

8. Indeed, some have proposed that political centralization originally arose for economic reasons, e.g., that the chiefdom arose to perform a central redistributive function. Karl Wittfogel's "hydraulic hypothesis" some years ago suggested that the state was created to fill the need for a central power strong enough to manage the irrigation projects of the early agrarian economies.

> Lines and tasks laid down by central authority do not leave much room for free choice in making decisions within an enterprise. The maximum energy could be used only for the purpose of fulfilling to the utmost possible degree the tasks of the plan, while leaving no great possibilities for correcting eventual discrepancies, or—which is more important—for an effective utilization of the possibilities and advantages which a centralized plan could not foresee. . . . [If] the economy develops, and if development proves to be an increasingly complex process, then strictly centralized planning and administrative management becomes less and less capable of making effective use of the numerous possibilities offered by the complex life of a modern economy. (quoted in Apter, 1965, p. 448)

If the game on the 3-D chess board boggles the mind, perhaps artificial augmentation of the powers of the mind could bring the modern economy within the grasp of central control. The tremendous potency of computer technology, it has been hoped, might overmatch the complexity of the task. Heilbroner wrote about this some years ago:

> A widely held opinion among Russian planners was that more detailed and better integrated planning performed on a battery of computers would solve the problem. Few still cling to this belief. The demands of planning have grown far faster than the ability to meet them: indeed, one Soviet mathematician has predicted that at the current rate of growth of the planning bureaucracy, planning alone would require the services of the entire Russian population by 1980. (1970, p. 627)

Whether subsequent technological progress has substantially improved the prospects for central planning I do not know.

The problem of ignorance is a major reason why a number of centralized economies (e.g., Hungary, the People's Republic of China) have been decentralizing in recent years, sacrificing ideological purity for the demonstrably more efficient regulatory mechanisms of a market system.

The advantages of decentralization in the economy have limited implications for other aspects of power. We return to the image of the vector. Ignorance hampers centralization in all spheres. In an economic system, the costs of ignorance can be decisive when the purpose of the system is to grow in magnitude regardless of direction. The efficiency of the market system maximizes GNP with no one governing its composition. Where it is necessary to maximize the vector of a society's competitive power, however, there can be no substitute for centralization of power. In a market society like the United States, decisions for allocating resources for defense are made in the capital (head) by the ruling groups. The vector needs a director. In such arenas, the advantages of a central controller outweigh the costs of his ignorance. A military organization may delegate some discretion to its sergeants when it needs to, but it will never cut them loose from the command structure to be military entrepreneurs.

B. Lack of Motivation

Pope Benedict XV wrote in his Encyclical *Ad Beatissimi:* "Force subdues the bodies of men, not their souls" (quoted in Leslie White, 1959, p. 325). Herein lies a weakness of many centrally controlled systems.

For a system to run at full power, friction should be kept at a minimum. A system based on coercion provokes resistance. Compliance may be compelled, but obedience against the will squanders those potent energies which derive from human dedication and enthusiasm. A hundred plodding slaves are less able to move a mountain than a handful of the impassioned faithful. A fighting force without morale lacks the punch of one with real esprit. And enforced unity can crumble when it is most needed. (For example, the Soviets, who need not worry about support of their allies in peacetime, must wonder in which direction their "allies" will fire in the event of war.) A power system therefore has an advantage if it can combine central power to direct the whole with the means of inspiring its members to want to do what the system requires of them. Individuals in that system become not merely the objects of central power but also its agents.

The challenge of making the will of individuals serve the needs of a power-maximizing system can be approached in several ways. One is to use ideology to make individuals identify with the aims of the whole as enunciated by the rulers. By controlling the flow of ideas and information, rulers can make their people "choose" values and actions which in actuality have been chosen for them. Ideologies of patriotism and nationalism can rechannel the energies of self-interest to the service of the society. Group identification submerges the self, and the will of the leader becomes one's own (cf. Freud's *Group Psychology and the Analysis of the Ego*). Religious teachings, which generally inveigh against selfishness anyway, can easily be turned to serve power in this way. By winning "the hearts and minds" of the people, a centrally controlled system can overcome the problem of motivation.

Another approach is to so construct the arena of action that the pursuit by individuals of their own selfish ends is harnessed to further the overarching interests of the system. This capacity to harness self-interest (of which there is no shortage) is the source of the dynamism of the market economy. A centrally controlled economy, by contrast, has difficulties in this area. Where "incentives" are not instituted, perhaps because of their ideological repugnance, productivity suffers. For example, the state-run farms of China and the Soviet Union have been remarkably less productive than the small, private plots that the state has begrudgingly let farmers cultivate for their own use and profit. Problems arise, however, when incentives are artificially created to harness the interests

106

of individuals for collective ends. One Soviet tractor factory, given a quota to meet measured in tonnage of tractors produced in a year, produced tractors so heavy that they were useless.

A third approach is to socialize individuals so that the commandments that serve the power of the system are "inscribed" upon the psyche, that is, internalized. The superego, which in psychoanalytic theory is an introjection of what was originally an external authority, can act then as a deputy of the central power—or even to some extent as its replacement. This even helps solve the central power's problem of ignorance, for each individual monitors himself. Internalization helps to illuminate two aspects of ostensible decentralization in some modern societies: capitalism and democracy.

Capitalism.—The market economy has been described as a decentralized system, and structurally it is. Yet the psychological dimension of capitalism presents a picture of internalized authority. The motivations of the "economic man" of capitalist theory are not so naturally given as those theorists would have us believe, and the rise of capitalism is associated with a particular sociohistorical personality structure. In the development of "the spirit of capitalism," we can see the internalization of a relationship like that between master and servant. That great spokesman of the capitalist ethic, Ben Franklin, captured well this image in "The Way to Wealth": "If you were a Servant, would you not be ashamed that a good Master catch you idle? Are you then your own Master, be ashamed to catch yourself idle, as Poor Dick says" (quoted in Van Doren, 1938, p. 69). As D. H. Lawrence perceived, Franklin's man is not so much free of being ruled as he is ruler and taskmaster over himself. A psychological structure has been created which is driven toward work. In his famous work on the subject, Max Weber quotes Nikolaus Zinzendorf: "One does not only work in order to live but one lives for the sake of one's work, and if there is no more work to do one suffers or goes to sleep" (1958, p. 264 n. 24). It sounds like a slave's existence, but now with the bondage internalized the central powers need not worry about resistance: they have, as it were, a deputy to oversee for them. Resistance is transformed from a political to a psychological conflict. Adam Smith's invisible hand seems to have been aided by an invisible iron fist. Central authority no longer needs to enforce sacrifice, for internalized authority requires individuals to do it voluntarily. Said the Protestant theologian Richard Baxter: "You may labour to be rich for God, though not for the flesh and sin" (quoted in Weber, 1958, p. 168). The fruits of your labor are not for you to enjoy, but for a higher authority.

Democracy.—We equate democracy with freedom and rightly so, but only in part. We have learned since World War II that not all peoples can make democracy work. Perhaps the reason is that in the absence of an overriding power above us—in our large, heterogeneous and powerful societies—social order requires a psychic structure of discipline and self-control. We are less in need of being compelled because we have brought the compulsion within ourselves. "Where liberal institutions have been successful they seem to have been dependent upon some past discipline maintained by coercive authority" (Barbu, 1956, p. 50). First comes power in its raw form from above, and then it is internalized. Woodrow Wilson declared that those who opposed the ruthless use of force in the Philippines failed to understand that

> liberty is the privilege of maturity, of self-control, of self-mastery—that some people may have it, therefore, and others not. We cannot give them any quittance of the debt we ourselves have paid. They can have liberty no cheaper than we got it. They must first take the discipline of law, must first love order and instinctually yield to it. (quoted in Rogin, 1971, p. 567)

Again we are our own "masters." And again, we should recognize that the internalized discipline that makes us "free" entails a cost in another kind of freedom. A Russian once said to John Maynard Keynes: "You don't need the police because you all have mental straitjackets" (Andrzejewski, 1954, p. 131).

Internalization of this kind is in part an escape from central control, but in part also it is an extension of it. Internalization, like bureaucratization, represents a way of bringing the demands of power closer to where the commandments must be obeyed.[9]

C. Stagnation

Finally, central control over a system may carry with it the disadvantage of relative cultural stagnation. To see this, we can contrast the civilization of China with that of Europe. Well over two thousand years ago, China passed through its Warring States period and was consolidated under a single imperial rule. For the most part, it remained unified thereafter. Unmatched in its part of the globe by any system of comparable power, the Chinese could regard themselves as the Middle Kingdom—a stable center in the cosmic order. By contrast, European civilization sprouted forth in a politically fragmented fashion. The nations of Europe, under no unifying power, grew out of strife and have continued their ceaseless struggles against one another into recent memory. The parable of the tribes asserts that competition among sovereign entities drives much of what is called progress. The comparison between these two civilizations—

---

9. The issue of internalization is explored in greater depth in chap. 5, "The War Within."

China, isolated and unified, versus Europe, competitive and fragmented—provides an illustration of this thesis.

One striking fact is that several inventions that, in European hands, helped usher in the age of modern power, originated in China, for example, gunpowder and the compass. In the centrally controlled Chinese civilization, power-relevant innovations were regarded with suspicion by rulers wanting to preserve the status quo. Carlo Cippola says of these rulers: "Fearing internal bandits no less than foreign invasion, the [Chinese] Imperial Court did its best to limit both the spread of the knowledge and the proliferation of artisans versed in the art [of firearms]" (quoted in Walle   1 Wallerstein adds: "In Europe with its mu   re was no hope of limiting the spread of ar   vas still possible, and hence the centralized s   ical advance essential in the long run for the   wer." The central rulers of China not only I   but were actually motivated to retard chang   tism of culture was accentuated by centra   there was no one to control power, the rapi   mizing technologies was not only possible fo   so mandatory for each actor in the system. I   ve stagnation came due for the Chinese. H: ions as novelties to the backward European   mselves under the gun from modern Europ   eas in their compass-guided ships.

This illustra   ntrol is better for harnessing than for gene   On the one hand, a given system at a gi   power if it is under central control. On th   ractive systems of competing parts are mos   f power (if these competing parts do not fi

10. This persp   Europe raises the question: why is it that the civilization of I   ied as China did nor developed the dynamism of Europe   nswer this question in depth, but a few relevant ideas may

The history of   riod the familiar pattern of unification/ centralization thro   ect to the Vedic period. The unification culminated roughl   ishment of the Mauryan Empire, which was closely knit an   ost-Mauryan India, what became normal was a looser, "feud   le may say disorganization. The question arises about post-]   conflict-ridden India could continue as stably as it did.

Bashan confr   the history of India differs so from that of China, i.e., why   id not lead to the building of a permanent empire over the w   nswer, he says, was that "no king of India

Dynamism may also be impaired by centralization within economic systems. Clearly, market societies have developed the crucial innovations on which modern economic (and military) power depends. On one hand, perhaps the competitive decentralized structure of these economies makes them more effective at innovation. This is less than completely clear, however, since cultural and historical differences confound the variables. On the other hand, even if the market economy enjoys advantages over a planned economy in its powers of innovation and, as we have argued, in its efficiency, it is nonetheless handicapped in its ability to harness that economic power for intersocietal competition. Thus far, we have considered economic power as a magnitude without direction. The economic capacity, as measured by GNP, was treated as a measure of the contribution of the economy to a society's power. Thus, in this century, we have had what have been called "GNP wars," which were "won by the side which was able to supply its millions of soldiers, sailors and airmen with sufficient food and clothing, and the most military equipment—ships, planes, tanks—over a four- to five-year period" (Dalton, 1974, p. 104). But GNP does not translate automatically into competitive power. To paraphrase Herodotus more than two thousand years ago: War is not won by gold, but by the swords it can purchase; nor by grain unless it is made food for armies. Aron puts the same point in more modern terms: "War is carried on not with steel but with guns and tanks. The country

---

was able to develop a bureaucracy capable of functioning without a strong guiding hand." He contrasts it with the bureaucratic culture developed by Confucian China (p. 123). But the main factor, he says, "which prevented the unification of India was the martial tradition itself" (p. 124). An earlier military ethic in India, articulated in the classic text of the *Arthasastra*, regarded war as a continuation of policy by other means, an activity whose main motive is "gain and the building up of a great empire" (p. 125, 126). In post-Mauryan India, a new ethic gained predominance saying that "war should be waged for glory and homage rather than sordid aims such as wealth and power" (p. 124). War, says Bashan, became a sport. That ethic helped preserve Indian fragmentation.

Bashan does not ask why (unlike in Europe) the chronic conflict did not impel Indian minds toward power-enhancing innovations. Perhaps, however, a part of the answer can be drawn out of another aspect of Indian culture that seems kindred and connected to the military ethic just described. It concerns the political culture and, in particular, the political consequences of victory and defeat. "When decisively defeated in battle," Bashan writes, "a king might render homage to his conqueror and retain his throne" (p. 94). "The degree of control over overlord and vassal varied much. . . . Many claims to homage and tribute amounted to very little" (p. 94, 95). The picture suggested is that war was a sport, so being conquered was not intolerably burdensome. Perhaps when even the worst can be borne, the spur of necessity is not so sharp as to induce the dynamism of a highly inventive culture.

These reflections on India serve to underscore the nondeterministic nature of the parable of the tribes (chap. 1, "Power versus Choice in Social Evolution"). The selection for power can govern in the long run because it is patient and tends to work consistently and cumulatively. In the short run, idiosyncracies of individual cultural systems can retard the growth of power. India's fragmentation, ultimately, contributed greatly to its vulnerability to manipulation and domination by a comparative handful of British men. By the time India threw off the British imperialists, India had in the process become one of the great nations of the world. Plagued though it still is by centrifugal forces, India stands as the dominant power of its region, developing something of an empire of its own (see Alumni Magazine Consortium, "The Rise and Fall of Empires, 1982").

that has steel will have thousands of tanks at the end of a year or two, provided it has not first been crushed" (1954, p. 90). This proviso is now more important than ever before. With the technology of modern warfare, a decisive blow can be struck in a matter of hours or days. A centrally controlled economy like that of the Soviet Union, for all its drawbacks, sees to it that its steel takes the form of tanks. Regardless of the deprivations its people suffer, the regime employs whatever economic resources it needs to maximize national power. The economies of the West dwarf that of their Soviet rival, but with less direction they are unreliable in matching the vector of Soviet force. Should Soviet tanks strike for the Rhine, millions of Mercedes cars and color television sets will not even slow them down.

6. The Adrenalin Society

A threat to survival is an emergency. To survive that emergency, a system must organize and orient itself to deal effectively with the threat. We can get a picture of what this requires by looking at how our own bodies respond to an emergency. Adrenalin is secreted into the body and acts, among other ways, (1) to increase the alertness and coordination of the central mental and sensory systems that monitor the threat and determine the proper response, (2) to anaesthetize the body so that stress and injury to the peripheral body parts will not hinder the necessary actions, and (3) to mobilize the strength of the body to make it capable of forceful action against the threat.

Since the rise of civilization, human societies have been condemned to live in a chronic emergency. Their survival threatened by an unending intersocietal struggle for power, civilized societies have evolved steadily toward a structure and posture analogous to the adrenalin response. We have explored how the external threat has focused energy on a centrally controlling part, and how the growing power of the head in the body politic has brought with it the capacity of the system, when acting as a whole, to ignore injury to the other parts. And to these structural changes we can add adrenalin-like changes in the spirit of the social organism: an increased capacity for aggressive behavior, and a stepped-up level of activity generally.

The first section of this chapter showed how Mars rose with civilization. The struggle for power and the selective process it generated changed the temper of human societies from peaceful to belligerent. In *The City in History*, Mumford relates how the aggressiveness of the new urban civilizations was a contagion infecting the peoples of "once peacefully disposed" more primitive societies, so that "Under the aegis of the city,

111

violence became normalized" (1961, p. 63). Yet as the emergency has continued, more and more of this social evolutionary "adrenalin" has seeped into the bloodstream of history. And again, the emerging adrenalin society, leading the way for mankind, throbs with the pulse of violence. Writes Robert Osgood: "The whole astonishing explosion of modern Western civilization is linked with a distinctive bellicosity in its organized political life" (Osgood and Tucker, 1967, p. 5n). The selection for power seems to entail the spread of a kind of social rage. "It appears that the less aggressive nations of the past are showing a capacity for learning how to be more aggressive than they had been" (Thieme, in Fried et al., 1968, p. 19).

The activation of the adrenalin society has transcended the purely combative dimension. Typically for the cutting edge of social evolution, the Western civilization that has been transforming the world in recent centuries has been quicker in its pace, more dynamic in its approach to the world, than those it has transformed. The selective process favors the restless spirit over the more content and self-contained. Denis de Rougement, in *Man's Western Quest,* attributes to the restlessness of Western man the fact that it was the Europeans, and not the better equipped Arabs, who set out at the end of the fifteenth century on a quest of exploration. And William Woodruff writes in *The Impact of Western Man:*

> It was this vigour, this spirit of inquiry, this urge to expand, this sense of adventure, which enabled the European to set his impress upon the world. . . . This emphasis upon purposive action which Goethe expressed in Faust might be used to describe the genius of European civilization. It is not discovery or originality that marks off the European from those who preceded them, it is energy—an almost daemonic energy to mould the world to its will. It was this which enabled Europe to arise out of darkness and enjoy its moment as the leader of the human race. (1966, p. 7)

Civilization evolves toward the adrenalin society.

An essential aspect of this selection for the "adrenalin society" cannot be derived from my organic analogy. Our bodies are designed to be capable of the adrenalin response as a temporary measure after which we return to "normal" because the threats are presumably temporary. The evolution of civilization, however, has allowed no reversion to a prethreat normalcy. Rather, the level of mobilization required has continually escalated. What emerges is a more and more stressed adrenalin society always poised as if to meet a *perpetual emergency.* This is true not because the threat to a civilized society is constant, any more than it is to an individual creature. It is because (*a*) cultural innovations constantly escalate the terms of competition, (*b*) a society's wartime power depends largely on its peacetime structure, and (*c*) the level of mobilization of power in peacetime societies must therefore escalate also. Social evolution is like the turning of a rachet, allowing movement in one direction (further toward power) but not in the other (back toward a less powerful social type).

Peace becomes but war pursued by other means. A society cannot afford to be much different in peacetime than what it must become in wartime. Thus, even peacetime society must embody the adrenalin structure required by war. McNeill says of the Sumerian polity that "extraordinary powers delegated in war became normal in peacetime" (1963, p. 43). This statement can be taken as a motto on the banner of civilization, with escalation rampant on a field of power struggles. Political structure becomes permanently fixed like a central nervous system poised to strike or defend. "The habits of command and obedience generated by the needs of war," writes Andrzejewski, "tend to persist in times of peace" because "preparedness means being organized in such a way that war could be waged without lengthy reorganization" (1954, p. 93). The stressful stimulation of the adrenalin society has become more and more extreme as societies have progressively increased their capacity to focus all social resources on the projection of power. The accelerated march toward total war in the nineteenth and twentieth centuries has made peace structurally less and less distinguishable from war. Jouvenal was quoted earlier as saying that the Prussian victory of 1870 made Europe field peacetime forces as large as the forces at the height of the Napoleonic wars. Osgood writes of this same circumstance that the efficiency of Prussian preparation persuaded all governments that "The game would be won or lost by what went on before the war" (Osgood and Tucker, 1967, p. 81). Today's democracies look apprehensively across at their totalitarian rivals, worried that, as Aron says, the tight centralized systems of their foes confer the advantage of more immediate readiness for conflict. Total war has meant the increasing involvement of the entire social body in mobilization, not just the political head and the military arm but also the economic guts which nourish the power system. The selection for the adrenalin society has mandated frenetic economic transformations as well, so that what sometimes is called progress can be seen in retrospect as mobilization:

> Down to 1910 it could be said with great apparent force that even if the transformation of our [American] economy was inevitable, it had proceeded too fast. Why such reckless speed? Why not more time, more caution, more moderation? Today this view appears dubious. Had our pace been slower and our achievement weaker, had we not created so swiftly our powerful industrial units in steel, oil, textiles, chemicals, electricity, and the automotive vehicles, the free world might have lost the First World War, and most certainly would have lost the Second. (Nevins, 1953, viii–ix)

113

Powers required in wartime become embodied in the peacetime adrenalin society.

So the rachet turns. The escalation of power forever raises the necessary level of mobilization.[11] Thus the parable of the tribes accounts for the evolution of the adrenalin society, always organized and oriented toward the requirements of the intersocietal threat. The demands of war have condemned civilized peoples to have no peace.

7. Common Denominator: The Homogenizing of Cultures

The necessity of power has shaped civilized society in size and structure, in technology, and to a degree in the spirit that animates its motion. If this shaping of power is regarded from a vantage point that encompasses all mankind, another dimension of the process becomes salient: the homogenizing of cultures. In a system of competing societies, the rule of power mandates certain cultural ways, precluding other cultural choices. As cultural homogenization is (largely) the fruit of intersocietal competition, the emergence in modern times of a single global competitive system brings all human cultures now toward convergence.[12] Loren Eiseley writes of an aspect of this convergence:

> Increasingly there is but one way into the future, the technological way. The frightening aspect of this situation lies in the constriction of human choice. Western technology has released irrevocable forces, and the "one world" that has been talked about so glibly is frequently a distraught conformity, produced by the centripetal forces of Western society. So great is its power over men that any other solutions, any other philosophy, is silenced. . . . (I)t is as though instead of many adaptive organisms, a single gigantic animal embodies the only organic future of the world. (1969, pp. 38–39)

The historical and accelerating convergence of cultures has been noted by many people, but the role of power in this process is seldom recognized. Many cultural ways do diffuse through human choice, of course,

---

11. Actually, although the overall trend of history is toward the growth of power, there are times—the most notable of which is the "fall" of the Roman Empire—when systems of power collapse. The fall of empires by no means ends the struggle for power—indeed the more pervasive anarchy may intensify it—but it can have the effect of temporarily lowering the level of power an actor in the system needs to survive for competition. For a discussion of how the cyclical patterns of the rise and fall of power systems fits into the essentially linear view of the parable of the tribes, see chap. 7, "The Death of the Unnatural."

12. Akira Iriye, in his book on the Japanese-American conflict in World War II, writes that "the war required greater effort at industrialization and urbanization, efficiency and productivity, and utilization of resources, as well as scientific and technological innovations, than ever before. To that extent, *the very act of fighting obliterated differences between nations*" (1981, p. 95), italics added.

spreading because they are generally regarded as improving the human condition. Yet, when we look at the elements of civilization that have spread and endured the most we must be struck by the prominence among them of the ways of power.

It is not necessarily that power is the preoccupation of those who undertake to spread their own culture. To them, frequently, superior power is simply an instrument by which superior vision can be introduced. This is captured well in the statement, made in 1683, by an artillery captain named Mieth: "Before the discovery of gunpowder, both the Indies were in the jaws of hellish Satan and in the very darkest obscurity, more like cattle or wild beasts in customs and beliefs than like reasonable creatures of the great God. Gunnery has been the only means by which the command of Christ could be performed (Luke 14:23: 'Urge them to come in that My house may become full.')" (quoted in Vagts, 1937, p. 45). Yet, in the workings of social evolution, the technological/power medium became the message while the intended spiritual message became lost. In Asia, according to A. Grenfell Price in *Western Invasions of the Pacific and Its Continents,* the Christianity important to Western colonizers made few inroads whereas their technology did. And Woodruff observes that "Paradoxically, the Christian Church and its foreign missions had a greater degree of success in transmitting Western materialism, with its growing emphasis on superior weapons, productive methods, and an ever-widening commerce, than it did in transmitting its own spiritual message" (1966, p. 6). The Western invaders certainly were fully armed with materialist intentions as well as spiritual. But any contradiction between intention and result appears paradoxical only if we regard history as a story made by people "speaking" rather than by impersonal selective forces "listening." The parable of the tribes is a theory to account for the selective listening in the transformations of civilized societies. Herbert Butterfield notes:

> When we speak of Western civilization being carried to an oriental country like Japan in recent generations, we do not mean Graeco-Roman philosophy and humanist ideals, we do not mean the Christianizing of Japan, we mean the science, the modes of thought and all that apparatus of civilization which were beginning to change the face of the West in the latter half of the seventeenth century. (1961, p. 179)

We mean, that is, the spread of the new springs of power the West had begun to tap.

What spreads most surely is what made colonial conquest possible in the first place: power. It is not that the tools of power are at the heart of the conquering culture, despite the notions of the economic determinists. Nor is the apparatus of power less alien to the cultures of the conquered than is the spiritual dimension of the invading culture, for the transformations demanded by power are disruptive enough. Power is what spreads because power is a necessity for social survival: for Japan, as we saw, "it was industrialize or be gobbled up like the rest."

The thesis that the selection for power leads to cultural homogeneity rests on two premises: (1) to survive, a society must have sufficient power to avoid destruction in intersocietal competition, and (2) only a narrow range of cultural possibilities is consistent with achieving the required power. Let us look more closely at this second point. Just how narrow is the range of viable cultural options? How much is the whole society determined by the requirements of power? These questions are important if one believes, as I do, that cultural diversity is a valuable treasure for mankind.

Consider some of the requirements for "modernization." Simon Kuznets, upon acceptance in 1974 of the Nobel Prize in economics, suggested some of the cultural requirements for implementing modern technology:

> If technology is to be employed efficiently and widely, and, indeed, if its own progress is to be stimulated by much use, institutional and ideological adjustments must be made to effect the proper use of innovations generated by the advancing stock of knowledge. To cite examples from modern economic growth: steam and electric power and the large-scale plants needed to exploit them are not compatible with family enterprises, illiteracy, or slavery—all of which prevailed in earlier times in much of even the developed world, and had to be replaced by more appropriate institutions and social views. Nor is modern technology compatible with the rural mode of life, the large and extended family pattern, and the veneration of undisturbed nature. (1974, p. 247)

To a degree, therefore, Eiseley is justified in speaking of "the technological way." George Dalton also indicates some "structural transformations" required of a modernized society "regardless of whether the economic institutions employed are capitalist or communist: a) the growth of non-agricultural employment and output . . . b) the growth of cities and towns . . . c) the use of machine technology and applied science in new and old economic sectors . . . d) mass literacy, training and education; e) the intensification of national economic, political and cultural integration" (1974, p. 206). Whether or not competitive power is the motivation for such modernization, long-run social survival seems to depend on having a modernized society. This entire chapter has delineated some other broad dimensions of social morphology to which a society must conform to survive.

Yet the question remains: how broad are we to consider these requirements? Is the selection for power indeed shaping—in Eiseley's expression—a single cultural animal? A look at the world today reveals differences as notable as the convergences, even among the great powers. The United States and the Soviet Union, although they share much of the machinery of power, remain very different. The requirements of power do not mandate that all societies live in identical cultural houses. A more apt image is that power requires that every structure achieve a certain minimal height: a stone temple, an office building, and a stadium may all suffice. They might suffice, that is, for a particular moment in history, before the escalation of power leads to still higher demands. According to this image, the spread of the ways of power does not mandate convergence toward a simple kind of culture, but is consistent with genuine cultural differences.

But perhaps the coexistence of the stone temple and the office building is only a temporary state. Perhaps the slow workings of the parable of the tribes allows atavistic remnants of diverse historical traditions to survive awhile before they are ground finely and finally by the homogenizing mills of history. After all, consider how far toward convergence have come American, Russian, and Japanese societies in a mere century. David Kaplan writes: "It seems merely a matter of time before all of the cultural systems of the world will be different variations, depending upon divergent historical experiences, of a single cultural type" (in Sahlins and Service, 1960, p. 92).

And then one more problem: how important are those aspects of culture determined by the requirements of power in comparison with those areas where cultural choices remain open? Living in a stone temple is different from living in an office building. But from the standpoint of one who wishes to live down on the ground amid the trees where the birds sing, may not these edifices be much the same? Are the differences between Sparta and Athens more important than the power-producing similarities? If Kaplan is right, how important will the "variations" be in comparison with the singleness of the one type? To answer those questions seems to require a God's-eye view of what is central and what is peripheral in human life. I can offer no answer.

What does it matter whether or not cultural diversity persists?

One answer is suggested by Eiseley's image that rather than many adaptive cultural organisms, "a single gigantic animal embodies the only organic future of the world." Cultural homogeneity is a version of the blunder of putting all one's eggs in the same basket. The maintenance of a variety of cultural options seems only prudent in view of the uncertainty about what cultural resources human survival and well-being may require in the future. The danger of having but one "single cultural type"

117

is especially acute when that type designed by power is especially prone to contain the seeds of its own self-destruction.[13]

A second answer is that no single cultural way can fully capture our humanity. Born an unfinished creature, the human being takes finished form according to the image promoted by his culture. Any single rendering of the human being realizes only one part of the full spectrum of the individual's potential humanity. People and peoples different from ourselves can perform for us an essential visionary service, revealing to us fuller dimensions of our own humanity than we can easily recognize in ourselves. To squander the diversity of cultures, to break this fuller mirror of our potential, is to endanger still further our precarious awareness of ourselves. Cultural homogenization threatens to narrow human consciousness.

Some who note the disappearance of differences *between* cultures suggest that increasing differences *within* them might compensate. Lenski, for example, writes: "Compare, for example, the way of life of an advertising executive living in a modern metropolis like New York with that of an illiterate migrant farm worker in Texas or California" (1970, p. 99). It seems to me, however, that differences within societies that grow with increasing division of labor are of a fundamentally different nature than those being lost between societies. The differences between societies that have developed autonomously represent different visions of human life. By contrast, the differences growing out of the division of labor within societies, mandated in large part by the rule of power, are more like the differences between parts in the same machine. Differences like these do little to illuminate the human spirit. We will not be saved by a society that produces Alphas as well as Gammas in its human factory.

These first two arguments for cultural diversity would apply to any kind of cultural homogenization. A third answer relates to the specific kind of culture which the rule of power creates. Power compels all cultures toward a common denominator; even if this common denominator is not necessarily the lowest, it is not the culture we would choose if we could. Not, as I said in chapter 1, that the cultural transformations dictated by power maximization are invariably hostile to human needs. They are simply indifferent.

An ideal cultural system for humanity would be founded upon what people need for fulfillment. Upon that foundation, a variety of societies might be constructed to accommodate a full and rich human existence. The design of the society and the principles governing how the human elements of the social system interact would be determined by values

13. As argued in chap. 7, "The Death of the Unnatural."

rooted in a profound vision of the meaning of human life. The inter-societal system in that ideal world would then function to enhance the viability of those human societies and the richness of human experience. Ideally each system would serve and nourish what it encompasses, and human needs would be at the core.

The parable of the tribes demonstrates that powerful social evolutionary forces operate in exactly the opposite direction with predictably inhumane results. At the foundation of the structure of caused determination is an intersocietal system the anarchy of which makes the struggle for power inevitable for all civilized human life. As civilized societies are shaped by this enveloping struggle into ever more efficient machines of power, their human members are compelled to serve these power machines. People are condemned to become mere means to social ends determined not by the human spirit but by the selection for power. Cultural homogeneity shaped by forces like these is not to be desired.

Flesh and blood strive constantly not to be ground up in the machine. And, indeed, not all power has demanded the degradation of humanity of a Gulag Archipelago. But the inescapable requirements of power maximization are constant threats to our hopes for a truly human existence. To the extent that people are compelled to act as instruments of a social power machine, we can ill afford to be sanguine about the terms of human life. In *The Human Use of Human Beings*, Norbert Wiener writes:

> [The] aspiration of the fascist for a human state based on the model of the ant results from a profound misapprehension both of the nature of the ant and of the nature of man. I wish to point out that the very physical development of the insect conditions it to be an essentially stupid and unlearning individual, cast in a mold which cannot be modified to any great extent. I also wish to show how these physiological conditions make it into a cheap mass-produced article, of no more individual value than a paper pie plate to be thrown away after it is once used. On the other hand, I wish to show that the human individual, capable of vast learning and study, which may occupy half of his life, is physically equipped, as the ant is not, for this capacity. Variety and possibility are inherent in the human sensorium—and are indeed the key to man's most noble flights—because variety and possibility belong to the very structure of the human organism.
>
> While it is possible to throw away this enormous advantage that we have over the ants, and to organize the fascist ant-state with human material, I certainly believe that this is a degradation of man's very nature, and economically a waste of the great human values which man possesses. (1954, pp. 51–52)

A striking aspect of this passage is the utilitarian basis for the argument against the fascist degradation of the human being: to use a person as an ant is, like using a camera to drive in a nail, a waste of the instrument's capability. Perhaps this means that the totalitarian approach to civilized life will be selected against because its costs in wasting human resources will exceed its benefits in social control and militance. Such societies, however, have shown some ability to draw upon their members' human capacity for performance while simultaneously demanding antlike narrowness in matters of values and the spirit. Perhaps our own freedom and concern for human welfare will prove too costly in terms of social power. At any event, the record of power's growth allows one little comfort from Wiener's analysis. For, although civilization will not waste what proves to be essential, it will not be deterred from a course of development simply because it degrades man's nature.

Even if the more humane Western route to power is favored, causes for alarm certainly remain. It is not necessary to look forward to a future *Brave New World* to see in the modernized culture spreading around the world a kind of mechanization of human life. The machinery of power developed by the West may eschew wanton cruelty, but it still seeks to transform flesh and blood into components of the machine. "Want of principle," wrote Hazlitt, "is power." A handicap in the pursuit of power is integrity, that unity between the ground of one's existence and one's values and one's actions. Power systems are therefore hostile to integrity and to the humane cultural traditions that provide an orientation to help people achieve it. The power that erupted in the West has from the outset sought the disintegration of the cultural principles that stood in its way. Hannah Arendt writes that Europe, in exporting its technology and "the grandiose development of the natural sciences and the victory of the nation state over all other forms of government," exported also "its processes of disintegration": "The same forces which took centuries to undermine the ancient beliefs and ways of life, and which have their place in the continuous development of the West alone, took only a few decades to break down, by working from without, beliefs and ways of life in all other parts of the world" (1968, pp. 82-83). The disintegration of culture allows more mechanical principles to enter the social body and govern it. (I think of the image from the film *The Invasion of the Body Snatchers* [Allied Artists, 1956] in which people are replaced, when they fall asleep, by look-alikes from outer space who have their functional abilities but lack all feelings and values.) Erich Kahler views the emerging cultural homogeneity in this way, a single global culture determined not by genuine human values but rather by the mechanical necessities of production:

> In our day the life of people all over the world is, for the first time, on the point of following an immediately universal pattern and not, as in former periods, pursuing distinct modes of life which had originated in and expanded from a particular human attitude. The present forms of living as generated all over the globe by Western civilization are not a genuine style of life; they

are abstract standards [as opposed to values] imposed by objectively tested experiences, by scientific and technological precepts, by industrial production. . . . What determines the conduct of people today is, in a rapidly diminishing degree, tastes and preferences, but more and more the inexorable, factual and practical necessities of collective work and the collective facilities it produces. (1957, p. 207)

Admittedly, this is but one part of the picture. Our flesh and blood seeks continually to inject meaningful and humane values. But our machines of power persistently threaten to shape our lives to their inhumane pattern.[14]

Shaped by power, our systems are in many ways not our tools. Indeed, they press us to become instruments to their ends. The needed integrity between human needs on the one hand and cultural design and practice on the other remain far from realization in a world ruled by power. The challenge to us is to find a way to act with integrity and with an understanding of the antagonism between the human and the power system. The opposite of integrity is opportunism, which is the willingness to allow the environment to govern one's course. Like water flowing downhill, the opportunist takes the course of least resistance. In an ideal world, opportunism and integrity could be the same thing. But as long as social evolution is governed by forces that threaten to drag human well-being down, the only responsible course is to labor against the current. At the same time, in a world filled with grave necessities, one cannot survive by simply going against gravity. For integrity to be more than gesture and martyrdom, it, too, must find its opportunities. In a complex and dangerous world, the path for individuals and for societies between self-destruction and the loss of soul is at best narrow but not straight.

14. The hero of E. M. Forster's story "The Machine Stops" cries out: "Cannot you see . . . that it is we who are dying, and that down here the only thing that really lives is the Machine? We created the Machine, to do our will, but we cannot make it do our will now. It has robbed us of the sense of space and the sense of touch, it has blurred every human relation. . . . The Machine develops— but not on our lines. The Machine proceeds—but not to our goal" (in Allen, 1971, pp. 172–173).

Epilogue to Book I

Power and Choice in Our Times

I

It is a common illusion to believe that one's own moment in history represents a turning point of epochal proportions. World War I was the war to end all wars (it did not have a "I" after it then). A generation ago, the end of the age of scarcity was said to be at hand. The record of millennial hopes bids one be cautious about claims of incipient salvation.

Nonetheless, as the evolution of civilization tends to move forward into new territory, we need not assume that all change simply means more of the *même chose*. With respect to the problems of intersocietal competition central to the parable of the tribes, modern developments have indeed created unprecedented dangers and opportunities. The main unprecedented danger, obviously, lies in the fact that our technology of destruction today is many orders of magnitude larger than that of all previous historical eras. Less visible are the sources of opportunity to create a more whole civilization, although the parable of the tribes helps to bring them into focus.

First, all the societies on earth are being knit into an increasingly dense web of interaction and interdependence. Contrary to much recent discussion of "interdependence," one cannot assume that increased inter-relatedness leads to increased harmony. Dependency can as often be a motive for conflict as for cooperation. The coming together of a single global civilizational system, however, does make it conceivable that the disastrous fragmentation of the intersocietal system can be eliminated. Power has been so virulent a contaminant because the body of civilization has lacked the integration necessary to mobilize resistance against small intrusions. Thus the disease in one small part could progress until it afflicted the whole: if in one corner of the world a community of societies managed to end the struggle among them, they remained vulnerable to eventual invasion from some remote part of the earth where the struggle raged unchecked. Now, all human societies are in constant contact with one another and, barring the possibility of some Wellsian invasion of extraterrestrial forces, for the first time in history all powers can assemble and come to grips with civilization's problem of power in its entirety.

Clearly, as long as civilization is comprised of more than a hundred sovereign nations, the end of the system's fragmentation is only partial and potential. But the anarchy suggested by the multiplicity of sovereign actors is mitigated by another aspect of the contemporary international system: the predominance of two superpowers.

The parable of the tribes relates the hypothetical story of ten tribes, showing that it only takes any one of the ten to poison the whole system. It is vain, the model suggests, to hope that all ten would choose the way of peace. (Indeed, in history the number of potential competitors has been far higher than ten.) But in the post–World War II world, the achievement of far greater global peace and relaxation has required not the improbable ten out of ten, or a hundred out of a hundred, but a more reasonable two out of two. That is, if both the United States and the Soviet Union were truly devoted to leading the world beyond the chronic struggle for power, the inhumane forces described in this work might have been (might still be) significantly weakened. The superpowers do not control all other actors on the world scene, but so great is their dominance that if they cooperated in creating an atmosphere of peace and trust, and if they dampened rather than inflamed the inevitable local and regional conflicts, the climate of the world community would be greatly (though assuredly not completely) pacified.

It may be reasonable to hope for two out of two, but of course that is not what has happened. The rubble of World War II had scarcely settled when a new struggle for power between the two erstwhile allies developed and, with varying degrees of intensity, has continued ever since. Their bitter struggle has poisoned the world, even without outright conflict, and threatens to inflict catastrophe upon it. A momentous op-

123

portunity in world history has not been seized and, as of 1982, there are no signs it will be.

The world did not get two out of two, and there are many who would say that what it got was zero out of two. The question of who is responsible for the cold war has been the subject of much study and controversy. Surely, the self-righteous American view—popular in the 1950s and held in high offices now—that everything the United States has done is blameless cannot be accepted. The record shows that American ambition and hypocrisy (as well as naiveté and diplomatic incompetence) have played a considerable role in exacerbating world tensions. But to depart from the orthodox cold warrior's view that the Soviets get 100 percent of the blame is not necessarily to conclude that the fault lies mostly with the United States, or even that responsibility must be apportioned 50–50. Many believe that reversing the usual ethnocentric bias, as some cold war revisionists do, is a sign of enlightenment. In this case, I believe, it is not.

There are several reasons to be skeptical about evenhandedness in the assignment of responsibility for the cold war struggle. First, the democratic processes of the United States—the rather free flow of information and the periodic accountability of leaders—act as a decisive check on the ability of leaders to sacrifice or risk humane values to slake their thirst for world power as an end in itself. Such checks are unmatched in the Soviet Union (which is why Afghanistan cannot really be the Soviets' Vietnam, and why their military budgets can remain fat regardless of how lean the Soviet society becomes). Second, and related, the moral quality of Soviet and American leadership when the postwar struggle was set into motion is hardly comparable. The record of Stalin's rule is now fairly clear, and it shows that "Uncle Joe" was as ruthless a human being as can be imagined. Willing to murder millions of human beings for his own purposes, including his compatriots, his colleagues, his wife, obsessed with extending and protecting his power, Stalin contributed more to the barbarism of our century even than Hitler (see Bychowski in Wolman, 1971; and Grenier, 1982). He was not the kind of man who would have helped bring on the day when the lamb might safely lie down with the lion, whatever the posture of American diplomacy. Although Stalin's successors have been less monstrous, the men who sent tanks to crush freedom in the streets of Budapest in 1956 and in the streets of Prague in 1968, and who menaced the green shoots of Polish liberty in 1980–81, have shown themselves to be truly the heirs of Stalin in their orientation toward brutal power to order human affairs. Even though the quality of American leadership has been far poorer than one would wish, the moral differences between the regimes remains substantial, as represented in the different postwar fates of Eastern and Western Europe. Third, the traditional American world view contains, along with its self-righteous ruthlessness, a generous admixture of generosity, tolerance, and an idealistic belief in a cooperative world order, whereas the Russians have emerged from their darker history with a tradition of oppression and xenophobia. (To these it may be added that as a status quo power, the United States had less motive to create a struggle where it might be avoided.)

On the basis of these general reasons, and of the more detailed evidence of the history of the cold war, I venture to say that if both superpowers had been like the United States, there would have been real possibilities for substantial progress toward a peaceful world order; whereas if both had been like the Soviet Union, the history of the postwar period would still have been one of continuous struggle. (If both superpowers had been like the Soviet Union in its relative steadiness and cautiousness of policy, however, the ensuing struggle might have been less dangerous. That is, a less erratic course might have facilitated the establishment of a modus vivendi with less possibility of perilous episodes like the apparently superfluous brinksmanship the United States employed in the Cuban missile crisis of 1962.)

The parable of the tribes is a vision of possibilities restricted by the imposition of necessities. According to this view of the cold war, the Soviet Union had more benign possibilities available to it than it chose to pursue or was able to perceive. In turn, the conduct of the Soviet Union imposed upon the United States necessities harsher than it was inherently disposed to meet. And the fact remains, I would argue, that the principal, though far from the only, stumbling block in the path of the world's moving toward more human possibilities can be removed only by a transformation of the Soviet Union's approach to the world.

This analysis does not suggest a distinction of moral black and white, but of two different shades of gray, neither close to white, yet one perceptibly darker than the other. Moreover, to attribute to the Soviet Union a primary share of responsibility for the global struggle of the past generation is not to suggest that Soviet conduct represents some extraordinary evil: lamentable as that conduct may be, in the historical record of internationally powerful actors, the Soviet Union's relentless drive to expand its power appears not at all unusual. On the contrary, the Soviets have fortunately shown themselves to be rather prudent and careful. Finally, this view of the problem of power in our times does not imply that other nations are entirely helpless about improving the international climate. In particular, the pursuit of a wise, balanced, and coherent diplomatic policy by the United States toward the Soviet Union might help effect real improvements. But American policy has been confused, and at the heart of this confusion has been a failure to grasp the tragedy of power illuminated by the parable of the tribes.

II

The essence of tragedy is that its truths are dual, and the two sides of those truths are in conflict. People like their truths simple, and the pursuit of simple truths in a tragic world is perilous. Consider recent vicissitudes of American policy.

In the 1970s, from the protracted disaster of American policy in Vietnam, Americans learned one side of the truth—that the struggle for power is ugly and pernicious. Many Americans recoiled from destroying a country in order to "save" it. They saw the hypocrisy of embracing brutal dictators as allies in the defense of the "free world." And as they experienced the other ongoing American trauma of the era—Watergate—the citizens of this country saw that the fetish of "national security" could threaten at home the very values of freedom and justice under law that they were presumably struggling to secure.

Because these perceptions gained ground in American public opinion, the 1970s saw a progressive American retreat from the struggle for power in favor of other, more (immediately) humane goals. The retreat was far from complete, but it was significant. To enhance the quality of life domestically, the United States deemphasized military spending in favor of social programs. The United States dismantled some of its intelligence apparatus to protect its own democracy and to respect the rights of self-determination of other peoples. In the name of human rights, to some extent the United States refrained (during the Carter years) from embracing regimes which might have furthered American aims in global competition but which repressed and/or exploited their peoples. And in the hope that there might be an alternative to the dangerous and ever-escalating power struggle between the superpowers, the United States sought to establish a detente with the Soviets that would signify a new code of superpower restraint.

The world should allow a nation to make such choices. But this is a tragic world in which the pursuit of power is not only an ugly business, but also a necessity.

The experience of the 1970s showed the limits of the range of American options. Many, including myself, had held a hopeful belief about Soviet intentions: what they want is not domination but equality and security. In the first Strategic Arms Limitation Treaty, the United States voluntarily ratified strategic parity to replace its once considerable superiority and unilaterally also reduced its spending on weapons in general. But as the Soviet Union gained parity it did not break stride. With half the American GNP, the Soviet Union appears to have spent more on defense than the United States for a decade, modernizing and expanding its weapons systems in every category far beyond the requirements for mere security. The relative American withdrawal from the global chess game simply meant the Soviets could make a few unanswered moves (in Africa, in Afghanistan). By the end of the 1970s, the hopeful hypothesis about the Soviets appeared untenable. And the means and will of the United States to protect Western interests were in doubt.

Americans sensed that the world's current was running rapidly against them, and the balance of public sentiment shifted to embrace that other side of the truth—that power is necessary. President Carter and his idealistic policies and pieties appeared discredited by the reversal and humiliation during the hostage crisis in Iran, and by his belated self-confessed discovery about the nature of the Soviet Union after it invaded Afghanistan. This shift in opinion led to a shift of national leadership to a new administration, to a group of men who delight in the struggle for world power.

The Reagan group had no difficulty with the tragic lesson of the parable of the tribes—that a society threatened by a power-maximizing rival cannot preserve its way of life without sacrificing it. Defense spending leaped forward, at the expense of programs in human services and with considerable strain on the budget and on national economic health. These men seemed to understand the bitter truth of the parable of the tribes that in order to avoid being swallowed or destroyed by a threatening society, a nation is compelled to transform itself more into the image of its enemy. The administration sought to reequip national intelligence agencies with powers like those that had so recently proved subversive of democratic liberties at home. Scorning the idealism of Carter's human rights policy, the realists of the Reagan administration were prepared to make common cause with gangster regimes in Central America. This group had no need to awaken to those harsh realities about what a dangerous, and often cruel place the world is.

Unfortunately the change was not from folly to wisdom but from one unbalanced truth to another, like the proverbial swing of the pendulum. The Reaganites showed no sign of tasting the bitterness of the truths they grasped. It was with no visible repugnance that the administration supported the fascist regime in Argentina (giving comfort that may have emboldened the junta to embark on the Falklands fiasco), or to the killers holding power in El Salvador. The nomination of an Ernest LeFevre to run American human rights policy revealed more than just a recognition that human rights cannot be an absolute in the formulation of foreign policy. More than just an understanding of the strategic importance of the Philippines is demonstrated by the farcical enthusiasm of an American vice president for Marcos's practice of democracy. And more than mere acceptance of the importance of armed might is reflected in the administration's extraordinary and dangerous tardiness in embarking upon arms control talks with the Soviets.

The one-sidedness of the Reagan administration's handling of the two-sided problem of power is already regenerating its polarized opposite. This is true with regard to the struggles in Central America, where the Reaganites' disregard for human aspirations and moral values has encouraged the opposite view which disregards the necessity at times to choose among evils. But this is especially true in the nuclear arms race.

The evidence of the past decade cannot support the contention that the United States is the power responsible for the present acceleration of the arms race. The readiness of Western governments to augment their military forces is a sign not of belligerence but of self-defense. Otherwise, it would not have the support of such men as Helmut Schmidt and Francois Mitterand. But the Reagan administration's first year of apparently unambivalent relish for the arms race gave great impetus to the rise of a "peace movement" in Europe and the United States with strong currents of anti-Americanism, unilateralism, and unrealistic forms of pacifism.

The peace movement embraces a diversity of opinions. An absolutely vital truth that all its elements express is that the prevention of nuclear war is a task of utmost priority, and that complacency in the face of a potentially destablizing arms race is intolerable. It also correctly underscores the changes that weapons of massive annihilation make in the venerable equation between increased military strength and increased national security. But a strong current of unilateralist, antimilitary sentiment in the peace movement ignores the opposing truth that deterrence is what has kept the peace for thirty-five years, and that deterrence is based on displaying that one has the means and the will to defend oneself against attack. In order to preserve the illusion that policy can be based on simple truths, some in the peace movement argue that if the West were to disarm itself, the Soviets would feel morally compelled to follow suit. As the *Economist* has observed, absolutely no evidence supports that expectation: "The Russian response would pretty certainly be a grateful, if puzzled, smile" (August 8, 1981, p. 10). Another illusion is that through the peace movement, the people can pressure their governments to abandon the madness of the nuclear arms race. But as Max Lerner argues in his review of Jonathan Schell's *The Fate of the Earth*, "only the governments of the West will be vulnerable to the storms of antinuclear protest" (1982, pp. 28–29). (The one genuinely popular peace rally in the Soviet Union was terminated within a few seconds with the confiscation of a banner and the arrest of the few people involved.)

These movements of protest against unbalanced policies seeking a purely military solution to a complex political and human problem in El Salvador, and against policies in the nuclear weapons field, serve a useful purpose in checking the follies that grow out of the current administration's dangerously simpleminded view of the world. Protest has probably retarded the administration's descent into the abyss in Central America, and has probably been instrumental in getting President Reagan into negotiations with the Soviets (though it remains to be seen whether either side is prepared to do more than grandstand in front of Western public opinion). But this vectoral addition of skewed directions does not lead to the kind of balanced approach that is required if this nation is to help move the world toward a more humane kind of order. Nor does a quadrennial swing between unworldly idealism and unprincipled pursuit of power fulfill this nation's responsibility to grasp both sides of the dilemma of power. A pendulum may seem to correct itself, but it is always on its way to an extreme position.

Clearly, Americans as a people are of two minds on the issue of power. Balance, however, is not achieved by having two minds. Balance requires, rather, an integrated consciousness that comprehends at once our nation's need to have and to use power, and mankind's need to escape from power's dominion. It requires a recognition of the validity both of the Sermon on the Mount and of Machiavelli. Indeed, there is not much profit in gaining the world at the cost of one's soul. But it is far from clear that one gains if to preserve the purity of one's soul one allows one's quite impure adversaries to become the rulers of the world.

Simple truths lead to tragedy. A tragic truth, like the parable of the tribes, may help lead elsewhere.

BOOK II

THE NATURAL AND THE UNNATURAL

Introduction

The Natural and the Unnatural

According to some people, everything is natural. Nothing can be unnatural. Human beings are a part of nature and therefore everything we do must be natural.

Of course, words can be defined however we wish. Thus the concept of the natural can be all-encompassing. Such a definition, however, has important costs: by making "natural" and "unnatural" both meaningless, it obliterates some useful distinctions.

We should recognize the fundamental cleavage between a beaver dam and the Hoover Dam, between an ant colony and the People's Republic of China, between the predation of lions upon antelopes and the conquest of American Indian peoples by Europeans. With all their connotative freight, the terms "natural" and "unnatural" are appropriate for designating that distinction, for indicating an important division between the systems out of which civilization emerged and the systems civilization has created.

I hope to clarify that distinction and to demonstrate its importance. For it is into the gap between these two that mankind has stumbled, and it is in that gap that we experience that extraordinary (and unnatural) anguish of the civilized human animal.

132

PART ONE

A HOUSE DIVIDED:
THE HUMAN CONDITION IN CIVILIZATION

Prologue

A Zoo Story

Not so long ago people in the Western world knew little about the nature of baboons or, indeed, of other species of monkeys and apes that are the closest relatives to man among the animals.

About half a century ago, a man named Zuckerman undertook to study baboons, specifically a large colony of hamadryas baboons living in the London Zoo.

What he saw when he began to observe them was most disturbing. The colony was beset by violence. The fighting was chronic and brutal, the carnage ultimately claiming the lives of a third of the original members. Adult males were the main offenders, and their victims included not only one another, but females and young as well.

When Zuckerman told the world what he had seen, many drew the obvious conclusions: baboons are unrestrainedly violent by nature, and baboon society is a bloody battleground. To many the mystery of baboon nature seemed solved.

Some years later, a different picture of baboon nature began to emerge. Other investigators had gone off to observe baboon behavior not in the zoo but in the savannas of Africa, the animals' natural home. Under the conditions where the baboon had evolved and lived for millions of years, the baboon still showed a pugnacity of character. But aggression was a game primarily of threat and retreat. Its occurrence was quite occasional and its injurious effects almost nonexistent. The elements of conflict and dominance that had proven so disruptive and destructive in the zoo were, in the savanna, part of the means of maintaining the tight social order that protected baboon survival.

What was seen in the wild cast the murders in the zoo in an entirely new light. In nature, baboons establish a hierarchy as they grow up; by the time they are fully armed with the formidable teeth of adulthood, it has already been established who has priority and who will back down. In the zoo colony, dozens of adults from different baboon troops were suddenly thrown together; the baboons' natural repertoire of behavior gave them no way of establishing order peaceably. In nature, the baboon who loses a confrontation can signal his defeat and escape the victor by retreating far from the fray. The zoo society was enclosed, preventing the retreat that would end the fight without bloodshed. What Zuckerman saw were baboons in a state of high agitation and confusion, encountering problems that baboons had never faced before and for which their natural responses were wholly unsuitable.

The history of primatology shows that the baboon story is not unique. Again and again, the agonies of life in the zoo have been found to exaggerate greatly the bloodiness and misery of life in the wild.

For baboons, and for other species of primates.

Chapter Four

Human Nature and the Evaluation of Civilization

1. Out of the Cold:
Beyond Value Neutrality

As a theory to explain the evolution of civilization, the parable of the tribes can be accepted (or rejected) regardless of one's attitude toward the reign of power. This picture of social evolution as dominated by the selection for power need not be part of a critique of civilization. That model can be presented or assessed from a value-neutral standpoint. Indeed, somewhat similar ideas about the triumph of the powerful in the struggle for survival were entertained in the last century by Social Darwinists in a spirit of enthusiasm for what they regarded as the selection of "the most fit." Questions of truth can be separated from questions of value.

The predominant philosophic bias of our times, however, argues more than that: according to this view, truth and value not only can be considered separately but they also cannot meaningfully be brought together. Concern about value, it says, is not a legitimate component of the search for truth. This legacy of positivism declares reality to be external and objective, whereas judgments of value are "merely" subjective. Being subjective, value judgments are also merely idiosyncratic. These judgments, therefore, have no status in reality and afford no basis for assessing their validity. They are, in a fundamental sense, meaningless. A meaningful science, for this reason, can tell us about the ways things *are* but can say nothing about the way things *should be*.

This view of value must be rejected. For one thing, we find it repugnant because it runs against our nature. For another thing, it is fallacious.

Value may be defined as the basis for choice. In the absence of values, any alternative is as good as any other. Indifference reigns. To be or not to be can be no question, for there is no basis for answering. Values are implicit in any choice, and choice is required for any action. If action requires choice, it is no wonder we need values, because to live it is necessary to act. That is why the value-neutral universe of positivism seems lifeless and therefore repugnant.

To enter the cold universe of positivist value-neutrality is as if to recede in time through billions of years to a universe in which everything is dead. If there were nothing alive, no one to care, what could it then matter what happened? Whether the universe exploded or collapsed, burned or froze, would be matters of complete indifference. In such a dead world, "the way things were" is indeed meaningful in a way that "the way things should have been" is not. But then life developed, and in time there emerged creatures like ourselves with the capacity for joy and suffering, creatures whose will to live coexisted with the possibility of death. With the emergence of such life, something essential has changed. The shell of universal indifference has been breached, and into the world has stumbled a sacred new reality: value. No longer are all things the same, because they are not all the same to us, or to the other sentient creatures who have and feel needs and wants. No longer does indifference reign, for feeling creatures are not indifferent. Hot blood changes the cold universe.

We feel within ourselves a profound commitment to value. To begin at the heart of the matter, we cling to life and fight death. When a living, feeling creature regards judgments of value as meaningless, it is as though somehow the heart of things has been cut out. This positivist concept of reality, we feel, runs counter to the reality of what we are. Indeed, there seems a paradox in the very notion that if people want to say anything *worth* listening to, they should speak only of matters of objective truth and not about value.

It would hardly be persuasive to a positivist, however, to argue that value-neutrality should be rejected because it goes against our natural inclinations and feels alien. Feelings share with judgments of value that second-class status of the "merely subjective." It is necessary to confront the argument on a logical basis.

2.   A Theory of Natural Values

The crucial distinction between the objective and the subjective must be examined. On the one hand, it is meaningful to discuss an objective fact ("There is a tree in the yard") because it concerns a shared reality in the world out there. On the other hand, we base our judgments of value ("It is good to have loving relationships") ultimately not on the objective world outside us but on the feelings and attitudes within us. These being part of a private world, it is argued, it is not possible meaningfully to argue the judgments based on them. I will not dispute the contention that a tree exists independently of human subjectivity whereas the goodness of loving relationships does not. But it is fallacious to conclude from this distinction that our values are therefore less legitimately a part of our objective and shared human reality.

If our subjective world were merely idiosyncratic, there would indeed be little meaningful basis for arguing that something such as the selection for power in the evolution of civilization was either good or bad: idiosyncrasies afford no basis for common cause. But our reactions, while subjective, are not merely idiosyncratic.

We return to the evolutionary perspective for insight into the nature of things.

The near perfection of the living body is, according to evolutionary biology, the legacy of ages of living history. For countless generations, life has experimented with various forms. At each step, some have survived to produce successful offsprings whereas others have not. Because only the survivors determine the organismic future of their species, the cumulative effect of this ceaseless and ancient process of selection is the evolution of a body intricately designed for survival.

The body evolves not a static design, but one in action: to survive, an animal must do what is necessary for survival. In its interaction with the outside world, the organism must get what it needs for life (the survival-positive) and avoid what could destroy its life (the survival-negative). Thus, survival requires the right behavior, the right behavior requires the right choices, and the right choices mean positively valuing what helps survival and negatively valuing what hurts it. Value, therefore, is vital to survival. And as the requirements for survival determine body structure, the body is structured with an intrinsic system of value.

To the extent that our values are embedded in our nature, so also must be our feelings. *Feelings may be defined as the experience of value.* The cold shell of a value-neutral universe is cracked by the emergence of creatures capable of experiencing joy or suffering. It is because things can matter to some feeling creatures that anything can matter. One important dimension applicable to feelings is positive-negative: some feelings are experienced as good-satisfying-pleasant and others as bad-frustrating-unpleasant. We are designed to have feelings to motivate us to choose the course of action necessary for survival: the pain from stubbing our toes induces us to be careful with our feet, the discomfort of hunger motivates us to obtain food, the pleasant aura of love leads us to wish to take care of each other, the pleasure of sex serves the continuation of the species. Writes David Hamberg: "Tasks that must be done (for species survival) tend to be pleasurable" (in Washburn and Jay, 1968, p. 254). In all these cases, feelings are grounded in the structure of the body and tied up directly with our natural system of value: those experiences which have been survival-positive for our species tend to feel positive and those that have been survival-negative tend to feel negative.

Our natural system of values is no more idiosyncratic than our anatomical structure. We are not identical physically to one another, but our similarities far exceed our differences. The late Professor Theodosius Dobzhansky once argued (in class) that there is no such thing as "human nature," that there are instead 4 billion unique human natures. But one could equally well argue that there is no such thing as human anatomy. In fact, however, all human beings share an extensive heritage: just as doctors can study the human body, so can we speak of a basic shared inheritance of natural values embedded in our organism.

Experience admittedly shapes our subjective domain of feeling and value. (For that matter, experience can mold our inherent anatomies and physiologies.) Depending upon one's experience, for example, one person may directly express anger where another will turn it inward; one person may be taught to repress his sexual impulses where another is encouraged to fulfill them. Experience can be idiosyncratic (and can differ from culture to culture), leading to idiosyncrasies (and cultural differences) in values. However, the capacity of human beings to adapt themselves to different environmental influences does not disprove the existence of underlying natural values we share as a species. Any value system can be instilled only if it roots itself in the organismic experience of the person: socialization (with its encouragements and rewards and discouragements and punishments) must begin with the intrinsic value-feeling system of the human organism. Despite differences superimposed upon us by experience, the bond of shared natural values remains embedded within us.

The evolutionary perspective transforms our vision of the subjective realm in two significant ways. First, we must recognize the objective reality of values. The true foundation of our value judgments is not "merely subjective" but is a part of our nature as creatures: our values are not mere chimerical fancies but are as inextricably rooted in the objective nature of things as trees are. Second, to the extent that values are grounded in the body, they are not idiosyncratic, for a particular body is a mani-festation of a general species type. Within a species, the intrinsic system of value means shared values. Thus value—or at least the fountain of our values—is not a merely private matter but is a domain of shared experience with our fellow human beings. It is not shared in precisely the same sense as the world out there but in a sense that is just as valid and meaningful.

Values are inextricable from our lives, from our living bodies. We are molded from value-neutral dust to positively value life and the things that have served life. Our repugnance for a "reality" stripped of value proves to be an expression of our natural wisdom that knows that values are the blood of human reality. We have now discovered a bridge between the domain of factual reality and the domain of value. In our species' natural system of values we are given a basis for meaningfully appealing to one another on matters of value (a basis that, indeed, people have always used). We have a basis for inquiring "What is good for mankind?" We have found a terra firma upon which a critique of civilization can stand.

But first, there is one essential part of our foundation which must be reinforced: the fact and importance of biologically evolved human nature.

3.   The Question of Human Nature

The idea that we as a species are endowed by our evolution with an inalienable system of natural values is dependent upon our having a substantial inborn nature. But this assumption is widely questioned. The image of man one discovers in many contemporary portrayals is of a creature whose essential nature is a lack of an invariant nature. According to that view, it might make sense to speak of natural values with respect to "lower" creatures, whose behavior is ruled by instinct indelibly in-scribed upon their natures, but not with respect to man, who has evolved to present his environment a veritable tabula rasa upon which anything can be writ. Human nature, in this currently predominant view, is a mere drop of biological necessity in a sea of human adaptability.

In contemporary thinking this tabula rasa argument commonly takes two forms.

A. The "Uniqueness Is Essence" Assumption

In our cultural tradition, setting man radically apart from the other animals is an ancient and deep-running current. We find in Genesis the special creation of man. In today's anthropology, most of the inconsiderable time spent on the question of human nature is used for extolling the special qualities of our species. What is man? His essence, we are told, is what differentiates him from all other animals: his unique intelligence, flexibility, and culture. If we regard as "human" what is distinctively human, then our indeterminateness is our nature, as the tabula rasa case propounds. But this approach stems from the fallacious assumption that the true nature of something resides in its unique qualities. If a shipment of identical new cars arrives and we place upon one a special hood ornament, have we thereby transformed in a single stroke its essential nature? No, it is still basically the same as the others. The illogic of this view of man should alert us to the likelihood that clarity is being sacrificed for ideological purposes.

Of course, human evolution has differentiated us from other species. But how different are we? In particular, how plausible is the idea that our nature, unlike that of other creatures, has become essentially indeterminate?

The "human" phase of our ancestral development, that in which our "true" nature of plasticity would have had to develop, has been relatively brief. Our ancestors, it should be remembered, do not begin at some dramatic branching of the tree of life: they include one-celled animals, aquatic vertebrates, and then the animals evolving on land leading through reptiles eventually to mammals, primates, and finally the line of *Homo*. And evolution has a memory: though modified by gradual change, the structure of an animal is like a living record of the aeons of living history during which it has developed. Thus, our blood to this day reflects the salt concentrations of the sea our ancestors left many millions of years ago. And our glands are the result of the ages of transformation of a fish into a mammal. In evolution, what has been does not quickly disappear. The old is not neatly extirpated and replaced by the new, the way the army can discard the mule for the jeep with no sign of a tail on the jeep. This persistence of ancient nature pertains as much to the dynamic aspects of a creature, the way it acts and feels, as to the static structures that survive in fossils.

From the relative brevity of our strictly human evolution, we can infer that it was not so long ago that our ancestors needed as ingrained and substantive a nature as other creatures have. In a world demanding that energies be well directed, survival as mammals required a deep and complex emotional and cognitive nature, not a blank sheet. Thus, if our nature is a clean slate, it had to be wiped clean.

From the tendency of evolved structures to persist, we may infer that this ancient animal nature would not have quickly disappeared. Would the roughly one million years since the earliest beginnings of culture have sufficed to substantially eradicate what must have been a deeply inscribed animal nature? Here it should be noted that the period available for such an erasure is of a duration several orders of magnitude shorter than for the transformation of gills into glands. But an even more important point needs to be made. For almost all of this already brief period, as was argued in the first chapter, the emergence of culture did not greatly transform the conditions of human life. From this we can infer that the ancient animal nature of our species remained essentially compatible with the demands being made on people by their environment. Consequently, there would be no great pressure to wipe clean the slate of human nature. It is unlikely, therefore, that the substantive nature of our species would have been selected against before culture had brought about major changes in the demands of human living. The period for wiping the slate clean would not be the one or two million years of the emergence of the cultural animal, but the few thousand years of the evolution of civilization. And during that period, it is generally agreed by those who study human evolution, we have changed genetically insignificantly, if at all, from our paleolithic ancestors.

It seems most plausible, then, to imagine our ancient animal nature to have survived within us largely intact. Our more recent acquisition of plasticity might better be seen less as a replacement for our substantive nature than as a superimposition upon it.

This image of superimposition enables us to approach a second source of the tabula rasa argument.

B. Cultural Diversity as Proof of Indeterminacy

If man's nature were given in his biological organism, some argue, this inherent nature would give rise to uniformities between independent human cultures. What we find instead is a wide range of cultural diversity. History and anthropology demonstrate that human beings can fit into enormously varying cultural environments with correspondingly diverse demands upon their human members. Cultural diversity, in this view, stands as proof of the lack of substantial content in the inherent nature of man: human nature is plasticity.

Although this argument is fairly plausible, ultimately it is not compelling.

In the first place, a substantive human nature would not imply cultural uniformity but only discernible tendencies in human culture. Man requires culture to give his nature finished form. Man naturally walks upright, but the style of walking varies from culture to culture. It is natural for people to smile and laugh, but the precise ways and meanings of smiling and laughing are culturally modified. Man is naturally an over-hand thrower, but what he throws and the style of delivery are influenced by culture. So, too, with love between people and with contact with the sacred. To the extent that cultures should be regarded as expressions of human nature, the various cultures will tend to be not identical but variations upon a theme.

In the second place, it is perilous to view all cultures as direct expressions of human nature. To the extent that forces other than those arising from human nature have molded cultures, the logic of this tabula rasa argument fails. And the parable of the tribes demonstrates that a major subset of human cultures (civilization) has been shaped by such forces. We cannot accept, therefore, the suggestion by the famous anthropologist Alfred Kroeber that human nature be defined by the limits of all the cultures known to us (1966, p. 207). For in the light of the parable of the tribes, we cannot view an isolated hunting-gathering tribe and a totalitarian empire as equally representative and free flowerings of the nature of our species. Among primitive societies we might find a mirror of our nature. But the inescapable selection for power has so warped our civilized culture that they can afford only a most distorted image of ourselves.

The case for the tabula rasa at last falls back on the incontrovertible fact that human beings indeed have fit into a wide spectrum of different societies, the massive power system as well as the primitive society. If man did possess a substantial inborn nature, how could socialization fit people into such an apparently limitless variety of social environments? We must present our cultures a carte blanche to allow them to write so freely upon us.

The plasticity of man is not, however, proof that man lacks a substantial organismic nature. The proponents of the tabula rasa view would have us conclude from our evident flexibility that we are each born like a lump of wet clay without any intrinsic shape of our own. But I propose a different image: our flexibility is like a wire of spring steel capable of being bent in many directions but always straining against the pressure, always trying to assume its original shape.

We reach here the heart of the human dilemma: the coexistence of our natural needs and values with our unique flexibility. As the neocortex in our brains flowered above the enduring mammalian and reptilian structures, so did we acquire plasticity superimposed upon our given nature. The human species grew more adaptable to serve its own survival, to fulfill the needs of human nature. Plasticity did not arise in conflict with our given nature; culture for ages embellished without warping the lives of human animals. But evolution cannot look ahead. It only rewards what has worked in the past. Without planning, one can fall into traps. Our capacity to learn became so great that we became capable, in Rene Dubos's phrase, of overadapting, of learning too well for our own good. It became possible for us to conform to an environment antagonistic to our nature.

Yet another metaphor helps convey our condition, a metaphor more apt in some ways than either clay or spring steel for it captures our pain: the image of the bound foot of the traditional Chinese woman. We are plastic enough to develop into the stunted form that the forces imposed on us demand. But how painful not to grow into our true human shape!

4.   Eden: The Natural Environment

Having plausibly confirmed the substantiality of human nature, we may return to building upon the foundation provided by the theory of natural value. This theory gives us a basis for inquiring "What is good for mankind?" To begin with, we can deduce from it the image of the Garden of Eden: the goodness of a creature's original, natural environment.

The natural environment for an organism is that in which its species has evolved. The body is designed by evolution for survival. Survival, however, involves not just an organism but an organism in an environment. The ongoing processes of natural selection constantly mold each species according to the opportunities and hazards for life in its particular environment. Each creature, therefore, is naturally a projection of the world around it, its body crafted to fit intricately with its natural environment.

This fit has implications about the goodness of the natural environment. If a species is endowed by nature with an inherent system of values according to which what has been survival-positive is good, and if that species has been designed for survival in a particular environment, it follows that this environment will be good for the species. This goodness is not something wholly intrinsic to the environment itself. Rather, it is the fruit of the match between organism and environment. And the positive judgment is from the standpoint of the organism's own inherent values. The environment, one might say, creates creatures who will like it.

Each creature, then, evolves in an Eden. But we must not get carried away by this paradisaical image. Although its natural environment is good for a species, it is hardly perfect. Death was in the Garden well before man first sinned. One reason for it does not detract from this view of the natural environment as good for the species: ultimately death is our lot by design. For creatures like us, the optimal strategy for our species includes the mortality of individuals. The long-term survival of our kind has been best assured by giving each of us a short-term lease on life. But death stalks our imperfect Eden for two other reasons.

First, evolution has been finite and has found no invulnerable solutions to the problems of preserving life: flesh can be cut or crushed, burned or bruised, for living tissue cannot thus far be both viable and indestructible. The longer a species lives in a given environment, presuming that environment to be reasonably stable, the better adapted becomes the species to its environment and correspondingly the better is the environment from the standpoint of the species. Yet life remains vulnerable to slings and arrows.

A second and probably more important reason for the imperfection of a species' natural environment is that life feeds upon life. Although the ecosystem is synergistic in the sense that all living things depend upon the maintenance of a harmonious balance among all the elements of the whole, the aspect of competition and struggle is nonetheless also present, with one species living off the flesh of another, with nature red in tooth and claw. One creature's meat is another creature. There is no escape from the dilemma that even in the natural environment, either the predator will feel the pain of hunger or the prey the pain of death. Thus although evolution invents incredible harmonies for the preservation of life, the wholly opportunistic nature of the evolutionary process necessitates that these harmonies be constructed out of the conflicts of interest among living things. No solution perfect for all is possible, so the resolution is imperfect for each species.

From the point of view of any one species, improvements in the natural environment are possible. The jagged edges of rocks can be smoothed, the parasites and predators deterred.

Yet though improvements are possible, most environmental change is apt to be detrimental. That the natural environment falls short of perfection warrants far less emphasis than how close it comes. Genetic mutations can be favorable—that indeed is how evolution can occur. But just as the near perfection of biological design assures that the overwhelming majority of random mutations in genetic structure are detrimental, so also does it imply that most changes in a species' natural environment would be harmful rather than beneficial. Any species will thrive better in its own environment than transplanted to almost any different one. Environmental changes have often occurred from forces extraneous to the living system, as from climatic disturbances and fluctuations. These changes have generally led to genetic adjustments by species, which is to say the more frequent death without propagation of

146

the original majority genotype than of a few fortunate mutants. Not infrequently, environmental changes have led, especially when they were rapid, to the extinction of species (as—according to most current theories—in the sudden disappearance of the dinosaurs). The wages of change are, usually, an acceleration of death.

Leaving one's natural home, like leaving Eden, is generally a step in the wrong direction.

5. The Fatal Mismatch

In ten thousand years, the conditions of our lives have changed whereas the demands of our nature have remained the same. If we assume a fit between our needs and our environment in our natural state, we can see how a change on one side alone could create a fatal mismatch. The critique of civilization can thus be based on the widening gap between human nature and the unnatural environment of civilization: the same logic that establishes the goodness of the natural suggests also the evil of the unnatural.

Even if one grants the theory of natural value and its corollary argument about the goodness of the natural environment, however, one need not conclude that our present unnatural environment is less good. Since improvements are possible, civilization may indeed advance human welfare. The changes that have been made may not have opened a gap between the human environment and human nature but may instead have brought them closer together. Let us consider some arguments the defender of civilization might present.

One argument might run: if what is good for a species is what promotes survival, then clearly civilization is good for human beings. Civilization has promoted human survival both at the aggregate level (increased human population on the earth) and at the individual level (increased life span). If survival is the criterion of goodness, then civilization is good.

This argument, however, distorts the theory of natural value. What is good for an organism was defined not as what promotes survival but as what has promoted survival during the evolution of the species. This apparently miniscule distinction reveals, upon closer examination, a fundamental point. Value enters the universe not automatically with the appearance of life, but with the emergence of life capable of experience. Admittedly, it is for the preservation of life that this sentient capacity is created by selection. Nonetheless, it is only inasmuch as things matter to feeling creatures that things can matter at all. Our theory of value directs us to look not at life per se but at the experiential quality of life. Sentient

147

creatures are so crafted that positive experience lies on those paths which during the aeons of their species' evolution have led toward survival. It is possible for other paths to lead to survival over experiential terrain quite different and less fulfilling.

The preservation of life, therefore, is a necessary but not a sufficient criterion for the goodness of a creature's environment. This point can be readily and intuitively grasped with respect to both (1) the proliferation and (2) the extension of human life.

(1) The defender of civilization might ask: "Who among us would choose to return to our natural conditions which would support less than one in a thousand of those now alive? This alone is proof that civilization has bettered the human condition." But what if centuries hence the technology were developed whereby human beings could be kept alive by the use of tubes for nourishment and respiration at a density of one person per square foot? Could not the above argument be made with unimpaired logic? All of us, I am sure, recoil at the thought and instantly recognize that the quality of human life must take precedence over sheer quantity in our judgments of value. This understanding is reflected in the increasingly universal consensus that our current geometric population growth is a threat to human well-being and not a sign of it. The argument for civilization based on numbers, therefore, fails. All things being equal, more life may be better than less, but if all things are not equal we are compelled to judge where the degradation of quality balances the increase in quantity and, ultimately, at what point that degradation transforms life itself into an evil rather than a good.

(2) It is clear how the same considerations relate to our individual longevity.[1] An extended life is not necessarily a better one. A dog can be kept alive inside a cage, without the love or activity it desperately (and naturally) wants: its "survival needs" taken care of, it can still be miserable. Sometimes the failure to satisfy apparently inessential needs leads to death, as was revealed by R. A. Spitz's studies of the mortality rate of well-fed but unloved institutionalized infants. But it is possible within limits to set up an environment for some animals which better guarantees their survival than their natural environment but which is nonetheless ultimately less satisfying—less good—from their standpoint. Again, contemporary thinking reflects an awareness of the distinction between life per se and a life worth living. As medicine makes it possible for the terminally ill and the very elderly to continue essential life processes beyond the point where life has meaning, it is becoming increasingly acceptable to allow death to come.

---

1. It should be noted, however, that civilization's ability to extend the human life is extremely recent. Not until relatively modern times did the life expectancy of civilized humanity begin to diverge markedly from that of primitive peoples (see Eberstadt, 1981).

We who live in less visible cages than kennel dogs should not assume that long life compensates for the inability to run free. Nor is it clear for many who live in this unnatural environment that those civilized systems that maintain their life processes are doing them a favor.

The first argument—equating goodness with sheer survival—does not prove the goodness of civilization. But neither does refuting that argument suffice to refute the more fundamental point. Civilization's defender might turn here to a second argument.

If we wonder about the value of civilization, this argument would run, conclusive evidence is not hard to find. We need only introspect a moment to realize that we would choose civilization over the primitive living conditions of our natural environment. In our affluent society, the preferability of civilization is obvious. Who among us is prepared to choose life without flushing toilets, thermostated homes, and television? If value is defined as the basis for choice, and if our choice is to hold onto the comforts and entertainments of our civilized life, does this not prove the goodness of civilization?

I am not sure that it does. The counterpoint is also based on introspection. I admit that the more rugged life of the primitive would probably leave me pining for running water and well-stocked libraries. But I remember myself at the age of five and I believe I would have chosen differently then. The choice of the five-year-old may well be the more significant, for he stands closer to our nature. We as civilized adults are taught to need and appreciate civilization. We learn not to rely on those satisfactions that, however important, are unavailable or scarce for us, like community with other people and close, harmonious contact with the natural order. Our socialization channels our energies so that we are prepared to fill the roles required by civilized society and to find our enjoyments among the goods civilization provides. We adapt to our environment so we can find whatever fulfillment is possible under the conditions. If those conditions require us to overadapt, a part of the cost is a warping of our nature and a corresponding distortion of the basis upon which we make our choices. Our choices in favor of what civilization has taught us to choose cannot therefore resolve the issue.

If we have lost the wisdom of the body, perhaps we can regain it with the help of the mind.

We have come a long way from our good but imperfect Eden. Most paths away from Eden are downhill. For a change in its natural environment to be good for a species, it is almost certainly necessary that the force determining that change be most solicitous of that species' needs. In the light of the parable of the tribes, we can find little basis for optimism about the solicitude of social evolutionary forces. To the extent that the selection for power has been the force impelling us away from our Eden,

149

this unnatural environment we call civilization must at least be suspect of being badly mismatched with the needs of our nature.

The parable of the tribes—the entire argument of Book I—shows how civilization has been (largely) shaped by forces beyond human control and indifferent to human needs. The theory of natural value now combines with the parable of the tribes to provide an explicit and reasoned basis for arguing that civilization does not provide a good environment for human life. The gap between the natural and the unnatural is the second key for unlocking the mystery of the human condition. Throughout history, as much as people have extolled the blessings and achievements of civilization, they have lamented the anguish of human existence. Whole world views have been constructed around the problem of human suffering and misconduct. But we discover now a key to the evils of our existence which has no need for such concepts as original sin or maya. We see that the agony of human beings under the aegis of civilization derives from the fact that we evolved to live in one kind of environment yet are compelled to live in a vastly different one. Torn between the demands of his new unnatural environment and the inclinations of his inborn nature, civilized man lies tormented upon a social evolutionary rack.

6. The Original Sinner: Evaluating Human Nature

Through the ages, the evils of our world have hardly escaped notice. Nor is it novel to observe that there exists a gap between man's inclinations and the demands of his environment. Usually, however, this gap has been used as a measure of man's moral shortcomings. Confronted with the riddle of evil, many have sought the answer in man himself. I have embarked here upon a critique of civilization. But is it not as appropriate to conclude from the fatal mismatch that the problem lies in fatal flaws of human nature?

It is again in the evolutionary perspective that we can find a clear view. This perspective, we must recall, is a comparatively new one. During the ages when the world views of the great civilizations were developed, the vision of civilized people could not transcend civilization. Civilization seemed the natural and only imaginable condition for human life. Without a vision of man separable from the civilized state, man seems inextricable from the evils that plague civilized life: thus one could easily conclude that man is the source of the evil. With the civilized environment taken as a given, the disturbing mismatch between organism and environment appears to be a problem in the organism.

150

The Darwinian revolution has shown us that man is separable from civilization. And the archaeological record shows civilization to be a recent eruption in the evolution of our species. In these longer perspectives, civilization is no longer a given in our efforts to understand the human condition. Indeed, the theory of natural value, which is based on that evolutionary perspective, suggests that in our search for fulfillment our own nature is what should be taken as a given. This is not just because, in a practical sense, it *is* a given, unless we are prepared to let the genetic engineers hack away at it (which I am not). More fundamentally, in a conflict between our needs and our environment the theory of natural value would question on what basis we would give our moral allegiance to environmental demands that injure us. If what naturally constitutes goodness for us is the fulfillment of our natural needs, it would seem a perversion (literally, turning around) of our natural perspective to base our solution to the riddle of evil upon a condemnation of our human nature.

The evolutionary perspective enables us to see that the natural state of all creatures is to live in an environment that is well designed to meet its needs and in which what they should do is identical to what they want to do. These two blessings of the natural state correspond with two components of the problem of evil which arise for human beings living in civilization. The first evil is that of human suffering, of evil endured. The second is that of human misconduct, of evil perpetrated. The ubiquity and apparent inevitability of human unfulfillment have led some to postulate a basic flaw in the human condition: by nature alienated from God, by nature neurotic, by nature a sick animal. Similarly, the bloody atrocities and rampant corruption that afflict human affairs have provided images of innate human viciousness: original sin, Ardreyesque savagery. The evolutionary perspective places these two evils in a different light: it is simply not plausible that man is either sick or criminal by nature.

If the conditions of human life demonstrably do not meet human needs, this discussion of natural environments suggests that the problem lies with our unnatural conditions. There is a Sufi saying that thirst is the clearest proof of the existence of water. Similarly, we may say that human needs were not likely to be created by evolution except as a means to assure their fulfillment. The image of a creature whose needs are systematically frustrated by its natural environment is an implausible one. This argument of evolutionary plausibility can apply also to the image of man as innately at war with himself. The theory of natural value might accept our condemnation of human nature if it could be demonstrated that by nature we frustrate ourselves, that we naturally contain such self-contradictions as to make our misery inevitable. But is it plausible that the parsimonious process of natural selection would make a blunder so

151

fundamental as to equip a creature with the disposition to thwart its own life-serving impulses?

We can take as illustrative of the nonevolutionary view the pessimistic visions of Freud,[2] for the shadow of his thought still darkens our view of the basic human condition. No one has done as much as Freud to direct attention to the conflict between human needs and the demands of civilized society. Yet, because he did not see the human condition in an evolutionary perspective, he, like the ancients, could not envision human beings separately from the agonies he saw around him. Thus, in *Civilization and Its Discontents,* Freud saw human unfulfillment as the inescapable lot of man. His argument, it must be noted, applies not really to civilization specifically but to any form of human social life. If humans are to live together, he says, their basic instinctual drives must be repressed. Yet we know that man is by nature a social animal, molded since long before he became human to live in tightly knit groups. For any creature with such an evolutionary history, its basic instinctual drives are certain to correlate deeply with the requirements of social life.

Freud accurately saw the fatal mismatch within the Victorian European culture of his own time, but his attempt to discover in that conflict an invariant feature of human existence cannot be accepted. The most general formulation of Freud's vision of man's inevitable neurosis is the idea that the pleasure principle within us is inevitably opposed by the reality principle: in other words, what we want and what the world offers and demands are fundamentally different. But as has been noted by others (notably Marcuse, 1966), Freud's image of the "reality" principle whose demands must be met is derived from the realities of his own specific era. A reality principle that changes with history illuminates better the historical human condition than the basic nature of man. And my previous argument led to the conclusion that the reality principle applying in our natural state was in harmony with our unvarying pleasure principle. Then, we might presume, id and ego were not so much at war as in partnership.

Yet the evolution of civilization has indeed transformed our realities, and the sufferings Freud described have become a part of the human condition. And it is a short step from man the sufferer to man the criminal. Indeed, the two are almost but two sides of the same phenomenon. If our environment seeks to thwart the expression of our nature, we suffer. If we do nonetheless express that nature, it is viewed as misconduct. Sex becomes sin. Independence of spirit becomes rebellion or heresy. Little boys who want to act like little boys rather than sit quietly at

---

2. John Bowlby also writes of Freud's "pre-Darwinian" assumptions (1973, p. 399).

their desks are called behavior problems.

Beyond that, the frustration of our natural impulses transforms them.[3] Instinctual frustration breeds rage. The devastation of World War I led Freud to postulate in human nature a death instinct at war with the life energies of Eros. Freud did not even inquire how that inherent dualism in our allegiance could have evolved. His Thanatos serves no adaptive purpose, as the lemmings' periodic migration into the sea at times of overpopulation developed to safeguard the survival of lemmingkind. It makes no evolutionary sense, I suggest, to imagine natural selection to have writ as a basic principle of human nature a purely life-destroying instinct. An attraction to death does make sense, however, for creatures whose circumstances have made life so tormenting that for some it ceases to be clearly of positive value. And an urge to destroy is comprehensible for creatures whose fulfillment is blocked at every turn.

Truly wild animals do not behave wildly. But escaped from its cage in the zoo an animal may go "wild" from being so long pent up. Then, too, it may be destructive because it is bewildered, because it is not prepared by nature to cope with so unnatural a circumstance.

The zoo becomes an apt metaphor for civilization, the unnatural environment. And as we view the record of criminality of civilized people, we may turn to Zuckerman's famous baboons to see to the heart of our dilemma. When our knowledge of baboons did not transcend the London Zoo, baboons seemed by nature bloodthirsty and destructive creatures. But these baboons were attempting to cope with a situation that would never occur in their natural environment, a bewildering situation which frightened and confused them and in which the usually life-serving impulses of baboon nature had life-destroying consequences. On the savanna, the undeniable baboon aggressiveness leads to threats, occasional scratches and wounds, frequent retreats by the subordinate or intimidated animal. In nature, the dominance hierarchy of baboon society emerges gradually, as the animals mature, and it helps insure a life-serving order in social relationships. In the London Zoo, in an unnatural society formed suddenly on unnatural terrain, baboon impulses led to multiple murders. So, are baboons by nature criminal?

3. This is illustrated by the dream of a forty-five-year-old woman: "Two veiled figures climb onto the balcony and into the house. They are swathed in black hooded coats, and they seem to want to torment me and my sister. She hides under the bed, but they pull her out with a broom and torture her. Then it is my turn. The leader of the two pushes me against the wall, making magical gestures before my face. In the meantime, his helper makes a sketch on the wall, and when I see it, I say (in order to seem friendly) 'Oh! But this is well drawn!' Now suddenly my tormentor has the noble head of an artist, and he says proudly, 'Yes, indeed,' and begins to clean his spectacles." About this dream, the Jungian psychologist Franz says: "(T)he dream reveals that the veiled burglars are actually disguised artists, and *if the dreamer recognizes their gifts (which are her own) they will give up their evil intentions*" (in Jung et al., 1964, p. 203, italics added).

The evolutionary view leads us to the belief that the source of the undeniable evils of civilized human life is not to be found in human nature. By this defense of human nature, however, I do not mean to imply that man is by nature "good." It is not my intent to cast man in the role of the Noble Savage. Regardless of man's innate aggressiveness, lovingness, selfishness, altruism, *man is by nature good enough* for the life he evolved to lead. Since we have by nature a degree of consciousness and range of choice not possessed by other species, the moral dimension would "naturally" enter into all human life in a way that it does not in the rest of nature. But if man were in his natural place, the question of whether man as a species is good or evil would not arise any more than we seek to judge whether baboons are better than gorillas.

The question of human good and evil arises because we are not in our natural place, and because our responsibilities have become unnaturally heavy. In our role in the world we have become like gods, and for that role we are not good enough. It is because our powers so exceed what we are naturally equipped to manage that we have become the world's first criminals: this is the moral dimension of the fatal mismatch. But this does not justify a condemnation of human nature. Tiger and Fox have written that if baboons wielded hand grenades, there would be no baboons left alive in Africa (1971, p. 210).

If we are to wield unnatural powers we are indeed compelled, lest we destroy mankind and livingkind, to become unnaturally "good." The moral anguish expressed in civilized religions is here illuminated. What kind of creature would it take to live harmoniously in such a world? Make yourselves into creatures like that, civilized peoples have been exhorted through the ages. We are thus torn between our nature and our need to take a new set of demands as a "second nature." The required goodness conflicts, to a degree, with our inherent system of value by which we naturally seek our own fulfillment. Yet in our unnatural circumstances, the ultimate fulfillment of what we naturally value requires that our values go beyond what comes naturally. Throughout history, the great religions—though without necessarily understanding the origins of the human dilemma—have sought to transport their believers across that moral gap. With the potential for evil now far greater than before, it is more necessary than ever that humankind accomplish that fundamental religious task of reconciling the apparently irreconcilable.

Chapter Five

Power and the Psychological Evolution of Civilized Man

1. The Re-creation of Man

Our brave new world of civilization has required a new man to go with it. Civilization has not just provided a different social environment for the same creatures. The new conditions demand human transformation as well. And if it is power that has largely determined the structure of civilization, the structure of the new man also has been molded by the requirements of power. The insistent hand of the selection for power has, in these five or ten millennia, wrought a psychological restructuring of the human being.

It is difficult to exaggerate the importance for the maximization of power of the psychological system. Certainly, the engines of power get much of their drive from social, political, and technological innovations. But in our times it is plain to see that the power-generating potentiality of each of those systems can be realized only by a people whose culturally molded psychological structure equips them to make these macrosystems run. Without "human capital," everything else is of little avail, and with such resources in the souls of men power can be created even out of ruins. The rapid postwar reconstruction of Germany and Japan has demonstrated this. As Boulding has noted: "The knowledge of the people was not destroyed, and it did not take long, therefore, certainly not more than ten years, for most of the material capital to be re-established. . . . By 'knowledge' here I mean, of course, the whole cognitive structure, which includes valuations and motivations as well as images of the factual world" (in Blau et al., 1971, p. 422). The external ingredients of modern power are no secret, yet modernization proceeds at vastly different rates in different societies. The machinery of power cannot run itself, so access to the U.S. Patent Office does not unlock the door to power. The evidence from development programs shows how indispensable a key is human capital.

In their postwar efforts to help other peoples modernize, Americans have been surprised by the intractability of human psychological factors. This surprise should alert us that we are in the proximity of an important blind spot. We tend to assume that the way we are is simply the natural human way to be, and that other people therefore necessarily will share our purposes, passions, and perceptions. Czeslaw Milosz, the Polish Nobel Laureate and emigrant to the United States, has written that "Americans accepted their society as if it had arisen from the very order of nature" (1968, p. 263). But our motivational, emotional and cognitive structures are enormously complex artifacts of history, as far from given in our natural humanness as the modern technology we employ. If recent experience has revealed us to be blind to the peculiarity of that psychological constellation which embodies our human capital, it implies that we are also blind to the extraordinary convolutions of the soul which the evolution of civilization has imposed upon our natural being. One purpose of this chapter is to bring vision to this blind spot, in particular to discover how the rule of power in the rise and development of civilization has led to a re-creation of man as the servant of power.

We may envision civilization in terms of the channeling of energies. Nature supplies the energies, civilization channels their flow. This is clearly true at the level of technology, and it is equally true at the level of psychodynamics. Man may have natural inclinations and preferences, but he is also designed to be able to respond differently to different situations. A situation that blocks the flow of human energies from following its natural course does not make that energy disappear. Rather, it rechannels the natural impulse and changes its character, the way the Colorado River can be diverted into the furrows of a lettuce field or stored in Lake Powell to be tapped for electric power. By determining the situations in which human character takes form and human action occurs, civilization can make of human energies a natural resource available for its own exploitation.

156

The human being enters this world equipped by nature to be prepared for nurture. This pronounced receptivity to fundamental learning, which granted even primitive man enormous adaptability, allows family and social institutions wide latitude in socializing their members. But, to repeat, socialization is not just a matter of filling in the blanks. The human infant arrives not just with receptivity but also with a natural set of needs and expectations. If every minute some human creature is born a sucker, nature intended him to be so with the expectation he would take in his mother's milk and not the trickery of this evolving circus of civilization.

Consider the infant-mother relationship, that most primeval and deeply formative socializing situation. This relationship can serve us as a limiting case regarding the capacity of culture to shape human experience and, thereby, human character. For it is here that the imprint of natural need is most indelibly impressed, where nurture is most clearly shaped by nature. If civilized society can impose its own purposes at the expense of human needs in this situation, we cannot doubt it can do so at any other point. If we can envision how the maternal relationship can be perverted to the ends of power, then we can still more readily imagine how socialization from other personal relationships and from social institutions can also mold human beings to those ends.

The infant brings to the maternal relationship intense needs for a continuous flow of love and emotional-tactile contact. This is a major thrust of John Bowlby's excellent and lifelong study of attachment (as well as separation and loss) in the mother-child relationship. Support for this image of powerful natural needs is found in those studies (e.g., by Margaret Ribble and René Spitz) on the deaths of institutionalized infants who received material but not emotional sustenance. A good deal of work in psychology has substantiated the idea that the indispensable foundation for healthy emotional development in the human being is the experience of love and trust in this initial emotional attachment.

Fortunately, nature is at work in the other side of the relationship as well. The way the sound of the infant's voice stimulates in the mother the secretion of the hormone oxytocin, which in turns prompts the flow of milk, can stand for an entire pattern of natural maternal responses.

But nature's system is not foolproof. Mothering can be inadequate. A mother's inadequacy can be the result of individual idiosyncrasy, as in the case of a first-time mother chimpanzee who was a neglectful mother and whose infant eventually died (described by Jane van Lawick-Goodall, 1967). But maternal neglect can also be an established cultural pattern, since the socialization process, like all aspects of culture, evolves under the force of various influences, not all of them congenial to man. Ashley Montague (1971) has described the tendency of many cultures systematically to frustrate the innate need of the human child for touching, and

157

Bowlby has written, in *Attachment,* that prolonged separation of infants from their mothers occurs only "in more economically developed human societies, especially in Western ones" (1969, p. 199). The neglect of human needs is not mere inadvertence. Cultural practice is reinforced by cultural teaching, revealing that the socializing culture is not just neglecting human nature but is indeed warring against it. Consider, for example, this sage advice given early in this century by John B. Watson, a major figure in the American study of the psyche, in *Psychological Care of Infant and Child:*

> There is a sensible way of treating children. Treat them as though they were young adults. Dress them, bathe them, with care and circumspection. Let your behavior always be objective and kindly firm. Never hug and kiss them, never let them sit on your lap. If you must, kiss them once on the forehead [to] say goodnight. . . . Try it out. In a week's time you will find how easy it is to be perfectly objective with your child and at the same time kindly. You will be utterly ashamed of the mawkish, sentimental way you have been handling it. (quoted in Frank Caplan, 1973, p. 87)

Under the pressures of culture, the natural relationship between mother and child can be sabotaged. Hospitals drug delivering mothers and whisk away the newborns into nurseries controlled by professionals, thus undermining a critical and irreplaceable moment for bonding. Until recently in this society, fathers were forcibly kept away, and breast-feeding was scorned and discouraged. These social practices also weaken the bonds between the infant and its parents. Under the weight of social teachings and policies like these, and shaped herself by a similarly unnatural process of socialization, the mother may well be ill-prepared to respond to the needs her baby got from nature the way nature designed her to. As R. D. Laing writes, somewhat hyperbolically: "From the moment of birth, when the Stone Age baby confronts the twentieth century mother, the baby is subjected to these forces of violence, called love, as its mother and father, and their parents before them, have been. These forces are mainly concerned with destroying most of its potentialities, and on the whole this enterprise is successful" (1967, p. 58).

The unnatural socialization experience rechannels the natural human energies. Depending on the nature and extent of the deprivation, the child's natural yearning for love can be transformed into frustration and rage, into desperate driven searching, into feelings of helplessness. Early in his career, Bowlby (with J. Robertson) studied the effect on young children of separation from the mother, necessitated by the child's hospitalization. They found predictable stages in the children's reaction: in the beginning there was protest, a call for an end to the separation; then came despair, the bleak and depressed feeling of aloneness; and finally came denial, an end to wanting for the relationship to be renewed. They describe this last stage:

> . . . he will gradually commit himself less and less to succeeding nurses and in time will stop altogether taking the risk of investing love and dependence in anyone. Instead he will become more and more self-centered, transferring his desires and feelings from people onto material things such as sweets, toys, and food. He will no longer show upset when the nurses leave. He will also cease showing feeling when his parents come and go on visiting day . . . he denies all need for mothering or intimate care. (quoted in Montagu, 1955, p. 216)

Under the impact of a psychological trauma, even the deepest and most instinctually based desires can be redirected and/or denied. The frustration of need which happenstance imposed on the children in the study, societies may impose upon their young by design.

Idiosyncratic trauma needs no explanation, but a cultural pattern of thwarting human needs suggests a cultural purpose. By systematically traumatizing its members, especially in their most impressionable and formative years, a society can recast the image of man to achieve its own ends. But what ends are served by frustrating human needs (in the maternal relationship or anywhere else in the socialization process)? One inevitable end of civilized societies is the maximization of power, and I show how the ends of power can be served by human suffering. A fulfilled person at peace with the world is an instrument of limited utility. But frustrate him enough, and his energies turn to rage which can be channeled for his society's power. Energize him with the activation that marks the uncomfortable, and he can become one of those driven people who accomplish so much. Teach him to eschew human intimacy, and he becomes available as a pliant servant of impersonal systems and an attentive manipulator of the material world. Drive him to an intolerable sense of his own helplessness, and he may be quickened with an insatiable thirst for power.

What hurts the individual human being may therefore be helpful to the power-maximizing system, helpful not necessarily despite the human injury but sometimes even because of it. Human suffering is not always an incidental by-product of the parable of the tribes. It is not just that the struggle for power grinds people up, or that the selection for power is indifferent to human needs. Beyond that, the evolving systems of power-maximization utilize human suffering as a major fuel to energize their operation.

Power demands better servants than human beings are as nature created them. Civilized societies need power, and thus they are compelled to re-create man. Socialization practices are the instruments by which social demands are translated into psychological structure, and we have had an intimation of how such practices may injure mankind to maximize power. Since the selection for power selects also for power-maximizing socialization practices, it is evident how the parable of the tribes could illuminate our psychological as well as social evolution.

The psychological structure that best serves power has many components. Moreover, as civilization has evolved, the demands by power upon the human psyche have evolved as well. In this chapter, I explore a few of the major dimensions of this painful recreation of man into the image of power. "(T)he phenomenon of an animal turning upon itself, taking arms against itself, was so novel, profound, mysterious, contradictory and pregnant with possibility, that the whole complexion of the universe was changed thereby" (Nietzsche, 1956, p. 218).

2. Fighting Mad

The Seeds of Rage

Power is not the fruit of violence alone; it is far more complex than that. Yet the parable of the tribes has dictated that the capacity for effective aggression is indispensable for a society's survival. Civilization has therefore required the creation of a warrior spirit among a least some of its members. How readily have people been recruited into the combative cadres of civilization? Are the bloody pages of civilized history but the nature of man writ large? These questions were brought up in the "Red Sky at Morning" section of chapter 3. I return to them here in a new context: to note the psychological transformation that accompanied the social transformation of the rise of militarism.

The crucial testimony must be that of the natural man. But where is he to be found? We may look at primitive peoples, whom civilized mythology regards as savages. Yet savagery better characterizes civilization. Erich Fromm, in *Anatomy of Human Destructiveness,* concludes from the data that "the most primitive men are the least warlike and the warlikeness grows in proportion to civilization. If destructiveness were innate in man, the trend would have to be the opposite" (1973, p. 150). We may look also at children, each of whom is, as it were, a message to civilization freshly sent by nature. Anna Freud, carrying on her father's work, has written: "Children have to be safeguarded against the primitive forces of war, not because horrors and atrocities are so strange to them but because we want them at this decisive stage of their development to overcome and estrange themselves from the primitive and atrocious wishes

160

of their infantile natures" (quoted in Bender, 1953, p. 138). It would seem that the atrocities of war mirror the atrocious impulses, endowed by nature, with which we enter this world. Yet others who have studied children have perceived them very differently. On the basis of work with more than nine hundred children, for example, K. M. Banham concluded that children are born with outgoing affectionate drives. The hostile drives she regards as secondary: "They only become preoccupied with themselves, withdrawn or hostile as a secondary reaction, when rebuffed, smothered with unwanted ministrations, ignored or neglected" (quoted in Montagu, 1955, p. 194). Lauretta Bender has argued similarly in her study of childhood aggression: deprivations and dissatisfactions in the child's experiences, she says, are the cause of the "amplification or disorganization of the [child's "constructive"] drives into hostile or destructive aggression" (1953, p. 149). If we accept these findings, human aggressiveness appears inevitable only if we regard the positive needs of the child as inherently impossible of fulfillment. But the work of Bowlby and others suggests quite otherwise. They suggest that, in its natural environment (in Bowlby's phrase, in its "environment of evolutionary adaptiveness" [1969, p. 50]), the infant's needs correspond well with the nurturing it is offered. It seems reasonable to grant that a degree of frustration and a corresponding degree of aggressiveness are naturally part of the human condition, but the extreme destructiveness wrought by civilized man is probably best seen as an outgrowth of the unnatural degree of frustration to which civilization subjects its members.

The problem of human aggression, we may reasonably believe, lies not in ourselves but in our environment. J. P. Scott argues against any notion of an inevitable aggressive impulse. There is no need to fight, he says, as there is to eat. The absence of food leads, in time, to a disturbed internal, physiological condition. By contrast: "A person who is fortunate enough to exist in an environment which is without stimulation to fight will not suffer physiological or nervous damage because he never fights" (quoted in Fromm, 1973, p. 119). Man has no need to pray, give us this day our daily killing.

Viewing a European civilization seething between two convulsive world wars, Sigmund Freud saw men as "creatures among whose instinctual endowments is to be reckoned a powerful share of aggressiveness" (1961, p. 58). But, it should be recalled, Freud as an observer was in a situation much like Zuckerman's. In such a zoo, it is no wonder that he sensed "a primary mutual hostility" among human beings. Yet as a zoo-dweller— whose vision of human life before the zoo, articulated in *Totem and Taboo*, was of a repressive paternal tyranny terminated by guilt-inducing patricide—Freud misread the relationship between human aggression and

161

civilization. "Civilization," he thought, "has to use its utmost efforts in order to set limits to man's aggressive instincts . . ." (1961, p. 59). But the alternative view is that the unnatural environment frustrates human needs, and chronically frustrated creatures grow enraged. When a child's positive needs are not met, Durbin and Bowlby write, "such frustration leads to a violent reaction of fear, hatred, and aggression. The child cries or screams or bites or kicks" (in Bramson et al., 1964, p. 91). Man, a child of nature, kicks against the cage that frustrates him. The zoo runs red.

Because of chronic injury, not God-given impulse, civilized man grows up with a chronic lust for revenge.[1]

Channeling Destructive Energies

It is not immediately evident how civilized societies can benefit from enraging their human members by inflicting upon them the pain of unnatural living. If these destructive impulses should be expressed wantonly throughout the range of social interactions, this pool of energy might more readily disrupt and fracture a civilized society than be instrumental to it. The order of civilized society is, in fact, frequently threatened by violence—domestic, criminal, or insurrectional. Like so much else of human potentiality, however, human rage can be a pliant resource available to be molded and directed for social ends. What is needed is a means to channel the Brownian motion of purely individual rage into an aggressive movement of the whole social mass.[2]

The natural impulse is to strike back at the source of one's injury. But when the source of injury is society or its agents, including the socializing parents, retaliation typically is forbidden. Permitting such revolt would be incompatible with establishing the habit of individual submission to social authority. When the child expresses its anger at being frustrated, write Durbin and Bowlby, it is further frustrated by punishment. "The child is slapped or beaten or subjected to moral instruction—taught that its behavior is wrong or wicked" (in Bramson et al., 1964, p. 91). A psychological version of the law of the conservation of energy operates: the impulses, however much suppressed, do not disappear. Denied their

1. Achilles says in Homer's *Iliad:*
>   Why, I wish that strife would vanish away from among gods and mortals,
>   and gall, which makes a man grow angry for all his great mind,
>   that gall of anger that swarms like smoke inside of a man's heart
>   and becomes a thing sweeter to him by far than the dripping of honey.
>   (XVIII. 107–110)

2. It should be noted that individual aggressive energies are not the sole motivational foundation for collective aggression. More altruistic feelings—like love and loyalty for one's people and country—are also often important ingredients.

natural outlet, they will find another. The discipline imposed by civilization has a paradoxical effect, at once domesticating him for its purposes and driving him wild. Nietzsche, seeing through the facade of domestication in Victorian Europe, wrote: "What punishment is able to achieve, both for man and beast, is increase of fear, circumspection, control over the instincts. Thus man is *tamed* by punishment, but by no means *improved;* rather the opposite" (1956, p. 216). And Durbin and Bowlby continue their analysis of the frustrated child: "The overwhelming fact established by the evidence is that aggression, however deeply hidden or disguised, does not disappear. It appears later and in other forms" (in Bramson et al., 1974, p. 92). What forms are socially the most useful?

One transformation of aggressive energies is a form of internalization, a redirection of hostility back against the self, discussed later in this chapter in "The War Within."

More pertinent to our immediate concern is a second transformation: displacement. With displacement, the aggressive energy remains outwardly directed but the object against which it is directed has been changed. The urge to strike is permitted expression, but the dangerous and forbidden object of this rage is replaced by another. This new object, though perhaps objectively irrelevant, can serve a cathartic function if it is draped in the proper imagery to make it appear the proper target of hatred. Man, risen to greatness by his symbol-forming abilities, is here hoist by his own petard. Because our rage can be vented upon scapegoats, the very systems that injure us as they grow in power can use our pain to empower themselves still further. Mumford writes of warfare in the ancient city: "Hence the sense of joyful release that so often has accompanied the outbreak of war. . . . (P)opular hatred for the ruling classes was cleverly diverted into a happy occasion to kill *foreign* enemies" (quoted in Becker, 1975, p. 98). Scapegoats can, of course, be internal as well. The common factor—whether it is a czarist state diverting hostility toward the Jews or a ruling class of U.S. southern whites channeling resentment toward blacks—is that it is often the very powers that create discontent that choose the target of the consequent rage. Civilized societies exploit hatred as armies do: the hatred for the brutalizing but unassailable officer is directed, given free outlet, against the enemy he points to.

As in ancient times, so in the modern world, the pent-up rage of society's members can fuel the engine of social power, by strengthening the ruling part and by fortifying the aggressive drive of the whole. The typical Western individual, Talcott Parsons writes, is subject in the process of growing to adulthood to emotional strains so severe as to produce "a large reservoir of aggressive disposition" which, as it cannot be directly expressed, is "susceptible to mobilization against various kinds of scape-

163

goats outside the immediate situation of its genesis" (in Zawodny, 1966, p. 384). Similarly, Durbin and Bowlby write that "It is natural" that the aggression provoked by the frustration of the socialization process "should be chiefly canalized by, and flow unimpeded through, the state organization of common endeavor and military adventure" (in Bramson et al., 1964, p. 99). Reservoirs, canals, flows: the human being is exploited like the Colorado River of which not one drop now reaches its natural outlet in the Gulf of California.

Displacement through collective social aggression serves two functions. From those who seek to explain the phenomenon of war, one usually hears of the cathartic function. Thus Mumford concludes about the ancient city: "(T)he greater the tensions and the harsher the daily repressions of civilization, the more useful war became as a safety valve" (quoted in Becker, 1975, p. 98). But the parable of the tribes discovers another factor by looking at the same connection from the other side: the more necessary for social survival collective belligerence became, the more useful became the tensions and harsh repressions of civilized life.

The Faces of Human Aggression in the Evolving Reign of Power

Social evolution has placed the civilized individual and the civilized society in very different positions with regard to aggression. While the society needs to harness the aggressive energies of its members to maximize its own power, it also needs for its members to be subordinate to its authority. As social evolution has progressed, tighter social orders have emerged with more stringent demands that individuals restrain their aggressive energies. The intersocietal system, by contrast, has remained anarchic and has continued to require of societies the capacity for effective collective aggression. This widening difference in the demands made by the respective environments contributes to the channeling of aggression into collective forms: energies repressed in the individual erupt in the conduct of the system as a whole.

The forces of social evolution have prohibited in the individual the assertiveness they have made mandatory for the society. Only society is sovereign; only it is permitted to stand tall. Consequently, the subdued individual with unfulfilled longings all the more readily identifies with his oppressor, seeking through that identification the vicarious satisfaction of the human pride and freedom which the system has denied him. Denis de Rougemont has written about patriotism:

> In truth, we have here again egotism, but so broadened as to become a virtue. It is taught in schools under the name "patriotism." It is accepted that every form of pride, every form of vanity, and even the most stupid boastings are

> legitimate and honorable so long as they are attributed to the nation in which one has taken the trouble to get born. What nobody would dare to say of his *me*, he has the sacred duty of saying for his *us*. (1957, p. 78)

An important word of qualification: the foregoing discussion asserts no single character type for civilized man. Identifying any particular national character is sufficiently fraught with peril without adding cross-cultural and transhistorical dimensions. This sketch is simply to suggest and illustrate the nature of the interaction between the demands of power and the transformations of human energies. A full investigation would reveal a vast array of different characters, not only because of idiosyncratic personality differences, but also according to social roles, cultural differences, and social evolutionary changes in the demands of power. Most pertinent to the concerns of this work is the effect of changes in the demands of power, and this effect might usefully be illustrated.

In primitive societies, anthropologists tell us, respect is gained through generosity and proven wisdom. We in modern liberal societies feel more affinity for those values than for the martial virtues which warrior societies have placed above all others. The nobles of feudal society, for example, considered it a virtue to be prepared to avenge any slight by spilling blood. Tocqueville writes of medieval Europe:

> The nobles of the Middle Ages placed military courage foremost among virtues and in lieu of many of them. . . . Feudal aristocracy existed by war and for war; its power had been founded by arms, and by arms that power was maintained; it therefore required nothing more than military courage, that quality was naturally exalted above others; whatever denoted it, even at the expense of reason and humanity, was therefore approved and frequently enjoined by the manners of the time. (1945, II, 245)

We reject such conduct and values. Yet, unlike them, we live in that age of tight social order where individual aggressiveness is prohibited. The nobles of feudal society lived in an era without strong central control. They retained as individuals a degree of sovereignty in an environment which, in turn, retained a degree of anarchy. In view of the anarchy that surrounded them, and the anarchy that in the first place allowed them to come to power within their domains by force of arms, we can see two aspects of the selection for power that would favor this unreasonable and inhumane emphasis on martial virtues. Our individual circumstances are very different, and so are the ethics surrounding our individual conduct. Before we too hastily regard that era and its values as alien from our own, however, we should look at that juncture of modern life where our ordered existence shares a border with anarchy. We may recall that strong national impulse—barely restrained by a larger view of national interest—to avenge with blood the insult to the United States of Iran's holding less than .00000025 percent of our citizens hostage. That comparatively trivial but visible and sustained insult, more than any other factor, served (in 1980–81) to rededicate U.S. public opinion to martial virtues in American collective behavior, and swept into power an administration promising that such affronts in the future shall be met with "swift and effective retribution." Beware, ye who would throw down the gauntlet before us *as a nation*. Fortunately, high among the martial virtues that selection for power favors in major nation-states is the capacity for prudent calculation.[3] We may hope, therefore, that the resurgent militance will be unlike that of the hotheaded feudal warrior.

Not only has social evolution moved the locus of aggressiveness in the modern world from where it was in feudal times but it has altered its spirit as well. The demands war now makes upon the soldier in combat are different from those of earlier eras. Pinchas Noy writes that "The soldier involved in battles in the past could not function without being motivated by aggression. He could not put his sword through the body of his enemy without feeling hate for him, or without enjoying the actual act of killing" (in Winnik et al., 1973, p. 121). Modern weapons, however, require a new psychology for the act of destruction: "The skillful operation of these technical instruments requires a coolheaded, quick-thinking and emotionally detached soldier. In a dogfight between two supersonic jets, for instance, when life and death depend upon the ability of the pilot to plan and decide his action within a fraction of a second, the one blinded by rage and hate would certainly be the one to lose" (ibid.). Perhaps the need for split-second timing is not the crucial change, for hand-to-hand combat has also required it, but rather the change from large muscular movements to the very minute ones required to work the controls that unleash the violence. (See also Newcomb on how sophisticated weapons displace pugnacity with detached serenity as the advantageous emotional state of the modern soldier.) Perhaps this change also reflects the distancing and intellectualization that the apparatus of modern power in general requires of those who tend it.[4] We destroy now in a less ferocious spirit.

We who, in modern times, coolly equip ourselves to annihilate millions of our fellow human beings in other lands are nonetheless repulsed by

3. Indeed, the predominance of prudence over mere violence has long been a part of the successful strategy for power maximization for large-scale systems. Edward Luttwak writes of *The Grand Strategy of the Roman Empire*: "With rare exceptions, the misuse of force in pursuit of solely tactical goals, or for the psychic rewards of purposeless violence, was avoided by those who controlled the destinies of Rome." . . . "The firm subordination of tactical priorities, martial ideals, and warlike instincts was the essential condition of the strategic success of the empire" (1976, p. 2).

4. The idea that the change in the demands upon the soldier parallels a more general change in the demands society places upon its members finds support in a contrast drawn by Norbert Elias: "Whoever did not love or hate to the utmost in this [medieval] society, whoever could not stand his ground in the play of passions, could go into a monastery; in worldly life he was just as lost as was, conversely, in later society, and particularly at court, the man who could not curb his passions, could not conceal and 'civilize' his affects" (1978, p. 201).

the brutality of earlier eras. The ancients who took great pride in their capacity for cruelty and ruthlessness do not evoke our admiration. But perhaps we, no less than they, reflect the ruthlessness our own times require for survival in a still ruthless world.

Warfare in its early form decreed that not the meek but the most ferocious and relentless would inherit the earth. Walter Bagehot observes: "Insensibility to human suffering, which is so striking a fact in the world as it stood when history first reveals it, is doubtless due to the warlike origins of the old civilization. Bred in war, and nursed in war, it would not revolt from the things of war, and one of the principal of these is human pain" (1956, p. 58). Yet most of us, in the face of wounds and suffering, retain that sensibility. Nonetheless, we have developed a new insensibility, a disembodied distancing. In an era when the technology of destruction allows us to kill by remote control, we become remote in the manner in which we contemplate the meaning of our actions. Unlike our more bloody-minded ancestors, we cannot look our carnage in the face. But, like Perseus slaying Medusa, we do it by mirrors of abstract intellectualization. No longer given to crude boasts of atrocities, we in the nuclear age think the unthinkable and speak dispassionately of megadeaths.

Finally, it is worth noting one more effect of the changing requirements of power upon the nature and role of aggression in the psychology of civilized people. In our era, in comparison with earlier times, the role of purely military factors in the generation of social power has diminished. The development of modern economic productivity has become so vital a component of a society's competitive power that the selection for power has channeled a greater proportion of human energies to purposes other than aggression. It is perhaps in this perspective that we might ponder Tocqueville's observation about the energetic structure of Americans which in a few centuries has made their nation a superpower and a principal molder of modern civilization:

> To clear, to till, and to transform the vast uninhabited continent which is his domain, the American requires the daily support of an energetic passion; that passion can only be the love of wealth; the passion for wealth is therefore not reprobated in America, and, provided it does not go beyond the bounds assigned to it for public security, it is held in honor. The American lauds as noble and praiseworthy ambition what our forefathers in the Middle Ages stigmatized as severe cupidity, just as he treats as a blind and barbarous frenzy that ardor of conquest and martial temper which bore them to battle. (1945, II, 248)

Barbaric frenzy yields to cupidity; the savaging of human flesh gives way to a rape of nature's bounty. Either way, the mentality of power, though it may change, deforms the human character. In making human energies the instrument of inhumane ends, the selection for power makes virtues out of vices.

3. Hierarchy and the Lust for Power

In the political realm, as in the military, the requirements for the survival of civilized societies have had frightening psychological implications.

As civilization brought war to mankind, so also did it bring hierarchical political and social structures. We have seen (chap. 3, "The Evolution toward More Effective Central Control") how intersocietal competition has mandated inequalities of power within society. Later (chap. 7, "Men Are Not Ants") I explore how an analogous anarchy within societies has led to an analogous intrasocietal selection for power, compounding the tendency for civilized societies to become polarized between a powerful elite and a subordinated majority. Thus with power uncontrolled in human affairs, the emergence of civilization cast human beings into the new roles of ruler and ruled. These new roles demanded new psychological structures among the players in the human drama.

In a world where power is suddenly a requirement, the appetite for power will be rewarded. Those societies will survive best whose rulers can most wholeheartedly and single-mindedly play the power-maximization game. (The consequences of the recent juxtaposition between President Carter's Christian piety in the White House and chess-playing-as-usual in the Kremlin illustrate this point.)[5] Within societies, those groups are most likely to dominate which most crave the dominating role and which find most congenial the means that lead to power. The selection for power thus gives the domineering personality a dominant place in the picture of civilized psychology.

How large a transformation is implied by the prominence of this lust for power? Just as there have been many who have seen the record of civilized warfare as the outgrowth of the natural aggressive instinct of our species, so also have many seen the lust for power as the inherent bent of the human creature. Thomas Hobbes, writing at a particularly anarchic time in English history, saw men in the state of nature as inevitably obsessed with gaining power. In order to secure himself, Hobbes

---

5. In the words of the ancient Chinese classic of Han Fei Tzu: "King Yen practiced benevolence and righteousness and the state of Hsü was wiped out; Tsu-kung employed eloquence and wisdom and Lu lost territory. So it is obvious that benevolence and righteousness, eloquence and wisdom are not the means by which to maintain the state. Discard the benevolence of King Yen and put an end to Tsu-kung's wisdom; build up the might of Hsü and Lu until they can stand face to face with a state of ten thousand war chariots—then Ch'i and Ching will no longer be able to do with them as they please!" (Watson, 1964, pp. 100–101).

wrote, a man must try "by force or wiles to master the persons of all men he can . . ." (*Leviathan*, chap. 13). Nietzsche—looking beneath the carpet of nineteenth-century European civilization and himself standing, many believe, as a harbinger of the fascist mentality whose season was soon to come—portrayed the Will to Power as the essential motive of the human animal. "All driving force is will to power. . . . Pleasure is every increase of power, displeasure every feeling of not being able to resist or dominate" (1967, nos. 689, 690).

Yet in the state of nature, we discover a very different human portrait. The egalitarian nature of primitive society has been stressed before. Such insignificant differences in status as we find do not derive from success in subjugating others but from more benign and modest services performed for the community. In the state of nature, we do not find every man for himself, against all others. Rather, reciprocity and sharing form the basis for social interaction. We can infer that a moderate dominance hierarchy probably characterizes natural human society, since dominance plays some role in gorilla and chimpanzee societies. Yet that Nietzschean cleavage of mankind into the strong and the weak mirrors a disturbed human condition, not a natural one. Seeing man in natural society, we would not posit the will to power as the engine of all human action. If civilization has given men an insatiable appetite for power, it has been through a distortion of our natural psychology. Men like Hobbes and Nietzsche have been looking at Zuckerman's baboons.

In the lust for power demonstrated by many of civilization's most prominent individuals, therefore, we find not human nature so much as psychopathology. An insight into one aspect of that pathology is provided by Fromm. With the rise of civilization, he writes, a "new principle" came to govern human life, and a substantial part of that principle derived from the sadistic character type. Sadism he describes as "the passion for unlimited, godlike control over men and things" (1973, p. 165). And the prominence of sadistic pathology in early civilization he discovers, for example, in the way the rulers of Egypt and Mesopotamia "boasted on their monuments and tablets of their personal feats in mutilating, torturing and killing with their own hands their chief captives" (quoting Mumford in ibid.). "To exert power in every form was the essence of civilization" (ibid.). Says the king in a medieval *chanson:* "By my troth, I laugh at what you may say. I care not a fig for your threats, I shall shame every knight I have taken, cut off his nose or his ears. If he is a sergeant or a merchant, he will lose a foot or an arm" (quoted in Elias, 1978, p. 193). Regrettably, we cannot be assured that civilization has outgrown this "new" principle of sadism as it has become older. The sadistic delight in playing the god of torment still leaves its grisly mark upon our world.

It is not just the barbarity of an Idi Amin or a Pol Pot which gives us concern. In Hitler and Stalin, two of the most powerful and advanced nations on earth were ruled by the ancient spirit of sadistic pathology. The equation of civilization with progress, which seemed so clear to many just a few generations ago, appears untenable in the light of Auschwitz and the Gulag. Solzhenitsyn writes, with characteristically searing eloquence:

> If the intellectuals in the plays of Chekhov who spent all their time guessing what would happen in twenty, thirty, or forty years had been told that in forty years interrogation by torture would be practiced in Russia; that prisoners would have their skulls squeezed by iron rings; that a human being would be lowered into an acid bath; that they would be trussed up naked to be bitten by ants and bedbugs; that a ramrod heated over a primus stove would be thrust up their anal canal (the "secret brand"); that a man's genitals would be slowly crushed beneath the toe of a jackboot; and that, in the luckiest possible circumstances, prisoners would be tortured by being kept from sleeping for a week, by thirst, and by being beaten to a bloody pulp, not one of Chekhov's plays would have gotten to its end because all the heroes would have gone off to insane asylums. (quoted in Feifer, 1980, p. 57)

We in liberal countries feel securely insulated from such nightmares. But in our world too the lust for power plays a large and often corrosive role. Among us, the craving for power often takes other more subtle and devious forms, as in the tyranny of bureaucrats and in the Vince Lombardian obsession with winning as the only thing.

As long as so many of the men who run our systems are people who would sacrifice anything to be on top, it is difficult to imagine how the world would not be screwed up.

This work suggests two ways of explaining the unnatural prominence of the lust for power in the psychology of civilization. The parable of the tribes can explain its spread: as people left the Garden to become as gods, selection would dictate that those with "a passion for godlike control" would rise to be historymakers. If power needed power lovers, civilization would find more efficient ways to generate that character type than mere reliance upon the creation by happenstance of occasional "rogue animals" among the human ranks. To understand the genesis of the lust for power, we must turn to the thesis more recently developed here that unnatural and therefore unfulfilling conditions for human life generate pathological distortions of human nature.

A suggestion of how the lust for power arises as the fruit of unfulfillment is found in Fromm's ideas about the compensatory nature of sadism. The sadistic urge to demonstrate omnipotence, he says, grows out of the experience of agonizing impotence. An emotionally injured person who has lost "the power to be" may compensate by seeking "power over" things and people. Both points support an image of sadistic motives as secondary or derivative, like the aggressive energies discussed earlier. They also clarify how the frustrations of civilized life could transform more constructive impulses into sadistic ones—again as was the case with aggression. A social environment which forbids the human being to be what he naturally is, and which renders him impotent in the face of the repressive power of society, would seem well suited for generating sadists. We again encounter that tragic irony that the very suffering inflicted by power systems upon human beings can be turned to strengthen those same injurious systems.

We have looked into the psychology of the dominant, but there is another side to be considered. The hierarchical systems of civilization require a mass of people who will submit to control. As Machiavelli said, the virtues of rulers and ruled are not the same. As power systems have need of wolves, so have they need of sheep.

The image of the sheep seems to fit well Redfield's description of the peasant as stoical and passive. A similar portrait of a subordinate type is drawn by Fromm in his delineation of the "receptive" character: "The receptive orientation is often to be found in societies in which the right of one group to exploit another is firmly established. Since the exploited group has no power to change . . . its situation, it will tend to look up to its masters as to its providers, as to those from whom one receives everything life can give" (1947, p. 79).

Even here the ideologies of civilization (more particularly, of course, of its dominant elites) have sought to present existing conditions as revealing fundamental nature. In *Politics*, Aristotle declares that "It is clear . . . that some men are by nature free, and others slaves, and that for these latter slavery is both expedient and right" (1. 5–6). He does not argue that all men whose legal status is that of slaves are natural slaves, though it is natural for "barbarians" to be slaves to the Hellenes. As ruling elites are in no position to argue that human nature per se is servile, they are compelled to posit a deep biological cleavage in the species. By a kind of ideological speciation, in many aristocratic societies, the noble born and the base born have been regarded as radically different creatures. God made these men as sheep so it is fitting that we fleece them. By nature they are dull and plodding as oxen, so like oxen they shall be yoked to our plow. The ruled are transformed into a higher form of domesticated animal. We know now that however useful such ideas may be in justifying and preserving exploitative social arrangements, they do not stand biological scrutiny. The Pharoah-god was made of the same

171

stuff as his slaves. The backward Britons of Rome's Empire came eventually to establish a still greater one. Nonetheless, the goose steps of the Master Race echo still in living memory.

It is the unnatural circumstance of enforced subordination that creates the subordinate character type. For men are not by nature sheep nor, to use Jefferson's slightly different metaphor, has "the mass of mankind . . . been born with saddles on their backs" (1939, pp. 18–19). The weight of long oppression is what shapes the human back for the saddle. Fromm presents his receptive type as the product of long oppression, and we may recall Redfield's account of the transformation of "folklike" people into peasantry by their absorption into the bottom of a hierarchical system. The natural pride and initiative of people can be stamped out, but only at great psychological cost.

At first glance, it may appear that people in modern liberal societies are free from the pressure of being saddled, but the dignity of democratic participation is not people's sole or perhaps even predominant experience. As anyone knows who has worked in the large hierarchical organizations that dominate our work world, the bureaucratic tyrants have a multitude of their subordinate counterparts. The pressures in these systems, where power flows only downward, do a good job in forming Fromm's "receptive" behaviors. People in a position to effect no change, and dependent upon their superiors for their livelihood, are induced to treat those above them as their masters and providers. Indeed, political analysts like Franz Neumann and A. D. Lindsay worry that this daily experience of subordination undermines the human spirit democracy demands. The large stratified systems of modern production, Neumann says, "must instill the virtues of discipline, obedience and subordination . . . the very virtues which every authoritarian system seeks to cultivate" (in Cooperman and Walter, 1962, p. 227; see also Lindsay, 1962, p. 183). If the masses of men have not maintained the dignity of naturally free creatures, it is because unnatural power systems have made it difficult.

Ivan Karamazov's Grand Inquisitor presents a profound human reality in his portrait of the people as a sheeplike mass. The people, the Inquisitor says, reject the freedom that Christ offers them in favor of the security of an authoritarian regime that unburdens them of their liberty and provides their daily bread. But this portrait gives insight not into pristine human nature, as implied, but rather into the fruits of long oppression. Even now as analysts in the West ponder the prospects of Dostoyevski's people rising against their repressive and stagnant system, the consensus is that, though discontented, they shall remain bowed. Since before Ivan the Terrible they have known only repression, and this still peasantlike people have learned to keep heads down. The long experience of powerlessness leads to deeply ingrained passivity.

This suggests a final integrating point. If the experience of power-lessness fosters the sadism of the rulers and also the passivity of the ruled, perhaps the "virtues" of the two groups are ultimately not so distinct as we have been regarding them. In some cases, today's passive victim is tommorow's victimizer. As in the rites of initiation in fraternities, the newcomer who at first must submit to humiliation and abuse later relishes the chance to wreak sadistic vengeance against some new innocent. Proverbs exhorts: "Envy thou not the oppressor and choose none of his ways" (3:31). Moral exhortations always lean against human inclinations, and thus serve to point them out. Power's crimes perpetuate themselves. Injury begets injury. Although the tables may turn, the game remains the same. The Russian people did not stay forever under czarist tyranny—revolution brought a new one, and the revolution of the oppressed gave forth a Stalin. The guillotine in the Place de la Concorde gave the old oppressors a taste of their own medicine and thus perpetuated the disease. Indeed, the experience of oppression seems the best training for tomorrow's oppressors.[6]

The ruler and the ruled are less like black and white than like chicken and egg. A saying of the classical world, articulated in turn by men like Solon, Plato, and Cicero, has it that the best preparation for command is learning to obey. The unintended truth of this saying may be the deeper part. Even without revolution, there is the turnover of the generations. Bagehot says that the Romans conquered the world in manhood because as children they were "compelled to obey their fathers." His point is that this "domestic despotism" prepared them in later life to submit to a "military despotism," which made them a disciplined and powerful force. But again there may be an unintended point to be found: that the chronic experience of submission gave the Romans a strong appetite for conquest. The British upper class were fitted for ruling the world, Montagu suggests, by the way they were (or were not) mothered: the emotional distance from which they suffered as children created a cool and unsympathetic detachment in them as adults which was well suited for the Olympian

6. If the successors of Stalin should be overthrown, should we imagine liberty would be the Russians' fate? A pessimistic answer to that question is suggested by Feifer's analysis of Solzhenitsyn, that charismatic denunciator of the repressive Soviet tyranny. "Imagine," Feifer suggests, "life and liberty under a Solzhenitsyn state." This idea, he says, is "not so farfetched as it may sound. . . . It is Solzhenitsyn who stirs Russian souls, as it is he who would be acclaimed as the new leader if let loose upon the hungry land." Based on a considerable amount of evidence from Solzhenitsyn's life, Feifer concludes that life and liberty would not fare so well in such a state. Solzhenitsyn himself has acted unjustly and tyrannically, it seems, and Feifer imagines that Solzhenitsyn's revolution would end in dictatorship, as did Lenin's before him: "Since the leader and Teacher would not trust independent voices, his entourage would probably consist of henchmen who never challenge authority—the kind who would quickly restore a dictatorship in the disastrous disintegration sure to follow his death. . . . It is a great pity that this hero has taken on so many of the characteristics of the tyranny he opposes; and a greater pity for that troubled country" (1980, p. 58).

173

role of world rulers. It is said that them that has gets. But in the domain of power, sometimes it is them that gets least that later grabs most.

The experience of powerlessness creates a lust for power. Revolution is one possible expression of this urge, but like the aggressive energies considered earlier these, too, can serve as well as rend the power system. The identification with the oppressor which revolutions so often reveal can, if properly channeled, be useful to the oppressor. Morgenthau writes: "The great mass of the population is to a much greater extent the object of power than it is its wielder. Not being able to find full satisfaction of their desire for power within the national boundaries, the people project those unsatisfied aspirations onto the international scene. There they find vicarious satisfaction in identification with the power drives of the nation" (1972, p. 95).

Civilization brings to us an unnatural disease, and nothing in our evolution prepared the human organism to fight it well. Although the disease provokes a reaction from the human beings it afflicts, the reaction is as likely to feed the malady as to cure it. To be sure, the heart of the problem of the rule of power does not lie in our reaction to it, but the selective process can fasten upon our species' collective autoimmune response and use it to intensify the disease of power.

4. Under the Yoke: Harnessing Human Energies

Like every other creature, man has always been fully employed in the occupation of living and of perpetuating his kind of life. When the reign of power began to impose upon human life new and unnatural purposes, man's natural life-serving tasks were displaced by new ones in the service of power. Civilization has proved a harsh taskmaster. With no inherent limit to the drive toward power-maximization, the demands of civilization for human labor to do its work are also unlimited. As long as power is a function of human productivity, civilization will tend to regard the free spirit as a wastrel and the dedicated drudge as a virtuous man. The selection for power places man under the yoke.

Civilization's escalating appetite for human labor cannot be satisfied by the free expression of human nature. The astute observer of life in the zoo detects the resistance these demands encounter. Writes Freud: "The great majority of people only work under the stress of necessity, and this natural aversion to work raises most difficult social problems"(1961, p. 27n). As a pleasure-seeking creature, according to this view, man only unwillingly does the tasks that need doing. In this observation from *Civilization and Its Discontents,* we encounter the conflict between the pleasure principle and the reality principle. But again, I will argue, Freud's analysis of human discontent derives from the unnatural reality of the zoo. Regarding all human energies as seeking sexual pleasure, Freud believed that basic life needs could be met only through human frustration and consequent sublimation: "For what motive would induce man to put his sexual energy to other uses if by any disposal of it he could obtain fully satisfying pleasure? He would never let go of this pleasure and would make no further progress" (quoted in Marcuse, 1966, p. 82). But human energies are naturally as manifold as the natural demands of human life. As the performance of necessary tasks has always been as essential to our species' survival as reproduction or any libidinal expression, man is naturally a worker. In contrast with Freud's remark about a "natural aversion" to work, David Hamburg says that "tasks that must be done [for species survival] tend to be pleasurable; they are easy to learn and hard to extinguish" (in Washburn and Jay, 1968, p. 254). The work demands of the natural reality do not conflict with the pleasure principle. The observed "natural" aversion or resistance to work's demands stems from the imposition upon mankind of a new and unnatural reality. And the parable of the tribes helps explain why man's "progress" has required human beings to let go of pleasure and earn their bread by the sweat of their brows (Genesis 3).

The Displacement of Pleasure by Work

In the mythology of civilization, the life of primitives was nasty, and part of this nastiness was the presumed ceaseless toil needed to eke out the merest subsistence. But anthropologists have challenged this myth with their discovery that for hunter-gatherers the work of survival leaves considerable time for the simple enjoyment of life. The portrait of the Pygmies of the Ituri Forest, drawn by Colin Turnbull (1963), reveals them enjoying considerable leisure. After spending the morning in collecting food and fixing equipment, the Pygmies have time for eating and sleeping, for playing with children, for singing and dancing. Similarly, James Woodburn has written that the Hazda require on average only two hours a day to obtain their food (quoted in Sahlins, 1972, p. 27). Even in a relatively barren terrain, the !Kung bushmen studied by Richard Lee found survival only a part-time job, leaving a good share of their days for resting, playing, and visiting friends (Pfeiffer, 1969, p. 344).[7] For many of the members of a human society to have much surcease from

7. It is worth noting that these bushmen manage to live this way on a desolate land to which they retreated in recent centuries as they were squeezed out of their more abundant South African homeland by the more powerful black Bantu people from the north and white Dutch settlers moving in from the south (Paton, 1980, p. 48).

toil recurs only recently in the evolution of civilization, and then only in the most affluent of societies. Even so, after an overview of the anthropological data, Sahlins generalizes in his *Stone Age Economics* that "A good case can be made that hunters and gatherers work less than we do . . ." (1972, p. 14).

They are biologically the same creatures whom we find, after the agricultural revolution, spending their waking lives working the land. The cultivator, writes C. D. Darlington, "had learnt a patience and industry unknown to the hunter" (1969, p. 79). And Lord Raglan contrasts the hunter and the herdsman: ". . .the hunter with his bursts of furious activity interrupted by idleness and dissipation and the herdsman who devotes his youth and manhood to his cattle with devotion that he never spares and labours that never cease, morning, noon or night" (paraphrased in ibid.). The rise of civilization required a steadier, more industrious creature. Man's natural energies were therefore rechanneled toward productive labor. The loose spontaneity of the primitive tightens into the measured pace of the long-distance worker.[8]

The next quantum leap in the productive power of civilization saw a further emphasis on work as the center and purpose of human life. At the birth of modern economic power we find the ancient ethic of patient drudgery transformed into a desperate and impassioned striving. No one has described the new work-centered ethic better than Max Weber. In the Protestant ethic that accompanied the rise of capitalism, not only was one expected to work hard at his calling but "even beyond that labour came to be considered in itself the end [i.e., purpose] of life, ordained as such by God" (1958, p. 159). As Zinzendorf, the Protestant theologian, said, "One does not only work in order to live, but one lives for the sake of one's work . . ." (quoted in ibid., p. 264n). This ethic completes an extraordinary reversal between work and life, between human means and ends. While early civilization increased the weight of means in relation to the ends of human life and fulfillment, the rise of modern economic power saw those means become ends in themselves. The parable of the tribes suggests that this reversal becomes explicable in light of another: man himself has been transformed into a means to the ends of his civilized power systems.

The selection for power spreads those ways of life which effectively channel human energies for productive purposes. If we see human ener-

---

8. In Mesopotamia, as the rise of civilization sentenced the mass of people to hard labor to support the elite few, a new theology was developed to reinforce the new human condition. Men, it taught, "had been created expressly to free the gods from the necessity of working for a living. Man was thus considered to be a slave of the gods, obliged to serve ceaselessly and assiduously under pain of direct punishment—flood or drought and consequent starvation" (McNeill, 1963, p. 34).

gies as having become instrumental for the machinery of power, we can understand why civilization has impressed such mechanical virtues upon its human members. As the modern world emerged, with its cosmic image of the clockwork universe, there arose also a new man as regular as clockwork. How was it possible to achieve this alchemy transmuting the organic into the mechanical? One way seems to be through the creation of what psychoanalytic theory calls the anal character type. The link between the anal character and the bourgeois virtues is frequently made, for example, in the chapter "The Excremental Vision," in N. O. Brown's *Life against Death* and in Reimut Reiche's *Sexuality and the Class Struggle*. Particularly in bourgeois society, Reiche says, during the anal phase of development, the repression of anal pleasure transforms it into orderliness and so on, virtues that provide "a powerful model for organizing . . . [the] initiation and continuation of production" (1970, p. 34). The sphincter tightens still further civilization's grip upon man's natural spontaneity.

The Displacement of the Present by the Future

No adult lives wholly in the present moment. Indeed, the capacity for looking into the future is sometimes identified as a distinguishing trait of our species and a foundation for our success. Yet, the rise of civilization has led to a shift in the balance in human consciousness between present experience and future anticipation. There is a truth in the Greek myth that presents the titan Prometheus (literally, forethought) as the culture hero who brings to mankind the means of civilization.

Hunters-gatherers must plan, but their planning is limited in degree and range compared with that required by the agricultural revolution. Grahame Clark and Stuart Piggott, in *Prehistoric Societies,* write that animal domestication and plant cultivation make a long-term view inevitable. Once a society undertakes a deliberate policy of selecting suitable strains for breeding, for example, "it is involved in a process which may extend not only beyond a year, but even beyond a lifetime. The achievement of this larger perspective is in itself a psychological advance of no mean order" (1965, p. 158). Modern civilization has shifted the time perspective of human actors still further toward the future. By contrast with the present, according to Lenski, planning in agrarian societies was only a very occasional activity. The modern world, he says, is marked by a "growing emphasis on planning in all fields of human activity" (1966, p. 306).

An eye to the future has been the key to productive power not alone through the cognitive process of planning but also through the related allocation of resources for investment. Investment occurs when time or material which might be used for pleasure now is transformed into labor or capital to produce more goods in the future. The shift to productive work from activities undertaken purely for their own sakes therefore can be regarded as one aspect of a shift from consumption to investment. Without the renunciation of present pleasure embodied by investment, no economic growth can occur. For example, David McClelland found correlations in ancient Greece between psychological changes in the orientation toward the future and impulse control on the one hand, and subsequent changes in the rate of economic growth on the other (1961). Since economic growth is a major key to the growth of power, the selection for power will favor societies whose members willingly forego present consumption to invest in the future. In light of the parable of the tribes, therefore, we should not be surprised by the historical trend discovered by Leonard Doob, who has studied the sociopsychological aspects of becoming civilized: "There appears to be a fairly marked difference between less and more civilized peoples with respect to the amount of renunciation willingly endured" (1960, p. 85). Elsewhere, he describes what modernization has demanded of the African: a major psychological alteration required by the modernizing challenge of European civilization is a greater ability to postpone present rewards for the sake of future gratification (in Zawodny, 1966, p. 501).[9]

As Europe emerged into the modern age, there emerged with it this ethic of production and renunciation, of work and future orientation. The injunction "Live for your work" combined with the admonition "Labor to be rich for God, but not for the sin or flesh." As Weber observed, the inevitable practical result of this combination is the rapid accumulation of capital. A religiopsychological system conducive to rapid investment was evolving. There was even a responsibility to direct one's capital to its most efficient use. If you fail to do this, said the Protestant theologian Baxter, "you cross one of the ends of your calling, and you refuse to be God's steward and accept his gifts and use them for Him when He requireth it" (quoted in Weber, 1958, p. 168). It appears that the moral demands of Almighty God provide an amazingly effective strategy for power-maximizing civilization. It is notable that the development and expression of this motivational structure was coincident with the rapid rise of European power in the world. So potent was this ap-

---

9. So great can be the pressure to sacrifice the present for the future, that morality becomes equated with the delay of gratification. As the Victorian Samuel Butler wryly observed: "Morality turns on whether the pleasure precedes the pain or follows it. . . . Thus, it is immoral to get drunk because the headache comes after the drinking, but if the headache came first, and the drunkenness afterwards, it would be moral to get drunk" (Auden and Kronenberger, 1966, p. 367).

proach to life that it spread rapidly within Europe[10] and subsequently across the globe. It may be added that an ethic similar to that identified by Weber in Europe arose indigenously in the culture of Japan, the only non-Western society yet to achieve economic (and, by World War II, military) power comparable with that of the nations of the West (cf. Robert Bellah, *Tokugawa Religion.*) Material power is not the fruit of the material sphere alone. The soul of man, too, has been bent to fit the ever-improving designs of power's machinery.

This view of the Protestant ethic takes no side in the controversy over which element of culture determines the shape of the others. Whether the ethic Weber described created the conditions for capitalism or whether the capitalist economy wrought a religopsychological superstructure to its needs is not at issue here. (I suspect a model of mutual interaction is more enlightening than any determinist model.) The parable of the tribes, as a theory of selection, asserts that once a system like this emerged anywhere, for whatever reason, it would be likely to spread. This theory is concerned not so much with why a particular warping of human energies might be espoused by some small sect (such as the Calvinists) as with why a particular psychological structure among all those tried on this globe comes to play a major sociohistorical role.

As with aggression and the lust for power, the trend toward human bondage may appear to have been reversed by the progress of more enlightened societies. In the United States, for example, the Puritan ethic of hard work and saving has been deeply eroded by a new ethic of leisure and hedonistic consumption. However oppressive may have been the demands of earlier stages of civilization, contemporary civilization appears to offer liberation. The question of modern liberation is an important and multifaceted one. In this context, let me repeat that not every direction in which a particular society evolves proves ultimately to be compatible with its long-term survival. Whether the emergence of the consumption-oriented society is to be understood more as a free expression of the human desire for material pleasures or more as the consequence of capitalism's need at a particular stage to create the demand for its abundant production, there are now indications that competitive pressures from other societies are pushing American society back in the other direction. The decline of savings and investment over the past generation has contributed to an economic stagnation that perceptibly erodes national power. In Washington now (1983), foreign policy think

---

10. The spread of this ethic in Europe was due in part to the power it conferred in the struggle among nations, but in part also to its selection in another, purely economic system. See Chap. 7, "The Market as a Power System."

tanks pursue projects to study the problem of declining U.S. economic competitiveness. And after half a century of Keynesian policies focusing on the maintenance of adequate demand, a new (old) breed of "supply-side" economists is in office, proposing national economic policies designed to induce us to work harder and save more. Those whose orientation to the world centers on the need to prevail in competition are telling us it is again time to take on the yoke.[11]

The Human Cost of Production

An overriding theme of this chapter is that the unnatural demands of power make people suffer. In developing this theme, we have found the converse also to be true, that human suffering has itself fueled the engines of power maximization. The placing of civilized man under the yoke illustrates both themes.

The more obvious point is that civilization's demand for maximal productivity has gone painfully against the human grain. This can be inferred from the prominence throughout history of coercion in securing the cooperative participation of the masses of mankind in the productive regime. Hard labor has usually been forced labor. The coercive exploitation of the masses by ruling elites is as old as history. The ancient institution of slavery is one clear example of such coercion, but it has taken other more subtle forms. The peasantry of the great premodern civilizations were locked into exploitative social arrangements in which mere subsistence was the full reward for exhausting work. In much of the world, nothing fundamental has changed in this respect. In today's collectivized societies, workers are still compelled to devote to production that portion of their lives their rulers demand and to accept for their efforts that portion of the value of their production their rulers choose to give. Investment, like work, has been achieved by coercion. As we saw in our investigation of central control in chapter 3, rulers have forcibly expropriated surplus production for capital investment. The whip of the overseer is a sign that natural human inclinations are being overridden. When people are forced to act like ants, they suffer.

11. This is especially evident in the recent American turning to Japan as an economic model. As American enterprises are overtaken by Japanese competitors, a literature has emerged depicting Japan as "Number One," as the wave of the future, and as a model that Americans are exhorted to emulate. If the United States is to regain its economic supremacy, some argue, its educational system must become more like the Japanese, where a competitive process of extraordinary intensity dominates the lives of children even from nursery school years. American workers, among whom the Protestant ethic of labor as the purpose of life has withered considerably, must become more like their Japanese competitors, of whom Robert Ballon of Sophia University has written: "a Japanese does not work for a living, he considers work a way of life" (in Cook, 1981, p. 128).

But people do not always require the whip on their backs. The selection for power-generating productivity has seized also on certain psychological structures which substitute an inner compulsion for the compulsion of the taskmaster.

To mainstream thought in capitalist societies, it is self-evident why free men and women would strive to maximize their productivity in a system that gives material rewards corresponding with material contribution. According to this view, social production in free economies is maximized by harnessing man's natural unbounded desire for wealth. That we are thus driven reflects not perversion or rechanneling of human energies but their direct natural expression. The rational man of economics is naturally a hard worker, for through work he obtains the means to satisfy his naturally unlimited material wants. His capacity to delay gratification is a form of maturity which allows him to maximize his long-term utility: his sacrifice of present for future is repaid, with interest. Once societies have freed people to pursue wealth through work and savings, a great abundance is produced, increasing human welfare. It is more appropriate, therefore, to stress the substantial human benefits rather than the costs of maximizing production.

Material abundance, of course, has important beneficial aspects, especially in relation to the squalid poverty many peoples have had to endure. When we look closely at the history of the genesis and spread of capitalism, however, we find good reason to question this benign view of abundance as the natural fruit of free people pursuing happiness. Two propositions, regarded by the mainstream view as self-evident, warrant further scrutiny.

The first is that man has a natural urge to accumulate wealth. About this assumption, Max Weber himself observes that

> A man does not "by nature" wish to earn more and more money, but simply to live as he is accustomed to live and to earn as much as is necessary for that purpose. Wherever modern capitalism has begun its work of increasing the productivity of labour by increasing its intensity, it has encountered the immensely stubborn resistance of this leading trait of precapitalist labour. (1958, p. 60)

The history of modern colonialism, in fact, reveals that capitalist societies frequently used force to compel native peoples to act "naturally," to maximize their income through selling more of the time of their lives than necessity required.

A second and related proposition is that the amount of material wealth one commands is a reliable index of one's satisfaction in life. Thus our "standard of living" is measured by our per capita GNP. Yet this index,

181

however convenient for measurement and however well its assumptions serve the expansion of power systems, is no reliable measure of human well-being. Tocqueville's description of Americans, for example, comes to mind:

> In America I saw the freest and most enlightened men placed in the happiest circumstances that the world affords; it seemed to me as if a cloud habitually hung upon their brow, and I thought them serious and almost sad, even in their pleasures.
>
> The chief reason for this . . . [is that they] are forever brooding over advantages they do not possess.
>
> A native of the United States clings to this world's goods as if he were certain never to die; and he is so hasty in grasping at all within his reach that one would suppose he was constantly afraid of not living long enough to enjoy them. (1945, II, 144)

Affluence may insure the satisfaction of important human needs, but it is far from clear that the modern drive for wealth is best understood as a clean expression of human nature and the undistorted drive for fulfillment. In his study of the economies of primitive societies, the anthropologist Sahlins writes of "the original affluent societies": despite their low level of material consumption, hunter-gatherers felt they had enough, and they seemed happy. "For there are two possible courses to affluence. Want may be 'easily satisfied' either by producing much or desiring little" (1972, p. 1).

Much of the modern world has been shaped by internally motivated workers and savers. Although it is unclear how well their path leads to human fulfillment, it is quite manifest that it leads to power. As the psychological basis of productivity-maximizing economic man does not seem to have been handed down by nature, we may suspect that the selection for power has seized upon a perversion of human energies. Perhaps once again civilization has found in human distress a fuel for power's machine.

The first step in making the perfect driven worker is to make him despair of finding fulfillment in any other direction. It is easy to understand how one might follow Zinzendorf's injunction to "live for the sake of one's work" if one sees the alternatives as Zinzendorf does: "(I)f there is no work to do one suffers or goes to sleep" (quoted in Weber, 1958, p. 264n). At the foundation of the world-shaping Protestant ethic was an asceticism which, as Weber says, "turned all its force against one thing: the spontaneous enjoyment of life and all it had to offer" (ibid., p. 266). The economic man, who two centuries later could be turned out in the garb of enlightened rationality as the natural man, was in fact nurtured in a bitter war against all the natural desires of the human creature. It was a war against the body, a war against feeling, a war against the natural human craving for loving contact with other people. "Every purely emotional, that is not rationally motivated, personal relation of man to man easily fell in the Puritan, as in every aescetic ethic, under the suspicion of idolatry of the flesh" (ibid., p. 244). Blocked at every natural outlet, the energies of the human animal were "liberated" for productive enterprises: "(T)he sharp condemnation of idolatry of the flesh and of all dependence on personal relations to other men was bound unperceived to direct this energy into the field of objective (impersonal) activity" (ibid.). The way toward the inward goal of fulfillment being closed off, the energies come outward through work—with a vengeance. If we say, "Get thee behind me!" to our natural energies, they may be transformed into demonic forces that pursue us (see chap. 4 n. 3). Robert Bellah, in tracing an analogue in Japanese culture to the Protestant ethic described by Weber, quotes from Naito a passage reminiscent of the work-or-suffer image from Zinzendorf: "When engaged in meditation, all kinds of bad thoughts arise and do not stop for a minute, consequently our breasts are more disturbed than when we do our work in the world, and it is appropriate to compare it to tying a mountain monkey to a post" (1957, p. 119). As the Datsun commercial proclaims, "We are driven." If we are driven, it may be less pertinent to look at what we are driving toward than what we may be running from.

The preclusion of the natural payoff of inner satisfaction illuminates also the extraordinary willingness to delay gratification and, in general, to orient toward the future. In all these dimensions of human psychology under the yoke, what requires explanation is the degree of orientation. There is indeed a reality principle that the human being incorporates in the normal course of maturation. It is natural for the human adult, in contrast with the child, to be willing to bear responsibilities, to exercise prudent restraint on momentary impulse, and to take cognizance of future as well as immediate needs. But in the production-maximizers this development tendency has been carried to an extreme, as can be inferred from the judgments that representatives of these hyperproductive cultures frequently made concerning the adult members of conquered cultures: these adults appeared to their conquerers to be "just like children" in their spontaneity, their laziness (i.e., their orientation toward enjoyable activities), and their refusal to make the present moment entirely subservient to future advancement. (Elias, speaking of a different change in behavior required by the escalating demands of *The Civilizing Process,* says that "because emotions are here expressed in a manner that in our own world is generally observed only in children, we call these expressions and forms of behavior 'childish.'" [1978, pp. 200–201].) Although pru-

183

dence and planning are important, an incessant focus upon the future is inevitably incompatible with fulfillment. The present, after all, is the only time there is. The indefinite delay of gratification makes a certain sense, however, if psychic injuries have crippled one's capacity to experience pleasure. If undriven activity offers no pleasure (suffer or sleep), one's yearnings can be projected into a future that never arrives, either in another world (heaven) or in this one (return on investment). At the individual level, the image of the future serves to divert one's attention from the pain and emptiness of the present, while at the level of the power-maximizing system, a psychology like this serves to free the fruits of production from such irrelevant purposes as making people happy. ("You may labor to be rich for God, but not for the flesh and sin.")

This crippling helps explain also the unnatural obsession with wealth. For those whose socializing forces warred against "the spontaneous enjoyment of life and all it had to offer," the impossibility of genuine pleasure creates a demand for some symbol of it. Money is such a symbol, a promissory note the promise of which gives solace even if never redeemed. Money as a symbol of unrealizable pleasure can become an end in itself.[12] The confusion of ends and means—one lives to work—is the result of the inabilty to pursue the naturally joyful ends of human life. "Time is money," says Ben Franklin, the apostle of capitalism, neatly revealing the subordination of the real to the symbolic, of ends (the time of one's life) to means. The earning of more and more money, writes Weber, "is thought of so purely as an end in itself, that from the point of view of the happiness of, or utility to, the single individual, it appears entirely transcendental and absolutely irrational. . . . Economic acquisition is no longer subordinated to man as the means of the satisfaction of his material needs" (1958, p. 53). Weber goes on to say that this apparently irrational reversal of "what we should call the natural relationship" is as "definitely a leading principle of capitalism as it is foreign to all peoples not under capitalistic influence" (ibid). The irrational reversal may be explicable at the psychological level in terms of the pathology of the emotionally injured creature. We can understand why those who have embodied this unnatural relationship have played so prominent a role at the macrohistorical level once we grasp that the selection for power has favored not the delay of gratification but its indefinite postponement, in fact, its cancellation. A power-maximizing society can utilize human

12. Schopenhauer described money as "human happiness in the abstract." The person unable to enjoy happiness in the concrete, then, "devotes himself utterly to money" (quoted in Auden, 1970, p. 266).

beings who will desperately pursue what for them is but a symbol of unattainable fulfillment but what for the society is real capital for the expansion of productive power.

Again we see that in the unnatural world where power reigns, it is not the healthy who inherit, or, rather, it is not they whose ways become the cultural inheritance of humankind.

As the case of Franklin shows, the ethic could survive the dropping away of the original religious garments woven of God's injunctions and man's sins. A secular ethic can suffice to generate secular power. If by now that ethic has eroded without a corresponding drop in wealth and power, that does not mean that a world ruled by power has grown safe for pleasure-seekers. McClelland's studies of the "achieving society" demonstrate a lag of about fifty years between the rise and fall of the motivational structures that foster economic growth and the subsequent rise and fall of growth rates. In power, as in other things, the generation of people who "go now, pay later" may merely be living high off the capital their driven forebears accumulated.

Let us consider one final way the selection for power not only injures people but even contrives ways to make the injuries useful. To outfit human beings to serve as components of power's machine, it furthers power to increase the creature's activation level.

The productive apparatus will achieve more if the human machine can be revved up. It has frequently been observed that advancing civilization entails a more rapid pace of living, and this activation of the organism may be the basis of that quickened tempo. Philip Slater, in his critique of American society, *The Pursuit of Loneliness,* refers to a remark by Konrad Lorenz that "in all organisms, locomotion is increased by a bad environment" (1970, p. 82). Slater proceeds to conjecture that instinctual frustration by a civilized society may serve to increase people's locomotion. Not all kinds of suffering have this activating effect (just as not all people who have renounced pleasure have channeled their energies into productive work). But selection may favor those bad environments that have this effect. R. Lynn reports the general finding in "Anxiety and Economic Growth" that the level of anxiety among a nation's people is highly correlated with its rate of growth. Again, power-maximizing civilization capitalizes on the very injuries it inflicts, the way throwing an irritating grain of sand into the tender part of an oyster can induce it to make a pearl.

The selection for power turns human life inside out. Man becomes mere means to the systems that surround him. Man the worker becomes part of the productive machine. The comic image of Chaplin in *Modern*

185

Times comes to mind. Siegfried Giedion's *Mechanization Takes Command* chronicles the subordination of the living body to the mechanical apparatus of production. Biological time gives way to clockwork time—in toilet training or in factory discipline. Of discipline, Weber writes that "the psychophysical apparatus of man is completely adjusted to the demands of the outer world." As the selection for power sacrifices inner fulfillment for production, the inner world is shut down. Means become ends, master becomes servant.

> The horseman serves the horse,
> The neatherd serves the neat,
> The merchant serves his purse,
> The eater serves his meat;
> 'Tis the day of the chattel,
> Web to weave, and corn to grind;
> Things are in the saddle,
> And ride mankind.
>   (Ralph Waldo Emerson, "Ode" inscribed to W. H. Channing, 1950, p. 770)

Saddle, yoke: man becomes a beast of burden. The cornucopia we have produced is not altogther what it seems.

Afterword: The Fighting Machine

This subordination of the internal process to the external demand, which constitutes the essence of discipline, serves power in the military as well as the economic spheres. Indeed, Weber says that it was in the fire of war-making that the iron discipline of civilized men was forged: "The discipline of the army gives birth to all discipline. . . . No special proof is necessary to show that military discipline is the ideal model for the modern capitalist factory, as it was for the ancient plantation" (in Gerth and Mills, 1958, p. 261). Mechanization perhaps first took command in the building of the fighting machine. Earlier in this chapter in "Fighting Mad," I discussed the provocation in man of the aggressive spirit, but we also know from chapter 3 the indispensability of organization as a component in the maximization of competitive power. The energy of rage is important but insufficient; it must be disciplined by subordination to the larger apparatus. Writes Robert Bigelow: "Human wars are not won entirely by blind ferocity in the individual soldiers. Romans were probably no more ferocious, as individuals, than Carthaginians or Gauls. But Roman legions were not disorganized agglomerations of ferocious brutes; the legionnaires co-operated, often with spine-chilling effectiveness. Such cooperation required great emotional restraint . . ." (1969, pp. 23–24).

186

As inner restraint serves outward power, selection favors the culture of discipline.[13] Weber goes through a long list of military victories determined by superior discipline, and concludes it thus:

> Cromwell's victories—despite the fierce bravery of the Cavaliers—were due to sober and rational Puritan discipline. His "Ironsides"—the 'men of conscience'—trotted forward in firmly closed formation, at the same time calmly firing, and then thrusting, brought about a successful attack. . . . Gun powder and all the war techniques associated with it became significant only with the existence of discipline. (in Gerth and Mills, 1958, pp. 256–257)

Power has been increased by a kind of metallurgy that disciplines human energies into an iron resolve. Flesh and blood become part of power's machine.

5.   The War Within: Moral Internalization and the Social Order

Civilization, it was said in chapter 2, has made two great leaps in power. I have explored three aspects of the psychological transformation demanded by the first leap, the initial rise of civilization. The original transition from primitive to civilized society required man to become a warrior, a member of a dominance hierarchy, and a drone for productive labor. In the midst of my discussion of man the worker, I began to look at the psychological innovations of the second, the modern leap of power. Now, and in the following discussion of the power of reason, I continue this investigation of the psychological bases of modern power.

The best beast of burden is the one who is his own master. The same is true for the citizen. As the economically most productive nations have been those whose workers have internalized the ethic of productivity, so also does a social and political order based on internalization have great advantages. That order is a democratic one. The democratic way of life, as Zevedei Barbu observes, presupposes that the individual introjects social norms "so as to form in him, apart from the habit of conforming,

---

13. Discipline, according to Bernard Lewis, was at the heart of Islam's role in the great Arab conquests that followed the beginnings of that religion. Religion was important, he says, not in motivating the expansion so much as in effecting "a temporary psychological change" in a people "who were naturally excitable and temperamental, unaccustomed to any sort of discipline, willing to be persuaded but never to be commanded." Thus Islam, which means "submission" to the will of God, increased the power of its earliest adherents by making them "more amenable to control," disciplined parts of a fighting machine (1966, p. 56). Said Muhammad: "God loves those who fight in His belah in a line, as if they were a strongly constructed building" (quoted in Aho, 1981, p. 158).

the disposition towards voluntary action in the interest of his community" (1956, p. 48). The competitive advantages of democratic societies are several. If we investigate which among modern nations have been the most free from internal political disruption, the historically most democratic nations (e.g., Great Britain and the United States) are prominent on the list. Such stability protects nations from external predations and frees the human energies of the nation for productive purposes. Moreover, a sociopolitical system that can have the discipline of a more autocratic regime without its corruption and incompetence has distinct competitive advantages (see chap. 3). These factors help account for the fact that among the most prosperous and powerful societies of the modern world, a large proportion are democratic.

The survival of Western democracies appears to be one instance where the selection for power has served mankind as well. If moral internalization serves power maximation, it also grants people the blessings of liberty. After millennia of tyranny and exploitation, this is no small boon. Indeed, the benefits of living in a free society are enormous. But democratic society imposes costs as well, and the worst of these costs are hidden. Just as escape from the whip of the taskmaster entailed scars on the inside, so also with the liberation from the tyrant. As capitalism has psychological costs, so does democracy. We might profitably begin by looking at how those two systems—the economic and the political—are related.

It is not new to observe that democracy and capitalism have tended to occur together. The Marxist way of understanding this link does not seem the most enlightening. The connection may not be so much that democracy is the best political tool for protecting the interests of capitalism's dominant class (nor, as the conservatives would have it, that economic liberty is the prerequisite for political liberty). More important may be that both the economic and the political system are made possible by a particular kind of psychological structure.

One sign of this bond of the spirit is the correlation of both systems with Protestantism. The "Protestant Ethic and the Spirit of Democracy" remains to be written, but just as capitalism arose in Protestant nations and among Protestant minorities elsewhere, so also has the impetus behind the rise of modern democracy come largely from Protestants. The work ethic is but part of a more general picture of the emergence of a self-governing individual, of a person who imposes upon himself the discipline of civilized life. Protestantism, writes B. Brown, marks "a whole new stage in the complicated process of civilizational development by which compulsion has been progressively internalized in the form of inner constraints. . . . (I)t involved the creation of a 'performance principle' so firmly anchored in the mental structure of the individual that it no longer needed to be reimposed continually from without" (1973, pp. 87–88). Similarly, Henri Lefevre compares Protestantism with Catholicism, and declares that the former "performed the repressive function of religion with greater subtlety; God and reason were the portion of each individual, everyone was his own mentor, responsible for the repression of his desires, the control of his instincts" (quoted in ibid., p. 88). I have explored here some of the costs of an internalized "performance principle" wholly devoted to work, and of the "repression of desires" necessary for voluntary asceticism. But what are the costs of democracy? It is not so evident that a democratic order demands such stringent sacrifices. Indeed, Barbu presents a most sanguine portrait of the democratic man—liberated, integrated, the most internally harmonious there is. Is all the pain of self-government confined to the domain of work? Of self-governing people Barbu writes in a chapter entitled "Democratic Personality," "there is no inner conflict and repression in their minds" (1956, p. 187). Should we conclude that the maintenance of social order can be conflict-free?

Alas, no. The eruption of civilization with its unnatural demands upon its human members precludes that happy option. Our societies—so inhuman in scale, so often inhumane in their values, in so many ways hostile to our impulses and needs—can function only if they enforce upon us one way or another their burdensome demands. If a democratic society were so inexpensively bought, why have so few peoples proved capable of sustaining it? Are we to resort to calling the adults of other cultures "immature"? Woodrow Wilson justified the American use of force in the Philippines: the discipline of democracy, he indicated, does not come cheap. In view of this, we may regard Barbu's felicitous portrait as an example of what Dennis Wrong has called the "oversocialized" view of man in sociology (in Smelser and Smelser, 1963). This is a tendency to deny the tremendous conflict between the demands of civilized society and the natural inclinations of the individual. Even while using Freud's language, Barbu does not confront this essential Freudian insight.

To enjoy liberty, Wilson said, a people "must first take the discipline of law, must first love order and instinctually yield to it." By instinctual, he must mean habitual or automatic. If, indeed, it were an instinct, democracy would not be so rare a growth, so difficult to transplant, and so high in price. The order we must love is not our natural order. How much this civilized order we must embrace goes against our inborn nature we can, once more, infer from the original need for force to secure our obedience. Barbu himself observed that "Where liberal institutions have been successful they seem to have been dependent upon some past discipline maintained by coercive authority" (1956, p. 50). He uses for illustration the "tyrannical laws" of Puritan America which helped form in the individual's mind an inner authority. The demands of civilization are quite alien to our natures and can be pounded into human flesh only with considerable force and at the cost of much pain. This insight is to be found in Nietzsche's *Genealogy of Morals*. Although Nietzsche's view of man in the wild seems warped—his rage and lust for power seem like the injured zoo animal driven wild—he saw clearly the price man paid in being tamed for civilization. The severity of the penal codes of premodern societies, he says, gives us some idea how difficult it was "to drive into these slaves of momentary whims and desires" the principles of order required by their societies. After reviewing the grisly punishments of early European civilization, he goes on to say:

> By such methods, the individual was finally taught to remember five or six "I won'ts" which entitled him to participate in the benefits of society; and indeed, with the aid of this sort of memory, people eventually "came to their senses." What an enormous price man had to pay for reason, seriousness, control over his emotions—those grand human prerogatives and cultural showpieces! How much blood and horror lies behind all "good things." (1956, p. 194)

The liberty of democratic society is another of those "good things" that we enjoy as a legacy of violence and coercion. Wilson's reflections on democracy, we may recall, were made in support of a very bloody American campaign to control the Filipinos. This model of the requirements for internalization is, of course, quite incomplete, for not all coercive orders seem to lead to the kind of internalization that over the generations makes an uncoercive democratic system possible. But the essential connection is made: that democratic self-control brings within the individual a conflict which, when it was manifest in the external world, was brutal. The end of the coercive regime does not mark the end of the war against human nature. The war has simply moved within. "You don't need the police," the Russian said to the Englishman, "because you all have mental straitjackets."

I should not, however, overstate the pathology and pain of the democratic personality structure. The democratic order requires of its citizens a set of virtues—a capacity for compromise, a degree of geniality and empathy in interpersonal dealings, a sense of responsibility—of which the most disturbed and tormented psyches would be incapable. A recognition that democracy demands a reasonably well-ordered psyche and that this order requires at least a degree of internal harmony, should be kept in mind to balance the following discussion of the pain that internalization entails.

The battle that had raged outside is brought within, allowing peace between the individual and his society but at the cost of painfully warping his psychological structure. Although this process occurs to some degree in all societies, its furthest development has been perhaps among the bourgeois "guilt" cultures of modern Europe and America. Elias's *The Civilizing Process: A History of Manners* presents a fascinating chronicle of the escalation and internalization of moral demands during the rise of modern Western civilization. He shows that over the past half millennium, ever-higher demands were placed upon an ever-higher proportion of the populace to control and conceal their passions, instincts, and bodily functions. As the moral demands became stricter, they changed in nature from an *inter*personal code designed for showing respect to others (especially one's social superiors) to an *intra*personal one: "Now habits are condemned more and more as such, not in regard to others. In this way, socially undesirable impulses or inclinations are more radically repressed. They are associated with embarrassment, fear, shame, or guilt, even when one is alone" (1978, p. 150). "This way of consolidating habits," Elias says, gained "predominance with the rise of the middle classes." Again we see that the same social transformation that lessened coercion and inequality at the social level required that the individual more radically repress himself. All these striking developments of the powerful civilization of the West form part of a cultural whole. It is, moreover, no coincidence—a point observed also by Elias—that out of the same cultural environment arose also a brilliant psychological theory focusing on the burden of intrapsychic conflict: psychoanalysis.

For internalization to characterize a social order, it must characterize the socialization process of its individual members. For insight into this process, we can turn to Otto Fenichel's *The Psychoanalytic Theory of Neurosis*, perhaps the clearest comprehensive statement of Freudian theory. The very image of internalization of conflict that I say is the foundation of the democratic social order Fenichel identifies as the root of neurosis: "An original conflict between the id and the external world must first have been transformed into a conflict between the id and the ego before a neurotic conflict can develop" (1945, p. 130). Neurosis occurs only because the external world is hostile to natural human impulses. Although the motives for neurotic defenses are "rooted in external influences," it is the internalization of the conflict that brings about repression: "(T)he external world as such cannot repress. It can only compel the ego to develop repressing forces" (ibid.). The external world thus "compels" the psyche to bring its enemy within, to establish "an intrapsychic institution that represents and anticipates the external world" (ibid.). In order to safeguard itself against painful conflicts with the surrounding world upon

191

which it depends for love and life, the psyche turns against itself: "Through the influence of the external world instinctual impulses have been transformed into anti-instinctual impulses" (ibid., p. 103). The hostile demands of the outside world turn man into his own enemy.

The human animal becomes the "sick animal" (Nietzsche's phrase) because of the unnatural demands made upon it. Psychoanalytic theory does not, of course, equate anti-instinctual demands with unnatural demands. The conflict between the id and the internalized superego is not, according to psychoanalysis, the least bit unnatural. As all human social life requires the control of impulse, the internalization of a moral authority is a natural part of human development. This is no doubt correct— to a degree. It is part of man's nature to have unprecedented latitude from rigid instinctual programming. This space has been opened up, as it were, to provide room for culture. Culture can give the species flexibility, yet within any given culture that flexibility cannot be allowed to become anarchy. To prevent the unprecedented human freedom from becoming destructive within the social order, each culture must bridge the gap in behavioral regulation by instilling a set of moral injunctions. It is entirely credible, therefore, to maintain, as does C. H. Waddington in *The Ethical Animal,* that the human creature is structured to incorporate a moral authority as he matures. The superego *is* part of man's natural psychic equipment. To have an internal battle between impulse and control is probably a natural part of the human condition. But, as before, it is a matter of how severe are the controls that are required, and thus how savage and painful is the war within. A degree of repression may be part of the price of being human, but what Marcuse calls "surplus repression" is a special surcharge by which man is taxed by civilization. While any human reality will require self-control, only the unnatural reality of an antihuman society demands controls so severe that they sicken. It is out of Victorian Europe that comes a theory of neurosis based on the fundamental hostility of the external world to human nature.

In such an unnatural world, the socialization process is an injurious mix of the natural and the unnatural. The parents, whose natural relationship to the child is probably the most altruistic and loving of human bonds, are also the agents of an unnatural society hostile to what the child is and wishes to become. As agents of social demands, and as products themselves of a painful socialization process, the parents employ their natural bond to effect an unnatural psychic development. Writes Fenichel: "The instinctual attitudes of the children toward their parents are turned into forces hostile to the instincts by an introjection of the parents" (1945, p. 103). The introjection of the parents creates the superego, the parent within. The parents supply the external forces in conflict with the id, and these forces are internalized. As at the macrolevel, internalization of the authority may require coercive restraints, but coercion alone does not assure internalization. A merely punishing parent may get obedience without ever having his voice internalized by the child. "A severe conscience," Freud said, "arises from the joint operation of two factors: the frustration of instinct, which unleashes aggressiveness, and the experience of being loved, which turns the aggressiveness inwards and hands it over to the superego" (1961, p. 77n). Again, the natural and unnatural mix into a harsh potion. The natural love of parents prevents rebellion. Useful too is the high level of frustration produced by the unnaturally harsh demands of civilized society. In "Fighting Mad," we saw how a person's impulse toward aggression generated by frustration can be channeled outward to make man a fighter for the very society that frustrates him. It can also be usefully turned inward to strengthen those same unnatural moral demands that provoked it. "It is remarkable that the more a man checks his aggressive tendencies towards others the more tyrannical, that is aggressive, he becomes in his ego-ideal" (Freud, quoted in Sampson, 1966, p. 36). The frustrated rage that the superego prevents from outward expression then becomes part of the superego's own arsenal for war against the id. The harsher the demands the more the frustration, and the more the frustration the harsher the internalized voice of those demands. Man is like an animal in a trap; the more he struggles, the deeper bite the trap's jaws into his flesh.

By bringing the voice of the enemy within, one can live at peace with the world around. The parents are pleased by the good behavior. One can be trusted. One has come to love the discipline and order that tyrants once imposed by the sword, and one becomes self-governing. There is peace. But, says Freud, the price of peace is pain. "Originally, renunciation of instinct was the result of fear of an external authority." In this situation, good behavior was enough to secure peace. "But with fear of the superego the case is different. Here, instinctual renunciation is not enough, for the wish persists and cannot be concealed from the superego. Thus, in spite of the renunciation that has been made, a sense of guilt comes about" (1961, p. 74). In the life within the mind, the wish is as good as the deed. Since the wish is part of human nature, like human nature it is there to stay. The war within, therefore, never ceases. The internal regime adds to the burden of continuous frustration the further burden of continuous guilt. The perpetual condition of guilt may be useful for power-maximizing systems, making human beings energized and driven creatures. But in terms of human fulfillment, the regime of guilt has real costs.

Between the mental straitjacket of internalization and the external brutality of the secret police, I have no trouble choosing. The parable of the tribes (and plain common sense) clearly points out the special dangers of external relations of dominance. Moreover, a society of self-governing people seems best able to ameliorate the harshness of civilization's demands, to choose where possible to allow humane values to triumph over those of power. But the social evolutionary problem of power's reign remains, and thus the war between inhumane demands and human nature remains also. Here is Freud's striking image of the internalized control over aggressive impulses: "Civilization, therefore, obtains mastery over the individual's dangerous desire for aggression by weakening and disarming it and by setting up an agency within him to watch over it, like a garrison in a conquered city" (1961, pp. 70–71). The regime of internalization may be the more benign, but it remains an image of the rule of power. One of its faces is liberty, a partial truce between man and civilized society. The other is the garrison within the permanent conquest by the forces of culture over natural impulse.

6.   Unreasonable Reason

The power of a people is determined by how they fight and work and rule themselves. And also by how they think.

The Powers of Reason

Said Themistocles to his fellow Athenians: "When men counsel reasonably, reasonable success ensues; but when in their counsels they reject reason, God does not choose to follow the wanderings of human fancies" (Herodotus, 1928, p. 448). God's preference, we find again, parallels the selection for power. Reason is the mode of thought that leads to power.

There is little so difficult for human thought to describe as itself. We sense that our minds are not all of one piece, but cannot easily identify what the different pieces are. The same mind that rationally plans action in the world by day, employs by night a very different logic and language to compose the strange inner world of dreams. How many different modes of thought are fundamental to our nature? Freud proposed a dichotomy between primary process (as in dreams) and secondary process (as in conscious rational thought). This dichotomy does not imply that our psychic life is tidily compartmentalized, for if Freud proved nothing else he proved how powerful a role the emotional logic of the dream plays even in our waking lives. Illuminating the mystery of our minds remains most difficult, for we see our thought processes as through a glass darkly.

Through the ages, one identifiable mode of thought has been called reason. Reason is akin to, if not synonymous with, Freud's secondary process. As ubiquitous as the term is, it is difficult to define. We might begin by saying that reason employs a framework of logic to manipulate intellectually a set of relationships in a way that is interpersonally persuasive and internally consistent. The statements of reason can be made (fairly) clear in meaning and can be communicated from one person to another with minimal misunderstanding. The processes of rational thought are subject to systematic and even mechanical application. For all these reasons, the mode of reason is ideally suited to the construction and continuous elaboration of great cultural systems of understanding: its clarity makes each statement useful as a basis for further statements; its communicability and the interpersonally valid nature of its logic allow the systems based on reason to be built cooperatively by many minds; and the susceptibility to systematic application allows cumulative elaboration through time, always building upon what has gone before.

Part of the power of reason lies in its public, objective nature. Its contributions are like building blocks capable of being absorbed into mighty edifices. The rational is thus distinguished from the mythopoetic faculty (akin to primary process). No matter how great a poem is, it is not so structured as to make it suitable for intellectual system building. Newton could stand on the shoulders of giants (and Einstein in turn on Newton's), but who has stood on Shakespeare's? Bricks may be no better than roses, but they are better for monumental works.

This conduciveness of reason to constructing monumental public works may be a necessary basis for explaining reason's power but it is not a sufficient one. Another element is missing from the picture. All the attributes of the rational mode described above apply to mathematics, which is perhaps the epitome of the operation of reason. Mathematics, however, is pure form. It is a tautology built upon precise definitions whose implications are systematically developed. If human logic were merely tautology, mathematics would be a world wholly apart. In fact, however, mathematics is the "queen of the sciences," which is testimony to the fact that the rational processes of the human mind correspond to the structure of the world of nature. The logic of reason is an objective logic. The relationships it manipulates inhere in the objects of the external world. Compare $E = mc^2$ with "My love is like a red, red rose." Each employs a kind of logic to state an equivalence. But the relationship in Burns's formulation has a validity inseparable from the realm of the poet's own experience, whereas Einstein has said something objectively valid, regardless of human experience.

In the correspondence of reason with (many of) the processes of the objective world we find an instance of a truth underlying the theory of natural values. In chapter 4 it was argued that the structure of a creature is a projection of the world it evolved in. The structures that human rationality naturally builds are not merely of the mind. As Waddington has written: "We have a mind capable of grasping logical structures because the universe exhibits regularities which make logical thinking a useful activity" (quoted in Hardy, 1965, p. 49). The human mind at play can create mathematics, but mathematics can work in the world. To bring rational logic and system to the observation of the empirical world opens the path to objective truth. The mathematical structure of scientific thought goes beyond disembodied tautology and places the objective world within man's cognitive grasp.

What man grasps he can move. Thus the explosion of power in the modern era was largely detonated by the explosive growth of modern science. Kuznets's account of the unprecedented global transformations of culture wrought by modern economic growth emphasizes the importance of this one factor (1974, p. 249). Modern economic power is not the fruit so much of harder work as of work given greater leverage by the technology modern science has created. Similarly, in the military sphere, it is less the spirit of the fighters than the rational-scientific powers of the weapons builders that has magnified the destructive powers of modern nations. (If the Apache do not rule Arizona today, it is not for want of warrior spirit when they encountered the whites.) It is the creature who reasons, not the lion or the shark, that dominates the earth.[14]

The movement of history has been toward the rationalization of human consciousness. Reason is undoubtedly part of human nature and of human life everywhere. But in modern civilization reason has become *the* cognitive mode. This shift in the balance of the human psyche toward the supremacy of the rational was inaugurated by the rise of modern Western civilization. Walter Weisskopf writes: "The role . . . which reason and rationality play, the importance attributed to it, and the degree to which other aspects of existence and other faculties of the mind are recognized or neglected, vary considerably from culture to culture and from period to period. Modern Western civilization is characterized by

14. In today's world, therefore, the cultivation of scientific rationality is required to feed the systems of power. When scientific and mathematical education declines, as it has recently in the United States, alarm bells go off. The issue, according to Iszak Wirzup, a University of Chicago mathematician who monitors Soviet-bloc science and mathematics education, "comes down simply to the need to develop a qualified workforce for industrial and military needs" (quoted in *The Economist*, Oct. 10, 1981, p. 104).

a prevalence of rationalism" (1955, p. 224). This rationalization of human life, once germinated in the West, has spread to become an evident trend of social evolution. The effort "to win the world over to an exclusively science-based reality principle" Theodore Roszak describes as "Western society's most distinctive cultural project over the last three centuries" (1981, p. 57). The parable of the tribes helps explain the extent to which this project to rationalize human consciousness has been successful.

Reason confers power, and in recent centuries those societies most heavily armed with reason's power have been able to spread their ways at the expense of other cultures with a different cognitive orientation. History, like God, did not choose to follow men's fancies, those mytho-poetic ways of relating to the world that the Enlightenment regarded as atavistic superstition. It was the hope of the Enlightenment that reason might come to rule the world. The light of reason would be compellingly attractive to those in darkness. Reason has indeed proved "compelling," but in a sense unintended by the philosophers. Rationality has prevailed through the might of rational organization and science. The rule of modern reason is a fiefdom within the greater realm of power.

Is It Progress?

The rule of reason, whatever its cause, sounds like good news. Many of the great thinkers of earlier ages exhorted their fellow men to let the faculty of reason govern. Whether or not that vision of the ideal man is a worthy one, however, the "rationality" of modern civilization is not identical with that espoused by the philosophers. Our "reason" today is a purely technical faculty, a "value-free" mode of manipulating infor-mation and relationships. It is severed from the fundamental commit-ment to certain basic values that the philosophers of old regarded as inseparable from reason. As late as the seventeenth and eighteenth cen-turies, the concept of reason retained a substantial content. To the rational philosophers of that time, "ideas such as justice, equality, happiness and democracy and freedom were based on reason, natural law, and consid-ered self-evident *truth*" (Weisskopf, 1971, p. 39). The "rationalization" of the world since then, as Weber has pointed out, has lacked this substantive dimension. Without this element to add human meaning to logical clarity, all that remained was "functional" rationality, that is, certain logical and scientific principles of organization growing increasingly dominant over government and industry, over every aspect of life (cf. Harrington, 1965, p. 164). The skeleton of the ancient "reason" remained without its flesh.

The power of reason, I said, derives from the mastery it confers over the objective world. The "reason" of the ancients could also act as a check on power, inextricably connected as it was with human values.[15] Modern functional rationality thus casts off the intrusive baggage of values while retaining the powerful tools of logical objectivity.

Still, we do gain a certain clarity of vision, do we not? Does not rationality, freed from the intrusions of the inner man, grasp all the better the nature of reality? We might approach these questions through an idea from Jean Piaget, a brilliant psychologist whose lifework focused on the development of the rational faculties of the human mind. He distinguishes between realism (a child's way of looking at the world) and objectivity. Objectivity, he writes;

> consists in so fully realizing the countless intrusions of the self in everyday thought and the countless illusions which result—illusions of sense, language, point of view, etc.—that the preliminary step to every judgment is to the effort to exclude the intrusive self. Realism, on the contrary, consists in ignoring the existence of self and thence regarding one's own perspective as immediately objective and absolute . . . it values the entire content of consciousness on a single plane in which ostensible realities and unconscious interventions of the self are inextricably mixed. (quoted in Silberg, 1967, p. 15)

Objectivity like this certainly seems a great step forward. Is that what modern objective rationality has given us? Piaget's statement conveys his own belief in the superiority of objective rationality, and in so doing it opens two doors for our critical scrutiny.

Consider first the "countless illusions" that result from the intrusions of the self. The preliminary step to every judgment, he tells us, is to exclude the self. One thinks also of Freud's handling of religion in *The Future of an Illusion*. The Enlightenment marches on with its banner proclaiming a single kind of truth—a rational and objective one. But how enlightened *is* the vision illuminated only from the outside? Life is experienced inwardly, even if it is lived also in the objective world. The same evolutionary processes that gave us reason gave us also the profound and complex mythopoetic faculties. Does this more subjective mode produce only illusions? Are we to conclude that the nature that gave us the clear light of reason gave us only a distorting mirror when it made us also to be dreamers?

The mythopoetic mode of thought apprehends an important reality. It is the means by which we apprehend and express the reality of our experience. An important contribution of C. G. Jung was to show that

---

15. See, however n. 18, below.

in dreams are to be found not just pathology and obfuscation but a profound and wise organic intelligence that gives us vision and guidance. The language of this intelligence may not well serve to master the world, but it does provide a meaningful vision of our lives. Robert Bellah, in his notable essay "Between Religion and Social Science," writes: "The canons of empirical science apply primarily to symbols that attempt to express the nature of objects, but there are nonobjective symbols that express the feelings, values, and hopes of subjects, or that organize and regulate the flow of interaction between subjects and objects. . . . These symbols, too, express reality and are not reducible to empirical propositions" (p. 252). Excluding the self may often be very useful, but it is essential also that we are open to judgments that emerge from it. Subjectivity may at times contribute to confusions and illusions, but a solely objective view of the world is no vision. This argument is not a case for the supremacy of the irrational, but for the integration of our humanity.[16]

Nature has given us intellectually a kind of stereoptical view of the world. To look only out of one side is to discard the capacity for depth. If we lose sight of ourselves, our mastery of the world will avail us little. "What is a man profited, if he shall gain the whole world, and lose his own soul?" (Matthew 16:26).

If the modern view underestimates the potential of "realism" for insight, so also can it overestimate the clarity of objectivity at least in its modern form. The cult of objectivity hardly "fully realizes" the intrusions of the self. It is not awareness of the self it manifests but fear and ignorance. In psychology, scientism gave us behaviorism which, at its origin, dismissed any reference to internal experience. Clifford Geertz has written of the abhorrence in some social scientific circles of any mention of subjective or mentalistic factors; appeal to such factors, he says, "is castigated as a lamentable failure of scientific nerve" (in Scher, 1962, p. 714). Modern rationalism seems at times bent on excising the human from our vision of the world. In modern parlance, "myth" has become synonymous with "false belief," and the "mystical" with the unreal.

But as elsewhere, the psyche strains against unnatural distortions. As Horace said,

> Naturam expellas furca, tamen usque recurret.
>   If you drive nature out with a pitchfork, she will soon find a way back.
> (Epistles I.x.24)

---

16. "Our course," writes Roszak (1981, p. 59), "is not to strengthen half the dichotomy against the other half, because *the dichotomy is the problem*."
"May God us keep," wrote Blake, "From Single vision & Newton's sleep."

Jungian psychology has shown that when vital aspects of the personality are ignored or misunderstood, they can turn destructive. What we attempt to disown can end up possessing us. Writes Bellah in *Beyond Belief*:

> Just those who feel they are most rational and pragmatic, and most fully objective in their assessment of reality, are most in the power of deep unconscious fantasies. Whole nations in this century have blindly acted out dark myths of destruction all the while imagining their actions dictated by external necessity. (1970, p. 254)

Our natures are not of clay but of spring steel. We may be bent to the ways of power, but not without strain. Nature comes back with a pitchfork of her own. Again, Bellah: "Concentrating so heavily on the mastery of objects, we have too long neglected what Anaïs Nin calls the 'Cities of the Interior,' and everywhere these neglected cities are in revolt" (ibid., p. 253). A lopsided vision of the world is not a clear one. It is not even safe.

Let us look briefly into some of the costs of this hypertrophy of rationalism.

The Loss of Meaning and Value

According to the theory of natural value, if nothing in the universe had feelings, nothing would matter. Similarly, for any human being out of contact with his feelings, everything is a matter of indifference. Life for him is empty, without meaning. Such an "existential vacuum," writes Viktor Frankl, "is epidemic in the modern world." Frankl, the author of *Man's Search for Meaning*, says that more and more people are "complaining of an inner emptiness, a sense of total and ultimate meaninglessness in their lives" (in Koestler and Smythies, 1970, p. 399).

The modern overemphasis on functional rationality may play a role in this loss of meaning. The experience of meaning requires connection between thought and feeling, between perception and passion. Functional rationality is "disembodied" thought; passions, meanwhile, are rooted in the body. The light of rational thought is a cool light, in contrast with the warm charge of feeling with which the thought of myth and dream is imbued. The gift of reason is man's crowning glory, but it threatens also a fatal disconnection of man from himself. Physically, man is indeed crowned with a recently mushroomed neocortex, that most advanced part of the brain that gives us our special intellectual powers. According to Paul MacLean, it is not the neocortex but the more primitive mammalian part of the brain that is integrated with the affective dimension of our experience. Perhaps, he says, the neocortex has developed with such extraordinary speed (as biological evolution goes) that its connections with the rest of our psychic apparatus are not very richly developed. While recognizing how much the human brain and consciousness remain a mystery, we might conjecture that this link between our cognitive powers and our full experience as human animals—if it is so tenuous—is an area of vulnerability in our inherent constitution. Like a pipeline lying exposed crossing the desert, this frail connection can allow outside forces to disrupt the economy of human energies. Rationalized modern civilization has been an external force of this kind. Applying pressure against our weak link, civilization breaks our potent cognitive equipment away from our intractable humanity. This connection ruptured, we become alienated from ourselves; our moorings severed, we float freely with the currents around us.

This loss of meaning, this alienation, is one side of the coin. The loss of values is the other. If meaning is the felt valuation we give to our own experience, values are the principles of meaning we apply to our world generally. Although values can be held as intellectual principles, unless they are well integrated with the person's experience of meaning they will lack the force to guide his conduct in the world. Most people have some knowledge about right and wrong, but "knowing" is a matter of many levels. The modern "explosion" of objective knowledge may be less important than the modern disintegration of the subjective knower. Disembodied knowledge has no footing and thus no leverage to move human beings. Knowledge that matters in human terms must be integrated with the whole human being. A psychotherapist may have to wait months or years to tell a person what might have been said in the first meeting. A Zen master could tell his disciples the "answer" to a Zen koan. But an intellectualized understanding of one's character or of a religious insight is worthless unless it grows out of one's organic experience. Civilized people may be trained to pass an "objective test" with flying colors, yet remain ignorant at the fundamental level. Along the path of intelligence, S. Ferenczi has said, "which is a function of the ego, really nothing in the way of conviction can occur" (quoted in Lowen, 1958, p. 20). A civilization of people whose intelligence is but poorly connected with their full humanity is likely therefore to lack conviction. When reason loses its "substantive" content, "rational" people can pursue unreasonable purposes. Nothing matters, so anything goes.

Alienation within allows evil without. Camus's Stranger is a man whose disconnection from his own and all humanity is so extreme that the death of his own mother does not move him, nor does his murder of another man. When civilization teaches us to become "strangers" to ourselves, the way is cleared for the doctrine of value neutrality. In many domains of modern life, we are taught that it is unnecessary to ponder questions of moral responsibility. In the market economy, the invisible hand will insure that good comes. In international affairs, reasons of state are considered reason enough. In science, the pursuit of truth and mastery are self-justifying; the intellectual sphere is permeated with the paradoxical teaching of the value of "value neutrality." In each of these areas, the freedom from moral concerns has its valid justifications. Each also reveals a spirit of opportunism that animates many of our powerful systems. Opportunism alone, however, cannot explain the receptivity to these principles of valuelessness of the individuals who labor within these great systems. People can march off behind the piper of value neutrality because they have been made deaf to a more vital music. Fritz Perls, for example, makes this connection between the academic ideology of value neutrality and the underlying psychological condition: "There is no indifferent, neutral reality. The modern epidemic scientific conviction that most or even all of reality is neutral is a sign of the inhibition of spontaneous pleasure, playfulness, anger, indignation and fear . . ." (in Perls et al., 1951, p. 233). People who cannot experience their own ultimate purposes provide a vacuum to be filled by the purposes inherent in their systems. Functional rationality deals with means, not ends. The ideology of value neutrality justifies and extends that vacuum, telling us (in Leo Strauss's words) that "we can be wise in all matters of secondary importance, but have to be resigned to ignorance in the most important respect." The idea, he says, that "we cannot have any knowledge regarding the ultimate principles of our choices" places us "in the position of beings who are sane and somber when engaged in trivial business and who gamble like madmen when confronted with serious issues—retail sanity and wholesale madness"[17] (1953, p. 4). These ironies make sense in the light of the reign of power. The wholesale madness serves the mad growth of power. The human incapacity to attend to ends reflects the change of man's status from the purpose to the tool of his systems. The powers of reason have been made better instruments to achieve the irrational ends of power systems. Man is no longer so noble in his reason. Positivistic science and bureaucratic rationality magnify the vector of human power without guiding its direction. Power profits, for the triumph of functional rationality nurtures the breeding of functionaries. Ours is not to question why.

Evil is hardly a modern innovation. What is new is the cool dispassionate way in which modern civilized people can commit evils. In studying the worst atrocities of our times, Hannah Arendt discovered not

17. Says Captain Ahab in *Moby Dick:* "All my means are sane, my purpose and my goals are mad."

malignant passion but the "banality of evil." She found Nazi functionaries had done the most hideous things with cool efficiency. Surely irrationality played a major role in the Nazi nightmare, but the crimes of fascist Germany cannot be understood simply as crimes of passion. The defendants at the Doctors' Trial at Nuremberg asserted "that their 'objective and scientific' attitude was far more advanced than the opinions held by ordinary people" (1963, p. 110). The functionary mentality creates man as pure tool. As the satiric song went:

> "Once the rockets are up
> Who cares where they come down,
> That's not my department,"
> Says Wernher von Braun. (© 1965 Tom Lehrer. used by permission)

The discovery that some of the most intelligent, educated, and cultured of modern individuals could willingly serve the most abominable of power systems has resounded through our times like an alarm. Death came from the powers of darkness, but also from the light of unreasonable reason. The systems of power can dominate because of the human failure to integrate. "How lucky it is for tyrants that one half of mankind doesn't think, and the other half doesn't feel" (J. G. Seume, quoted in Auden, 1970, p. 369).

The case of Nazi functionaries is an extreme example of a more general problem. Our world is increasingly controlled by huge bureaucratic organizations in whose rationalized structures are placed innumerable specialized functionaries. Everything in the system teaches, "Yours is not to question why, not to concern yourself with the ends, but only to help provide the means." Nathan Leites has been one of the most perceptive observers of the progressive spread of amorality. "During the twentieth century," Leites writes, "there has been a steady rise in the level of political immorality. . . . Political acts increasingly disregard any moral obstacles in the way of what seems to be maximum efficiency. . . . A related trend is to take for granted 'jobs' which have somehow become part of one's life routine, i.e., to exempt them from any moral evaluation" (1977, pp. 82–83).

The way is cleared for the purposes of the systems to be adopted by people as their own purposes, rather than vice versa. Technology emerges as the trend of the modern world: rule of the tool.

Another of Erich Fromm's character types helps illuminate the ability of social systems to shape men to their purposes. Fromm sees the "technocratic" mode of character as the possible vanguard of American society as a whole. Shallow in emotion, this type "has no plan, no goal for life, except doing what the logic of technique determines him to do" (1973,

p. 350). As the world becomes rationalized, the social environment of civilized peoples increasingly takes the form of the machine. The functionary is the human part to fit that machine. The unreasonable rationalization of human consciousness helps to mass produce those parts. Perhaps the defendants at Nüremberg were correct in believing themselves to be the more "advanced" types. If the visionary imagination of science fiction writers is any guide, the future portends the progressive mechanization of the human being—flat affect, functional efficiency— or even our replacement by machines that possess our intelligence without our messy flesh and blood.

Our humanity has not yet, however, been eradicated. Although much of science proceeds on the assumption "if we can, we should," there are other voices: the fearsome potential of nuclear energy gave birth to the Union of Concerned Scientists; and the scientific community itself raised the issue of the possible necessity for restrictions on the research in recombinant DNA. In corporate boardrooms, concerns about "social responsibility" surface, not always simply with an eye to public relations. In the international arena, concern for human and sovereign rights is given lip service worldwide, and occasionally moral values do truly inhibit the unbridled pursuit of calculated national advantage. Some people still strive to make systems serve human purposes. But the danger remains that if our connection with our humanity grows more and more precarious, the ability of humane values to check the rule of power will wane. "The strong do what they can," said the Athenians, and the machinery of power grows stronger.[18]

---

18. This discussion of the dangers of "unreasonable reason" and value neutrality can be both enriched and corrected by Eli Sagan's profound work *The Lust to Annihilate: A Psychoanalytic Study of Violence in Ancient Greek Culture*. Sagan argues that the sophists of ancient Athens anticipated the modern employment of amoral reason: they "taught people how to argue rationally the case [for] cruelty" (p. 140). He cites Thucydides, in passages including several quoted in this work, as embodying in a new, "reasonable" form the ancient code of the Homeric warrior: the lust to annihilate is disguised as the reasonable and natural pursuit of interest (see his Chap. IX). The crime of dispassion is thus not completely an invention of modern civilization.

Nor is the evil perpetrated by apparently dispassionate, rational people, as "banal" as it may appear on the surface. Although value neutrality is in part a vacuum, Sagan reminds us that it is also in part a cloak. It can abet evil, therefore, in two ways—by creating a void to be filled by the purposes of the systems in which people are embedded, and by removing the checks against fulfillment of unacknowledged impulses buried within people's hearts. In a passage that resonates with Bellah's declaration that "Just those who feel they are most rational and pragmatic . . . are most in the power of deep unconscious fantasies," Sagan writes of Thucydides and of the Athenian character he typifies: "Lusting for violence, feeling both shame and guilt about that lust, he insists on a double denial; he denies that he has either that lust or a superego which condemns it" (p. 170). "Morality," says Sagan, "can only be repressed in the service of immorality" (p. 180).

As long as the demonic forces can masquerade as the dictates of logic, they remain beyond the reach of truly rational analysis. The impulses we fail to recognize can possess and destroy us. The Peloponnesian Wars that destroyed the flowering of Athenian culture were portrayed by Thucydides as inevitable, although "his own recital of the facts contradicts the assumption that war could not

Impersonality

Alienation inside implies alienation outside. In other words, a person who is out of touch with his own humanity will be estranged also from the humanity of those around him. "Love thy neighbor as thyself" is presented as a moral injunction, but it may also be regarded as descriptive of what naturally happens.

Forming deep bonds with other people is fundamental to human nature. In our natural condition, "society" was essentially an extended family. Intimate relationships of sharing and caring were at the core of our species' strategy for survival, and it is in such relationships that our deepest selves tend to be nourished. This is another aspect of "connectedness" that can strengthen the human in its struggle against the inhumane.

The rationalization of human consciousness tends to weaken the ties that bind. Many of the currents feeding the stream of modern civilization show this. The rational and the impersonal are akin: both involve stepping back, being detached. We recall the suggestion by the behaviorist John Watson that parents should treat their children "objectively." (Behaviorism, the science that regarded the human being as a learning machine, was itself a manifestation of the thrust of rational-industrial culture.) In the production of the modern consciousness, the breakdown of the interpersonal bond and the emphasis upon the objective outlook have historically reinforced each other. We may recall also Weber's observation about Calvinism that "the sharp condemnation . . . of all dependence on personal relations was bound unperceived to direct this energy into the field of objective (impersonal) activity." From the same roots grow the culture of radical individualism (where it must be protested that no man is an island) and the epochal growth of objective and rational science. If the current of modern individualism has helped undermine intimate bonds, modern collectivism offers no contrast. Indeed, the collectivist

have been avoided" (1979, p. 177). "As for Athens and Sparta, war was inevitable because they were in love with it" (ibid.)

Reason arose as the instrument of violence because, says Sagan, for the first time in the history of Greek culture a "revolutionary moral view" had gained sufficient power to challenge the ancient, war-loving ethic of sadism and brutality. Perhaps we are now at a similar juncture. In our own time, as we watch rational men in the military-industrial complexes of the superpowers retreat from doctrines of nuclear deterrence and speak dispassionately of the likelihood of nuclear conflicts that can be kept limited and that must be won, we should ponder the lessons the rational men of Athens have bequeathed us.

Remember that Hitler, too, loved "ice cold" reason. In 1941 he said, "I would prefer not to see anyone suffer, not to do harm to anyone. But then I realize that the species is in danger and . . . sentiment gives way to the coldest reason" (quoted in Waite, 1977, p. 40). Just those, said Bellah, who feel they are most rational are most in the power of deep unconscious fantasies. War appeared objectively inevitable, said Sagan, to those who were in love with it.

states of our era perhaps present a still more extreme case. Barbu, himself a refugee from Stalinist Eastern Europe, has described the ways in which the communist state seeks to destroy both the interior life of the individual and the emotional bonds within the family. Perhaps this is another intimation of the connection between rationality and impersonality. Communism is often described as the most uncompromisingly rationalistic approach to the problems of civilization. Bringing "science" to the design of the social machine, the Soviets have attempted, according to Barbu, to displace the "emotionality" of the child, "naturally captivated by his parents," onto the distant and impersonal apparatus and leadership of the Party. Reason makes society into a machine, and the machine works best when each person is a-part. *Gemeinschaft*, in Tönnies's famous formulation, steadily gives way to *Gesellschaft*.

In the rationalized organizations of the modern world, people are treated impersonally, "objectively," that is, as if they were objects. This advanced civilized consciousness contrasts strikingly with the primitive view of the world. The historically most significant feature of primitive life, writes Diamond, is *personalism*, a view that "extends from the family outward to the society at large and ultimately to nature itself. It seems to underlie all other distinctive qualities of primitive thought and behavior. Primitive people live in a personal, corporate world, a world that tends to be a 'thou' to the subjective 'I,' rather than an 'it' impinging upon an objectively separate and divided self" (in Montagu, 1968, p. 127). (Similarly Martin Buber writes of primitive man that "Everything is to him full of sacramental substance.") Out of the primitive parts of the mind, that richly associative "primary" process, comes a connectedness with all the world that makes of every thing a "thou," an entity with which one stands in a relationship with potentially sacred significance. Consider the contrast with rational civilization. Whereas the primitive regards its "its" as "thous," the impersonal rationality of modern civilization teaches us to treat other people as "its." Anyone who has worked in large institutions knows how difficult an environment they are for genuine interpersonal caring. An Indian sociologist, Purnima Bhatt, said to me: "American institutions are so impersonal, there is so little real human contact in them compared with what is still the practice in India. But I don't fault America for this so much as I see it as a sign of where the whole world is heading."

In his interaction with nature, with what science regards as the world of things, the primitive is constrained by his feeling of relationship from exploiting nature ruthlessly. Where people too are seen as things, a big barrier is removed from the exploitation of man by man. What is injurious in human terms is again in the service of the power system. People are treated impersonally in modern systems because this facilitates their being used to achieve organizational ends. In a section entitled "The Appearance of Scientific Management," Giedion describes the pioneering time/motion work of Frederick Winslow Taylor.

> In Taylor's work: The human body is studied to discover how far it can be transformed into a mechanism. Taylor once constructed a great steam hammer, whose parts were so finely calculated that the elasticity of its molecular forces served to heighten its efficiency. . . . Similarly does he proceed in the study of human efficiency: He approaches the limit of elasticity. . . . The stretching of human capacities and the stretching of the properties of steel derive from the same roots. . . . By constant observation wrong or slow-working methods are replaced by rational ones. . . . Taylorism demands of the mass of workers . . . automatization. Human movements become levers in the machines. (1948, pp. 98–99)

In scientifically managed modern institutions, what Parsons calls the "expressive" dimension of leadership (caring about the internal, emotional state of people) is eclipsed by the overemphasis on the "instrumental" dimension (concern with external performance on the collective task). People are instruments.[19]

The "personalism" of primitives is an example of what Piaget would call an "illusion." The psychological evolution of civilized man has allowed us to advance beyond such illusions.

In our struggle for a truly human civilization, our fellow human beings are our natural allies. This alliance, however, is weakened by the unmitigated dominance of rationality in the modern psychic system. It is not through our rational mode that we discover our love and identification with one another. The rational ego of the Enlightenment is an isolated self, clearly aware of the boundary between 'I' and 'not I.' As Durkheim, as a rational child of the Enlightenment, pursued the study of society, he discovered a most irrational element to be the glue that holds society together. The core of society, he found, consists of a set of collective representations which are impressed upon the minds of group members at times of especially intense group activity. These times he characterized

---

19. Another way that the breakdown of bonds among people may sever the hindrances on power's free play is suggested in this passage by Albert Schweitzer, written between the world wars: "There has been created a social mentality which discourages humanity in individuals. The courtesy produced by natural feeling disappears, and in its place comes a behavior which shows entire indifference. . . . The standoffishness and want of sympathy which are shown so clearly in every way to strangers are no longer felt as being really rudeness, but pass for the behavior of the man of the world. . . . We have talked for decades with ever increasing light-mindedness about war and conquest, as if these were merely operations on a chess-board; how was this possible save as the result of a tone of mind which no longer pictures to itself the fate of individuals, but thought of them only as figures or objects belonging to the material world? When the war broke out the inhumanity within us had a free course" (1960, p. 15).

as "collective effervescence," a term applicable to the ritual gatherings of primitives and to such intensely emotional periods as the French Revolution. This concept of collective effervescence does not fit well into the rational pattern of the Enlightenment, according to Bellah: "it could almost be called a social unconscious" (1970a, p. 239). Where a people lose the capacity to integrate into their social lives their more primitive nonrational modes of experience, the humanizing bonds of fraternity are forfeited, and society may grow still more mechanical. A vital balm upon the wounds of humanity has been the mystic apprehension of the Brotherhood of Man. This experience derives from our irrational, "Dionysian" side. In Schiller's famous words to Joy:

Deine Zauber binden wieder,	Thy magic binds again
Was die Mode strengt geteilt,	What the world's ways has rent apart
Alle Menschen werden Brüder	All men become brothers
Wo dein sanfter Flügel weilt.	Where thy gentle wings rest.

Where men are brothers, the strength of love blocks the ruthless workings of the world's way. But divide and conquer works here as elsewhere. The unbalanced identification of individuals with their rational egos hinders their identification with each other, and makes each a more willing instrument of impersonal systems.

Reason is indeed a noble gift of man. Yet what makes the reasonable man wise is a sense of balance and proportion. Reason unbalanced by the rest of our humanity is unreasonable and foolish. If its growth is unchecked by any sense of proportion, even reason can become a cancer.

The predominance of functional reason in human consciousness remains far from total. In areas like religion and the arts, the mythopoetic dimension still powerfully shapes experience for many people. But the rationalization of the mind seems a distinct social evolutionary trend. And we may recall, it takes a drop of only a few degrees in the global climate to plunge the earth into an Ice Age.

7. Conclusion: Possibilities

Several factors might diminish the persuasiveness of this overview of our psychological evolution under the aegis of civilization.

Its brevity, inevitably, means oversimplification. To paint a portrait of so complex a subject as "civilized man" in a single chapter demands that each brush stroke be bold, each line implying a thousand subtleties. If well done, it is evocative, like a figure of Picasso. But it will also be less, if perhaps also more, than true to life.

208

Its one-sidedness is another perhaps more troublesome source of inaccuracy. Any portrait is selective, but selectivity in the service of a single idea makes the portrait a caricature. Here the vices of civilized man have been depicted to the neglect of his virtues. The hope is that the failure to tell the whole truth will be redeemed by the effort to tell nothing but the truth.

These two drawbacks seem inescapable here, and thus bear no more than mention.

A third possible factor, however, may fruitfully be discussed. This is the question of the credibility of the premise implicit in this chapter, that conforming to the demands of civilized society causes us severe psychological injury. It is a matter of our vision of human possibilities.

How rich a life is man's birthright? My vision is that we—most of us, most of the time—realize but a shadow of our natural potential. Our life energy moves through us as if we had atherosclerosis of the soul. The life we were born to is much more deeply nourishing than what we have. It is also my perception that we are—most of us, most of the time— profoundly incapable of grasping the severity of our sickness of the soul. We are like the inhabitants of Plato's cave who mistake the shadow of ourselves for our reality, and never dream how illuminated our being could be. Chronic injury produces numbness, and chronic numbness creates amnesia of the natural strength of our life-force. Conventional consciousness, therefore, regards as deluded utopians those whose voices cry out that our growth as human beings is being stunted. Our day-to-day mundane existence is regarded simply as the way life is. Only when the wounds become visible in the actual shedding of blood is a problem recognized (though even here the reaction is often flat). Life in the cave. I have not been able to make my own home in the full light of the sun, but the visits I have made there make me cling, even as I lapse back into the cave, to the more real vision of the natural fullness and richness of human life.

Rejecting the vision of human potential as utopian illusion serves to conserve our dystopian reality. Social conservatism is marked by its pessimism about man, believing always that the coercive systems of society save us from being still worse than we are. The conservative view of the world is marked also by its exceedingly narrow goals for human life: survival is sufficient; one's stance in the world must be defensive. To seek a reality that is not mundane, to strive for heightened aliveness, is scorned.[20]

20. This scorn was illustrated in America in the 1970s, for example, by the conservative counterattack against the counterculture. High aspiration is apparently so great a threat that the errors of that movement were constantly used to discredit even its ideals.

The great majority of us are conservatives in this respect, consoling ourselves for our experiential disabilities with the thought that experience offers nothing more. And so we leave unmolested the world that injures us.

It is difficult to prove that the unnatural demands of civilization have made our lives less whole and fulfilling than nature intended for them to be. Some suggestive evidence, however, exists. To begin with, we retain within ourselves signs of a natural wholeness far superior to our conventional constricted consciousness. The Hindu teaching and practice of transcendental meditation, for example, reveals a natural tendency of the mind to seek pleasure, bliss. Meditators report (and I can confirm by experience) a sudden suffusion of good feeling, a sudden expansion of being. Without effort. For me also, the experience of dreams gives an intimation of a larger self, of a natural capacity of consciousness to achieve a greater wholeness of experience. Is this wholeness an intimation of our natural state? For clues, we can look to those last remaining embodiments of our natural selves, the primitives.

Those who have studied them tell about the lives of primitives with something closer to envy than to pity. Hunting-and-gathering peoples, writes Carleton Coon, seem to be "less subject to continuous anxiety" than do we civilized peoples (1971, pp. 9–10). Stanley Diamond, whose work has aimed at bringing back to civilization lessons that primitive societies can teach about human life, draws the more general conclusion that "*If the fulfillment and delineation of the human person with a social, natural and supernatural (self-transcendant) setting is a universally valid measure for the evaluation of culture, primitive societies are our primitive superiors*"[21] (in Montagu, 1968, p. 136). The example of the primitive expands our view of our natural selves, and challenges the narrow and pessimistic view of the conservative. Writes J. C. Smuts: "When I look at history, I am a pessimist . . . but when I look at prehistory, I am an optimist" (quoted in Fromm, 1973, epigraph).

To apprehend that we are naturally endowed with the capacity for much fuller lives is a profoundly radicalizing experience. It does not necessarily, however, justify radical action. Radicals also have their portion of illusion, and conservatives their part of the truth. Grasping that something is radically wrong, the radical is often reckless in the pursuit of

---

21. It is, of course, impossible to step inside the skin of another person, much less a wholly different way of life. But according to bioenergetic psychology, the psychic condition of a person is manifested in the structure and motion of his body. Says Alexander Lowen, the founder of bioenergetic analysis, "The body does not lie." The pictures of primitives, according to Dr. Edward Muller, a prominent bioenergeticist, reveal them to be on the whole better integrated and better grounded than civilized people (personal communication).

radical change. History shows that millenarian movements lead to disaster more reliably than to any other destination. Revolutions in the name of freedom too often bring only new tyranny. It seems simple enough to storm the Bastille, but breakdown creates anarchy, and anarchy brings us back to the root of our evils. The illusion is that the simple yearning for liberation must be matched by a simple way to get there. But we are now so far from home that it is not enough to strike out blindly in that direction. To do so is to be like a prisoner on the island of St. Helena who seeks to escape by running toward France. About our inherent possibilities for a free human life, true realism makes us radical. But regarding the possibilities for getting there from here, the realist must adopt a good measure of conservative caution.

The conflict between these two realities is also a part of the agony of our civilized condition.

PART TWO

POWER AND THE LOSS OF WHOLENESS

Chapter Six

Systems of Nature and of Civilization

1. Synergy and Viability: Dimensions of Wholeness

The Search for Natural Law.—For other living creatures, questions of good and evil do not arise. They simply follow the law that evolution has inscribed upon their natures. Human life, by contrast, is full of moral uncertainties. Because of man's unfinished nature, the inborn voice speaks less distinctly about what it means to be human. Culture implies a degree of uncertainty. Then, in addition, human beings were swept along by the evolution of civilization, which has taken humankind still farther from its natural state. With civilization, not only "How should we live?" but also "How should the world be?" become open questions.

Some believe that the answers are to be found ahead, further in the direction of our escape from the order of nature. The good person is he who overcomes and renounces his natural animality. The good system is one that nullifies the "law of the jungle." Nature, to them, is no moral guide.

One tradition in philosophy, however, looks to nature for moral wisdom. In the tradition of natural law, the good human life is one that fulfills our human nature. This work is in that tradition. The theory of natural value, developed in chapter 4, provided a basis for a critique of the unnaturalness of civilization: an unnatural environment is not good for us to the extent that what it offers and demands fails to correspond with the needs of our human nature. This chapter extends to a new level the search for moral principles to be derived from an understanding of nature. While the theory of natural value sought to prove that goodness is ultimately grounded in experiential fulfillment at the level of individual creatures, here I search for the essential properties of systems which best assure such fulfillment.

Two of these properties, I propose, are what can be called *synergy* and *viability*. These are dimensions of wholeness in living systems which far better characterize biologically evolved systems than those of civilization (see "Nature and Civilization Contrasted," below). Moreover, these concepts help identify what it is about the systems of civilization which makes them so problematic (see chap. 7).

Synergy and Viability.—A system can be defined as an aggregate the elements of which interact. Because of these interactions, no element of the system can be entirely understood in isolation. Each element is a part of a larger whole. For example, the movement of the earth can be understood not in terms of the earth alone but only in the light of the earth's place in the solar system. (Indeed, as the solar system itself moves in ways dictated by its place in the galaxy, even this whole is also a part, and a complete view of the earth's movement reflects this fact.) Another example is the psychotherapeutic concept of the "identified patient," that is, the member of a family system whose pathology dramatizes a problem of the whole family's interaction pattern.

With a system of living things, it is possible to speak of the welfare of the different parts. According to the way the interaction within such a system is organized, the welfare of the parts may be served well or ill. The optimal pattern of interaction is synergistic, that is, one in which each part functions in a way that enhances the welfare of the other parts as well as its own. The term for synergy we use in speaking of human affairs is "cooperation." When people cooperate well, each is better off than he would have been without the actions of others. The absence of synergy is exemplified by the zero-sum game. In a zero-sum game, like poker, the total of winnings and losings of all players is zero: one player's gain implies another player's loss. In some interactions the sum is less than zero, as in the panic of people in a theater on fire, where the actions of each trying to serve his own needs add up to a disaster for all. The opposite of a synergistic system is a *corrupt* one. Corruption characterizes a system to the extent that parts of the system seek or serve their own

216

interests at the expense of the overall well-being of the system.

In any living system, a degree of conflict of interests among the parts is inevitable. Perfect synergy is therefore impossible. It is nonetheless possible to differentiate between resolutions of these conflicts that are more or less synergistic and therefore more or less advantageous to the whole.

A second dimension of wholeness—viability—characterizes a living system to the extent that it is able to maintain without diminution whatever it is upon which its continued existence depends. Viability requires, therefore, a balance between input and output: a viable system must either replace an equal portion of what it uses or it must reuse indefinitely what is not replaced. In the earth's biosphere, for example, indefinite reuse is exemplified by the continuous cycling of essential substances (such as oxygen and nitrogen) throughout the system. Only energy once "used" is dissipated, and thus the viability of the biosphere depends upon a continuous "income" of energy from the sun. In addition to having to maintain the availability of what it needs, a viable system must also not accumulate what is toxic to its well-being. In the case of our own bodies, death from thirst illustrates a failure of input and death from uremic poisoning a failure of output. The opposite of a viable system is a decadent one, one that lives beyond its means and destroys the conditions for its healthy continuation.

Synergy and viability are not identical, but they are related. One may say that synergy is cross-sectional whereas viability is longitudinal, that is, that synergy describes the health of a system at a given time, viability over time. As the future is a function of the present, viability depends in part on synergy: a system where individual parts injure the whole will ultimately not remain viable. For example, when a corrupt ruler like Emperor Bokassa (late of the Central African Republic) lavishes many millions of dollars of his impoverished country's resources on his own coronation, he leaves that society in a sicker condition.

Both these analytic concepts have moral import. Both help describe what is healthy in a living system, what is conducive to the fulfillment of the living creatures within them. A system so structured that its parts serve each other in serving themselves is clearly a good system for its members. And since goodness depends upon life, the long-term fulfillment of all creatures requires that their systems be so structured as to perpetuate the conditions essential for life.

With these concepts of what is good in living systems, we can now compare those two different kinds of living systems the world has seen, the systems of biologically evolved nature and those of civilization, the natural and the unnatural.

217

2. Nature and Civilization Contrasted

A. Natural Systems

(1) *The body.*—The body of a living creature epitomizes the wholeness of natural systems. The human body, for example, can be seen as a system of many parts—cells, organs, subsystems of digestion and respiration, and so on. We begin as a single cell which proceeds embryologically to grow and differentiate. This genetic unfolding itself demonstrates the fundamental synergy of the body: the development of organisms, write G. G. Simpson et al., "is controlled by the entire set of genes acting cooperatively" (quoted in Koestler, 1967, p. 124). Throughout life, the parts act together to preserve the health of the whole and all the other parts: stomach, lungs, heart, brain, kidneys, each perform functions essential to the continued survival of all the others, and the various actions are intricately coordinated for maximal well-being by messages of various sort from the central nervous system, the endocrine system, and so on. The magnificent synergy of the body is well illustrated in such classics as Walter Cannon's *The Wisdom of the Body,* and Fritz Kahn's *The Human Body in Structure and Function.* It is also the basis of Aesop's fable of the abortive revolt of the members of the body who resented the stomach's getting all the food and formed a disastrous conspiracy to stop feeding it. When the body does sacrifice a part, it is to preserve the health of the whole. A phagocyte dies in fighting an infection; the extremities get frostbitten if the body is exposed to prolonged cold, so that the most indispensable parts of the body can continue to be nourished. Such sacrifices demonstrate not an indifferent exploitation of one part by the others but a wise assessment of which parts must be given up to preserve as well as possible the life and well-being of the whole.

The elaborate synergy of the body is the result, of course, of a long evolutionary process by which natural selection has favored those best equipped for survival. The body is synergistic because synergy promotes viability. The body is designed to maintain and to pass on life. Maintenance requires preserving conditions within the fairly narrow range that life requires. Besides a balance in inputs and outputs, this maintenance requires elaborate internal homeostatic mechanisms. "Somehow," writes Cannon, "the unstable stuff of which we are comprised has learned the trick of maintaining stability" (1963, p. 23).

Yet, as we know, the viability of our bodies is limited, the maintenance of stability breaks down. We die. This is not, however, a failure of design but a component of design: we are programmed to self-destruct. Our mortality is not an indication of the failure of natural systems to achieve wholeness. Rather, it demonstrates that our individual bodies are parts of a larger natural system that, from the standpoint of the long-run preservation of our kind of life, is ultimately more important. Individuals are designed to die that the species may live, that it may maintain adaptability.

This leads us to the next level of natural systems.

(2) *The species, especially natural societies.*—The members of a species form a synergistic whole. Yet they are also often separate and autonomous creatures seeking their own ends, sometimes in competition with one another. The ambiguity of partness and wholeness is present throughout biological nature. Even our own bodies consist of cells capable, under the right circumstances, of continuing the processes of life on their own. In his famous work, *Cells and Societies,* J. T. Bonner reveals the spectrum of ambiguity stretching from seeing the individual body as a society of cells to seeing the natural society as a single superorganism. There is, for example, his description of the life cycle of the slime mold Dictyostelium, which at one point consists of a collection of separate amoebas that then come together to form, for reproductive purposes, essentially one multicellular organism. At the end of the process, the many one-celled organisms "arrive at a condition of rest, of dormancy, that is the final fruiting body in which the stalk cells have become essentially dead, trapped in congealed cellulose walls, and the spores lie in hibernation, waiting for favorable conditions in which they can again feed as separate amoebae" (1955, p. 110). These living things have cooperated in the perpetuation of their kind, the many playing a sacrificial role to allow a few of their kindred to pass on the sacred design of their lives. Another work in which we glimpse the larger wholeness of which individual creatures are parts is Lewis Thomas's *Lives of a Cell.* An individual ant, Thomas suggests, is a creature of little intelligence. "It is only when you watch the dense mass of thousands of ants, crowded together around the Hill, blackening the ground, that you begin to see the whole beast, and now you observe it thinking, planning, calculating. It is an intelligence, a kind of live computer, with crawling bits for its wits" (1974, pp. 12–13). It is the whole—the species, the society—which is the primary bearer of life, and thus in nature the individual creatures which form parts of that whole act in synergy.

The synergy within a species is often, however, far from the whole picture. Bonner's slime mold and Thomas's ants may illustrate a fundamental truth about nature, but they are not altogether typical species. In a great many species, individuals' lives involve far less cooperation. Beyond that, there are often genuine conflicts of interests among individuals which are expressed in competition for scarce resources such as food, territory, mates, and status in a hierarchy. Such competition was the primary focus of many early evolutionists. But we can now see that in their preoccupation with competition and their emphasis on the individual as the unit of biological evolution, they revealed more about their own cultures than about the workings of nature. For modern evolutionary theory has shown that intraspecific behaviors, even of a competitive nature, are less comprehensible in terms of a struggle for individual survival than of a strategy for the preservation of the collective whole.

The character of relationships between members of the same species is part of the evolved nature of that species. No pattern of interaction could emerge unless it served the survival of the whole. Writes Bowlby: "Whether the individual outcome is food-intake, self-protection, sexual union, or defense of territory, the ultimate outcome to be attained is always the survival of the population of which the individual is a member" (1969, p. 56). Because selection acts upon genetic populations, the "ultimate outcome" even of competition within such populations is synergistic. When individual animals compete for territory or mates, this should be understood ultimately not as the crossed purposes of individuals but as an inadvertently cooperative effort to optimize the chances for species survival. The form of competition often shows that the system is designed to minimize its destructive impact. In many species, a fight ends when the defeated animal signals surrender by exposing its vital and vulnerable body areas to the teeth of the victor—yet the bite does not come. Consider what this demonstrates about the intraspecific system. "What," asks Arthur Koestler, "is the *individual* survival value of not hitting (or biting, goring) below the belt?" (1967, p. 157). This leads to the issue of "altruistic" behavior among animals of which another example is the alarm signal many animals give to their fellows at the sight of a predator, dangerously calling attention to themselves. "These alarm calls," says N. Tinbergen, "are a clear example of an activity which serves the group but endangers the individual" (quoted in ibid.). One may also cite the instinctual suicidal migrations of the lemmings which serve to control against overpopulation. The male baboons who go forward to meet the leopard, and protective maternal behaviors in countless species, also illustrate the altruistic nature of intraspecific interactions. This altruism points to the essential nature of the evolutionary process. What is happening is a process of group selection which leads, in R. H. Crozier's words, "to the maintenance of traits favorable to populations and communities, but selectively disadvantageous to genetic carriers within populations" (in E. Odum, 1971, p. 274). As J. B. S. Haldane is said to have declared, "I would willingly lay down my life for more than two brothers, four nephews or eight cousins" (Pulliam and Dunford, 1980, p. 98). Group selection brings about design for the whole, and this means that the interactions among the parts are ultimately synergistic in nature.

Just as individual death is part of a larger strategy of life, individual competition is part of a larger synergy to serve the long-term survival of the whole. (As recent ethological observation has underscored, however, this overall synergy is not so protective of individuals as to prevent all instances of intraspecific killing: Haldane may be willing to sacrifice himself for two brothers, but a victorious stallion may by the same token harass his newly acquired pregnant mares into aborting.)

(3) *The ecological system.*—Just as in moving from the individual body to the larger whole of the species there is an increase in the manifest conflict of interest among the parts, so also in going from the species to the overarching ecological system does the element of strife become more visible. The early evolutionists, describing the "struggle for survival," saw nature "red in tooth and claw." Creatures do, indeed, feed upon one another; they constantly battle each other in zero-sum games where winning and losing are matters of life and death. The vision of such unrelenting conflict fostered the idea of "the law of the jungle," which in the domain of biological nature is the equivalent of the parable of the tribes.

Yet, again, the manifest strife overlays a more basic synergy. Because life emerges in a wholly opportunistic fashion, nature reveals no scruples about protecting the rights and well-being of individual creatures against their injury by other life-forms. Nature, that is, does not side with the prey against its predator or the host against its parasite. Anything that works, goes. On the other hand, nature is remarkably exacting about what "works." Because the process of evolution sifts through very gradual changes over vast stretches of time, no part "works" unless it is embedded in an intricate network of synergistic interactions with the living system as a whole. Predatory relationships evolve in time into a balance that protects against overpredation, an eventuality injurious to predator and prey alike. The predator may even become necessary for the long-run survival of the prey species; for example, the elimination of the predators may allow a herbivore species to overgraze its habitat, damaging the plant and soil resources upon which its life depends. It is frequently remarked that when a parasite kills its host it is a sign of a new relationship, one that given time will move toward a more benign interaction conducive to the survival of both species.[1] Eugene Odum writes:

---

1. Lewis Thomas writes: "There is a tendency of living things to join up whenever joining is possible: accommodation and compromise are more common results of close interaction than combat and destruction" (1981, p. 52). As evidence for this proposition, Thomas cites the photosynthetic chloroplasts (inside the cells of green plants) which give our atmosphere most of its oxygen and which are "almost certainly the descendants of blue-green algae"; and the mitochondria in our own cells, which we require in order to be able to use oxygen for energy, and which are "the direct descendants of symbiotic bacteria."

> A cardinal principle is that the negative effects tend to be quantitatively small where the interacting populations have had a common evolutionary history in a relatively stable ecosystem. In other words, natural selection tends to lead to a reduction in detrimental effects or to the elimination of the interaction altogether, since continued severe depression of a prey or host population by the predator or parasite population can only lead to the extinction of one or both populations. (1971, p. 220)

More fundamental than the conflict of interests among species are some inescapable common interests. In a universe that is probably largely lifeless, life is a kind of miracle. It demands special conditions. All species have a common interest in the maintenance of the conditions that make life possible. And out of common interest, with time and natural selection, comes synergy. Creatures large and small become inadvertent collaborators in the creation and maintenance of the great body of the biosphere. So intricate are the balances of the living system, that it is hardly the case that anything goes. Species "must be connected with input and output flows to survive," writes Howard Odum, "otherwise they are shortly eliminated, for they run out of raw materials or energy." He goes on: "Not only must the selection continue those populations most suited to the system's efficient function, but it must also pick those that properly contribute to the total long range order and energy flows of the system in which it is embedded" (1971, p. 150). The patient process of biological evolution produces synergy because only highly cooperative interactions preserve the viability of the whole upon which all depend. Life is clearly a plus-sum game.

Living systems are structured to serve life. If one posits life to be good, this structure of natural systems commands our moral allegiance. Am I suggesting that biological evolution moves toward "the best of all possible worlds"? Not necessarily, for it is hard to establish a calculus of the value of well-being for all the earth's living things. But if one adopts something like the Hindu belief that all life is sacred and that all living things possess some degree of spirit (however akin or alien to ours), then in the thrust of the ecosystem something is sacred and good.

This is substantiated, for example, by a look at the nature of ecological succession. Any ecosystem, if left undisturbed, will move through a process of succession to an ecological climax. A climax community represents a kind of optimum, for it maximizes (a) the amount of living material, (b) the cooperative "symbiosis" among species, and (c) the stability of the entire system (E. Odum in Boughey, 1973, p. 14; Cox et al., 1976, p. 52). That is, it maximizes life (as measured by biomass), synergy, and viability in the system.

Life has constantly worked to protect itself from the slings and arrows of outrageous fortunes that can befall it from the nonliving world. Thus, in the sucession toward climax, nutrients (matter) are absorbed "from the *abiotic* or non-living environment into the *biotic* component of the habitat," for having such essential materials under the control of the living system better protects against their loss to the system and thus protects its long-term stability (Cox et al., 1976, p. 53). In other ways as well, life has sought to extend its control over nonliving nature. Organisms not only adapt to the physical environment, says E. Odum (1971, p. 23), "but by their concerted action in ecosystems they also adapt the geochemical environment to their biological needs." Similarly, according to Lamont Cole, "our atmosphere as we know it today is a biological product . . ." (p. 6). The biosphere as a whole can be said to have exhibited an evolutionary thrust similar to the movement of succession. In "The Strategy of Ecosystem Development," E. Odum discerns a "strategy" of long-term evolutionary development in which the biosphere has moved toward "increased control of, or homeostasis with, the physical environment in the sense of achieving maximum protection from its perturbations" (in Boughey, 1973, p. 14).

Certainly, this protection of life against nonlife is quite incomplete. This limit on the control by living systems over their own fates is the reason for the occasional widespread destructions of life that are evident in the archaeological record. Most current thinking about the wave of extinction that erased the dinosaurs devolves not on failures within the living system itself—deadends of evolutionary development—but on catastrophic disruptions of the biosphere from beyond the earth. For example, a recent theory suggests that upon its impact with the earth a huge meteor cast into the atmosphere so much dust and debris that the earth's climate drastically altered for a few years, killing off plant life and thus many of the animals that depended upon it, so that by the time the dense cloud had settled the dinosaurs had perished. Cycles within the sun may account for the ice ages that have also brought waves of extinction. One more example of a force beyond the control of terrestrial life, but with great impact upon it, is the drifting of the continental plates. When North America collided with South America, which had long since parted from Africa, the new land bridge at the Panamanian Isthmus allowed a sudden mingling of species from the two continents. The species of placental mammals from the north had competitive advantages over the marsupials in the south, so that on account of this geological accident many South American animal species were suddenly extinguished.

But these very cataclysms, coming as they do from beyond the realm of life, only serve to underscore how marvelously the structure of living systems serves to protect life. Evolution shows constant change, but it tends to be gradual and free from catastrophe and destruction. Where there has been destruction, it has been wrought by forces from the non-living universe; living creatures, by their own actions individually and collectively, tend not to destroy the system even when by their own evolution they change it.

Not, that is, until the coming of civilization. With civilization, for the first time, destructive forces have come from the domain of life itself. For the systems of civilization are not characterized by the dimensions of wholeness, the synergy and viability, which are the essence of the biologically evolved systems of life.

B. The Systems of Civilization

Civilized systems differ markedly from those of biologically evolved nature. Ultimately, the most essential difference is the destruction by civilization of systemic synergy and viability.

(1) *Overarching systems: ecological and intersocietal.*—A civilized society, like a natural society, is embodied in an ecological whole. There is, however, another surrounding system that forms part of the "environment" of a civilized society: the intersocial system.

The *ecosystem* has been changed by civilization. To be sure, the old natural structures remain recognizable on the terrestrial landscape. But with the power of civilization over nature steadily growing, the old structures are subverted and replaced at an accelerating pace. The ancient and time-proven patterns of cooperation give way to a regime of domination. Where previously all were free though unwitting actors in a collective drama of mutual survival, with civilized man there arrived on the scene a single player to write the script for the whole. To secure a place in the old synergistic system, a life form had to serve the ecosystem as a whole. But, increasingly, the prerequisite for a continuing role in the drama of life is service to the single dominant animal. If you impinge upon the interests of man, out you go: wolves and bears and lions, who like the meat that man wants for himself, are eradicated or at best are forced to retreat to refuges. If you are useless to man, however teeming with life, you will be swept aside in favor of something that better serves the master: the magnificent forests are felled and replaced by the more paltry but more "useful" growths of man's cropland. The grains and cattle that fill men's bellies—these thrive and prosper. Life comes to be governed by a calculus that is fundamentally corrupt. The well-being of man is what rules, regardless of how small may be the human benefit in relation to the costs in well-being to others of God's creatures. Never before has a creature had the power to arrange the pattern of life for its selfish ends, so never before has the ecosystem been corrupted. So pervasive is the assumption of the human right to selfishness in the ecosystem—might

224

makes right—that even the arguments for human restraint tend to be couched in terms of human self-interest: natural environments have recreational value; species we extinguish might have proved later to have unforeseen usefulness to man.

There is one more case for restraint based on enlightened self-interest. Just as synergy is nature's tool for long-term viability, so also the wages of corruption are the long-run decadence and death of living systems. Man uses up the bases of his life. Look at civilization's most ancient homes: once fertile places, many of them now lie denuded of life's basic nutrients. Around the Mediterranean, across the "Fertile" Crescent, deforestation and overgrazing broke the grip by which the living system clung to the sacred soil. The spread of the deserts is accelerating. And for each bushel of corn that comes from Iowa, more than a bushel of its precious soil washes away. Man's corrupt pattern is feast and famine. In that order. The world's fisheries are overfished. The fragile forests of the tropics are recklessly harvested. Across the board, we take in for our use more than we or nature can replace. We have a strip miner's approach to our planet.[2]

The decadence of civilization as a living system is demonstrated by the nonrecycling of its outputs as much as by the nonrenewal of its inputs. For every other living thing, its outputs function as essential inputs for others: the oxygen/carbon dioxide exchanges of plants and animals, the buildup of soil by the leaves that drop from trees and by the excrement of animals. Before civilization, life produced no toxic wastes. Now, our insecticides threaten birds and other species. Our burning of fuels may bring climatic disaster. Our output of fluorocarbons may expose us and other living things to harmful solar radiation. This generation is producing mountains of nuclear wastes that hundreds of generations to come

2. The most prominent current instance of civilization's unviable input structure is the energy crisis, which is a confrontation between the increase in human demand and the exhaustion of the earth's supply of oil resources. Civilization is the only living system to require for its existence the using up of nonrenewable terrestrial resources. Jerome Rifkin, in *Entropy*, correctly points out that the crisis involving petroleum is not civilization's first energy crisis, that the exhaustion of wood resources in Europe, for example, helped stimulate the breakthroughs in energy technology that facilitated the Industrial Revolution. (Necessity, again, the mother of invention.) He is less illuminating, however, in viewing civilization's recurrent problem of resource exhaustion in the light of the concept of entropy. The second law of thermodynamics applies to the nonliving systems of the universe. While biologically evolved living systems do not violate that law of entropy, within their own domain they work against it—creating more order rather than less, raising energy to a higher state rather than lower. These systems can appear counterentropic only because of the steady income of energy from the sun. Eventually, the sun would grow cold and entropy would claim earth's biosphere as well (as vividly pictured in Wells's *Time Machine*). But without civilization, life on earth could develop without entropy being a problem. If, even now, any of earth's injured ecological communities could be freed from the intrusions of civilized life, it would immediately begin to progress in a counterentropic direction, that is, toward the greater buildup of life and order. Given the sun, life is a perpetual motion machine. We therefore can best understand the resource and energy problems of civilization by seeing them not as a continuity of the laws governing inanimate systems but as a discontinuity of the laws governing *living* systems. The exhaustion of essential resources marks civilization as it has existed thus far as an aberrant, and unviable, living system.

will have to live with, and perhaps die from. And as frightening as radiation is, many warn us that we have more to fear from the countless tons of "conventional" wastes that lurk in thousands of dumpsights across the land. Out of the womb of civilization, down through countless Love Canals, issues forth death.

Civilization has shattered the intricate web that stabilizes the flows of life. Awareness of this problem has grown dramatically in just the past generation. But the direction of the biosphere's movement under the continuing impact of civilization is still toward degradation and decadence. So rapid is the growth and spread of civilization's power that the pace of death has, if anything, accelerated. All life is so interdependent that either we must stop the decline of the biosphere or fall with it, and we must be quick about it. Either quick, or dead.

The ecological problems of civilization, and their relation to the parable of the tribes, are discussed in chapter 7, "Man's Dominion."

The *intersocietal system* of civilization, as we have seen in Part I, is an arena for unregulated conflict. Civilization created conflict by opening for each civilized society possibilities that fostered conflicts of interest among societies, and by creating an anarchic situation that mitigated against synergistic action on the basis of interests shared by those societies. The consequent ceaseless struggle for power has been unsynergistic in several ways.

First, conflict gains its role in the intersocietal system even against the wishes of mankind. The parable of the tribes shows how even if all or almost all wish to live in peace and safety the structure of the intersocietal system prevents this optimal condition from prevailing. As the general historic plague of war comes to mankind uninvited, so too there occur specific wars no one wanted and other wars that whether wanted or not, benefit no one. As I write, a war is ongoing between Iraq and Iran of which it has been said, "It is a war both sides are losing."

Second, even when some benefit from the conflict, the struggle for power is almost invariably a minus-sum game, one in which the net gains of the winners are more than offset by the net losses of the losers. War is costly to wage, and the destruction wrought by it leaves the whole less than it was at the outset. But beyond those factors is a more important one akin to the economic idea of diminishing marginal utility: in most human affairs the movement from some to much gives less benefit than the movement from none to some. It follows that the movement from some to none does more harm than the movement from some to much does good. Thus the conqueror who now governs two lands may be better off, but his gain is not commensurate with the loss of the vanquished who is dispossessed. The profit of gaining a slave is far less than the debit of losing one's liberty. Yet, the history of civilization is full of just such exchanges imposed by uncontrolled force. The pursuit of such conflict may be "rational" (in, again, the economic sense of the pursuit of self-interest) from the point of view of the stronger party who stands to gain, but it is irrational and unsynergistic from the point of view of the system as a whole. In natural systems, such choices do not arise, for the power to injure the whole for the sake of oneself is granted no one.[3] The unprecedented anarchy of civilization's intersocietal system breaks down the order of synergy, making room for the corrupt regime of power.

Third, the immediate costs of the corrupt rule of power are compounded by the long-term social evolutionary costs. Out of the strife comes a selective process leading people along a path different from what they would have chosen. The absence of an overarching synergy to assure that intersocietal interactions serve the common interests has condemned mankind to domination by ever-escalating power systems largely indifferent to the well-being of human beings or other living creatures.

This unsynergistic determination of our social evolutionary destiny clearly endangers the long-term viability of the system. Never before has a living creature had in its repertoire of possible actions the virtual destruction of itself and other life on earth. Always, there might have streamed out of the indifferent heavens some giant meteor or comet or asteroid to burst the thin film of life's bubble on this planet. But living things, having been designed with no other options, always served life. Now two superpowers are capable of raining down upon the earth something like ten thousand warheads, each one of which is many times more destructive than the bombs that leveled Hiroshima and Nagasaki in seconds. If we are still here in fifty years, it is likely that the destructive capacity of that time will dwarf our own as ours does that of World War I, a war that seemed so catastrophic to its participants that they thought it must be the war to end all wars. For the first time in more than three billion years of life, a living system is relentlessly creating the means not of self-preservation, but of self-destruction.

I examine further the intersocietal system in chapter 7, "The State of Unnature."

(2) *Social systems: governmental and market.*—Unlike the intersocietal system, a civilized society is not, or at least need not be, anarchic. A society is regulated by a political order (as well as, in a different sense, by custom

---

3. When the deer forfeits its whole life that some lions may enjoy a single meal, there is a kind of imbalance; yet for the carnivore, the death of the other is required for the life of itself; and the system as a whole reflects the imbalance of each immediate transaction between lionkind and deerkind by arranging the food pyramid so that there is a counterbalancing disproportion in the numbers of the prey species and of the predator species who can, at any given time, live.

and religion). In many societies, this political order controls economic activity. In others, economic transactions are left free within certain limits of governmental regulation by deliberate choice out of a belief in the value of the economic order created by a free market system.

A *governmental system* makes it possible for a civilized society to be structured in a synergistic fashion. Laws can be designed and enforced to promote the common good. From a feeling of community and a sense of common interest, the members of society can cooperate for the general welfare: the greatest good for the greatest number, or some other synergistic principle.

Societies do achieve this synergy to a degree. But corruption is also a large part of the picture, perhaps more often than not the larger part. Certain elements of the social whole, often far from a numerical majority, devise ways to arrange social interactions to meet their own wants at whatever cost to their fellows' well-being and to the health of the society as a whole. Marx's work eloquently described how much the history of civilization is the history of the exploitation of the many by the few.[4] Whatever the shortcomings of his diagnosis of the root of this corruption, Marx's description of the symptoms had great acuity. Historical analysis has shown that in the typical archaic civilization, a mere one percent of the population would contrive to live in splendor and luxury while most of the rest groveled at the level of mere subsistence, with nonmaterial goods distributed with similar disproportion. Throughout the world, the part still sacrifices the whole for its own sake. This corruption takes many forms. The Marcos family in the Philippines and the Shah's family in Iran grew rich from their positions: the part that claims to serve the whole is in fact a parasite on the social body. Those who have followed Marx have certainly not solved this ancient problem of social corruption. It is not just the limousines in Moscow or the villas in the Polish countryside. The Gulag too is a monument to corruption: one must be far gone in the Party line to believe that most of these millions of "enemies of the state" were more of a threat to the well-being of the social whole than those who murdered them to protect their positions of dominance. Even in the relatively democratic societies of the West, each day's newspapers show how private interests suck like leeches the vitality of the social body: the revolving door in the United States between public regulators and the private institutions they regulate, the economizing upon food for the poor while rich agribusiness in the Western states gets subsidized water. The list is endless. Those who struggle against corruption are many, and their work has effect. But it is like rolling a ball uphill:

4. See chap. 7, "Men Are Not Ants."

the natural flow in civilized systems is down, toward corruption. The functionalist view of society as a (synergistic) whole never captures more than part of the reality.

The value of conceiving these age-old plagues of civilized society in terms of synergy (and its absence) lies less in its revelation of new injustices than in the new light it sheds on the problem of injustice. First, it underlines the contrast between the corruption of civilized society and the synergy of its natural counterparts. Hobbes also notes this contrast, identifying as the difference between human societies and those of ants and bees that in the latter "the common good differeth not from the private" (chap. 13). But without the evolutionary perspective, Hobbes could not see how aberrant is the human side of that contrast, what a recent departure our condition is from what we were embedded in for so very long. Many people have long seen in nature less a contrast than a reflection of the problems of civilized life, as in Aesop's tyrannical lions and rapacious wolves. Indeed, the triumph of the mighty over the weak is a phenomenon of societies other than man's. But in the light of the concept of synergy, we can see the difference between the warrior's sway over feudal society, on the one hand, and on the other the selection through combat of the stallion who leads the herd or of the alpha male baboon with preferential access to food and mates. This is the second point illuminated by synergy: that the problem of corruption is the degradation of the whole; that what is unique in civilization is not the split into victor and vanquished, nor even perhaps into oppressor and oppressed. It is the failure of these splits to serve an essential life-sustaining function for the collectivity as a whole. Human injustice is injustice because it is not a strategy for life but a disease of decay.

In chapter 7, "Men Are Not Ants," the problem of the corruption of civilized polities is explored further. There it is shown that the problem in this system resembles that in the others: that the rise of civilization gives rise to a kind of freedom of action; that this freedom in the part creates anarchy in the whole, and anarchy allows power to govern; that to the extent that power rules a system, even if embodied in a government, its functioning will be corrupt.

And what about the viability of the civilized society? That specific societies can rise and fall has been a central preoccupation of many theorists of history (such as Spengler and Toynbee). That phenomenon is explored in chapter 7, "The Death of the Unnatural." Internal corruption is certainly part of the explanation of the decline of specific civilized societies.

The *market system* has been promoted, from its first and most persuasive advocate Adam Smith to the present, precisely as a means of harnessing synergistically human activity. The market economy in Adam Smith's analysis does resemble the living ecosystem as I have described it: leave people alone, he says, to pursue their self-interests and their selfish actions will be combined "as if by an invisible hand" to maximize the wealth and well-being of all. This point of view has many believers still, some in very high office in the Anglo-Saxon world.

Any clear-eyed and dispassionate observer of the market economy must be struck with two important truths. On the one hand, the capitalist system is enormously successful in the production of wealth, as Adam Smith said, and in satisfying certain human needs. On the other hand, an unchecked capitalist economy seems blindly destructive of certain important values, creating a rich but hardly ideal society. The synergy of the invisible hand seems real but quite limited. (The limitations are explored in chapter 7, "The Market as a Power System.")

(3) *The civilized human being.*—The human organism still enters this world a child of nature. A few thousand years of civilization, no matter how explosive its evolution, have not had any appreciable impact upon our genetic heritage. The Stone Age baby, however, faces a world rather different from the one its biology has prepared it to meet. This agonizing encounter, explored in chapter 5 and particularly in "The War Within," suggests how the concept of synergy might apply to the human organism. More than the other living systems, the natural body was marked by harmony and cooperation among its components. Conflict played a role in the larger systems of nature, but within the individual organism synergy was fairly complete even at the manifest level. For the human being, civilization has sundered that natural harmony. Civilization implants within us commandments that war against the inclinations nature has given us. "(I)n the course of the civilizing process," Elias has written, people "seek to suppress in themselves every characteristic they feel to be 'animal'" (1978, p. 120). This statement may be taken as an emblem of an intricate pattern of conflict between the "parts" of the civilized human creature, between those parts given the human animal by nature and those instilled by civilization through socialization. A natural, if not perfect, peace gives way to unnatural internal war. Unpeaceful of mind, Saint Paul wrote:

> For I delight in the law of God after the inward man:
> But I see another law in my members, warring against the law of my mind, and bringing me into the captivity to the law of sin which is in my members.
> O wretched man that I am! who shall deliver me from the body of this death.
> (Romans 7:22–24)

One part works against the other.

Yet it is not entirely satisfactory to describe the change from harmony to conflict as one from synergy to corruption. Corruption has been defined here as the sacrifice of the well-being of the whole for the sake of the part. In one sense, this change is clearly against the interests of the whole. The excessive predominance of one part (reason, or spirit, or superego) over another (appetite, the flesh, the id) makes man a sick animal. But the injury to the whole is not necessarily for the sake of the part. The part, indeed, may be inflicting the disease of neurosis upon the organism to protect it from still worse fates. For what seems from one point of view a form of pathology is from another a strategy for survival. Given that man finds himself trapped in the systems of civilization, becoming a "sick animal" may be necessary adaptation for the human being. Even at the individual level, neurosis may be better understood less as sickness and more as a means of coping with a dangerous world: neurosis "makes sense" as a way of being, at least under the circumstances of its formation. Therapeutic change makes sense because people continue their neuroses beyond the formative situation into others where much better options are available. We say that in many ways the human response to the agonies of civilization can compound the inhumanity of the human environment. But ultimately, the unwholeness of civilized man's neurosis is less a corruption of the individual system than a reflection of a genuine dilemma imposed upon that system from without.

To describe the loss of wholeness of the human system a different concept is needed. It may be called *experiential wholeness*. The enjoyment of experiential wholeness has several dimensions. Most essential to it are to experience all of oneself and to experience oneself as a harmonious whole. When Saint Paul speaks of his "members" he speaks as if of something other, distinct from the "I" who wills the more spiritual course. When Freud names the human natural impulses the id (= "it") while calling the conscious and rational part of the self the ego (= "I"), it clearly reflects an identification with a part of the self over another. One of the goals of a humanistic psychotherapy is to help a person come to recognize and experience his whole being as himself, neither denying nor projecting it beyond the boundaries of self-awareness. Another goal is to help resolve the conflicts among the parts, to bring peace of mind where neurotic wars have been fought. It may be that by nature the human being falls short of such wholeness, but certainly the wrenching demands of civilization magnify the unwholeness of human experience.

Another dimension of experiential wholeness could be the experience of oneself as harmoniously connected with the surrounding social and natural worlds. It can easily be shown that these bonds of connectedness are strong in primitive societies and have been progressively undermined in the course of civilization. The opposite of this connectedness can be called alienation, or anomie, the feeling of oneself apart.[5]

Paul Tillich has written that the human being lives in a state of separateness—separated from oneself, one's fellows, one's God. This state he calls sin. A thesis of this work is that the problem of sin is not so much original to our natures as it is the fruit of the circumstance of our leaving Eden.

3.   The Turning Point:
Biological Evolution versus Social Evolution

Introduction: The Problem of Discontinuity

The preceding section drew a sharp contrast between the systems of nature and those of civilization. With the coming of civilization, an ancient intricate pattern of wholeness began systematically to be demolished and replaced by a new pattern governed less by the needs of life than by the dangerous logic of power. This is a vision of radical discontinuity in the unfolding of life on this planet. This emphasis on discontinuity, as much as any other single point, is what differentiates the parable of the tribes from other theories that have attempted to illuminate our present human condition in the light of the biological evolutionary processes that created us.

The Social Darwinists, for example, were apostles of continuity who equated the competitive struggles of civilization with the "struggle for existence" which Darwin saw in nature. The parable of the tribes challenges that equation, maintaining that the power struggles of civilization reflect a fundamental anarchy unique to civilization and alien to the Law of the Jungle, and that in the absence of an overarching life-protecting order such struggle, unlike those in nature, can be destructive of all life-serving values.

More recently, the sociobiologists have committed the "continuity fallacy" in the construction of a new theoretical perspective. They instruct us to regard the observable behaviors of civilized human beings as fairly direct expressions of our genetic heritage. The parable of the tribes shares with the sociobiologists the view that man has an important inborn nature but denies that the human condition under civilization affords anything close to a clear and undistorted view of that nature. The way the sociobiologist infers the hidden messages of our genes from the manifest

5. See chap. 5, "Unreasonable Reason."

practices and attitudes of our civilized social life is reminiscent of the naïve overextrapolations many made from Zuckerman's observations of the baboons in the London Zoo. Our history has a break in it, a rapid journey from, as it were, savanna to zoo. Our condition is distorted by our having been trapped within two evolutionary processes, the second of which emerged from the first, but differs radically from it.

The fruits of the two evolutionary processes have here been contrasted in the starkest terms. This dichotomy may seem implausible to some. For one thing, the belief in continuity seems to die hard: all is one, everything is natural. For another, biological and social evolution do indeed exhibit strong parallels. Even if the Social Darwinists were mistaken in their conclusions, they correctly perceived that civilization, like biological nature, is shaped by a selection for what is best able to survive. Thus, even if one grants the validity of the parable of the tribes as descriptive of (a large part of) the evolutionary dynamic of civilization, the question still arises: how *could* two evolutionary processes, in some ways rather alike, create results structurally so different? To make more persuasive the present critique of civilization as breaking from and undermining the ancient wholeness of living systems, I delineate the important ways in which the two evolutionary processes differ. From the differences in the shaping processes derive the differences in the shape of the systems.

Different Mechanisms of Change

One of the most obvious differences between the two evolutionary processes is in the source of novelty.[6] New genetic possibilities arise more or less randomly (at least until the civilized technology of recombinant DNA), through the process of mutation. Random mutations are generally deleterious and disappear. In social evolution, by contrast, conscious human purpose creates new possibilities (Simpson, in Washburn and Jay, 1968, pp. 141–142). The entry of purpose into the generation of the material for selection means a much higher proportion of new forms will have adaptive usefulness. The new teleological forces accelerate the process.

That acceleration, which the new way of generating innovations begins, the new way of transmitting them greatly compounds. In biological evolution, only the direct descendants of a successful mutant can utilize a given advantageous change. Sexual reproduction has advantages over asexual reproduction in this respect in that it allows different advantageous strains to combine their advantages. But the transmission of cultural innovations is exponentially more efficient. Waddington writes: "The

6. See chap. 2, "The Mother of Invention."

233

major weakness of the biological system from an evolutionary point of view is that, although it ensures some mixing of hereditary qualities from different individuals, it limits the number of individuals which can participate in this mixing to only two. . . . This restriction of hybridization is greatly reduced in the human socio-genetic system" (in Banton, 1961, p. 117). In "The Human Evolutionary System," Waddington goes on to discuss how the means of transmitting cultural innovations has become increasingly efficient, allowing those innovations that can be conceptualized to be communicated even without person-to-person contact, through writing and other processes. We have now reached the point where an important and apparently advantageous innovation achieved anywhere in the human cultural system can be disseminated throughout the whole system almost immediately. Cultural dissemination is a far more efficient means of spreading information than biological insemination.

These first two factors together yield an important characteristic of social evolution: its unprecedented speed.

Another new aspect of the process of evolutionary change is directly connected with the problem of power: the ascendancy, with the rise of civilization, of direct competition. In biological evolution, species or varieties within a species generally compete with one another indirectly. Indirect competition is a long-term process through which those living forms which prove more viable spread and displace the less viable with little direct conflict.[7] In social evolution, different forms are likely to compete directly through active confrontation with one another. By analogy, the indirect competition that is more characteristic of biological evolution is like a game of golf whereas the direct competition between civilized societies is like a boxing match. Why would direct competition play a larger role in social than in biological evolution? One part of the answer may be the consciousness of the competitors of the fact of competition. Wheat and rye competing in a field do not know they are competing. A mutant strain of bear will compete with the older type without any of the participants knowing that a test for superior viability is being conducted. The awareness of human beings that the spread of their society conflicts with the needs of another society makes people more likely to join that conflict directly.

An investigation of the new factors—the emergence of consciousness and purpose, the omnidirectional transmissibility of new forms, the (consequent) dramatic acceleration of the rate of change, and the tendency for alternative forms to compete more directly—illuminates some of the most prominent, and troublesome, characteristics of civilized systems.

7. E.g., the displacement of marsupials by placentals when North and South America joined was principally by such indirect means. The marsupials were "outfed and outbred" (see Gould, 1981, pp. 293–295).

Evolving Different Kinds of Structure

The extraordinary efficiency with which new cultural possibilities are generated and spread would appear to be of great benefit. Cultural evolution does not need eons to spread its improvements.

But fast change is dangerous change. Eugene Odum writes of the "principle of the instant pathogen," referring to the markedly negative effects that often come from sudden, large-scale change in an ecosystem (1971, p. 200). Homeostatic control and balance in an ecological system "comes only after a period of evolutionary adjustment" (p. 35). The suddenness of man's impact on his environment is a major source of his destructiveness. A fungus from China quickly destroys America's magnificent chestnut forests. The sudden introduction of goats onto an island soon renders it barren. When a host is killed by its parasite, as was said earlier, one knows the relationship is of recent origin. Civilized man upon this earth seems like such a parasite.

> The biosphere with industrial man suddenly added is like a balanced aquarium into which large animals are introduced. Consumption temporarily exceeds production, the balance is upset, the products of respiration accumulate, and the fuels for consumption become scarcer and scarcer. . . . In some experimental systems balance is achieved only after the large consumers are dead. (Howard Odum, 1971, p. 18)

Nature, Leibniz said, does not make leaps (*Nature non facit saltus*). Civilization does, and it has no way of looking first. A new form in biological evolution will spread very gradually through the genetic system,[8] and will become general only if the short-run advantages that allow it to survive and spread at the outset are combined with long-run advantages, or at least long-run viability. In the cultural system, by contrast, new forms can spread rapidly without their ultimate viability having been demonstrated anywhere. The hyperefficiency of transmission can make civilization like a cancer. Even without the parable of the tribes, the ability of the untested to become the universal would make civilization dangerous. The necessary tests, like those of ponderous biological evolution, may take time far beyond human ken or patience. So many strategies have benefits that are immediately clear, but costs that, though eventually catastrophic, are paid only after many generations.

The suddenness of the changes wrought by civilization also affects competition within the system: abrupt change intensifies competition. In

8. The attack, by Stephen Jay Gould and others, on the "gradualism" of Darwinian orthodoxy does not really challenge the point of view presented here. What Gould argues for is rapid origin of new forms (within small populations) (1981, pp. 182–185). What is pertinent to the issue here is the rapidity with which genetic innovations spread—a matter with which, as I understand it, the model of punctuated equilibria is not concerned.

235

biologically evolved situations, according to Cox et al., "species that compete for food or other resources have evolved means of reducing the pressures of competition and of dividing up the resources between them. This is mutually advantageous since it reduces the risk of either species being eliminated and made extinct by competition with the others. This is an advantage not only to the species directly involved but to the whole community of species in the habitat . . ." (1976, p. 67). When nonliving nature forces sudden changes upon living communities (as in the joining of North and South America) interspecific competition can become intense and, until a new equilibrium is reached, destructive. With the rise of civilization, life itself has created a sudden disequilibrium and the precipitous plunge into catastrophic competition. A big question about civilization is whether it will make it to a later stage of synergistically minimizing competitive pressures. The extraordinary transmissibility of cultural forms is dangerous not only because of the suddenness of the changes it makes possible but also because of the structure of the system it creates.

If new forms simply descended through direct descendants, as in genetic transmission, the unviable might ultimately die out and leave behind the more viable alternatives. But in cultural evolution, all lines can converge. This cultural homogenization (see chap. 3) is a "trend in cultural evolution which is almost totally absent in biological evolution" (Kaplan, in Sahlins and Service, 1960, p. 73). Indeed, the entire thrust of development in biological systems is toward diversity. The ecological climax, C. Barry Cox says, entails the greatest diversification of species (1976, p. 53). The numerous species, each with its own adaptations, none so numerous as to displace the others, "result in a greater degree of stability for the community" (p. 67). But the "climax" of civilization's evolution seems to be that state where, as Eiseley was quoted earlier as saying, "instead of many adaptive organisms a single gigantic animal embodies the only organic future of the world." It is the danger of one basket for all one's eggs.

This rapid and convergent evolutionary process might be reckless even without the problem of power. But when one adds to these factors the problem of direct competition and the selective process it creates, we can see that not only does social evolution put all its eggs in one basket, but it chooses a basket that is rotten.

A powerful civilized society can be like a rabid dog—doomed itself to die, yet able to impose its disease on others whom it contacts. Over centuries, many agricultural civilizations have destroyed the land from which they gained their livelihood and power, all the while spreading their ecological and other ways outward, displacing ecologically sounder cultural approaches. The superiority of power in systems with direct competition need only be quite temporary. The selection is for power maximization, and what generates the most power in the short run may lead to ruin in the long. Rome stripped Italy's rich forests to build its fleets: triumph now, pay later. In Brazil right now, primitive peoples with viable ways of living in the Amazon jungle are being displaced, their ways of life destroyed, by potent but unsustainable "development" (D. Price, 1981). With power uncontrolled, the criterion for selection is an advantage that need only be momentary, like an injection of "speed" to charge up the system now only to crash hard later, but the drug enters the common bloodstream of mankind. Even after the unviable systems crash, they leave their pathology in those who remain: there are no meek left to inherit. The apparent boon of efficient transmissibility, when combined with the contagion of power maximization, makes civilization a disease.

Rapidly converging toward a single cultural option designed through intense competition for the immediate maximization of power, civilization is a uniquely unwhole living system.

The Agony of the Torn

In the ancient world, for example, in the time of Alexander the Great, one grisly form of execution consisted of bending two trees to the same spot, tying the legs of the condemned to each, and releasing the trees. Part of the problem of civilization is like that.

Although part of the problem of civilization is that its evolutionary process differs in character from that of nature, another part lies in the simple fact that there are two simultaneous processes. (That execution would not work the same with only one tree.) With the appearance of civilized man, for the first time in the history of life on earth a species is in the grasp of two distinct and not necessarily harmonious evolutionary processes. Between the demands of his nature and those of his civilization, man is torn.

This unprecedented possibility for conflicting demands strikes at wholeness in two ways. It undermines what was called experiential wholeness, and it casts creatures for the first time into roles they cannot be relied upon to play. Human nature always tries to express itself; civilization constantly demands that it do otherwise. Aside from the pain it causes the human creature, this conflict also threatens the effective functioning of the system. (For example, a creature evolved only for the responsibilities of egalitarian groups may, in a position of power in a

civilized society, act corruptly and weaken the whole.) A system that requires a continuous redirection of energies from their natural flow is on
an uphill course. By a kind of entropy, such systems are likely to roll
back to the bottom.

4. Artificial Wholeness:
Justice as the Antidote for Power

The Restraint of Power

Power acts like an instant pathogen, in E. Odum's phrase. It is a sudden
new phenomenon in the living systems of the earth, and it works as a
poison eating away at the health (O. E. *hàelp,* whole) of those systems. To
restore that health, mankind must find a way of restraining power. In
the old regime, all forces could flow unrestrained because the synergistic
evolution of those forces effected a kind of prior restraint. Civilized
people and their systems, however, have sprung forth armed with powers
that no whole order has granted or reviewed in advance. "Surely the
mountain lion," writes Gregory Bateson, "when he kills the deer is not
acting to protect the grass from overgrazing" (1972, p. 504). Yet when
those among us who are like lions kill those who are like deer, none but
the lions profit. There is for us no way back into the old regime where
creatures can be free in action because they are controlled in design. We
humans who have redesigned our own powers for action must construct
also our own system of restraints.

This restraining system must allow something other than power to
rule the conduct of civilized systems. The design of restraints has two
components, one practical and one moral. The practical aspect derives
from the paradox that, to a significant extent, only power can control
power. It is necessary therefore to design systems with "checks and balances" so that powers cancel each other out and make room for other
factors to govern. (The wholeness of the ecosystem too, derives from
checks and balances of a sort.) But if we ask what kind of order is desirable
to replace the regime of power, we are led to seek some moral principle
that we wish to characterize the workings of our systems. Also, as we
probably cannot manage so to arrange powers that all are canceled, we
require a moral principle by which those who do wield powers should
act. Leaving aside the practical problems of system design, I investigate
now that moral dimension of the desired regime of artificial wholeness.

Morality is only a human problem, for only humans can subvert wholeness by doing what comes naturally. We attempt to introduce moral force

to check the natural drives of self-interest that prove dangerous in the unnatural conditions of anarchy. We want the play of power to be checked by a moral principle that leads away from corruption to synergy.

Consider two rules to comprise this synergistic principle. (*a*) Where power is exercised, I say, it should not be used to benefit the wielder of power at the expense of the health of the system as a whole; and (*b*) where different parts of the system have conflicts of interest, the conflicts should be resolved not by their differences in power but by some moral principle which, if always followed, would ultimately be to the benefit of all in the system.

Justice as Synergy

We do not need to invent a name for this synergistic moral principle, because the rules described above capture the essence of a virtue central to philosophic thought for millennia. That virtue is called *justice*.

Over the ages, the concept of justice has had many meanings. It is nonetheless clear that its use here as a specific moral antidote to the problem of power is not idiosyncratic but lies near the heart of this ancient and important concept. To see the essential connection between justice and power we can turn to Plato's *Republic*, that classic inquiry into the meaning of justice. The first definition given there is that offered by the character Thrasymachus who says that "the just is nothing other than the advantage of the stronger" (338C). This makes a good starting point, for basically it is a way of eliminating the idea of justice, of depicting the way of the world unconstrained by moral principle. What happens, happens, Thrasymachus says in effect. Earlier we encountered a similar defining away of the moral into the amoral, when Thucydides quoted the Athenians as saying: "You know as well as we do that right, as the world goes, is only in question between equals in power, while the strong do what they can and the weak suffer what they must" (5. 90). The idea that "might makes right" is a denial of the relevance of the moral dimension. If "right" is in question only between equals in power, it is never really in question at all. What the Athenians are describing is concern not with a moral principle but with striking advantageous bargains, and this is but a continuation of the amoral principle of getting what one can. If "justice" is whatever the strong impose upon the weak, then there is no basis for a moral critique of the corruption of civilized systems. Though they sweep away the problem of what *should be*, these ideas describe well what *is* (or at least what tends to be): the rule of power. And they serve for us the useful purpose of showing that moral concepts like rights and justice are specifically concerned with restraining the rule of power.

Just as the problem of power is the target of justice, so also are the two synergistic rules mentioned above at the heart of traditional views of what justice requires. (*a*) Justice requires that the whole not be subverted for the more powerful part. Thrasymachus again helps out, succinctly describing the injustice of the world: "(E)ach ruling group sets down laws for its own advantage. . . . (A)ll declare that what they have set down—their own advantage—is just for the ruled, and the man who departs from it they punish as a breaker of the law and a doer of unjust deeds" (338E). This is the reality that, when we can depart from the realm of hypocrisy and arrive at a genuine morality, justice changes. (*b*) At the heart of the battle of justice against corruption is a notion of impartiality, of the need for rules that would ultimately benefit all because in any given case they are indifferent to whom they benefit. Justice with her scales is blind, determining rights without regard to the power of the parties in conflict before her. The rules of justice are those we would choose if we had no interest in the case, or rather if we did not know which of the conflicting interests would be ours. This essential aspect of justice is illustrated in John Rawls's *A Theory of Justice*. Rawls's hypothetical just society would be governed by principles that "free and rational persons concerned to further their own interests" would agree to in a situation where "no one knows his place in society, his class position or social status, nor does any one know his fortune in the distribution of natural assets and abilities, his intelligence, strength and the like" (1971, p. 12). Blind choice engenders a disinterestedness that makes possible the emergence of rules to maximize the interests of all. At the essence of the concept of justice lies a commitment to synergy in human affairs.

It can therefore be seen that the moral principle by which the rule of power might be restrained for the sake of synergy is the venerable principle called justice. As synergy is an aspect of that wholeness we find in natural systems, the synergistic principle of justice can be viewed as part of a system of natural law; in our unnatural dilemma, we can turn to nature for moral guidance and imitate her natural wholeness with an artificial one.

Justice is the moral antidote to the poisonous rule of power. As the parable of the tribes shows power to be the primary problem of civilized life, so correspondingly, according to Rawls, "Justice is the first virtue of social institutions" (ibid.).

Limits to the Scope of Justice

It is not, however, the only virtue. Justice is a specific remedy for the ills caused by the abuse of power. Even where power is wholly controlled for the sake of synergy, other ills will remain the correction of which is not required by justice or, to put it another way, which must be addressed in the name of other moral virtues. We want justice to protect the weak from the powerful, but it beclouds an important idea to make it protective of everyone from misfortune of every kind. We rightly are concerned whenever we find a person lying injured upon the ground. But we are right also in regarding differently the case of the person who has fallen from a tree from that of the person who has been beaten by thugs. We bring the doctor to each but the officers of justice only to the latter.

Justice has limits. Justice is a principle for *governing the interactions* of the parts of a system. At those junctures in a system where the parts have an impact upon one another, we wish to be sure that the impact is not unjust. A system was defined as an aggregate of elements which interact and which cannot therefore be entirely understood in isolation. But, as the pervasiveness of the interactions can vary, systemhood is a matter of degree, and the parts of a system also exist as wholes in themselves, with their own spheres of autonomy. Consider, for example, what might be called "the global system of civilized societies." In, say, the eighteenth century, a global system might be said to have existed—the British were in India, the New World was colonized, and so on. Two thousand years ago, however, the great civilizations of Rome and China had only the most tenuous and indirect connections with each other, and the Old World and the New proceeded in virtually complete isolation from each other. Today, the degree of interaction weaving all societies into a single system is more extensive than ever before, and still increasing. As systems can vary in the intensity of their interactions, the applicability of the concept of "justice as interactions governed justly" will also vary.

Justice, therefore, will have a greater or lesser role in a system depending on the degree to which it *is* a system. The misapplication of justice can result in injustice in either of two ways: its overapplication, beyond the domain of actual interaction, unjustly trespasses upon the proper domain of autonomy of the parts; its underapplication, leaving some interactions unregulated by justice, simply leaves intact some of the original injustice to which civilized interactions are prone. The error of overapplication can be called the collectivist fallacy, that of underapplication the individualist fallacy.

A collectivist principle of justice is exemplified by Marx's dictum: "From each according to his ability; to each according to his need." Implicit in this statement is the assumption that everything belongs to the social whole, that the individual exists entirely as a part of a larger collectivity and is not at all a whole in himself. To some extent, in our times this vision of the relationship between individuals and society has become a self-fulfilling image: in countries where Marx's vision prevails, individuals have been denied autonomous spheres protected from governance

241

by the whole; they have been freed from the necessity or right of shaping their own destiny. But human beings are not simply the creatures of their collectivities. An excessively collectivist approach not only deprives people of an important ingredient of their full humanity but also exposes them to the most profound injustices at the hands of the presumed representatives of the collectivity. An overly collectivist view of justice leads readily to the injustice of a Gulag.

Only a limited concept of justice is capable of governing the complex and multilevel structure of the universe of human interactions. Mankind must be seen as a tiered structure consisting of parts which are also wholes and which are therefore partly responsible for their own destiny. Individual, family, nation—the well-being of each is in part a function of its treatment within a larger whole, but is in part also its own to determine. If I am pushed in front of a truck, I have justice on my side to compensate my injuries; if my own carelessness put me there, I do not.

"To each according to his need" will not do as a comprehensive principle of justice. If we earthlings were suddenly to encounter four billion other creatures living elsewhere in the solar system, but within reach, who were suffering from starvation, would justice require that we share with them our food? No, for as their problems anteceded any contact between us, it is impossible that we are responsible for them. Justice involves the paying of debts, a restitution of what is owed. Where justice is not in question, it becomes a matter of charity, of giving what is not owed. We might feed our starving space neighbors out of love, or charity, but not for the sake of justice. The distinction is important, for justice is traditionally obligatory and, where possible, it is enforced, while charity is given freely. A terrestrial version of the same dilemma is the North-South conflict. In some people the collectivist vision (combined perhaps with self-interest) has fostered the assumption that the wealth of the rich nations was taken from the poor so that the poverty of the poor is the responsibility of the rich. ("Property is theft," by implying that gain is invariably a function of power interaction, is an idea that feeds the collectivist vision.) If that were so, and the evidence suggests that it is so only to a rather limited extent, then indeed justice would require that inequalities of wealth among societies be rectified. If we see these differences as consequences of unequal productivity within societies rather than of unjust distribution among them, the transfer of wealth from rich to poor becomes a matter of charity, or perhaps even of enlightened self-interest, but not of justice.

To demand that justice ensure universal equality of outcome is to chain everyone to a universal collectivity, unjustly robbing all of an essential human property—autonomy and the responsibility that goes with it.

242

The idea of Justice, Ltd. is more congenial to the individualist vision, which indeed was formulated to protect human freedom and autonomy from tyrannical authority. Individualism, however, is prone to excesses of its own. The individualist tends to depict a human reality in which interactions consist only of the making of contracts—discrete transactions into which autonomous individuals, responsible for themselves, freely enter. Where the collectivist commits the fallacy of making the human being wholly a function of the society, the individualist commits the opposite fallacy of making society wholly the creation of completely autonomous individuals. The idea of a limited social contract freely formed in the hypothetical past by individuals living wholly outside of all society casts an inappropriate degree of legitimacy over existing social relationships in individualist societies. Indeed, our "state of nature" was never so individualist, and the fabric of interactions (just and unjust) has always been densely woven.

No society is only a market where deals are freely struck. An individualist principle of justice may be stated: "From each according to his ability to contribute, and to each according to the value of his contributions." There is indeed a "justice of the market." But just as the collectivist tends to overestimate the degree of interaction, the individualist tends to underestimate it. Not all interactions consist of such identifiable, free, and mutually beneficial transactions. When the capitalist pays the worker a competitive wage, the justice of the marketplace can overlay an intricate network of other social, political, and historical interactions that make that instantaneous transaction an extension of injustice. Blindness to this intricate web of interaction stretching through time leads to blindness also to the ways that the play of power, like a shuttle across a loom, weaves injustice into the social fabric.

The task of justice is both large and subtle.

Justice and the Future

Synergy was one of the dimensions of wholeness, that is, that pertaining to the nature of interactions within a system at a given time. Justice, I have tried to show, provides for that synergy which the rule of power tends to subvert. But what of the other dimension, viability, which pertains to the maintenance of wholeness through time? Can justice help protect also the wholeness of a system into the future?

It is clear that the past, present, and future represent a system, for the present is a function of the past, and the future a function of the present. A society (or any other system) at t_x cannot be understood without reference to the state of that society at t_{x-1}. The apparent unidirectional

243

flow of time makes the systems created by time exceptional in their structure because the interactions among the parts of the system are inevitably one way. Posterity is dependent upon what we do, but we cannot be dependent upon what posterity will do. This unidirectional character of interaction implies a clear inequality of power. One is reminded of that definition of power as the ability to speak, whereas weakness is the necessity to listen. Between present and future, the present does all the speaking while the future cannot be but mute. And as one would expect with such inequalities of power, the injury to wholeness is predictably that the civilized present uses its power to rob the future. Après nous, le deluge. People spend the goods of their system—topsoil, aquifer water, minerals, forests—as if there were no tomorrow, because for themselves as individuals there is not. Fortunately, people's loving identification with their children (and eventually, perhaps, with their children's children) moderates the exploitative relationship between present and future, but generations yet unborn still generally get short shrift. After all, as Kenneth Boulding has put it, "What has posterity ever done for me?"

All the ingredients are here to make the application of justice appropriate. That the "parts" of the system are different times has altered neither the fact of interaction nor the problem that the abuse of inequalities of power yields injustice.

The application of the principle of justice, therefore, can serve also to protect the viability of systems. By requiring the people of the present time to restrain their power, justice protects the future health of human systems. If the needs of the future are made by justice to weigh as heavily as those of the present, despite the inequalities of power, the tendencies of civilized systems to become degraded with time will be checked.

In the man-made concept of justice, therefore, civilized peoples can find an apt moral and analytic tool for reinstating into systems plagued by the problem of power a kind of wholeness which nature no longer can protect.

Chapter Seven

The Parable of the Tribes and the Loss of Wholeness

In chapter 6, the loss of wholeness was briefly described for each of the several major civilized systems. In this chapter, each of these systems is explored in greater depth: (*a*) to describe more fully the loss of wholeness and its costs; and (*b*) to demonstrate the extent to which the parable of the tribes can help explain these destructive transformations of systemic structure.

1. Man's Dominion: Power and the Degradation of the Ecosystem

A. Paradise Lost

A New and Dangerous Regime.—Civilized man, the revolutionary creature, has overthrown the natural order and established a new regime. It is a regime of tyranny.

Earlier I wrote that power "is a sudden new phenomenon in the living systems of the earth" (p. 238). The validity of this statement depends on extending the concept of power beyond the original definition as the ability to impose one's will regardless of the will of others. Surely, the lion imposes his will upon the zebra. What is different about man's ecological power?

An important difference is one of degree. Howard Odum writes that while there may be in the natural system some "locally overpowering units" like the tiger or the killer whale, "their power is still a small part of the total power budget" (1971, p. 213). The power of these species is small because the magnitude of the role of the individual animals necessitates their being thinly distributed throughout the system as a whole. Stable natural systems are characterized by "much decentralization of control" (ibid.). The regime that civilization has imposed upon nature is like an organized horde of tigers swarming across the land.

A second difference was stressed earlier: man alone has had the power to define his own role outside the control of an overarching order. Ultimately this confers upon man the unique power to structure the system according to terms of his own choosing.

The Unbound One.—This chapter examines how regimes based on power injure the natural wholeness of living systems. Injury is certainly an evident consequence of man's rulership of nature. Freed from biologically evolved constraints, civilized man has exploited and wounded the natural order in several ways:

Uncontrolled in his dealings with other living things, man has exterminated species, stripped the land of trees and grasses, and left the world more dead than he found it. *Homo* has proved more *faber* than *sapiens.*

With no order to regulate his interventions into the cycles of essential nonliving materials, man has poisoned the waters, polluted and altered the atmosphere, and maximized immediate productivity at the sacrifice of resource maintenance. Man's strategy for exploiting nature, as E. Odum points out (1971, p. 21) is the opposite of nature's strategy for itself. And as the strategy of nature is designed to maximize the stable flourishing of life, the strategy of civilization seems to threaten the opposite result.

Man's unprecedented global mobility allows him to introduce disruptive novelties, whether they be natural living creatures placed in settings unnatural to them (rabbits in Australia, gypsy moths in North America) or unnatural substances injurious to living cycles (e.g., DDT, PCB, Kepone). Man's power in nature is not like that of an effective governor but like that of the proverbial bull in a china shop.

With his way of life not set, man's numbers on earth are also ungoverned, with dangers both to mankind and to the environment as a whole. Bertrand Russell described "every living being [as] a sort of imperialist, seeking to transform as much as possible into itself and its seed" (quoted in

Leslie White, 1959, p. 37). But only in man can this "imperialism" be translated into an empire, an empire that threatens the long-term degradation of the living environment.

Corruption as Suicide.—"And the prosperity of fools shall destroy them" (Proverbs 1:32).

As is often the case with the tragedy of civilization, man's very glory is also his undoing. Nothing enduring can be built without a stable foundation. The tragic paradox of human power is epitomized by H. Donald Hughes's statement in *The Ecology in Ancient Civilizations:* "The rise of civilizations depended upon the increasing ability of people to use and control their natural environment, and the downfall of these same civilizations was due to their failure to maintain a harmonious balance with nature" (1975, p. 29). He documents this proposition with respect to various specific civilizations.

The dangers of self-destruction which plagued the ancient world are even more pronounced today with the greatly magnified powers of modern civilization. Cole, for example, argues that we have been lucky so far. Had DDT possessed certain conceivable properties, he warns, "it could have brought an end to life on earth" (in Helfrich, 1970, p. 4); and perhaps one of the half million chemicals we carelessly dump into the soil, air, and water could so interrupt the nitrogen cycle as to "cause the extinction of life" (p. 7). The new regime would appear to be engaged in playing biospheric Russian roulette.

Like most corrupt rulers, man uses his powers to satisfy his wants regardless of the cost to others. But such is the interdependence of living systems that one ultimately does to oneself as one does unto others. Life played right is a plus–sum game; played wrong, it is minus–sum. The power regime is life played wrong. When one plays that way, therefore, to win is ultimately to lose. As Gregory Bateson writes, "A creature that wins against its environment destroys itself" (1972, p. 493).

Sinning Freely.—A central issue of chapter 1 was whether the evolution of civilization and the manifest problems that accompanied it are best understood as governed by human choice or by unchosen forces. This work stresses the latter, and shortly will explore the role of the parable of the tribes in shaping the evolution of civilized man's relationship to nature. Of all the problematic dimensions of civilization, however, the ecological problem is the most explicable in terms of human freedom.

By their intelligence and creativity, human beings discovered the means to choose new ecological arrangements. Where the choice was between life and death, people (understandably) chose life and, with this escape from fixed natural limits imposed by death, human numbers have swelled.

247

Even today, we can see nature's old regime being overthrown by choices of this sort: in Africa, for example, where modern public health procedures and other factors diminish the diseases that formerly checked population growth, some of this earth's last great primeval ecosystems are rapidly being overtaken by agricultural expansion needed to feed the new millions.

The ecological threat posed by the free creature is not, however, confined to the preservation of mere survival. If one emblem of ecological degradation is the famished peoples of the Sahel picking their land clean of the last vestiges of wooded growth, another is the rich woman in the snow leopard coat. Where the choice is between abundance and super-abundance, people still choose more. Those who eat of the dwindling whale population are not starving. Those who grow and those who eat the bounty of America's eroding fruited plains do not have starvation as their only alternative to the present less expensive but needlessly wasteful methods of tillage. Those who enjoy furniture made of the lovely wood from the earth's vanishing tropical forests would not otherwise lack for all comforts. People choose, and in their freedom to choose they place their own wants and needs above all else.

If human choice has proven destructive of ecological wholeness, it would seem that human folly and wickedness are largely to blame. Folly in the sense that human understanding, however great by any previous terrestrial standard, has consistently lagged behind the reach of human impact on the environment. Who in the early civilization of the Fertile Crescent could have known, for example, that the magnificent irrigation networks that made the land green were slowly salting the soil and leading to desolation more bleak than before man's intrusions (see Hughes, 1975, p. 34)? But wickedness, too, in the sense of a willingness unjustly to serve oneself without regard to the costs to others. The problem of salting from irrigation is now known, but the process goes on. The willingness of the present unjustly to impose its costs upon the future is revealed in countless ways, in the careless dumping of hazardous wastes, in the depletion of fisheries, the scarring of the land by stripmining. Unjust and wicked too is the calculus by which the costs to nonhuman forms of life are slighted when there are human profits to be made. An image comes to mind which captures all too much of man's relationship to nature. The carcass of a rhinoceros rots in the African sun. It is intact but for its great horn, which has been severed by the murdering poacher who will enrich himself from its sale as an aphrodisiac. The rhinoceros is threatened with extinction. The aphrodisiac property of ground rhinoceros horn is, by all evidence, an illusion.

Man eats of the fruit of knowledge that he may play god, and death enters the Garden—not the death of individual creatures, which has always been there, but death of the Garden itself.

The Justification of Injustice.—To this way of viewing the loss of wholeness in the ecosystem, the parable of the tribes is irrelevant—but clearly the problem of power is not. This has been evident from the description of a man as a tyrant in the new regime of nature, and of the injustice that human exploitation of the environment entails. Power here corrupts the system not through its workings among people but between people and the other elements of the ecosystem.

For many people who despise the tyranny of some people over others, man's exploitation of nature seems perfectly natural and justified. But perhaps the clear parallels between the justifications given for human dominance over nature and those given for other tyrannies can persuasively suggest that man's dominion is merely another example of corrupt exploitation based on superior power.

The ruler always proves his rule is just that. This justification in the West, which has furthest advanced the human exploitation of nature, goes back to our cultural roots, which reach primarily back to Israel and to Greece. The Judeo–Christian tradition wastes no time in establishing man's dominant position. It is in the first chapter of the first book of the Bible. Scarcely has the natural order been created, with a special creation of man in God's image, than God grants the first man and woman "dominion over the fish of the sea, and over the fowl of the air, and over every living thing that moveth upon the earth." Man thus enjoys a divine right of king over nature. From Athens, a similar image of nature as inherently hierarchical can be found, albeit drawn in a medium intellectually wholly different. Quoth Aristotle:

> We may infer, after the birth of animals, plants exist for their sake, and that the other animals exist for the sake of man, the tame for use and good, the wild, if not all, at least the greater part of them, for food, and for the provision of clothing and various instruments. Now if nature makes nothing incomplete, and nothing in vain, the inference must be that she has made all animals for the sake of man. (*Politics* 1, 8, 1256b)

At the foundation of Western culture, therefore, we find a distorted image of the natural regime. For, contrary to Genesis and to Aristotle, natural living systems are ordered without rulership, and while the "lower" elements of the system may be necessary for the survival of the "higher," no element exists "for the sake" of the others. In part this distortion of nature as hierarchy may be a projection onto the wider cosmos of the power relations that had come to pervade human relations in the human

249

microcosm (just as the Creator, in such an environment, becomes imaged as King of the Universe). But this image also has the look of propagandistic rationalization. It has helped smooth the way for the new regime of hierarchy which, though neither God-given nor logically required, civilization has increasingly established over nature.

Man proceeds in his conquest of other creatures. Students of war have often noted that conquest is psychologically facilitated by creating an image of its object as wholly different, alien and inferior. When nations go to war, their propaganda dehumanizes the foe. Colonial powers mere decades ago justified their domination by portraying the native peoples as lesser beings. Americans proclaimed the inferiority of blacks to justify their enslavement and of Indians to establish the right of expropriation and extermination. These devices are still employed against our fellow animals.

It is difficult to be ruthless toward those with whom we feel kinship. We thus exaggerate our difference from other animals. What the "special creation" does in theology, our incessant self-definition in terms of our uniqueness does in anthropology—tool-using, laughing, symbol-making, and so on. This stress on man's distinctions overlooks our considerable evolutionary kinship with other animals (see Hallowell, in Tax, 1960, p. 317). Distortions of reality betray our motives. Like the dehumanization of the enemy, our de-animalization of ourselves removes inhibitions to our ruthlessness. What is different from ourselves always counts for less. Americans seem more moved by the deaths of dozens in Ireland than by the deaths of hundreds or thousands of different-looking people in Asia. And what is the calculus for weighing the lives of animals against those of people? This question is not intended as a challenge to the human carnivore's eating of meat: let us say that man is entitled to the rights enjoyed by the lion and the shark. But there are other concerns. All across the world, animals are sacrificed in experiments to yield knowledge that may (or may not) prove helpful to people. The heads of drugged cats are dashed against a wall to study the effects of the impact. How many cats' lives are worth expending to save the life of a single human being? Is there any limit? All respect for the animal's experience is discarded, as increasingly mechanized food-production methods transform hens into immobilized machines for the conversion of grain into eggs, just as the pig becomes simply the means of making pork. Not just in death but in their perverted lives as well these animals are wholly sacrificed to human ends.[1] It is a sign of unjust systems that the wants of those with power are overvalued while those of the powerless are disregarded.

---

1. In the words of a current commercial, "It takes a tough man to make a tender chicken." Especially tough on the chicken.

The typical assumption is that human beings count for more because we are better. It is notable that we believe the most appropriate criterion of value is the quality we possess to a greater degree than any other species—intelligence. Such a criterion should be suspect, the more so in view of the ubiquitous tendency of ruling groups to base their superiority on similarly self-serving criteria: plutocrats see wealth as the basis of value, aristocrats see manners and eminent ancestors, lighter-skinned peoples ruling darker see fairness as a sign of superiority. When we are exhorted to spare other creatures like whales, porpoises, or apes on the basis of their manifest intelligence, it is reminiscent of racist societies in which blacks with lighter skin are granted higher status than their darker fellows. Better to be an octoroon than a quadroon. According to the natural theory of value, a creature's capacity for joy and suffering is a more appropriate basis for weighing the importance of its well-being. While this may be correlated with intelligence, it is far from equivalent. My impression about cats (the animals I know best, after humans) is that they are extremely sensitive at the level of feelings, not markedly less so than people.

Our most evident superiority is, as in the other cases, superiority of power. And as is so frequently the case, power corrupts the way values are weighed. A recent work argues that "damage to penguins, or sugar pines, or geological marvels is simply irrelevant until the human costs of pollution or controls are determined" (from Columbia University Press advertisement for *People or Penguins* by William F. Baxter). Even among people most concerned that the environment be protected against wanton human destruction, the appeal is often for a more enlightened view of human self-interest than for a voluntary restraint of self-interest for the sake of other worthy but powerless creatures. A major international environmental conference, for example, issued a resolution declaring that "It is important that we urge the adoption in law of the principle that every *person* is entitled by right to the environment free of elements which infringe *human* health and well-being and the nature's endowment [sic], including its beauty, which shall be the heritage of the present to future generations . . ." (from the Tokyo Resolution, reported in Leontief, 1970, p. 25, italics added).

The system of nature under civilization remains a regime of power. There are many voices—for example, Richard Wagner (1971, p. 318)—calling for respect for the *rights* of other creatures, for voluntary human restraint. But man continues to exercise dominion, insufficiently checked even by enlightened self-interest let alone by consideration for the interests of others. These others—unlike the enslaved and colonized peoples of this and other eras—are powerless to throw off the yoke of our unjust rule. There is no prospect, therefore, of revolution. Yet one should

251

not assume for that reason that the animal with the hubris to eat of the forbidden fruit shall reign unchallenged forever. Bateson says, from his ecological vision, "the systems are . . . punishing of any species unwise enough to quarrel with its ecology. Call the systemic forces 'God' if you will" (1972, p. 434).

B. *The Evolution of Technology and the Parable of the Tribes*

To explain why the ecosystem is troubled by civilized man, Genesis would suffice. But man's freedom to choose good or evil is not all that makes him dangerous. The creature who might freely have subverted ecological wholeness has also been compelled by social evolutionary forces to take the path of maximal exploitation of nature. To Genesis, therefore, we must add the parable of the tribes to get a more complete picture of the forces shaping man's evolving relationship with the natural environment.

Technology and the Growth of Civilization.—To cross from the Garden, where man sins freely, back into the domain of the inescapable rule of power, the first part of the bridge is established with the point: that man's dominion over nature is a cornerstone of that whole edifice of human power the growth of which the parable of the tribes seeks to explain.

The ways in which people modify their natural environment to achieve their own purposes can be defined as their *technology* (see Lynn White, quoted in Forbes, 1968, p. ix). There can be no doubt that the development of technology has been a central factor in the overall evolution of civilization. The entire process was inaugurated by the largely technological breakthrough designated the Agricultural Revolution, and more recently the technological breakthroughs of the Industrial Revolution have facilitated and accelerated cultural changes of all kinds (see chap. 2, "Two Great Waves of Change").

The importance of the technological dimension is the major thrust of the social evolutionist Leslie White. From White we can learn to regard technological development as a limiting factor on the overall evolution of civilization. "Cultural development would not have gone beyond a certain level," he tells us, had not primitive peoples found some way "to harness additional amounts of energy per capita" (1959, p. 43). Thus: "After hundreds of thousands of years of relatively slow and meager development during the Old Stone Ages, culture suddenly shot forward under the impetus of augmented energy resources achieved by agriculture and animal husbandry" (1959, p. 372). Of the later major technological leap, White asserts the similar idea that had the energy of nature not been tapped in a new form, "human culture would never have gone substantially beyond the peaks achieved prior to the beginning of the

Christian era" (1949, p. 383). White is correct in stressing that the extent of a civilized society's exploitation of nature sets limits on other aspects of development.

To grant that the harnessing of nature determines the range of cultural possibilities is not, however, to follow White (and some others of his school) into the position that technology governs the evolution of civilization. This distinction is essential for disclosing how the parable of the tribes incorporates and transcends White's analysis of social evolution. To reuse a metaphor, it is important not to confuse one of the chief sails upon the mast with the wind that drives the ship. A thorough critique of the technological determinism found in White and, some say, in his mentor Marx, is a complex undertaking. In brief, the essential points in the critique are these.

(1) It is insupportable to maintain, with White, that "The technological factor is . . . *the* determinant of a cultural system as a whole" (ibid., p. 399), that social systems, philosophies, and so on are "mere functions of technologies." White regards this as "little more than obvious." History shows, however, that societies with substantially the same levels of technological development can be culturally very different. Consider ancient China and Rome. Whatever differences in technique there may be between the two societies would seem insignificant in Whitean terms in comparison with their common agrarian approach to the problem of subsistence. If the differences in social organization surrounding the technology are absorbed into the concept of technology, then "technology" has been so broadened as to make this technological determinism tautological, and therefore meaningless as a theory. But if the profound differences in these ancient cultures are to be regarded as insignificant compared with those similarities which stem from their common agrarian "base," either this too would make the proposition tautological or would seriously distort the nature of human life, for in human terms the differences between China and Rome are hardly trivial. Thus, when we see that the same x leads in different cases to very different ys, we must reject the proposition that $y = f(x)$.

(2) Technological determinism fails as an explanation of change. The idea that $y = f(x)$ implies that it is changes in x that lead to changes in y. The first problem with this is that where x is technology and y the rest of the cultural system, it just is not so. White asserts that "culture evolves as the amount of energy harnessed per capita per year is increased" (1959, p. 42). If this statement is not tautological, it would seem to be in important respects false. Kent Flannery, for example, indicates that the most striking difference between state societies and simpler ones lies not in "matter and energy exchanges" but in the realm of decision-making and

253

organization (1972, p. 412). Similarly, Karl Wittfogel (in Streuver, p. 558) and a good many others have noted that the beginnings of industrial capitalism were instigated not by changes in technology but in the realm of reorganization. Major cultural transformations, it seems, have originated in the supposed "superstructure." These changes in the "dependent variable," in the example of the Industrial Revolution, set forces in motion which led to major breakthroughs in the supposedly independent variable: a different social and economic structure acted as a stimulus to the development of the new technology.

This leads to the second problem with a theory like White's in explaining change: it does not really describe any mechanism to account for the movement in the supposed engine of the whole process. Why, for example, after thousands of years of agrarian civilization, which had reached its peaks "prior to the Christian era," did technology suddenly reach another breakthrough? If technological change grows out of the technological system itself, why did industrial technology emerge in one region of agrarian development rather than in others, in some of which the first breakthrough had occurred far sooner? On this, the White approach is mute. Ultimately, White's theory of social evolution appears less explanatory than merely descriptive, and the perspective from which cultural development is described appears to reflect less the conclusions reached from a study of the movements of history than the assumptions of an essentially materialistic view of the nature of human life.

The parable of the tribes can be enriched by White's perceptions of the important role of technology in the development of social evolution without being encumbered by the theoretical shortcomings of his technological determinism.

(1) As indicated earlier, the parable of the tribes has no need to posit any element of the cultural system as more fundamental than the others, no need to reduce important dimensions of culture to the status of mere superstructure. The mutual influences between spheres—material and spiritual, economic and social, technological and ideological—may be fully reciprocal, or may be unbalanced in one way or another, or may vary in direction from one era (or society) to another. With respect specifically to technology, what is important is the recognition that the extent to which a society can make the natural world serve its ends is an important determinant of the range of its cultural possibilities.

(2) The parable of the tribes is not reductionistic because it locates its central determinant of change not within civilized societies themselves but in a dynamic selective process that stands outside the cultural organisms. Cultural changes may take place for an infinite variety of reasons

at different times and places. If in the meanwhile a selective process is occurring according to reasonably stable criteria, a systematic transformation of the whole comprehensive cultural system can occur. The parable of the tribes asserts that within the system of civilization such selection has occurred with the criterion being competitive power. Technology's role in the evolutionary process described by that theory grows out of its relation to power. By setting limits upon the range of a society's possibilities, technology thereby also sets limits on its capacity to generate power. Any technological breakthrough that extends those limits escalates the struggle for power within the system of civilization. Thus, to the extent that the parable of the tribes governs social evolution, the evolution of technology can be seen as so much grist for the mill of the selection for power. Or: technology not as engine, but as sail.

We see the uniquely free creature ravaging his Garden. But as we withdraw to gain a wider perspective, we see that the shadow of the rule of power casts a different light on this destruction. The creature freed of certain ancient natural constraints is being driven by new necessities. Where the old regime of nature compelled creatures toward synergy, this new regime of power necessitates, among other things, environmental destructiveness.

The Selection for Power and the Evolution of Technology.—Technology is a component of power. Much of the power men wield is the force of nature which they have harnessed. This point has been so recurrent a theme in this book that it needs but little elaboration. (1) If a society's power is a function of human numbers (chap. 3, "The Evolution toward Larger Societies"), population growth has in turn been substantially a function of technological advances. "There seems to be little question that the first two major revolutions in man's control over his environment, the agricultural and the industrial, brought in their wake significant increases in the rate of population increase" (Richard Adams, 1975, p. 146). (2) If power is a function of superior organization, of division of labor (chap. 3, "The Evolution toward More Complex Societies") and of effective central control (chap. 3, "The Evolution of More Effective Central Control), this too has been facilitated by technological developments. Increased productivity allows greater division of labor, and the technology of communication and transportation makes possible effective administration of large areas. (3) If the ultimate test of power is in war, the importance of technology is obvious. We might start with the man on a horse, a primitive but effective way of harnessing natural forces which often differentiated the dominant from the dominated. The conquests by the mounted over those on foot lie very far back in time (e.g., in China, though more recently among the tribes of the American plains),[2] but their legacy can still be seen in the designation of one Roman class as Equestrian and in the code of "chivalry" for the medieval European ruling class. Then there was the technology of metals, which helped societies with more advanced metallurgy, like the iron-armed Assyrians, to triumph over others (Bozeman, 1960, p. 39). The military importance of technology in the twentieth century hardly needs to be emphasized, when every month brings news of feverish efforts to develop new weapons like radar-proof aircraft, laser-beam antiballistic missile systems, and on and on.

The advance of power through the development of technology can largely be seen in terms of the natural energy harnessed, the aspect of technology stressed by Leslie White. Of course, not all technological advance is a matter of increasing energy flow: the silicon-chip revolution in microprocessors, for example, is a matter of more being accomplished with less energy expended. Nonetheless, the two great revolutions did involve quantum leaps in the amount of energy available to serve human ends. The increase in population is explicable partly in terms of the enhanced ability of human beings to convert available energy into human substance. (Ludwig Boltzman: "The whole web of life is . . . a struggle for free energy, whether it be between shrub and tree for a place in the sun, between a locust and a rabbit for the energy-yielding compounds of leaves, or between lion and tiger for the flesh of an antelope" [quoted in Leslie White, 1959, p. 34n]). Yet energy harnessed by civilization can be used for other purposes as well. When the Industrial Revolution made fossil fuels available to do human work, it allowed the labor of (say) a coal miner to be multiplied manyfold. A man who mines five hundred pounds of coal a day (which, incidentally, is very far below current productivity levels) makes available for use five hundred times the heat value of the food he burned up in getting it. Granting considerable inefficiencies in the human labor and in the engine that burns the coal, Fred Cottrell computes that by his day's work the miner will magnify the labor available by a factor of a couple dozen or more. James Fairgrieve computed four decades ago that the average British family gained, through the burning of coal in British factories, the equivalent of more than twenty Helots (Greek slaves) working for them (quoted in Morgenthau, 1972,

2. The horse was important in the Aryan conquest of India. A passage in the Rg Veda says of the war-horse:

> And at his deep neigh, like the thunder of heaven,
> the foe men tremble in fear,
> for he fights against thousands, and none can resist him,
> so terrible is his charge.

(in Bashan, 1954, p. 36)

p. 358). Energy harnessed is a means, and the choice of ends can of course include competitive social power. James Watt told King George III that he dealt in an article of which kings were said to be fond—Power. Power in the sense of kilowatts is not equivalent to power in the sense of the parable of the tribes, but they are related.

Given the role of the exploitation of nature in the generation of power, and given the role of power in human affairs, it is not surprising that, in the words of C. S. Lewis, "Man's power over Nature means the power of some men over other men with Nature as its instrument" (1946, p. 178).

As the parable of the tribes would predict, the struggles among human societies have inexorably spread power-conferring technologies. The more numerous and powerful food producers have driven away the food-gathering societies (Cottrell, 1955, p. 24; Kaplan, in Sahlins and Service, 1960, p. 74). And technological advance played no small role in granting the nations of Europe the capacity to westernize the other cultures of the world, and to spread thereby their own powerful ways of exploiting nature. Among the explanations of the West's rise to dominance, a variety focus on technological superiority. Europe expanded in the sixteenth century, says Lynn White, because for the past seven centuries it had progressively outstripped the rest of the world in the technology of agriculture (1967, p. 52). Cottrell calls attention to advances in "the use of the energy of the sail. . . . It was with the sailing ship that a few small nations of western Europe developed control over the trade of the world and gained such power as to subordinate many times their own numbers to the political and economic ends they sought" (1955, pp. 77–78). And Forbes writes more generally, in *The Conquest of Nature*, that "The expansion of Europe, beginning with the discovery of the New World, was actually based on Europe's high consumption of energy in the expanding applications of technology, which engendered productivity and military power" (1968, pp. 38–39). Even as the power of Europe has receded in this century, the role of power in dictating the spread of Western technology has continued undiminished. The nations of the third world, Toynbee wrote, are "hell-bent" on following the technology of the West "because they feel that unless they get even with us in technology, which means in material power, they will be at our mercy and we shall continue to abuse our power and exploit them" (in Urban, 1971, p. 42). Whatever the role of power in leading the first innovators to create more potent and aggressive means for exploiting nature (see chap. 2, "The Mother of Invention"), it appears that power has been a significant factor in spreading these more exploitive technologies.

With more exploitation comes more ecological damage. The working of power systems sweeps away what is more ecologically sound, for example, slash and burn in tropical jungles (D. Price, 1981), traditional rice-growing techniques in the Philippines (Sears, cited in E. Odum, 1971, p. 513), and replaces it with what is immediately more productive but ultimately less sustainable. It may be that the more powerful technology is more destructive simply in proportion to the magnification of man's role: that is, as man's power doubles, so also does his injury to the environment. But the increase in destructiveness may exceed the growth in human powers. For with the development of more potent technologies has come, at least until quite recently, an increasingly wanton disregard of the sacredness of the natural system. A change in cultural attitudes may have compounded the injurious effects of the changing technological practices.

The Serpent's Tooth (the selection for attitudes toward nature).—There is more to "man's relationship to nature" than mere behavior. We who were born children of nature have also a profound psychological and spiritual relationship with our Mother, the earth and its living systems. As our behaviors are in general reflective of our inner feelings and values, so also are the technological practices of various societies reflections of important attitudes concerning nature and man's proper role in it. Thus, a society's power is a function not only of its ability to exploit nature, but also of its willingness. The selection for technologically powerful societies therefore tends also to be a selection for certain attitudes toward nature in preference to others. Man did not spring forth out of the natural order already schooled in the ethic of human tyranny over nature. That is a teaching that, in the workings of the parable of the tribes through history, power has gradually fashioned and spread.

The earlier discussion of Genesis and Aristotle suggested that civilized, and particularly Western, peoples have long justified their position at the top of the natural order. Yet this right of dominion has not been without limit. To the ancients, the indiscriminate exploitation of nature was regarded as a sacrilege, as a violation of a higher law to which people felt bound (Nef, 1950, p. 132). Agricultural folk (such as that in the Yucatan described by Redfield) felt an obligation to take only what was needed from nature, and to take less than all that was available: "When the honey is taken from the hives, a little is left. . . . These offerings return in part and in symbol what is essentially the property of the gods and which is by them ceded to men of pious conduct" (1953, p. 116). Such attitudes were embodied also in the Commandments followed by the Hebrews, as where Leviticus says, "But in the seventh year shall be a sabbath of rest unto the land" (25:4). Mark Graubard, in "The Frankenstein Syndrome," reviews ancient and traditional cultures and discovers a profound theme concerning the proper limits to man's place in the natural order: man must not in his pride trespass beyond the place given him by the "superior and omnipotent law of nature," for if he does his hubris "can lead only to chaos, evil, and destruction" (1967, p. 423).

Only comparatively recently has unbridled human ambition to rule and exploit nature became sanctioned in a major civilization. The emergence of modern Western civilization was accompanied (rather, it was fostered) by a new attitude that facilitated the more complete overthrow of the natural order for the enhancement of human power.[3] In England, before the Industrial Revolution had begun, Francis Bacon helped launch the new science that would put the reins of natural forces into the reigning hand of man. Wrote Bacon: "The end of our foundation is the knowledge and the secret of things, and the enlarging of the bounds of human empire to the effecting of all things possible" (quoted in Forbes, 1968, p. 42). In France, René Descartes established a major thrust of modern philosophy with a perspective and a program by which "We might thus render ourselves the lords and possessors of nature" (quoted in Nussbaum, 1953, p. 2). Meanwhile, in Germany, an image was current of a man who sold his soul to the Devil to gain powers otherwise beyond human reach, an image that Goethe would develop into the heroic figure of Faust whom some have seen as a fitting symbol of our whole ambitiously striving, world-molding civilization. "What is characteristic of the cultural revolution of modernity," Philip Rieff has written, ". . . is the abandonment of limits" (in Urban, 1971, pp. 52–53).

This ideological change is inseparable from the technological revolution that so explosively has escalated the growth of power. Those who can eye nature with an uninhibited urge to use her are far more likely to discover the techniques for manipulating her. And those who hold to an ideology that encourages the unlimited exercise of power are the more likely to put their knowledge to use.

The selective process that has favored the technologically advanced has therefore also favored the spread of the less pious, more exploitative and rapacious attitude toward the natural order. George Bernard Shaw wrote in *Man and Superman* that "The reasonable man adapts himself to the world: the unreasonable one persists in trying to adapt the world to himself. Therefore all progress depends on the unreasonable man" (1951, p. 739). Where "progress" is governed by the parable of the tribes, we can see how this is true. Max Weber contrasted Confucianism with Pu-

---

3. Even relatively early in the European Middle Ages, according to Lionel Casson, "technology became elevated into Christian virtue." Lynn White describes a ninth-century work of art depicting preparations for battle between David and the righteous against the ungodly: "The Evildoers are content to use an old-fashioned whetstone. The godly, however, are employing the first crank recorded outside China to rotate the first grindstone known anywhere" (in Casson, 1981, p. 42).

ritanism thus: whereas "Confucian rationalism meant rational *adjustment* to the world," Puritan rationalism meant "rational *mastery* over the world" (quoted in Parsons, 1966, p. 77). When intersocietal competition intruded to select which was the way of progress, it was the cultural attitude of the traditional Chinese that gave way. Rebounding from more than a century of traumatic experience of imperialism, China revolutionized itself. Among the revolutionary changes was the replacement of the traditional emphasis on harmony and adjustment with one on dialectical conflict and struggle. Of this, Rhoades Murphy writes that "In no respect was this radical change more important than in the attitudes toward nature" (quoted in Glacken, in Helfrich, 1970, p. 139). More generally, the imperialistic triumph of Western civilization can be regarded in part as the triumph of an attitude toward nature. Writes Woodruff: "It is the idea of a continuous, cumulative expansion of man's power over his environment, and perhaps even over his own destiny, which most sharply distinguishes the European from other civilizations. It is the most powerful idea that Europe has put abroad"(1966, p. 1). The constriction of human options by the rule of power goes on. Recently, I participated in a discussion in which a prominent American national security analyst cited the decline in the American people's "belief in the value of controlling the material world" as a source of growing national vulnerability in America's competition with its superpower rival.

The way that power selects what man's relationship with nature will be is demonstrated clearly in the history of the North American continent. All the European powers seeking empire in North America were more aggressive and less reverential in their attitudes toward nature than the native cultures that the Europeans replaced. Yet among the Europeans themselves, there were differences. The attitudes of the English settlers, writes E. F. Murphy, "precluded the sort of accommodation with nature" that marked Spanish and, to a lesser degree, French settlements in North America (1967, p. 7). In time, the English largely squeezed out the others in the settlement of the continent. Among the English, in turn, there again were differences in attitudes. This is well illustrated in Leo Marx's *The Machine in the Garden*. Two images competed in the English cultural attitude toward nature: "To depict the new land [as did some English literature about the New World] as a lovely garden is to celebrate an ideal of immediate, joyous fulfillment. . . . To describe America as a hideous wilderness [as did another strain of literature], however, is to envisage it as another field for the exercise of power" (1964, pp. 42, 43). Marx adds that "It is hardly surprising that the New England Puritans favored the hideous wilderness image of the landscape. The competing images correspond somewhat to the well-known historical conflict between the Jeffersonian and Hamiltonian images of America's future, between an image of a pastoral America with yeoman farmers and the Hamiltonian design for a technologically developed nation of ascendant power. Regarding the outcome of this struggle, we can recall Michael Chevalier's judgment in the nineteenth century that to form the American character one would take one part of the Virginian and add to it three parts of the Yankee. The role of power in deciding this outcome is not confined to the necessities imposed by the intersocietal system, though it is worth noting that Hamilton's intentions, as revealed in his *Report on the Subject of Manufactures* (1791), is to create "the economy best suited to the establishment of America's supremacy among nations" (quoted in L. Marx, 1964, p. 168). The competition was largely intrasocietal. The literature of the nineteenth century, Marx says, expresses sentiments on both sides of the issue of whether to allow the "machine" to advance into the "garden." But those against that advance tended to be more peripheral to the powers governing society while the advocates of technology appeared in journals "which on the whole represent the views of the governmental, business, and professional elites." That which determines the chooser determines the choice.

In its various workings, power has played a major role in shaping the evolution of man's relationship to nature, in attitudes and in practice.

Beyond the Question of Master and Servant.—

> Only let the human race recover the right over nature which belongs to it by divine bequest, and let power be given it; the exercise thereof will be governed by sound reason and true religion.—Francis Bacon, *Novum Organum*

The optimism that helped propel the growth of technology has in the twentieth century begun to fade. There has accumulated simply too much evidence of the destructive effects and the still more destructive possibilities of man's harnessing the forces of nature for human purposes. Technology has made possible the unprecedented repression of the totalitarian state; it has created the means for waging total war of annihilation; it threatens the biosphere with gradual poisoning and deterioration. All the good it has also made possible notwithstanding, technology has abetted too much evil to nourish the assumption that the exercise of human powers over nature will be "governed by sound reason and true religion."

The troubled history of the uses of technology has led to a debate about whether technology is man's servant or his master. Some have sought to solve the riddle of evil by depicting technology as a force in itself, a Frankenstein monster out of control wreaking havoc. A spokes-

261

man of this view is Jacques Ellul who says that "Technology has become autonomous. It has fashioned an omnivorous world which obeys its own laws. . . . (T)echnique pursues its own course more and more independently of man" (quoted in Florman, 1975, p. 54). Against this view are arrayed the still numerous disciples of Bacon, such as Samuel Florman who regards Ellul's position as making "absolutely no sense." "Technology," writes Florman, "is not an independent force but is merely an activity in which people engage because they choose to do so" (1975, p. 57). A similarly sanguine view of man as master of his tools is put forward by R. J. Forbes: "Man is not only free to choose his technology; he can also control the rate at which it absorbs previously human functions" (1968, p. 96).

These statements are representative of widely held views. The problem with which they wrestle is, in turn, representative of the overriding puzzle confronting civilized peoples: to understand the source of civilization's destructiveness. Yet neither side offers a satisfactory insight. The "technology as master" school recognizes the apparent human inability to choose a constructive direction of development; but it fails to give a sensible explanation of how the tool can rule. The "technology as servant" school recognizes the shortcomings of the other view but fails adequately to account for how much greater has been the technical skill in harnessing nature than the "sound reason" for governing its use.

The parable of the tribes cuts through the master/servant dichotomy. Technology is not master—it is but a tool. But neither is man the master (or at least not wholly so) for the context of human actions greatly constricts the range of human choices, grants an unchosen and unrepresentative few the power to choose for all, and compels people to serve systems of power. Technology is not in itself a demon or an autonomous force. But because it is so intimately connected with power, and because the unchosen selection for power helps direct the evolution of civilized systems, certain technologies and attitudes will tend to spread without necessary regard to the general opinion of mankind or to the impact on the well-being of human and other life.

In an understanding of man's problematic and destructive relationship to nature, man can be seen both as sinner and as victim. We act in freedom in some respects, we are bound by necessity in others. Where the parable of the tribes is the root, the problem of man's power over nature can be solved only by solving first the problem of power among people. Where civilized peoples destroy out of folly and wickedness, change requires a change of heart. If we are to rule, we must become more like the ruler described by Socrates who does not "consider or command his own advantage rather than that of what is ruled" (*Republic*, 342E).

Or perhaps, with the problem of power solved, and mankind released from the compulsion to strive for godlike powers, we can abdicate the throne usurped and become again the children rather than the lords of nature.

Beyond Hubris.—It is the modern fashion to regard the humility of traditional peoples before the "sacred" natural order as a childish state reflective of the ignorance of premodern peoples. Modern man has outgrown the belief that some powers are meant for the gods alone. The deeper we have bitten into the fruit of knowledge, the deeper has become our conviction that we have become as gods. A nineteenth-century American advocate of technology's unlimited advance, Timothy Walker, said: "From ministering servant to master, mind has become the powerful lord of matter. Having put myriads of wheels in motion by laws of its own discovering, it rests, like the Omnipotent mind, of which it is the image, from its work of creation, and pronounces it good" (L. Marx, 1960, p. 186). Man pronounces himself God.[4]

But perhaps the more profound ignorance lies in this proud modern consciousness. The idea of hubris may turn out to reflect not superstition and ignorance but a deep awareness of the fundamental nature of things. One of the more profound scientific visionaries of our times, Gregory Bateson, was quoted earlier as saying that a species that quarrels with its ecology is eventually punished by systemic forces—"call [them] 'God' if you will." We must recall that man's lordship over nature is progressively undermining the ecological bases of human life. The ancient sense of sacred limits may contain deep wisdom.

In the classical myth of Actaeon,

> a hunter, a vigorous youth in the prime of his young manhood, who, when stalking deer with his dogs, chanced upon a stream that he followed to its source, where he broke upon the goddess Diana [Gk: Artemis] bathing, surrounded by a galaxy of naked nymphs. And the youth, not spiritually prepared for such a supernormal image, had only the normal look in his eye; whereupon the goddess, perceiving this, sent forth her power and transformed him into a stag, which his own dogs immediately scented, pursued, and tore to bits. (told by J. Campbell, 1969, p. 62)

The man of power who has harnessed nature (in the form of hunting dogs) to gather nature's yield (in the form of deer) encounters that sacred spirit to whom he owes his powers. In his arrogance, he eyes even the

---

4. Hubris is a climbing that leads to a fall. In a Midrash on the book of Genesis, Rav Yehoshua of Siknin (speaking in Rav Levi's name) depicted the temptation that snared our species: "The serpent began speaking slander of his Creator saying: He ate of this tree and created the world, He therefore ordered you not to eat thereof so you will not create other worlds, for every person hates his fellow craftsman" (*Bereishes Genesis*).

goddess in a mundane, perhaps predatory, way. As punishment for this irreverence, the aggressive hunter's form is transformed by the goddess into that of a vulnerable creature. Whereupon he is destroyed by the very tools of his power.

A change of heart might be not only good for the soul but necessary for survival as well.

2. The State of Unnature: The Problems of the Intersocietal System

The problems of the intersocietal system being at the heart of the parable of the tribes, they have been touched upon repeatedly throughout this book and require only very brief treatment here.

Horseman of the Apocalypse

That the ubiquitous strife among nations is a major human problem is clear to everyone. Especially in this age of weapons of mass destruction, the costs of the intersocietal struggle for power are of universal concern. Even without war itself, the global cost of armaments exceeded (in 1970) the total income of the poorest half of mankind (Lester Brown, 1972, p. 249). (This implies that without those expenditures, half of mankind could enjoy twice their current material benefits without the other half being worse off.) Despite these costs, despite the shadow of annihilation stretching over us as a species, and despite the evident fact that the various regional and superpower arms races ultimately fail to enhance the security of anyone, the struggle for power and advantage goes on.

To many, this frantic struggle is evidence of mankind's monstrous folly. Since the costs are so huge, the dangers even more so, and the benefits for mankind so hard to see, is it not obvious that the arms race is a symptom of our insanity?

Such a judgment is based on a fallacious perspective. Surely, if we look at mankind as a whole, this conduct of nations makes no sense. But mankind lacks the means to act as a whole, and this is the heart of the problem. Rather, humanity is fragmented into numerous interacting but autonomous decisionmakers, each of whom must act to survive in an environment that can guarantee nothing about security. We return to the image of a panic in a burning theater in which each actor, though sane, may have no choice but to contribute to a destructive collective insanity. The pattern of conduct that would be optimal for the system as a whole

264

may not be a realistic option for any of those acting at the level where decisions can actually be made.

Once we recognize how the structure of the international system limits the choices of those acting in it, we are compelled to acknowledge that the problem of war is as legitimate a human dilemma as any. Seen from that perspective, the distinction implicitly made by many in the West between worthy problems (like the population explosion) and the unworthy problem of security is unjustified. That human armaments grow uncontrolled, just as that human numbers do, is a regrettable but unavoidable consequence of our present civilized condition.

If we are to escape the dilemma of the struggle for power, it will not be so much by exhorting the present actors to act sanely—for the policies of most are already more or less sane, while for most the policy of unilaterally forswearing the use of force would be folly—as by finding ways to transform the structure of the overarching system in which all must act.

With the intersocietal system, unlike with the ecological, civilization did not subvert an original wholeness. Before civilization, an intersocietal system hardly existed: primitive societies lived in relative isolation, and the comparative absence of widely overlapping domains of action contributed to their apparent relative peacefulness. The rise of civilization increased the scope of each society's potential area of control, and thus increased the potential utility for each society of the resources (territorial, material, and human) that neighboring societies possessed. Civilization thus magnified the potential conflicts of interest among human societies (see chapter 3, "Red Sky at Morning").

But more important, the kind of intersocietal system that emerged with civilization made it exceedingly difficult for the independent societies to act synergistically on the basis of their considerable body of common interest. The structural impediments to intersocietal synergy lie at the core of the parable of the tribes, and were described in the first chapter. The emerging intersocietal system is characterized by an unprecedented anarchy, unregulated by nature's law and still beyond the reach of any enforceable human law. The system is subject to corruption first because individual societies have the capacity to subvert synergy by their unregulated pursuit of self-interest. But far more destructive of the chances for intersocietal synergy is that once introduced from any source into an anarchic system, power acts as a contaminant that inexorably spreads to infect the whole.

In an ordered system like the body, the resources of the whole can be mobilized to stop a pathogen at its point of entry. In an anarchic system like that of civilized societies, the pathogen of power never encounters the resistance of the whole. (Machiavelli describes how the fragmentation of the Mediterranean world enabled the Romans to come to rule them all. Romans demonstrated, he writes, that while the "potent prince" is making war upon one, the "other powers that are more distant and have no immediate intercourse with him will look upon this as a matter too remote for them to be concerned about, and will continue in this error until the conflagration spreads to their door, when they will have no means for extinguishing it except their own forces, which will no longer suffice when the fire has once gained the upper hand" [*Discourses* 2.1].) One aggressive and potent actor upon the scene can impose on each of the others the necessity of gaining the power to protect itself, or the inevitability of becoming absorbed into the power of another. Thus, because power acts as a contaminant, it is also in such a system a necessity. "The instinct of self-preservation, in a world made up of independent nations, operates to make each desire power in order to secure itself against the danger of external aggression" (J. Allen Smith, quoted in Morgenthau, 1972, p. 158n). Says Morgenthau: "Whatever the ultimate aims of international politics, power is always the immediate aim" (ibid., p. 25).

Human societies become obsessed with power because, in that unnatural Hobbesian state of nature, so deep are the insecurities that no one can feel certain of having enough of it to assure survival. Inevitably, the conditions of chronic insecurity make the actors in the intersocietal system distrustful of one another, and the atmosphere of suspicion further clouds the chances for nations to cooperate together in the service of their common interests. The more that conflict rather than synergy governs intersocietal relations, the more the gains of one's neighbors imply a threat to oneself. Circumstance thus tends to thrust civilized societies into unceasing competition with one another, a mode of interaction based not upon the premise of synergy but upon that of the zero-sum game. "(D)uring the time men live without a common power to keep them all in awe," wrote Hobbes in *Leviathan*, "they are in that condition which is called war; and such a war, as is of every man, against every man" (1960, p. 82).

This dilemma of anarchy and the inevitable struggle for power, though well recognized by many in the field of international relations, bears stressing not only because of its profound and unobvious consequences but also because it is a truth that many in the West, perhaps because it is so unpleasant, have chosen not to confront. That anarchy in a system implies a state of chronic insecurity and conflict was a major premise of the case for union put forward in *The Federalist* against those who hoped that the preservation of their local sovereignty was compatible with the assurance of systemic tranquility. Wrote Hamilton:

> A man must be far gone in Utopian speculations who can seriously doubt, that if these States either be wholly disunited, or only united in partial con-federacies, the subdivisions into which they might be thrown would have frequent and violent contests with each other. . . . To look for a continuation of harmony between a number of independent unconnected sovereignties, situated in the same neighborhood, would be to disregard the uniform course of human events, and to set at defiance the accumulated experience of the ages. (*The Federalist*, no. 6)

Of course, in the two centuries since then that experience has, regrettably, continued to accumulate, for the anarchy that those States managed (largely) to avoid through becoming United still plagues human civilization as a whole.

It is thus the structure of the system, not man's insanity, that has given that fearful horseman such free rein. "All history shows that nations active in international politics are continuously preparing for, actively involved in, or recovering from organized violence in the form of war" (Morgenthau, 1972, p. 35).

Everybody Loses

Conflict first takes root in the gaps in the common interest, and then by its uncontrolled growth it undermines the common welfare. As argued in the preceding chapter, the rule of power has both (*a*) immediate and (*b*) long-term costs.

(*a*) The immediate costs are divisible into the ways in which all lose and the ways in which the gains of the victors are incommensurate with the losses of the defeated.

An important dimension of the way in which all lose is that though everyone is scrambling for security, the net effect may be that no one obtains it. He who lives by the zero-sum approach is condemned to an existence where the gains are finite and precarious. The strong states in the system, Klaus Knorr writes, have been only relatively more secure than the weak. Although anarchy "gives predatory opportunities to the strong," he continues, "it is a risk and a burden to all members" (1973, p. 26). All can lose in the anarchy of the intersocietal system just as all can lose in a panic in a fire. But the anarchy of the intersocietal system, it must be conceded, is mitigated somewhat by a greater luxury of time than obtains in the burning theater. Even though "lacking a common power to keep them all in awe," the members of the system can meet and make pacts for the sake of synergy. An arms control agreement, for example, can be genuinely a plus-sum game. Nations can make peace and become good neighbors. Yet, power remains a contaminant in a system where contracts are unenforceable, so that the chances for synergy remain only as strong as the weakest link (least trustworthy, least desirous of synergy).

In human affairs, when the strong prey upon the weak, the result is unsynergistic because while the strong gain luxuries, the weak lose necessities. The way a God who loves synergy and justice would look upon such exchanges, which have characterized the relations among nations for millennia, is eloquently stated by the story of Nathan's visit to King David who, that he might satisfy his lust for Bathsheba, had arranged the killing of her husband Uriah the Hittite:

> And the Lord sent Nathan unto David. And he came unto him, and said unto him. There were two men in one city; the one rich, and the other poor. The rich man had exceeding many flocks and herds. But the poor man had nothing, save one little ewe lamb, which he had brought and nourished up; and it grew up together with him, and with his children; it did eat of his own meat and drank of his own cup, and lay in his bosom, and was unto him as a daughter. And there came a traveller unto the rich man, and he spared to take of his own flock and of his own herd, to dress for the wayfaring man that was come unto him; but took the poor man's lamb, and dressed it for the man that was come to him. And David's anger was greatly kindled against the man; and he said to Nathan, As the Lord liveth, the man that had done this thing shall surely die. And he shall restore the lamb fourfold, because he did this thing, and because he had no pity. And Nathan said to David, Thou art the man. (II Samuel 12:1-7)

Throughout history, the imperialists' rule that "Them that has, takes more" has subverted the well-being of mankind as a whole.

(b) I argue here that the cumulative, longer-term effects of the rule of power are of even greater consequence than the immediate, for the triumph of the strong over the weak directs the course of social evolution toward power maximization. Whether the selection for the ways of power is contrary to the well-being of mankind as a whole has been shown to be a complex question (chap. 2, "Two Great Waves of Change," and chap. 3, "Common Denominator"). Before modern times, imperialism was usually an unabashed expression of the conqueror's self-interest. The imperialists of the last century, however, often tried to argue that the forcible diffusion of their civilization served "progress" and the needs of subject peoples. This view of imperialism as altruism finds its most famous statement in Kipling's exhortation (1928, p. 373) to "Take up the White Man's burden . . . To serve your captive's need." This service was not, of course, of servant to master, but of parent to the less-developed child; for Kipling describes these "new-caught, sullen peoples" as "Half-devil and half child." Similarly, A. P. Snow describes the "trusteeship" of a civilized European state over a colony populated by people of non-European origin as being like "that of a guardian and ward." This analogy, he says, becomes "very close in the case of aboriginal tribes whose members, by reason of their lack of mental and moral development, occupy a relationship to civilized States akin to that which young children of civilized parents bear to the state" (1921, p. 110).

The beneficiaries of this paternalistic attention have rejected the imperialists' claims both to having given such kind treatment and to possessing the cultural superiority that justifies the dominant role. Spokesmen of the captive peoples refute the claims of beneficence, saying that crimes have been presented as good deeds (Hovénoux, an African) and that the Europeans created a charnel house of innocents. No wonder Kipling's captives were sullen. And many Third World theorists today turn this moral judgment around, seeing the imperialists as barbarous destroyers of valid non-Western civilizations (Hodgkin, in Owen and Sutcliffe, 1972, pp. 102–103).

It is not necessary to choose between the two sides, finding either the conquering or the conquered culture to be superior. Suffice it to say that the bases for one people's domination and transformation of another had nothing to do with superiority in morality, maturity, or the capacity to nurture full and rich human life. It lay simply in superiority of power. As even Bagehot, that nineteenth-century believer in progress, wrote: "Let us consider in what a village of English colonists is superior to a tribe of Australian natives who roam about them. Indisputably, in one, and that a main, sense, they are superior. They can beat the Australians in war when they like; they can take from them anything they like, and kill whom they choose" (1956, pp. 150–151).

Imperialism's reliable legacy is not well-being or progress but power. To equate the spread of power's ways with human progress in a moral sense is a perversion of values. Here we encounter some of the other justifications offered by nineteenth-century imperialists. The cultural transformations imposed by imperialism were defended as necessary to enable subject peoples to learn to "stand by themselves under the strenuous conditions of the modern world" (quoted in Rupert Emerson, 1968, p. 3). This justification appears to suffer from the spurious reasoning of the gangster who sells the people "protection" from himself. Also spurious is the reasoning used by Western militarists to justify their imperialist ways. Vagts describes their use of a kind of Darwinism:

> The foundation and justification of military institutions and practices were made immediately identical with the very explanation of human existence: the struggle for existence, "natural selection, and the survival of the fittest." . . . The more hostile life was conceived to be and the more "beneficient"

> the restless conflict in the jungle, the more armed combat appeared to me necessary, indeed defensible as a good thing in itself and as a way of raising the qualities of the fittest that survived. (1937, pp. 390–391)

This circularity of reasoning betrays the moral confusion of those who have picked up the burden that civilization has imposed upon man and embraced it as God's gift.

Not all cultural transformations, of course, have been dictated by power, and not all the changes power has required are detrimental to human welfare. But where power does govern, the value of the changes should at least be suspect. Clearly, the play of power in the intersocietal system has narrowed the range of social evolutionary options available to mankind. The choices lost in this way are the principal cost of power's reign.

Evil and Beyond

An incessant struggle for power, the predation of the strong upon the weak. These more than anything else are what make history a nightmare for mankind. Yet, as I have argued, the proper lesson of this bad dream is not an analysis of the human neurosis. Jay, in *The Federalist* (no. 4), suggests that it is "disgraceful . . . to human nature that nations in general will make war whenever they have a prospect of getting anything by it." But it is not so much a disgrace as a misfortune, the misfortune of chronic insecurity. In a system where war seems ultimately inescapable, everyone, as Rousseau noted, "is anxious to begin it at the moment which suits his own interests." In such a system, he says, even offensive wars should be seen essentially as "unjust precautions" (quoted in Waltz, 1959, p. 180). That the intersocietal system lacks the grace of synergy does not disgrace human nature.

To acknowledge this, however, is not to justify unbridled Machiavellianism in the international arena. The system may mitigate against the Sermon on the Mount, but it does not mandate *Mein Kampf*. The task of displacing conflict by synergy is a difficult but not impossible task: indeed, international relations contain much that is benign and constructive as well as the struggle for power. That the present world order is not *more* synergistic is a function not only of the system's structure but also of the refusal of more malignant nations to utilize opportunities for cooperation offered by the more benign (or less malignant). (See pp. 124–125 above.) Part of the process of improving the intersocietal system can, therefore, be dedicated to the transformation of individual national actors, changing their values, broadening and enlightening their perspectives. But the problem of evil nations, too, is in large part the fruit of inescapable systemic processes. Over the ages, the parable of the tribes has selected

270

for those kinds of societies and regimes most willing and able to succeed in the largely unprincipled struggles of the anarchic system. It should not be surprising that after millennia of life-and-death conflicts, many of those entities that remain on the scene bring to the international arena even greater relish for conflict than the present moment may require.

Although some states exacerbate the evils of intersocietal anarchy, there is little basis for the hopes many have held that some particular variety of social system might be isolated as the carrier of the disease of strife and imperialism and that the process of social evolution would spread some new social kind immune from such tendencies. Just as the twentieth century dashed those nineteenth-century hopes that the rise of bourgeois democracy was making war a feudal atavism, so more recently does the growth of the Soviet empire uncover the groundlessness of the Marxist notion that imperialism and belligerence are characteristics specifically of capitalist states, and that a world of socialism would be a world of harmony. A realistic theory of international conflict gives no large role to devils.

Out of a primordial dispersion of human groups, civilization has knitted together an intersocietal system the elements of which interact but do not constitute a synergistic whole. The overall progress of history has been in the general direction of more and more interaction over an ever-wider area. The area is now global, the interdependence still growing. Yet the dangerous anarchy remains. The knitting together must proceed further, until the destructive anarchy is replaced by some synergistic order. The beginnings of this process (in international values, in nascent international organization) are already evident, even as the world is still stalked by war, an ancient destroyer now armed with modern weapons. If mankind is fortunate and wise, the era of the parable of the tribes will prove a troubled interlude where peoples were neither far enough apart to live in peace nor bound together closely enough to live in harmony. If we are not fortunate, our ever greater collisions on our ever tighter planet will be our undoing.

3. Men Are Not Ants: The Problem of Power in the Body Politic

A. Intrasocietal Analogue of the Parable of the Tribes

If the disease of power is an outgrowth of anarchy, it would seem that the cure for the disease must lie in "archy," that is, government. Indeed, this is true to the extent that no solution for civilization's ills is possible without government. But government, far from being an automatic remedy, is often itself a part of the disease. All too often, that predation of the powerful upon the weak which afflicts the fluid condition of anarchy is not eliminated but merely fixed and hardened in the order of the civilized polity.

The corruption of the human social order by tyranny is another bitter fruit of the growth of civilization. In the beginning, human society was essentially egalitarian. No one was subject to the power of another. Activity was coordinated through spontaneous cooperation, and what leadership there was was granted on the basis of respect and exercised without power of command (Turnbull, 1962, pp. 266–267; Fried, 1967, p. 83; Service, 1975, p. 51; Hoebel, 1964, p. 82).

Such equality did not survive the rise of civilization. Larger and more complex social organisms require a more centralized "nervous system" for their coordination. The pressures of intersocietal competition in particular necessitated a more hierarchical structure of social relations. It is thus possible that the original differentiation between those who rule and those who are ruled, like the differentiation of the head in the evolution of animal structure, emerged wholly because of the needs of the social organism as a whole. Even if this were so, such inequalities of power in the unprecedented conditions of civilization inevitably became a breeding ground for social corruption.

In human societies, the differentiation between those with more power and those with less proves dangerous. Synergistic purpose is subverted by corrupt execution. Early in the evolution of civilization, institutions created to serve the needs of group life became instruments, "employed primarily for self-aggrandizement and exploitation" (Lenski, 1966, p. 168). Leaders became institutionalized as rulers. Individuals empowered by their fellows for their special qualities sought, for the benefit of their heirs and despite the costs to society, to perpetuate their advantage in the form of hereditary offices (see Service, 1975, p. 294). The dictum that power corrupts might more accurately be stated: one cannot rely on people with power using it synergistically. In *Power and Privilege,* Lenski observes that the record of history compels one to the conclusion that *"when men are confronted with important decisions where they are obliged to choose between their own, or their group's, interests and those of others, they nearly always choose the former"* (1966, p. 30, italics in original). Justice dispensed by mortals is rarely blind and thus rarely just.[5]

5. Hoebel concludes his account of the evolution of the Ashanti chiefdom and its legal institutions; "The [Ashanti] functionaries . . . had come to forget that the institutions had been created for the benefit of society; they had come to think that they existed to serve their own selfish interests" (1964, p. 234).

The key to understanding this curse of social corruption again lies in the unnatural state of civilized life. It is true that the power structures of civilization resemble some natural structures. But the synergy of the natural systems is despoiled in the civilized because despite the analogous appearances there are profound differences. For example, the class society of ants, unlike its civilized counterpart, is differentiated wholly in terms of function, not at all in terms of power. This exemplifies a vital difference between the way nature typically "governs" an order and the nature of civilized government: nature creates order through an intricate complementarity of roles, with the laws embedded in each element; civilization creates order by empowering a ruling part to dominate others, with the laws enforced from above. Thus the "queen" of an ant or bee society is not a ruler like a civilized monarch; she could more readily be seen as her society's slave. Where a natural structure does employ something more akin to power, as in the dominance hierarchy of a baboon troop, there is another essential difference. The dominant baboon is cast in a role laid down by nature, and biological nature is an author that composes always with the whole in mind: thus the power of the alpha male exists because its exercise serves the survival of the troop. The privileged human, by contrast, fills a role nature has left unwritten. This role, moreover, is one for which nature has not prepared human beings, their natural state being one of equality. Man's egalitarian origins do not predispose him to be a tyrant, but neither do they school him for the responsible use of power. Some cultural traditions, such as the Confucian, succeed to a degree in instilling synergistic values to mitigate the corruptive consequences of large disparities of social power. The liberal political tradition has emphasized a different strategy, relying on the equalization of power and the consequent tendency of competing powers to cancel and balance one another. Though ameliorated by such approaches, the disease of corruption is found in all civilized societies and, moreover, is not really to be found anywhere else.[6]

Again, the core of our ills lies in our unprecedented circumstances, not in the evil of our natures. "If men were angels," as Madison says, we would have no need for elaborate constitutional contrivances predicated on human untrustworthiness. Indeed, men are not angels, but it is only

---

6. In *Human Action*, the prominent theorist of competitive capitalism, Ludwig von Mises, redraws the old Darwinian image of "an implacable struggle for existence" as the natural relationship among members of the same species. By contrast, he says, "Man alone by dint of his reason substituted social cooperation for biological cooperation" (1957, p. 38). But the true evolutionary contrast is just the reverse. The fundamental nature of biologically governed intraspecific relationships is cooperative, designed to assure the survival of the species or natural society as a whole. Only man, by dint of the freedom derived from his reason, has the capacity to subvert the needs of the whole by the corrupt pursuit of self-interest.

(civilized) human beings whose circumstances require of them angelic morality. The problem with the human being is not that he is worse than the other creatures of nature but that he is not particularly better.

As before, the costs of the play of power in human affairs are twofold: (*a*) the immediate cost of injustice and (*b*) the long-term costs of distortions in social evolution.

(*a*) The mainstream view of society predictably emphasizes the synergistic bases of social differentiation. A well-known example of this mainstream, functionalist emphasis is the declaration by Kingsley Davis and Wilbert Moore that social inequality is an "evolved device by which societies insure that the most important positions are conscientiously filled by the most qualified persons" (in Laumann et al., 1970, p. 125). Differences in power, prestige, and wealth are described as "rewards" (Eisenstadt, 1971, p. 9), with the implication that they serve as a kind of quid pro quo offered by society for services rendered. To a significant degree, of course, civilized society *is* synergistic: the service of the whole requires individuals to play different roles, some of which are more important and more difficult than others; and differential rewards for different services and different levels of performance can be socially useful.

A man must be "far gone in Utopian speculations," however, and far removed from the bleak realities of most civilized history to believe that this functionalist view captures the essential nature and consequence of social inequalities. Even inequalities instituted for the sake of the whole soon tend to become corrupting forces; the synergistic giving of rewards becomes the corrupt taking called theft. In the words of Adam Smith: "All for ourselves, and nothing for other people, seems, in every age of the world, to have been the vile maxim of the masters of mankind" (1937, pp. 388–389). Lenski provides good documentation for this proposition in his review of the historical record of major agrarian societies. The governing class in these (e.g., China, Russia, France, and England) constituted about 1–2 percent of the population (1966, p. 219). This governing class, together with the ruling royalty, used various systems of taxation and rent to extract from the toiling people of their countries "not less than half" the total income of these societies (1966, pp. 228, 267). This is not synergy but exploitation. The ruling class typically wrung from the subjugated classes every last drop of sweat while leaving them only the merest necessities of life. (On this, in Europe generally, see Lenski, 1966, p. 270; on Poland, see Mosca, 1939, p. 257.) The corrupt calculus of such distribution is alien to natural societies. Although the aristocratic/monarchic structure of rule may be a thing of the past, corrupt distribution of social goods is not: to one degree or another, virtually every ruling group in the world, from Manila to Kinshasa to Warsaw to

Washington, tends to fatten itself on the body politic (generally in proportion to its power to do so). The free play of power saps the vitality
and well-being of the social organism as a whole.

(b) The unequal distribution of power within civilized societies has
several long-term social evolutionary consequences.

For one thing, inequality begets more inequality: them that has, takes
more (see Andrzejewski, 1954, p. 24). Eisenstadt has called social stratification an autonomous dimension, meaning that the evolution of a society's stratification system is partly governed by the workings of that
system itself (1971, p. 16). The way in which the powerful use their power
to extend their power is an important part of that autonomy. Once human
societies embarked upon the path of social inequality, a kind of gravity
of corruption impelled them further on that downhill course.

Another social evolutionary cost of inequalities of power within society
is a perversion of social values. In part, a society's values may represent
a synergistic, consensual view of human life. But in large part also, as
Marx argued, the ruling groups impose upon society as a whole values
that serve their class interests. Inasmuch as these interests tend to conflict
with justice, their values are likely to diverge in major ways from those
that would best serve human well-being. And inasmuch as these values
function to buttress a social structure that runs against man's egalitarian
origins, they inevitably tend to deny and pervert aspects of human nature.
It can hardly be to the benefit of mankind for values like these to be
given a disproportionate role in its evolving societies.

These factors would tend to apply to anyone placed in a position of
dominance. Except to the extent that selfishness is reined in by moral
values, the imposition of anyone's will and prejudiced vision will pull a
society from the course desirable for the whole. This problem, however,
is compounded by the fact that those who rise to the top are a nonrandom
group. Here we encounter the intrasocietal analogue to the parable of
the tribes: that the struggle for power within societies selects certain kinds
of people over others to have a disproportionate role in shaping the
future of these societies. That is, not only does power tend to corrupt,
but often it is the most corrupt who tend to gain power.

There are differences among civilized societies in the means by which
rulers and ruling classes achieve their dominant roles. But the process
of selection has been a humane one in only a small minority. Generally,
brute force and Machiavellian intrigue have been essential elements. In
extreme cases, for example, the Mughal Empire, "To become a ruler . . .
a man was obliged to wade through a sea of blood, including that of his
own brothers" (Lenski, 1966, p. 237). In our time, a Stalin can seize control
of a mighty modern nation and liquidate all possible rivals. One can

imagine how pernicious is the impact upon a society for it to be shaped by the vision of a human being capable of such conduct. (It is impossible to judge for how many of its scheduled one thousand years the Reich founded by Hitler would have endured had not the mad lust for power of its founder not overextended itself in the arena beyond Germany.) The ubiquitous domination of civilized societies by warrior classes—in more modern terms, by military regimes—raises similar concerns. The struggle for power thus is not confined to the intersocietal realm. Continuous struggles for power, writes Lenski, characterize the political histories of most civilized societies (1966, p. 217). Even where the struggle is not violent, it is often those whose overweening ambition is matched only by their ruthlessness who gain power. Thus the "history-makers" "selected" in such struggles to chart their people's destiny are often the last human specimens the people themselves might select.[7]

The selective process magnifies the problem of corruption. It is not just that men are not angelic. It is also that, because of an inhumane selective process that is difficult to prevent, positions of power fall frequently into the hands of the most diabolical among us.

Government thus stands in paradoxical relationship to the problem of power. Without it, people are prey to the calamitous Hobbesian state of nature where there is no justice but only the rule of power. Escape from that state, Hobbes said, requires a governing power to hold all in awe. Yet Hobbes's solution is no solution. Too often, the peace with which government replaces the war of all against all is only the surrender imposed by the conqueror upon the vanquished. Polity can thus be the continuation of anarchy by other means. Locke articulated this danger in his critique of Hobbes. For men to look to Hobbes's potent ruler for refuge from the dangers of anarchy, said Locke, is like taking care "to avoid what mischiefs may be done them by polecats or foxes" while thinking it safety "to be devoured by lions" (1939, no. 93). That man, says Locke, is in more danger who "is exposed to the arbitrary power of one man who has the command of 100,000 than he that is exposed to the arbitrary power of 100,000 single men . . ." (no. 137). Perhaps Locke gives insufficient weight to the value of order: one secure lion may tear

---

7. In this work, a recurrent statement of part of the problem of power is that no, the meek are not the ones who inherit the earth. Consider the recent horrible fate of that "Gentle Land," Cambodia. T. D. Allman writes: "'What explains this mania among the Khmer?' I found myself asking a Cambodian Provincial official one night. 'Not even Hitler killed his own people.' Then I fell back on what everyone who knew Cambodia in the past always said: 'Cambodia was always such a gentle country. . . .' 'That is the whole problem,' he replied, 'we are still so gentle. Where else could a few madmen successfully terrorize an entire nation? In the village where I was imprisoned, the Khmer Rouge didn't even have guns. They just shouted and waved machetes, and that was enough'" (1982, p. 53). But, it may be objected, the Khmer Rouge stayed in power only a few years. Yes, but it was not the Cambodian people who deposed them but their rather fierce and powerful neighbors, the Vietnamese.

276

less flesh than a hundred thousand polecats and foxes clawing and biting in their unceasing Hobbesian anxiety. But he is entirely correct in stressing that the achievement of order is far from equivalent to the protection of society's members from the destructive reign of power. Order does not imply justice. "(G)reat robbers punish little ones to keep them in their obedience; but the great ones are rewarded with laurels and triumphs, because they are too big for the weak hands of justice in this world, and have the power in their possession which should punish offenders" (no. 176). The words of an anonymous poet express this same recognition that the order achieved by civilized society is often but the maintenance of small justices in the perpetuation of a larger, all-pervading injustice.

> The law detains both man and woman
> Who steal the goose from off the common
> But lets the greater felon loose
> Who steals the common from the goose.
> (quoted by Lowi, 1969, p. 285)

True synergy in civilized society is exceedingly difficult to attain. While the natural tendency of biological orders is toward synergy, the natural tendency of unnatural civilized polity is toward corruption. The corruptive rule of power germinates freely in the environment of civilization, like mildew in a damp room. To cleanse the social order of the contaminant of power is a process that is at once complex and perpetual. Only special kinds of government vigilantly attended even begin to approximate the just society.

B. The Roots of Injustice:
A Critique of the Marxist View

No one has done more to call attention to the problems of intrasocietal conflict and exploitation than Karl Marx and those of his school of thought. Society, in Marxist thought, has been throughout history not a harmonious whole but an arena for the exploitation of the masses by some dominant class. Marx's work is a cry for justice. Marxism has become a natural home for oppressed groups and peoples around the world. It is, however, the wrong home.

Exposing the shortcomings of Marxism is an important element in the proper presentation of the parable of the tribes. This is true not in spite of but because of the fact that the two visions have certain fundamental concerns in common. Thus, for example, although functionalist theory tends to gloss over the elements of strife and power in civilized society, my critique of it here has been fairly brief, whereas that of Marxism is more thorough. The parable of the tribes challenges Marxism for the role it presently plays in the world. For one thing, Marxism is probably the principal reigning social theory, the single encompassing system of thought that most influences the way thinkers, even non-Marxists, view man and society. The parable of the tribes presents an alternative comprehensive vision. More important, however, Marxism stands as the most prominent theoretical basis for action against the manifest injustices of the world. The parable of the tribes is an alternative diagnosis of civilization's most debilitating diseases.

In the choice of diagnoses, considerably more is at stake than the prospering of one theory or another. If the diagnosis is misguided, so too will be the treatment. If those who recognize that something is *radically* wrong in civilization act on a theory that misses the *root* of the problem, their radical action will only create new problems. An erroneous radical theory is therefore of great service to the cause of injustice, for it harnesses mankind's natural energies of hurt and outrage and diverts them from the rectification of injustice to its perpetuation. Marxism is such a theory. It is not just coincidence that the revolutions guided by Marxist thought have led very far from the utopian visions of *The German Ideology*, that they have led not toward a heaven of human fulfillment and dignity but to the hell of the Gulag. Not coincidence, not incidental betrayal of the revolution, but a direct and predictable consequence of fundamental theoretical errors.

Marx misunderstood the root of injustice. He misconceived the problem of power. He failed to apprehend the true problem of government.

In Marxist analysis, the *economic* relations of production are fundamental. Other social relationships are built upon the economic foundation. Ownership is paramount, rulership and the means of coercion derivative: the economically dominant class constructs a political superstructure as a tool of its exploitation of the lower classes. Wrote Engels: "it is as a rule, the most powerful, economically dominant class, which through the medium of the state, becomes also the politically dominant class, and thus acquires new means of holding down and exploiting the oppressed class" (in Feuer, 1959, p. 392). Engels proceeds to apply this image of the state as created by an economically dominant class to "the state of antiquity," to the feudal state, and to the capitalist state. From analysis of this sort, it more or less followed for Marx and his followers that equalization of economic status (through collective ownership) would lead to a classless society. Equality at the substructural level would insure an end to injustice and exploitation. Since the state was but a superstructural device for class domination, it would be superfluous in the classless postrevolutionary society: an interval of dictatorship of the proletariat would taper into the withering away of the state. To quote again Marx's partner Engels: "The society that will organize production on the basis of a free and equal association of producers will put the whole machinery of the state where it will then belong: into the museum of antiquities, by the side of the spinning wheel and the bronze ax" (in ibid., p. 394).

Much of the error of Marxism derives from the primacy it gives to the economic dimension. Economics is, indeed, fundamental in the sense that to human life, as to all life, the economic processes of obtaining the means of sustenance are absolutely indispensable. In this sense, life without politics is conceivable whereas life without "economics" is not. But it does not follow from this that economic relationships among people are fundamental in determining the other dimensions of relationships within society. In the search for the roots of inequality and injustice, the parable of the tribes would direct us to attend to a different dimension of relations: the power to compel, ultimately the capacity to exert force.

At its core, as a theory of selection in the intersocietal realm, the parable of the tribes is nonreductionistic: the selective forces stand outside the systems being molded. (See chap. 1, "The Reign of Power.") Moreover, the manifest complexity of interaction among the dimensions of actual social life should caution us against regarding any dimension as a mere function of any other. This mutuality of influence is especially important where the problem of power does not prevent people from shaping their own destinies, and thus where the multiplicity of human values can come into play. Where power does intrude, however, certain directions of influence will tend to prevail over others; and the parable of the tribes, aside from presenting a model for a selective process, also affords a perspective on what it is in the civilized human condition that allows power to reign. If we were to seek, therefore, a reductionistic explanation of the problems of social inequality and injustice, that perspective suggests a foundation not in economic substructure but in underlying anarchy and the consequent triumph of raw power.

The primacy of raw power at the root of injustice is suggested both by logic and by the evidence of history.

Although food is a natural requirement of human life, under the unnaturally ungoverned circumstances of civilized life the sword becomes more basic in shaping human relations. Force is an irreducible form of power. Under conditions of anarchy, it governs. Violence can ultimately be controlled only by the capacity to commit more powerful violence. While control over material resources can be translated into the power to compel, those who have wealth without such power usually suffer spoliation (Andrzejewski, 1954, p. 25). Conversely, those who have raw power without wealth can directly use their power to take the resources of others less powerful, whether wealthy or poor.

The primacy of force points our investigation of the roots of injustice not toward economics but toward politics, for it is the state that manages the use of force within society. The unjust state is connected with the sword in two possible ways: (*a*) rule is often established by the sword, that is, previous inequalities of raw power become embodied in the political system; and (*b*) rule is invariably backed by the sword, so that granting any group superior political power ipso facto implies subsequent inequalities in the control of force within society.

(*a*) Unless very strong and widespread cultural influences are able to restrain the use of force among people, or unless a political order is already sufficiently established to domesticate the rule of raw power, those who wield the sword will be able to wield the scepter as well. Gaetano Mosca writes that "it is the unvarying fact" that among civilized peoples who have recently entered the agricultural stage the position of rulership is occupied by the "strictly military class" (1939, p. 258). And Arthur Livingston writes that "the human beings who have lived on this earth in security from the brutal rule of the soldier are so few in number, on the background of the whole human history, as hardly to count. The military tyranny in some form or other is in fact the common rule in human society" (introduction to Mosca, 1939, p. xxiii). In the world today, a great many regimes came into power through essentially military means, maintain their rule by the use of force, and can be changed only by the common phenomenon of the military coup or, under less common circumstances, by armed revolt. Again we see that what seemed a clear-cut distinction between the intersocietal arena, the unavoidable anarchy of which gives rise to the rule of power described by the parable of the tribes, and the "governed" intrasocietal realm is really rather blurred. Even within political boundaries, force tends to rule. "The history of national societies," Morgenthau writes, "shows that no . . . group has been able to withstand for long the temptation to advance its claims by violent means if it thought it could do so without too great a risk" (1972, p. 475). The relations among social groups tend too often to rest on a foundation of that irreducible form of power.[8]

The primacy of raw power in determining the balance of political power within societies is demonstrated by an interesting relationship: changes in the distribution of the capacity for violence tend to lead to changes in the distribution of political power. Lenski asserts the general proposition that "the greater the military importance of the peasant farmer, the better his economic and political situation tended to be, and con-

8. Is not the common pattern in civilization of domination and unjust treatment of women attributable in large measure to the superior physical power of the male?

280

versely, the less his military importance, the poorer his economic and political situation" (1966, p. 275). It appears that within societies, also, as the Athenians instructed the Melians, justice is in question only among equals in power. Historical substantiation for this view of the determinative role of raw power in the relations among social classes is found in Andrzejewski's *Military Organization and Society.* In ancient Egypt, when the Hyksos conquest impelled the Egyptians to adopt the capital intensive (therefore scarce) military technology of chariots and armor, a professional soldiering class was established with the consequence of considerably widening social inequalities (1954, pp. 42–43). Similarly, in medieval Europe, where the armored knight was the indispensable military asset and where several years' income of a whole village was necessary to equip a single knight, the "militarily useless" peasants "possessed no political rights" (p. 59). Conversely, history shows that where the means of force are widely distributed, creating mutual vulnerability, there tends also to be greater social equality. In classical Greece the change from armor and cavalry to the more generally available arms of infantry helped foster greater political democratization. In ancient China, the introduction of the reflex bow helped ameliorate social inequalities. Creel wrote, in *The Birth of China,* that this powerful bow, which could penetrate armor, kept the Chinese aristocracy from enjoying the invulnerability of European knights (cited in Andrzejewski, 1954). As a consequence, says Andrzejewski, the Chinese masses "possessed the power to revolt" (1956, p. 48). And in more recent centuries, as has frequently been observed, the coming of firearms and subsequently of mass armies significantly contributed to the rise of modern democracy.[9] Raymond Aron, for example, writes: "In the golden age of chivalry knights encased in steel dominated the battlefields. The harquebusiers, who delivered death at a distance—much to the indignation of the nobility—prepared the way for the fall of feudalism, which was completed when fortified castles could be destroyed in a few days by the artillery of regular armies. That victory heralded the birth of democracy"[10] (1954, pp. 85–86).

Not all governments are founded by force, nor is political power always distributed according to the capacity to inflict injury. Yet the lurking potential for anarchy in civilized systems makes the primacy of brute force a natural tendency. Only the careful construction of political edifices can elevate political relations above that level. Whenever the scaffolding of government breaks down, a kind of gravitational tug will plunge society

9. "'God did not make all men equal,' Westerners were fond of saying, 'Colonel Colt did'" (from magazine advertisement for books on the American West).

10. For thoughts on the implications of this line of thinking for the contemporary world, see pp. 287–289, below.

back into the base rule of naked power. (One thinks of the political gangsterism in the late 1970's in civil war-torn Lebanon.)[11] It is for this reason, too, that the radical perspective offered by the parable of the tribes suggests caution about that supposedly quintessential radical action, violent revolution. Since sweeping away the structures of order always risks a fall into the pit, it must be a particularly depraved and irredeemable regime to justify such a gamble. It was not Lenin and his Bolsheviks who overthrew the tyranny of the czar, but it was they who, in overturning the democratic provisional government of Kerensky, gathered the reins of power (Billington, 1980). Disorder, including revolutionary disorder, favors the ruthless.

(b) Because force can be controlled only with superior force, anarchy can be prevented only by a government that has a monopoly on the use of force, or at least a preponderancy of forces. This does not imply that all rule is coercive: any state governed only by force or the threat of it will function poorly; and most states need not rely primarily upon coercion to gain the day-to-day cooperation of their subjects. But no state is likely to survive long unless it possesses supremacy of forces within its domain.

From the fact that control over the state confers the power of coercion, an important conclusion follows: inequalities of political power create inequalities of coercive power. Therefore, even when a group achieves the status of ruling class without the use of force, the outcome in terms of force structure tends to be the same as in a polity founded by violence and conquest. However much the ruled may view the reigning power as vested with "authority," however "legitimate" the government may be in their eyes, to the extent that the free consent of the governed is not a condition for continued rule the scepter is ultimately but a metamorphosis of the sword.

Political power is, therefore, the next most irreducible form of power. In most civilized political systems, the sword and the scepter have tended to be manifestations of the same most fundamental species of power. Thus, in an ungoverned situation, those with raw power can seize control and govern, whereas in a governed society those who rule gain predominance also in that irreducible form of power. If society is divided into rulers and ruled, those who rule can translate their greater power into whatever goods the society has to offer. In particular, power permits its wielder to establish economic relations that are in his interest. For this reason economic power has tended throughout history to be derivative of political(-military) power.

11. The newly "elected" president of Lebanon is Bashir Gemayel, a man who rose to ascendancy by such means as murdering the families of his Lebanese Christian rivals. . . . A week later: no longer—Gemayel is assassinated by an enormous explosive.

This relationship is one the perspective of the parable of the tribes logically leads us to expect. But it is necessary to test this logic against the evidence of civilized history. That evidence, indeed, has compelled even some who approached history with a Marxist outlook to revise their assumptions about the primacy of economics at the roots of class differences. Service, for example, in *Origins of the State and Civilization*, recounts the disconfirmation of his original beliefs. Classes, he found, did not have "*material* (economic) beginnings" which "became gradually social, and finally political" (1975, p. 34). Rather, in the early civilizations "the two basic strata were the *governors* and the *governed*. Even in the earliest and simplest systems," he writes, "this political power organized the economy, rather than vice versa" (p. xiii).

The origins of class inequality evidently lie in the political, not the economic realm. As civilization emerged, societies had need of political differentiation. Yet as one group cannot be trusted to rule another, the power to direct and coordinate, which developing agrarian societies needed to invest in someone, becomes the power to oppress and exploit. Thus, historically, it is the political position of rule that has been the key to positions of economic domination. Similar to Service's findings about the earliest civilizations is Heilbroner's judgment that "*in premarket societies, wealth tended to follow power; not until the market society would power tend to follow wealth*" (1970, p. 32, italics in original). And Lenski likewise finds that in civilized societies until fairly modern times "*the institutions of government are the primary source of social inequality*" (1966, p. 210, italics in original).

Again, the perspective of the parable of the tribes places the problem of power at the heart of the human dilemma. This central problem grows not out of man's economic bases (which in a sense he shares with all creatures) but out of his unprecedented confrontation with anarchy. Anarchy enthrones force, and only government can place anything else on the throne. The ubiquitous plague in civilized society of exploitation among classes stems from *the failure of political systems* to wring anarchy out of the fabric of human society. In the economic "substructure" is to be found neither the root cause nor the true cure of social injustices.

The problem with Marx is that he drew rather general conclusions from a special case: capitalist society.

This is the one kind of society so structured as to enable economic predominance to translate fairly readily into other forms of domination. The bourgeoisie had indeed gained their place through their role in their society's economic life and eventually succeeded somewhat in shaping the political system to serve their class interests. But power could follow wealth (in Heilbroner's phrase) because some particular circumstances obtained.

In the first place, capitalist societies (such as England and the United States) had substantially domesticated the use of force through stable political systems. Unarmed wealth was therefore protected from the plunder to which anarchy would have exposed them. (One thinks of the fact that even in the United States today, the potential breakdown of order caused by a natural disaster requires the National Guard routinely to be called out to prevent looting.) In a stably governed system, it becomes possible for those without force to work for meaningful legal protections.

Thus, second, capitalist society had developed a system of laws which liberated economic activity from the shackles of political control (à la Adam Smith), a freedom for the economic realm which is historically exceptional. By granting the economic system an extraordinary degree of autonomy from control by other social and cultural forces, the economic system could become at once less derivative and more determinative than it had been among other forms of civilized society.

This autonomy was in part the work of the middle class seeking its own advantage, but this cannot be regarded as an adequate explanation. If a class "rises" it must first have been low, and its success suggests that higher classes must have refrained from quashing it. Thus, another factor in the evolution of a political order reflecting middle-class interests was that serving those interests also served the national interest. *The Wealth of Nations,* after all, is an argument for the maximization of national wealth. For the first time in millennia, economic performance was becoming a critical determinant of differences of power among civilized societies. The crown was therefore motivated to bless the market in order to fortify itself. The wisely wielded sword thus did not plunder or hinder the uniquely creative forces of production and industrialization, just as the wise man with a goose laying golden eggs refrains from gutting it.

In the context of this extraordinary set of circumstances which combined to give economic forces unprecedented social power, Karl Marx labored in the British Museum to present the laws of all history.

If one fruit of these labors was a critique of capitalism that, in many ways, was brilliant,[12] another was a general theory that failed to grasp the general problems of civilized societies. The theoretical failure led to revolutionary failure. Collectivization of ownership under the communist state cures the system of the plutocratic corruptions of the bourgeois polity, but it also readily plunges the postrevolutionary society into the depths of totalitarian oppression. That a Marxist revolution would lead to Stalin and the Gulag (also, in less dramatic but still pertinent examples,

12. This aspect of Marxist theory is critiqued in the next section, "The Market as a Power System."

to Maoist China and Castroite Cuba) is predictable in the perspective offered by the parable of the tribes. That the scratches of injustice inflicted by the "polecats" of capitalism would become the gaping gashes inflicted by the "lions" of a communist dictatorship is no surprise when we understand that the injustices of civilized societies have their root not in ownership of the means of production but in control over the coercive arm of the state.

Jefferson is thus a far better guide than Marx for the pursuit of the just society. Jefferson knew that equality of influence over the power of the state is the only basis for justice. The Jeffersonian revolutionary vision contains no illusions that any part of society can be trusted to represent "the people" unless the power of the people to compel that representation is built into the system and is vigilantly and incessantly protected. Jefferson would never have imagined that the state, becoming superfluous, would wither away. To begin with, in civilized society the state does not become superfluous: although the best government may be the one that governs the least, Jefferson would never have held, as Marx and Engels wrote in *The Communist Manifesto*, that "Political power, properly so called, is merely the organized power of one class for oppressing another" (in Feuer, 1959, p. 29); or said with Marx that after the success of the revolution of the working class "there will no longer be political power . . . since political power is simply the official form of the antagonism in civil society" (from *Poverty of Philosophy*, quoted in Hook, 1973, p. 271). Second, his sense of the root of the problem of power and of its temptations would never have made him sanguine that political powers would allow themselves to be dethroned, however unneeded they were. (Mao wrote: "'Don't you want to eliminate state authority?' Yes, but we do not want it at present, we cannot want it. Why? Because imperialism still exists, the domestic reactionaries still exist. Our present task is . . . to enable China to advance steadily . . . and to realize the state of universal fraternity" [in de Bary et al., 1960, p. 230]. Don't hold your breath.) A revolution based on such misunderstandings of the problem of power becomes the instrument not of liberation and justice but of the construction of some of the most dangerous concentrations of tyrannical power civilization has seen.

Contemporary evidence suggests that the approach of the liberal democracies gives mankind its best hope for freedom from oppression. To the extent that in the twentieth century the heirs of Jefferson, Locke, et al. have lost to Marxists their capacity to guide and inspire the world's huddled masses yearning to breathe free, it is due not to the failure of their liberating tradition but to their unwillingness to apply that tradition to the plight of other peoples. Many of these heirs have been seduced

285

by the temptations of world power and intimidated by the perils of intersocietal competition to betray the values of human freedom. Even the purest traditions seem to have a kind of half-life in which their morality is degraded into opportunism. (A few centuries after Christ, the cross led armies into battle.) The liberating glow of the message becomes obscured by the evident impurities of the medium.

The problem of power is unavoidable in human societies. No revolution will solve it finally. No civilized social structure can be immune to it. There is no class that, empowered, will lay to rest the evil of corruption. Inequalities of power lead invariably to corruption, and human affairs tend naturally to create inequalities of power. The task of counteracting these invariable tendencies is continuous and, at best, only partly successful.[13]

C. Modern Reversal of Trends?

Within societies, as between them, the problem of power arose with civilization. During the gradual transition from egalitarian bands to full-scale agrarian civilizations, social evolution meant ever-increasing social inequality (see Fried's *Evolution of Political Society*). Only in comparatively recent times has the evidence of history offered much ground for hoping that "progress" might bring greater social justice. Lenski writes that *"The appearance of mature industrial societies marks the first significant reversal in the age-old evolutionary trend toward ever-increasing inequality"* (1966, p. 304, italics in original).

This generalization needs to be qualified. We must ask: equality in what respect? Lenski's analysis focuses on equality in the distribution of national production. He shows that in modern industrial societies—liberal democracies and communist dictatorships—the proportion of product going to the most favored group is far less than in the "agrarian" societies of the past.

Distribution of wealth is important, but my analysis has led me to be even more concerned with the distribution of political power as the key to the problem of social justice. In this dimension, the category "industrial society" is too inclusive to be useful. In some industrial societies political power has been equalized, at least in contrast with societies of the past, but in others the masses of people are as powerless and as subject to coercive intimidation as ever.

13. The case for liberal democracy as a solution to the intrasocietal problem of power and the imperfections of that solution are discussed at length in my dissertation "The Parable of the Tribes," pp. 1007–1148.

The bright prospect of a social evolutionary trend toward equality and justice is thus beclouded.

Nonetheless, Lenski's assertion retains some validity, and it raises the questions: (1) Why should greater distributive equality and more widespread political participation blossom at this point in history among some of the most powerful and advanced societies? and (2) what are the prospects for the continued enjoyment of such blessings in the future? Here are a few thoughts on each.

(1) Among possible factors contributing to equality (material and/or political) are:

(a) In the world today, the ideology of democracy and egalitarianism is more ascendant than in premodern eras, forcing even coercive regimes to pay at least lip service to "the people." The question remains, however, why these values, which were heretical in many places throughout much of history, should rise to prominence now.

(b) Modern society is far more productive than its predecessor. With so much more to go around, the ruling groups may feel less impelled to keep "all for ourselves," as in the vile maxim cited by Adam Smith.

(c) The roles that modern society needs to have filled, requiring as they do mass literacy, specialized knowledge, and a degree of discretion and initiative, tend to reduce the feasibility of an organization based wholly on command, and to increase the dependence of those at the top of the organization on the good will and cooperation of those below them. Exploitation is thus tempered.

(d) A fourth factor (perhaps a special case of the third) in the rise of democracies may have been the development of market economies, with their emphasis on freedom of economic activity and on individual initiative. The market system, at least while the market is atomistic and not concentrated, tends to decentralize power and to hinder small elites from gaining complete control.

(e) Finally, there is the democratization of warfare, alluded to earlier: the rise of the mass army made the rulers of society more dependent upon the goodwill of their people, and so gave the people greater political leverage.

I explore the last point a bit further, not because it is necessarily the most important but because it extends the line of thought of this chapter into some provocative questions about a possible less benign reversal of the trend in the future.

The evolution of military organization and technology, it was argued earlier, has important effects on the evolution of political structures. Once the "democratic" revolution in France placed into the hands of Napoleon a mass army, the other nations of Europe were forced to resort to the same device simply to survive (see Vagts on this on page 99, above). Yet the very tool by which the old aristocratic order sought to preserve itself also threatened it: "Metternich, chief upholder of the traditional order, realized this perfectly; at the Congress of Vienna he insisted on the abolition of conscription" (Andrzejewski, p. 69). As is general in the history of power, a means of magnifying power, once discovered, will not forever remain shelved. Eventually, the European monarchies turned to conscription, but only after suffering decisive defeats: Prussia after Napoleon, the czars after the Crimean War, Franz Josef Strauss after the defeat of Austria by Bismarck (ibid.). Wider military participation seems to have been a factor in the wider political participation of the democracies which now characterize the European nations not under Soviet domination. Clearly, however, Nazi Germany and Soviet Russia demonstrate that mass armies do not necessarily lead to democracy. Still, Andrzejewski makes a good case for a major link between military structure and political structure.

(2) If that is the case, what does that link imply for the future of liberty in the West? The technology of warfare is rapidly evolving, and it would appear that contemporary trends are away from the democratizing, labor-intensive modes to the more elitist capital-intensive. In an age of nuclear stalemate and low-intensity conflict, it is not clear upon what military means national survival depends. Nonetheless, the exponentially increasing technological sophistication of the means of coercion carries the threat that the few could again hold in their hands the means to intimidate and control the many in their own society without sacrificing the power they could bring to bear against external enemies. One must therefore wonder whether that same military-political connection which seems to have helped nurture democracy in recent centuries may crush it in the era to come. It would not be the first time the evolution of power has given and taken away with equal indifference.

Against this malign possibility, a few counterpoints may be considered.

First, perhaps the demands of modern society (referred to in item *c* above) will mitigate against rule by coercion. The Soviet Union, however, demonstrates that coercion (although it has its costs) is not incompatible with modernity and with at least adequate efficiency.

Second, some hope that the leverage of terrorist violence might compel oppressive regimes to loosen their exploitive grip. This argument is based on the same link, but conceives the balance of power between the few and the many differently: whereas the guns of citizens may be no match for tanks and planes (Concord in 1776 turned out differently from Budapest in 1956), a single individual can construct and carry a single atomic device. The idea of a terrorist nuclear device, so fearsome in other contexts, appears here as a kind of twenty-first century Zorro against the dystopian tyranny of the future. It is for good reason, however, that liberal minds have learned to be skeptical of the use of terrorist violence for the achievement of liberation. It is the open society, not the closed one, that is vulnerable to the terrorist threat. This threat, if directed against a tyranny, is likely not to foster greater freedom but to reinforce the movement toward the repressive police state, toward an iron grip so firm that subjects lack the mobility necessary to strike against the state.

Third, many may hope that the structure of force has become irrelevant. Has not the use of force been subordinated to the political system in modern democracies, and does this not make the particular forms of force irrelevant to our political future? Yes and no. On the one hand, as long as we live in a well-ordered polity, changes in the nature of the force wielded by political authorities need have no impact on our society's internal power relations. On the other hand, any political structure is but a scaffold against the gravitational pull of anarchy. If the people in political power subvert the legitimate processes regulating their governance (as, for example, Richard Nixon recently began to do in the United States), or if some other group is able to gain control of the military and then to seize the state by coup d'état, the rule of the sword returns, and the chances of the people to regain their democratic liberties may depend on the nature of that sword. An ordered polity, in some ways, is like a sealed craft traveling through the changing medium of the facts of irreducible force. As long as the seal is intact, those in the vehicle can be comfortable whether the surrounding medium is air, water, or the vacuum of outer space. If the craft breaks open, however, the fate of the occupants depends on how hospitable is the environment that rushes in.

Changes in the forms of power can therefore increase or decrease the vulnerability of political liberty and justice. The preservation of democracy in the face of adverse changes in the structure of force is a challenging and delicate task. It requires vigilant maintenance of the political order, including the effective instillation of the cultural values of democracy so that structures of command (as in the military) cannot readily be employed for the subversion of that order.

D. Wheels within Wheels: The Class Struggle and the Evolution of Civilization

These days there are many histories but few theories of history. In the nineteenth century, more were willing to grapple with and try to explain the whole of human history. In its aims, the parable of the tribes is a spiritual descendant of those earlier efforts. A fundamental difference between the present theory and most of the others is that the parable of the tribes sees the crucial arena of social evolutionary activity as the encompassing system of interacting societies whereas the older theories typically looked within particular civilized societies to discover self-generated evolutionary forces.

One variety of these theories treated a civilization as if it were an organic entity with an intrinsic life cycle. Organic metaphors like this probably obscure far more than they reveal: civilized systems unlike other "organisms" have no genetic blueprint to govern them; having crossed the frontier of determined repetitive patterns, civilized systems unfold no inherent plan either in their living or in their dying. Thus, whatever patterns of rise and fall can be observed among civilized societies are best understood not through organic metaphors of the life cycle, but in terms particularly of the unnaturalness of the systems, as is argued in the final section of this chapter, "The Death of the Unnatural."

The Marxist theory of history is another variant of this focus on intrasocietal developments as the engine of social evolution. For much the same reasons as given earlier, it is the comparison between the Marxist theory of history and the parable of the tribes that warrants exploration. In the first place, the two theories are akin in their emphasis on conflict as the driving force behind social evolution: the role played by intersocietal competition in the one is played by the dialectical class struggle in the other. Second, even though few of the old social evolutionists are still influential, many people still look to Marx for a general framework in which to understand history. For both these reasons, and because I have not applied to the struggles for power within societies the general perspective of the parable of the tribes, it behooves me to step back and consider what place the class struggle should be given in a comprehensive theory of social evolution.

The claims of Marxist theory for explaining history are ambitious. Engels wrote that "As Darwin discovered the law of evolution in organic nature so Marx discovered the law of evolution in human history . . ." (quoted in Harris, 1968, p. 217). The heart of this "law of evolution" is expressed by the statement from *The Communist Manifesto* that "The history of all hitherto existing society is the history of class struggles" (1967, p. 79). These claims, of course, conflict with those of the parable of the tribes. Consequently, if the parable of the tribes is able to defend its own claims, it should be able also to refute, at least in part, those of Marxism.

The challenge to the adequacy of Marxist theory has several points. (1) The first point has already been made, that is, that Marx misunderstood the basic nature of the class struggle, that he mistakenly extrapolated characteristics of class relations in capitalist society as being fundamental to society generally. Thus, even if the class struggle were the key to history, Marx would still not open the way. (2) This deficiency connects with another, that is, that Marx's analysis of history is quite truncated in the time it covers. Although his theory of historical development touches upon the "primitive communism" of the egalitarian band and deals slightly with some of the forms taken by ancient civilizations, it does not seem to begin in earnest until it reaches the European Middle Ages. In "Socialism: Utopian and Scientific," Engels follows his "Let us briefly sum up our sketch of historical evolution," with "I. Medieval Society" (in Feuer, 1959). Marvin Harris has commented that "Marx's interest in the precapitalist economic forms is totally marginal to his consideration of the feudalism-capitalism transition, which in turn is marginal to his major concern, the analysis of capitalist society" (1968, p. 227). (3) This limitation in temporal scope is matched by an equally telling limitation in the geographical scope of the theory. The focal transition from feudal society to capitalist society had only occurred in a few societies in a single civilizational area. (Even in those societies, the "scientific laws" that were to carry them to the next culminating social evolutionary stage still remain unverified.) Thus, even if the Marxist analysis were wholly valid in the domain of its application, it would still illuminate social evolution for only a few centuries and apply simply to one part of the inhabited globe.

This suggests a major advantage of the parable of the tribes over a theory like Marxism: even if a theory like Marx's could account for the local origins of significant cultural changes, it is unable to explain the global pattern of their spread. Theoretical ideas about the intrasocietal dynamics of change cannot readily account for the wider processes that seem so central to the development of civilization. It seems clear that some of the most profound characteristics of social evolution cannot be explained in terms of the internal process of civilized societies, each society developing as if in isolation. By embracing the wide and now global context in which civilized societies develop, the parable of the tribes has the capacity to explain the overarching patterns of the evolution of the whole human civilizational system.

When the role of intersocietal struggles in generating change grew more and more evident, Marxism attempted to assimilate that fact without fundamentally changing its theory of history, by subsuming imperialism as a form or expression of the class struggle. If calling the conquest of one society by another a class struggle is simply a matter of greatly broadening the definition of class, then the proposition is tautological and only seems to say something of substance. This seems in part to be what Marxism has done. In part also, however, Marxism has attempted to subsume intersocietal struggles into its intrasocietal model by asserting that the former is a function of the latter, that is, that it is the class structure within the imperialist society which leads to imperialistic conduct of that society in the wider world. In my dissertation exposition of the parable of the tribes, I devoted a hundred pages to a refutation of the notion that nineteenth-century imperialism of European nations is primarily to be understood as a function of the capitalist domestic economies and classes of those societies. For the sake of brevity, I have here (in "State of Unnature" above) simply argued that the intersocietal struggle for power is far more a function of the nature of the overarching system than of the nature of its particular components; that since the beginning of civilization and all over the world since, discrepancies in power among societies have often led to imperialist conquest; and that the imperialism of the Soviet Union (not to mention Vietnam in Cambodia or China in Tibet) should have laid to rest any notion that ending capitalism would end the intersocietal predation of the strong upon the weak. Not that intrasocietal tensions of various sorts might not play a role in motivating a government to embark upon foreign adventures, or that some ruling groups may be hungrier than others to extend their powers. But no theory of the class struggle as such will be able to incorporate the role of intersocietal struggles as an engine of cultural change.

Indeed, perhaps a stronger case can be made in the other direction, that is, that intersocietal competition has a major role in the shaping of class relations within societies, examples of which I have already considered in this chapter. For example, changes in the organization and technology required for national power, altering the patterns of dependence and vulnerability among social groups, influenced the balance of equality and exploitation among classes. This relationship reflects the fact that, as Andrzejewski writes: "When faced with extinction the states usually adopt the most efficient military organization, even though it may be uncongenial to their social structure" (1954, p. 38). Also previously proposed was the idea that the importance of the bourgeoisie as a source of national power inhibited other still dominant social powers from crushing and plundering them, as they presumably had the power to do.

There are other ways in which the inescapable pressures of intersocietal anarchy and strife molded those very class relations upon which Marxism is focused. Heilbroner, for example, stresses the role of the insecurity and violence of life in feudal times in shaping the relationship between lord and serf:

> The peasant, although not a warrior and therefore not occupationally exposed to the dangers of continual combat, assassination, etc., was pre-eminently fair prey for the marauding lord, defenseless against capture, unable to protect

his poor possessions against destruction. Hence, we can begin to understand why even free men became serfs by "commending" themselves to a lord who, in exchange for their economic, social, and political subservience, offered them in return the invaluable cloak of his military protection. (1970, pp. 36–37)

As Hamilton said in *The Federalist* (no. 8), "external danger" is a "most powerful determinant of conduct." To be more safe, men are often willing to become less free. Vagts describes how subsequent evolution in European class relations was influenced by the changing nature of the wars of Europe (1937, pp. 407–408). His account of how warfare swept aside intervening loci of class dominance in order to strengthen the single dominant state power substantiates Jouvenel's generalization that the "intimate tie between war and Power is a constant feature of European history. Each state which has in its turn exercised political hegemony got itself the wherewithal by subjugating its people more completely than its rivals could subjugate theirs. And to resist absorption by their predecessors in hegemony, the other Powers of the continent were bound to get on a level with them" (1949, p. 142). Thus we can see that the arena of intersocietal competition described by the parable of the tribes, with its emphasis on the organizational imperatives for survival in that struggle, can go at least some distance in explaining the evolution of internal power relationships in civilized societies.

It is unnecessaary, however, to subsume either domain of power's play to the other. Both inter- and intrasocietal struggles go on, like wheels turning within wheels. Each has its own engine, and each can rub against the other affecting its motion. As a theory primarily of the spread of cultural forms, the parable of the tribes does not depend for its validity on the inconsequentiality of purely internal social processes in bringing forth novelty. The class struggle is indeed an important dimension of the human condition under civilization, and it is probably a creative factor in history, as Marx says. The parable of the tribes can encompass that dynamic arena within its own comprehensive perspective.

The parable of the tribes and its intrasocietal analogue ultimately blend into a single vision. The ungoverned intersocietal system and the ostensibly governed system of civilized society, we have seen, differ only in degree. Both are arenas for the same underlying unnatural human dilemma: that relations among human beings are, in a most fundamental and unique sense, unregulated; that the consequence of this anarchy is that power rules; that this rule of power means that most civilized human beings endure the impact of changes in their systems far more than they have a voice in determining those changes; and that the changes frequently tend, therefore, to be injurious.

4. The Market as a Power System: A Critique of the Capitalist Economy

A. Introduction

I have explored three major macrosystems of civilization in their relation to the parable of the tribes—the ecological, the international, and the political. Now it is time for the economic. To consider the economic system as an autonomous domain of civilized activity is to consider the market economy, because where there is no market the economic system has been subordinated to other systems, usually to the political (as in centrally planned economies) but often also to the sociocultural. An autonomous economy is a market economy.

What makes the market so intriguing in relation to the parable of the tribes is not that the market has proven an engine of societal power (although it has), but that the ideology of the market is like a reverse image of the parable of the tribes. The latter laments the way unregulated competition among self-serving entities creates systemic forces leading to unchosen and undesirable consequences. The advocates of the market, by contrast, advertise that in the economic realm the efforts of independent actors seeking only their own gain are combined as if by an invisible hand to promote an unintended yet synergistic end. Although the two theories relate to actions in different realms, by positing opposite results from analogous processes they stand in relation to each other like a man and his upside-down reflection in a pool.

The liberal ideology (given classic expression by Adam Smith) is a refreshing change from the tragic view of the parable of the tribes. Where the latter pictures us as trapped in systems that pervert our sacred energies for destructive ends, the other assures us that the system transmutes even our base and selfish motives into the golden rule of the common good. Where the one cautions distrust of civilized systems and calls for a barely conceivable wresting of our destiny from their machinations, the other comforts us with the certainty that a benign and invisible hand steers our course toward an ideal fate. How attractive a prospect! Synergy combined with freedom. People will act as they should act, not because they are coerced by an authority (an approach that is not only an affront to human dignity but dangerous to synergy as well), and not because they have been remade into altruistic angels (an approach that is unreliable as well as intrapsychically burdensome), but because the system so channels their energies. Man as he is leads to society as it should be.

294

This attractive view of the market was originally an extension of a vision of the world as governed generally by a beneficent natural order. The eighteenth-century physiocrats, for example, saw the economy as a self-healing system analogous to the body: remove the obstacles to free flow and health will ensue (Dalton, 1974, p. 45n). The atomistic society of Adam Smith's vision functioned like an efficient natural machine, a smooth-running and harmonious order like Newton's clockwork universe (Heilbroner, 1961, p. 5). Later, this laissez-faire ideology incorporated the new Darwinian theory: it was no wonder the unrestricted play of individual self-interest could produce the blessings of the free market, for the same laissez-faire competition had produced man himself (Keynes, 1927, p. 20).

By revealing the fundamental discontinuity between the natural and the unnatural, between the condition of creatures living in the systems of their biological evolution and that of human beings living in civilization, the parable of the tribes shows that no sound and sanguine view of the market can rest upon such extrapolations from the natural order. Adam Smith wrote that nature had "not only endowed mankind with an appetite for the end which she proposes, but likewise with an appetite for the means by which alone this end can be brought about . . ." (quoted in Cropsey, 1957, p. 4n). Creatures in nature may be so endowed, but with civilized mankind natural appetites seek satisfaction through unnatural means. The "means" of civilization are sudden inventions neither given nor tested by the synergistic order of nature. This discrepancy falsifies the equation between the "natural liberty" of the market and that of creatures in natural systems, and thus it precludes the easy deduction that from economic liberty synergy will naturally flow.

Disproving the premise, however, does not disprove the conclusion. It remains to be seen whether the market does indeed create a synergistic result. The purpose of this section is to examine this proposition.

A clear understanding of the market's functioning would be valuable. The market and its ideology remain potent forces in the world after more than two centuries. (In 1981, the president of the United States tells suffering peoples at home and abroad that their salvation is to be won not through official bureaucracies but through the free play of the market.) If, as I maintain, both the strengths and the weakness of the market are profound, it would be useful to have them clearly identified. A failure to do so has led (in many "mixed" economies today) to the double error of hindering the beneficial forces of the market while allowing its destructive tendencies to go unchecked. It should be possible to get rid of more of the dirty bath water without also dumping the baby.

B. Market Justice: Questions of Class Exploitation

The Market's Case Presented.—Many able writers have shown by clear economic analysis how the invisible hand works in the market system. In the interest of brevity, that analysis is not recapitulated here, despite the considerable beauty and validity of the argument and despite a regrettably widespread ignorance of this model even among educated people. Suffice it to say that the market is presented in liberal theory: as a marvelous mechanism for continuously processing an overwhelmingly complex body of ever-changing information, leading to a system of prices which truly reflects both the costs (on the producer's side) and the benefits (on the consumer's side) of an infinite variety of goods and services; as an unerring allocator of resources which, by translating "apples and oranges" into the common value language of money, can select among an infinite variety of possible market baskets the one that maximizes productivity and utility; as a stern taskmaster who compels those wishing to make profits to provide what people want and to strive unceasingly to do so more efficiently; and as a generous provider, allowing each consumer the greatest possible command of resources and choice of the form they will take.

That the hand is invisible means that the members of the market economy enjoy these benefits without the costs of coercion, that is, material advantage is wedded to economic liberty. The essential human interaction in the market is the free exchange, an act that, being voluntary, can be assumed to be mutually beneficial. The competitive system is comprised of so many separate actors that none can dictate the terms of trade to others. By making all powerless, in that sense, the market frees people from the unjust domination by others.

The market metes out both justice and welfare. It is just in that it gives people fair exchange for the value of their contribution. It promotes welfare in that it maximizes national wealth and this implies maximal utility and well-being.

Critique of the Marxist Critique.—These claims, of course, are hotly denied by many, especially by Marxists. It is important to distinguish among the many arguments against the market, both stated and implied.

(1) Some of the agonies described by Marx were functions not of the market system itself but of the wrenching transition from one kind of society to another as the market first emerged. (This point should also modify Karl Polanyi's critique of capitalism in *The Great Transformation*.) Indeed, rapid change is painful, but this does not necessarily reflect upon the intrinsic merits of the new organization of society. Modernization has been wrenching even when not driven by market forces.

(2) Implicit in other portraits of capitalist injustice sketched by Marx is that the distribution of wealth (in capitalist Britain) perpetuated the injustice of the old order. (One might think from some critiques that it was the capitalist revolution that had rendered the proletariat propertyless, but indeed that revolution found them in that condition [see Nussbaum, 1953, p. 223].) It is true that the market does not right previous wrongs. Adam Smith likened the pursuit of wealth in the market to a race in which all can strive to win within the limits of "fair play" (in Waltz, 1959, p. 94). But how "fair" can a race be which begins with some farther along the track than others, and with some having been crippled by their competitors' violence before the race began? Still, even if the market perpetuates old injustices, it would seem a big enough improvement upon the ways of the world if it simply did not create new ones: in time, broken legs can heal and the initial lead will recede in importance.

(3) The liberal ideology portrays the state as the impartial referee in the competitive contest of the market, providing only the assurance that fair play is adhered to and contracts freely made are honored. The Marxist view of the state as an extension of the dominant (in this case, capitalist) class rejects the notion of such impartiality. Certainly, Marx was in large measure right about the way the state actually functioned, for example, in early nineteenth-century Britain. (In many nations today in what American conservatives like to call the "free world" the state remains quite far from democratic, allowing the wealthy free use of the coercive power of the state to stack the deck in their favor.) And certainly, where the state makes and enforces laws in behalf of one class in the market economy at the expense of another, the market itself will not give justice. For these points to prove the injustice of the market system itself, however, it must be demonstrated that the market or capitalist system virtually prevents the establishment of a just polity. This proposition deserves consideration, but it is quite far from self-evident. (Marx's British proletariat has since been given the vote and with it considerable political power.) For the present, I assert that just government is possible in a market economy, and that where government is corrupted by the capitalist class it is best regarded as a problem in the political, rather than the economic, system. These assertions are reexamined shortly.

(4) Central to the Marxist critique of capitalism is the charge that the market economy is intrinsically exploitative of certain actors in the system for the benefit of others. In particular, it is argued that capitalism exploits (a) the working class in a domestic economy and (b) poor countries in the international economy. To clear the way for a genuinely helpful critique of capitalism, it is necessary to dispose of these two essentially invalid charges.

The first step in assessing the validity of these criticisms is to define the concept of exploitation. It is useful to define a relationship as exploitative if and only if both the following conditions apply: first, one party has a power over the other which gives him a greater say in establishing the terms of the arrangement; second, the terms established favor the stronger party.

Either condition can obtain without the other. The first without the second is exemplified by a good parent-child relationship, in which the parent, despite having a preponderant role in establishing the terms of the relationship, often chooses terms favoring the child's welfare because of love for the child. Advantage without power is enjoyed by a buyer arriving at the end of a yard sale: a desperate seller may accept sacrificial terms of sale in preference to no sale at all. While the buyer may be said to "take advantage" of the seller's plight, the seller is not being exploited because the buyer has no power over the seller. In this context, wherein the use of force is presumably excluded, power can usefully be defined as *the capacity to restrict the range of another's options.* The object of exploitative power would benefit from the disappearance of the exploiter, that is, his range of options would increase. The seller in a buyer's market does not want the buyer to disappear because the buyer adds to, rather than subtracts from, the seller's options.

If it is truly competitive, a market cannot be exploitative. Where there is a multiplicity of independent and noncollusive buyers and sellers, power is excluded. If anyone offers less for something than it is worth, in a competitive market the seller can reject the offer and hold out for a fair price. In such a market, the laws of supply and demand determine worth, and those laws give no power to any buyer or seller. Where anyone has the power to exclude competitors, the possibility of exploitation arises. Today's capitalism, of course, is far from purely competitive in many sectors, a fact that is central, for example, to John Kenneth Galbraith's critique of modern capitalism. Unless one concludes, however, that it is impossible to maintain meaningful competition, it remains worthwhile to investigate the workings of a genuine market. In this chapter, competition is assumed and the nonetheless important problems of market power (monopolistic and oligopolistic) are disregarded. With such competition, even the poor and the desperate will get a fair market price for what they have to sell.

(*a*) In his argument that capitalism exploits workers, Marx seems either to have misunderstood the workings of the market or to have denied that a real market functioned. In *The Communist Manifesto,* Marx and Engels wrote that "The average price of wage labor is the minimum wage, i.e., that quantum of the means of subsistence which is absolutely requisite to keep the laborer in bare existence as a laborer" (in Feuer, 1959, p. 22). Marx's view of the worker's situation has been likened (by both Galbraith, 1969, p. 65, and by Joan Robinson, 1966, p. 3) to the position of the beast who works for the farmer. But the beast, being the property of the owner, has no option about whose fields it will work in. If it did, and had the sense to make choices, its wages would not necessarily be the mere subsistence to keep it productive, but would be bid up in proportion to the economic value of its contribution. As. A. C. Pigou has argued, in a perfectly free competitive market, the wage rate is set at "the marginal net product of labor of a given quality . . . and if one employer offered a man less than others, that man would know that he could at once get as much as this value of his marginal net product from others" (1962, p. 557). The market determines the price of a workhorse, but not its ration, for the moment of purchase creates a perpetual regime of uni- lateral power relations. The same is true of the purchase and feeding of slaves. But it is not true of the wages of workers who retain the power of saying no to one and yes to another. Barring collusion and/or coercion, a multiplicity of employers will allow a worker to bargain like a human being, not like an ox.

The economic premise of the Marxist argument that labor is exploited and given only a subsistence wage was the "labor theory of value." Ac- cording to this theory, labor is what confers all value on goods. From this, it followed for Marx that the income from rents, interest, and profits is "surplus value," wealth legitimately belonging to the workers but stolen from them by the dominant capitalist class. That is, from the premise that only labor contributes to value, he inferred that economic rewards for any other factors of production were unjustified.[14] This idea is now rather universally discredited and even communist states have found that rational allocation requires that values be assigned to productive factors besides labor. Without the labor theory of value there seems no truly economic argument to substantiate the change of worker exploitation. Even deprived of its premise, however, the conclusion seems to live on (see, e.g., Oskar Lange, in Horowitz, 1969, pp. 77–78).

The capitalist does not get something for nothing. If he did, what would prevent any number of people, having nothing, from becoming capitalists and thus by their number driving the return on "nothing" to its proper level, zero? The answer, of course, is that the receivers of rent, interest, and profit possess a "something" that by virtue of its scarcity and its necessity for the productive process, warrants a return.

14. A much longer discussion and critique of Marx's argument is found in my dissertation "The Parable of the Tribes," pp. 1189–1216.

The laborer, too, gets a return in the free market according to the productive contribution and the scarcity of what he has to offer. If one accepted the Malthusian idea (held by many classical economists) of the "iron law of wages," that is, that population rises and falls with wages and thus keeps wages at the subsistence level, then the condition of labor scarcity would prove too unstable to confer upon labor any long-run benefits. But Marx did not accept this idea, perhaps for the very reason that liberation from the market could then offer no escape from the shackles of grim poverty. In any event, history has disproven the Malthusian notion that people inevitably breed in proportion to their wealth and has proven that wages can rise with labor's productivity. Nussbaum indicates that through the nineteenth century in England, France, and the United States, the increase in real wages corresponded to the increase in labor productivity (1953, p. 337). The market system, indeed, has proven to be the best protector of the worker from exploitation. Only in a truly competitive market can the relative vulnerability of the worker not result in a disastrous erosion of bargaining power. At an auction, the price a given good will yield does not reflect the seller's level of desperation. Where buyers and sellers must compete, exploitation is an unstable arrangement.[15]

(b) Similar arguments apply to the often-heard idea that the international market exploits poor countries. If we assume true competition among the buyers and sellers from rich countries, there is no reason why poor countries should have to pay more for goods they buy or receive less for goods they sell than they are worth.

Critics often charge that corporations make excessive profits from their investments in poor countries. If their work is open to competitive bidding, the level of return should be neither more nor less than in a fair one and many "less developed countries" have learned to utilize foreign corporations in this way as a valuable tool for performing economic services. If the return is high despite competition, it is presumably a reflection of the bidders' assessment of risk: no one who is sure of 10 percent elsewhere will accept 10 percent in a situation where (e.g., because of political instability) there is a real chance of no return or even of a loss of principal. And finally, if the government of a poor country has been bribed into making a corrupt contract with a corporation, the problem is not in the functioning of the international market so much as in the corruption of that country's political system. Even with no market

15. As in all market transactions, fairness between employer and employee depends on both parties having adequate information and a capacity for judgment to look after their own interests. When this is not the case—as when asbestos workers are not informed about the hazards they face—exploitation can occur.

economy in the world, the problem of political corruption and betrayal of public trust would remain.

Corporations are attacked for moving production to poor countries to take advantage of lower wages. Works like *Global Reach* (by Richard Barnet and Ronald Müller) condemn this as exploitation. But, in fact, it is an instance of market justice. Why should a worker in a rich country command a higher price for the same contribution than a worker in a poor country? The last quarter century of history has shown that the outreach of market forces into low-wage countries (like Taiwan, Hong Kong, South Korea, Mexico, and postwar Japan) has the effect of raising wages there. The losers are not the "exploited" workers of the poor countries but the previously protected workers of the rich who are now compelled to compete in a wider market where the average productive contribution of a worker is less than that within the confines of the rich nation alone. It is indicative of the confusion of many market critics that a work like *Global Reach* criticizes corporations both for taking jobs away from one country and sending them to another. One cannot have it both ways. It is regrettable that workers are faced with the choice of earning lower wages or losing jobs, but it is also a kind of justice: like justice, the market stands blindfolded, not favoring one nationality over another. The multinational corporations are criticized for being indifferent to the countries they operate in, for being wholly opportunistic. But this lack of loyalty or favoritism is just what makes the market yield an international justice in the prices it pays for economic goods. It allows peoples only recently severely impoverished to utilize the system of international trade to generate remarkable rises in material standard of living.

The international market system is attacked again for the dependency that it imposes upon the poor countries. Indeed, the market does encourage dependency. The division of labor, Adam Smith said, makes "man in constant need of the help of his brethren." He wrote:

> The taylor does not attempt to make his own shoes, but buys them from the shoemaker. . . . What is prudence in the conduct of every private family cannot be folly in that of a great kingdom. If a foreign country can supply us with a commodity cheaper than we can ourselves make it, better buy it of them with some part of the produce of our own industry, employed in a way in which we have some advantage. (1939, p. 424)

Every economics textbook demonstrates the concept of comparative advantage. They show that if each nation concentrates on producing the goods it can make relatively more efficiently and trades its surplus for other goods made by other nations, all nations end up having more of everything. Some political considerations (such as the possible impact on national security should external supplies of necessities be disrupted) may make it prudent to maintain self-reliance in some areas despite a cost in inefficiency. Except for such matters of international politics, however, specialization and trade are economically advantageous whereas self-reliance is costly. As Knorr has observed, impoverished Haiti is more self-sufficient than prosperous Japan (1973, p. 97). Critics of the international system bemoan the callousness of a market that can make a hungry nation produce cash crops like carnations rather than subsistence crops like corn. But the money from the cash crops could be used to buy from others more food than the same resources could have grown domestically. If the money is not used to buy the needed food, this is a very different matter (to which I will turn shortly) involving not specialization (and dependence) in production but distribution in consumption. There is no guarantee that even a crop of corn would be used to feed the hungry at home.

The functioning of the market maximizes wealth for all participants and dispenses justice of a sort. The abysmal poverty in the world is not the product of the market—poverty antecedes the market, and it is the pockets of wealth that stand in need of explanation. An overview of the world shows that wealth is far more to be found (even in the category that used to be called "developing") among those nations who have participated most in international markets than in those that have been closed to them.

The market has serious problems. But they are not best understood in terms of exploitation.

The Market Power of the Rich.—Two major claims made by defenders of the market are (1) that on the production side the market metes out justice and (2) that on the consumption side the market is ruled by human needs and facilitates their optimal fulfillment. The first claim was supported above. The second is now refuted, at least in part.

The market system is often likened to democracy: consumers, taking their money into the market, direct production according to their expressed preferences. The concept is called consumer sovereignty. Heilbroner writes that "in a world of pure competition, and only such a world, the public becomes the repository of most economic power. . . . (A) society of pure competition comes closer than any other form of economic organization to translating the general ideas of political democracy into economic reality" (1970, p. 537). In the democracy of the marketplace, the sovereign public can make its needs the true governor of the economic system.

This democratic model contains one essential flaw: in the market it is not people who vote but dollars. A person who brings $1 million into the market can "vote" a million times more than one who brings only $1. Moreover, it is in the nature of the market that even if people begin the competition on an equal footing, over time competition will create significant inequalities of wealth. Even if one believes that these inequalities are not unjust, one must recognize that such inequalities mean that the market's vision of human needs is significantly distorted by a lens shaped by the market power of the rich.

Because the market listens not to human needs directly but only as expressed by buyers, the market will produce yachts for the rich while the poor go without housing. The problem with growing carnations in a hungry world is on the consumption side of the economy, not the production side: a compassionate collective within the market will grow carnations to buy more food than it could grow itself; but it is the plutocracy of the market system that better rewards putting a carnation in a rich man's lapel than putting corn in a starving man's belly. The sovereignty of the consumer's dollar in a world of disparities of wealth directs production into the provision of luxuries when many lack the most basic necessities.[16]

There is no reasonable way to avoid concluding that the claim that the market is a tool for maximizing human welfare is seriously damaged by the market's responsiveness to the whims of the rich in the face of its deafness to the most essential needs of those without money. Some economists have tried to argue that one dollar spent must be presumed to give the same utility regardless of by whom or for what. It is impossible, they say, to make interpersonal comparisons of utility. How can we know whether a different distribution of goods would increase net welfare, whether the gain of some would offset the loss of others? Surely, this argument will not wash. We cannot accept as valid what has been described as the premise of the theory of consumer demand, namely that "the urgency of wants does not diminish appreciably as more of them are satisfied . . ." (Galbraith, 1969, p. 143). The principle of diminishing marginal utility can be applied not only to an individual's consumption of particular goods but also to his consumption of all goods and services (Weisskopf, 1971, p. 158). This reasoning leads those who wish to combine the great power of the market on the production side with optimal welfare on the consumption side to support the political redistribution of wealth within the market economy. (On this matter, see also Tinbergen, in Tinbergen et al., 1972, p. 43; Pigou, 1962, p. 89; Radomysler, in Arrow and

16. As one example, this is what Judith Randal writes of pharmaceutical companies: "The drug industry is not eager to produce medicines that won't be profitable. Either relatively few people need them or—as is true in the Third World—*millions need them to fight and relieve tropical disease but are too poor to buy them*" (p. 31, 1982, italics added).

Scitovsky, 1969, p. 91.) No doubt, the effort to compare the losses and gains in welfare of different individuals is a difficult undertaking. But to note its difficulty does not justify abandoning the effort (as Fritz Machlup [in Tinbergen et al., 1972] would seem to imply). Every political decision requires judgments of this nature—the weighing of costs and benefits falling on different people. To avoid murkiness in profound matters for the utmost clarity in trivial ones is to declare the fundamental blindness of one's economic vision.

There is a potential weakness, however, in the case for redistribution. Granting, for the moment, that net welfare maximization is the ultimate criterion of success in an economic system, and granting that the general welfare is enhanced more by devoting any given resources to meeting basic needs than to superfluities, it can still be argued that in the long run tampering with the market's distribution of rewards will diminish welfare. The fuel that drives the market engine is the self-interested drive for self-betterment, and redistribution can critically dilute that fuel. In other words, excessive reliance upon distribution to improve the welfare of the poorer people can be like killing the goose that lays the golden eggs. Defenders of the market properly point out that the key to the historical material betterment of peoples has been not redistribution so much as productivity growth. An equal piece of a small pie may be far smaller than an inferior piece of a larger pie. A conservative like Lenczowski argues that many poor countries only perpetuate their poverty by their redistributive policies, as in Tanzania where a marginal tax rate of 95 percent is imposed on any income above roughly $2,500 a year. If a level of national wealth is taken as a given, redistribution can be justified by the welfare argument. But in an economic system where the engine of growth can multiply that level, and redistribution can stall that engine, taking from the more productive to give to the less can lead over time to less for all.

This argument about incentives has validity, but convervatives like those making policy in the United States (in 1981) tend greatly to exaggerate it. Granting that some rewards are necessary to motivate people to take the risks and to devote the creative vital energies that make economies grow, one can still ask: how large do the rewards have to be? In the dynamically growing Japanese economy, for example, in 1970 the ratio of incomes of the highest quintile to the lowest was only just over half that in the more sluggish American economy (Vogel, 1979, p. 120). Not all rewards, moreover, are material. The corporate executive who earns from ten to a hundred times as much as his workers also enjoys higher prestige, more power, and more intrinsically rewarding work. It is hard to imagine that these enormous packages of rewards are necessary to motivate anyone to strive for achievement. Finally, there is the inescapable fact that, as the saying goes, you can't take it with you. Thus, beyond a certain point, what can be the rational motive for amassing enormous wealth? In reply to this question, the defenders of private property generally cite the love of family and the consequent incentive to leave to one's heirs a munificent legacy. This makes sense, but it also opens a crack in the psychological foundation of the market ideology. Self-interest, presumably, is the only motive that can be trusted to make people strive. If self-interest can be extended, through identification, to one's family and descendants, then conceivably the bubble around the atomistic individual may be more permeable still. Although the link with family is undoubtedly stronger and more reliable, perhaps people can strive to produce also out of love for a wider community. Here again Japan serves to illustrate: one theme of the literature of the Japanese economic success story is the predominance among the Japanese of group-centered rather than egoistic motives.

Thus, it seems most reasonable to conclude that some degree of sharing of wealth is compatible with a fully dynamic market productive system; and further, that even in the long term the unadulterated market does not produce the maximal possible human welfare.

The defender of the market can concede this, yet still oppose interference with the market for welfare purposes. All the foregoing discussion was based on the premise that human welfare is *the* criterion for evaluating an economic system. But an alternative view is that a system should afford justice, allowing a combination of liberty for individual actors with protections against the unjust use of power. According to this argument: if the market gives to autonomous actors their just rewards, the intrusion of state power to effect compulsory redistribution is unjust expropriation. Moreover, any such unjust intrusion opens the door to further collectivist tyranny.

I have granted that the market dispenses a kind of justice, and it is true that justice (as defined in chap. 6, "Artificial Wholeness: Justice as the Antidote for Power") does not require welfare maximization where no injustice has been done. (Recall the hypothetical case of earthlings encountering 4 billion starving space people.) Yet the atomistic image of society used by market defenders is overdrawn. The economic exchanges that lead to inequalities of wealth take place not in a vacuum but in a social and political context evolving over time. We are not each wholly autonomous entities. First, there are the injustices of the past: the disparities between the white executive and the black ghetto dweller in the United States cannot be understood without reference to a historical injustice; thus the cause of justice cannot now be left wholly to the market even if the market itself is not to blame. Second, there is the question whether even just differences between the fathers should be visited upon the sons, and even upon the sons' sons: if we believe that justice requires equality of opportunity for people as individuals, and not as perpetual familial entities, then such equality must be reestablished with every generation by the use of political power to undo the inequalities engendered by the market. And third, there is the tendency of economic inequalities to twist the ongoing political process in unjust ways: only if the rules governing the market are just does the market give justice, whereas to the extent that wealth confers political power the market will not only produce economic injustice but also threaten justice in the society generally. This question of the relation between the market economy and the truly democratic polity, deferred earlier, now warrants a closer look.

The Problems of Economic Inequalities and Political Equality.—The power of money appears to be different in kind from that power to compel which has been central to this work. The rich man, it seems, can have his way not against the will of others but by positively inducing others to serve his will. While the man with the sword takes options away from others—your money or your life—the man with a full wallet presents new potentially more attractive options: I will buy your land, I will pay you for your time, I will compensate you for damages and inconvenience. This positive kind of power is not incompatible with free choice for all the actors in the system.

This is not so, however, when the money corrupts politics. If a citizen is willing to sell his vote, no injustice is entailed. But if a senator sells his, then there is injustice. The difference is that in the first case, the seller gives up something that is his own in exchange for a different good for himself, whereas in the second the seller surrenders something he holds in trust for other people (whom he represents) in exchange for a reward just for himself.

The premise of democracy is that the well-being of each person is intrinsically as valuable as that of another and that each deserves equal say in the determination of collectively binding decisions. Where wealth is distributed unequally, and wealth can buy a disproportionate say in the political arena, the justice of democracy is subverted. The benign aspects of the market as an economic system are fatally transformed in two ways when private money enters the political arena. First, the positive power of money is corruptly transformed into the compulsory power of the state: that is, people's choices are unjustly taken from them. Second, and relatedly, the individualistic rewards of the market are transmuted into power over the collectivity.

Therefore, the argument for the justice of the market depends upon the ability of the political system to prevent wealth from being translated into political power.

There are those, such as F. A. Hayek and Milton Friedman, who argue that the liberty of the market is a necessary basis for the maintenance of democracy: the alternative to the market, they say, is state power, and the ultimate fruit of the concentration of power in the state is tyranny. I do not grapple here with the question of whether democracy can exist *without* the market economy, and ponder, rather, the problem of whether democracy can survive *with* it. That both questions can reasonably be asked is an indication of how difficult is the attainment of a just political system.

The evidence of history suggests that the plutocratic tendencies of the market system *are* a substantial threat to the democratization of political power. The deepest single flaw in the American constitution is its failure— and not, for the most part, by oversight—to protect the political process from influence by wealth. In the 1970s, after the corruption of Watergate floated to the surface of American political waters, legislative efforts were made to insulate politics from corruption by private money, for example, through public financing of elections. But the momentum of reform was quickly absorbed by the political power structures, and political office is still to too large an extent for sale. The U.S. Supreme Court has determined that limits on the role of corporate money in the political process is an abridgment of the right of free speech. As dedicated as I am to the sanctity of free speech, I nonetheless argue that the intrusion of private money into political campaigns is a violation of the constitutional guarantee of "equal protection under the laws."

More subtle than the role of money in elections is the role of money in the molding of the public consciousness which, in the long run, governs public choices in a democracy. It is patently not true that the intellectual life of a capitalist society is a straightforward expression of the interests of the dominant class. (This work, for example, which is intended more to challenge than to buttress the powers that be, has been funded from fortunes made in cereals and feeds [the Danforth Foundation] and in the manufacture of automobiles [the Ford Foundation].) Personal observation, however, has also shown me that where thought bears most directly upon public policy-making, as in the Washington think tanks, thought can be purchased to serve private interest. It is not so much that individuals tailor their thoughts to please their monied patrons, although this certainly often happens. More important, those whose views please those with money are the ones who gain the platform to publish their thoughts. Given the uneven distribution of money in society, and the nonrandom preference of the rich for certain ideas over others, the result is that a distorted image of mainstream thought can be wafted around public decision makers. (A specific instance of this is documented by Rothmyer, 1981.)

Thus, both directly (choosing the choosers and/or buying their choices) and indirectly (shaping the understanding that shapes choices) money is translated into power. To the extent that, in Congress as in the market, it is money rather than people whose votes count, democracy is subverted and class exploitation results. (And meanwhile the market itself becomes less just, as public lands, public waters, public health, and so on, are made to serve private greed.)

These plutocratic influences injure democracy, but they do not kill it. There seems no reason to assume that an alert and politically involved public cannot struggle with reasonable success to protect democracy from such corruption. If that is so, and if the market seems worth maintaining for other reasons, the solution to this political problem seems best sought in the political realm rather than in the wholesale abolition of the market. Besides, the evidence of history makes plausible enough the idea that democracy survives best in the company of the economic liberty of the market that we may reasonably wonder whether destroying the market to protect democracy might prove to be a case of departing the frying pan for the fire, or, to use an image from the preceding section, of retreating from the claws of polecats into the waiting jaws of lions.

C. Market Atomism and the Loss of Social Synergy

We have seen that the market ideology is premised on a highly individualistic view of human society. With that goes an atomistic model of human interaction: each actor (individual, corporation) is an atom unto itself, an autonomous entity that takes care of itself and that comes together with other social atoms only for discrete exchanges that are free and private. The previous discussion indicated that the facts of collective history and collective political decision-making must modify that atomistic view, and can bring into doubt the justice of the market. Now I will look at another, more purely economic critique of this atomistic vision.

Externalities.—I have considered the case for the market: "The market is just because each is allowed to mind his own business and prevented from minding the business of others. It is efficient because competition creates prices that truly represent the costs and benefits of the various goods available for exchange. The market thus gives synergy."

If society were wholly atomistic, these propositions would be true. But it is not, and to the extent that it is not these propositions are false.

The market treats a transaction as solely the business of the parties making the exchange. The costs that help determine price are the costs to the sellers, and the benefits those to the buyers. If you are not party to the transaction, the market ignores you. It is none of your business. The problem with this view is that people can be affected by business even if they do not participate in it. If my steel mill pollutes the air you breathe, my activity is, in a sense, your business. But your stake in the matter is wholly ignored in the market.

The market ideology manifests the common flaw in wholly individualistic approaches to social questions: it regards the whole as no more than the sum of its parts. But the whole is a network of interrelationships, a web of interdependence. No one's business is his alone; any transaction is apt to have ramifications beyond the immediate parties. But these ramifications fail to register in the market's magisterial information processing.

This is the problem of externalities, which can be defined as costs or benefits imposed by economic transactions on parties not involved in the exchange (see definition in Whitcomb, 1972, p. 6). Besides external costs (as in pollution), there can be external benefits (as to beekeepers from their proximity to others' orchards). Both kinds are "external" to the market's operation, both ignored in the market's pricing system. The price of steel does not reflect the cost in human wealth and well-being from poisoned air; nor is the keeper of the orchard rewarded for his contribution to honey making, much less for the beauty his trees bring to the countryside. To the extent that costs and benefits are ignored, the prices in the market cannot reflect the true values involved.

One might hope that in the long run it will all even out. After all, if I am the uncompensated victim of one transaction, presumably I will be the uncharged beneficiary of another; and if I am ignored when you mind your business, at least I can ignore you when I mind mine.

Unfortunately, the selective attention of the market is not such as to allow its oversights to cancel each other out. For one thing, we come to another aspect of the unjust advantage of the rich over the poor: since the system benefits transactors over nontransactors (it listens to the one while disregarding the other), those who transact the most (the rich) benefit the most, whereas those who are mostly bystanders are mostly victimized.

But more important, the selective concerns of the market lead to an imbalance because the values attended to and those ignored tend not only to belong to different individuals but also to be different in nature. The problem with the atomistic system is that it systematically ignores the dimension of interdependence. The very word "externality" is revealing: the entire network of connections that are the flesh of the social system is regarded as "external" by the market. The market listens to the wants of people as individuals but is deaf to their needs as an interdependent community: "the system proved to be deficient in the funds and institutions needed to supply the essential *public* goods—health, education, decent city design, public safety, environmental improvement—which did not offer benefits that could easily be broken down into saleable goods . . ." (Ward and Dubos, 1972, p. 20). The society as a whole suffers if a generation of city youth grow up alienated and unemployable, but the market does not hear their needs, and many free marketeers would leave the problem of jobs wholly for the market to solve. Perhaps everyone would most prefer an aesthetic and coherent urban environment, but the market creates unsightly commercialized strips. (This is especially visible in the cities of the American West where corporate capitalism has had unprecedented freedom to shape the urban landscape through atomistic market forces.) Jouvenel reports a suggestion he made to economists that

> the Parthenon was an addition to the wealth of the Athenians, and its enjoyment an element of their standard of life. This statement was regarded as whimsical. When I had made it clear that it was seriously meant, I was told that the standard of life is expressed by per capita Private Consumption of goods and services acquired on the market. Meekly accepting this correction, I asked my colleague whether when he drove out to the country on weekends, his satisfaction was derived from the costly consumption of gasoline, or from the free sight of trees and possibly the free visit of some cathedral (in Arrow and Scitovsky, 1969, p. 107).

The market can look only at the point of trade, and since some truly essential goods are not subject to discrete transactions between buyers and sellers, it is blind to important dimensions of human life. The subtle network of interdependence is what makes society a whole, yet by leaving the problem of wholeness only to the invisible hand, the market leads to fragmentation, to a society rich in its atomistic parts but poor in its organic wholeness. Since the market is incapable of attending to this vital dimension of utilities and disutilities, it is vain for us to wait for that system wholly to provide for synergy.

This again does not necessarily argue for rejection of the market. So useful a tool is it in its own proper domain that we may choose rather to correct it, as countries already do more or less fully and well, with politically determined inputs to compensate for the market's blind spots.

Public law can impose costs for external diseconomies (as by taxing polluting emissions) to enable the market to compute more reliably the true values involved. This approach has its difficulties. Aside from the problem of overcoming the plutocratic bias of the political system, there is the problem of computing the monetary value of things like beauty and health; there is the problem that it is more difficult to assure consistent attention to bureaucratically imposed values than to those the market is built for; and there is the problem that the power of market ideology tends to give the values of interdependence less standing than those that show up on profit reports. Thus, when people discuss the "costs" of pollution, they often confine themselves to such tangible factors as the cost of dry-cleaning curtains, of medical treatment for people sickened by bad air, of workdays lost, as if values were always objective and wholly economic and did not ultimately reside in the quality of human experience.

Other Dimensions of Market Inattention.—The market's attention only to the costs and benefits to the parties immediately involved creates problems akin to the problem of externalities.

(a) *Undervaluing nature.* I argued earlier that the market tends to pay labor according to its economic value. But the same is not true for the natural materials upon which labor operates. Indeed, the undervaluing of nature lies at the origin of the concept of the labor theory of value upon which Marx based his argument about the exploitation of labor. The labor theory of value came to Marx through the liberal tradition, and it was based (as Weisskopf shows) on the assumption that only labor is scarce. Locke began it, writing of a world where "there is enough" of land "and as good left in common for others" (quoted in Weisskopf, 1955, p. 23). Similarly, Adam Smith develops his discussion of price and value from the assumption of the original nonscarcity of natural resources. He uses the example that "If among a nation of hunters . . . it usually costs twice the labour to kill a beaver which it does to kill a deer, one beaver should naturally exchange for or be worth two deer" (1937, p. 47). If nature's goods are available in infinite abundance, the cost of those goods is simply the cost of harvesting them.

This assumption reflects the way the market tends actually to work. The market descends upon the brave new world of unexploited natural resources as though they will never become scarce. Nature is taken as a given, as something that came to us free and the intrinsic value of which is the same as its cost to us. Consider the case of oil. Until a quasi-cartel supplanted the market, the costs that went into establishing the price of oil were simply the costs of getting it out of the ground and to the market. Yet, as the case of oil illustrates, nature's bounty is not infinite. The well eventually runs dry, and as scarcity comes into the picture the price rises.

But meanwhile, the market has failed to recognize the finitude of supply, a finitude that always was there even if it was not always manifest. Consequently, it has undervalued the natural resource and encouraged profligate consumption. Over the centuries, it has done the same with the forests and topsoils given by nature; it has done the same with the fresh air and fresh water that seemed like infinite free goods to be squandered. As the farmers in the Plains drain the great but finite Oglala Aquifer, the price of their crops treats the water as free. The cost of corn does not reflect the precious earth that is washed away in its production; the cost of fish from the oceans does not reflect the damage from overfishing. The market's treatment of nature is as irrational as an accounting system that considers the cost of the check and ignores the loss of the capital it draws upon. Even when scarcity develops and the price rises, the rise reflects only the increasing cost of writing checks, not the further depletion of the earth's natural capital. Overfished species go up in price not because the costs of depletion are suddenly recognized by the market but because scarcity makes the writing of checks against the fisheries account more difficult and costly.[17]

The market cannot deal with nature responsibly by itself. The market tends perpetually to undervalue the earth we have inherited. It is God's labor that is exploited. Those who look only to the market for a picture of values cannot make wise choices. In 1976, the president of the United States vetoed a bill requiring strip miners to undo the damage their harvesting of coal does to the land. We could not, he told the American people, afford the measure, for it would raise the price of coal. Thinking like this fails to recognize that the increased price better reflects the true cost of the coal. If we cannot afford it, we cannot afford the use of that coal. To continue to pay only the market's price, subsidized by the market's incapacity to note the degradation of our natural heritage, is simply to impose upon future generations the costs we ourselves blindly refuse to pay for our present benefits.

(b) *Undervaluing the future.* In a way, the market's undervaluing of nature reflects its general tendency to give inadequate weight to the future in relation to the present. The market, as Tibor Scitovsky observes, is more effective in dealing with the way the economic situation is than the way it will be or might be expected to be (in Arrow and Scitovsky, 1969).

A tendency to undervalue the future is of course an attribute not only of the market but of human systems in general. As creatures, we are

17. The market's undervaluing of natural resources does point out a way in which the market tends to be unfair to "less developed countries," not because they are poor but because, having less sophisticated economies, a larger proportion of their exports consists of raw materials. Yet this burden can also fall on wealthy countries, such as the United States, with its large exports of food and forestry products.

inclined to give greater weight to a benefit today than to an equal benefit tomorrow. Even more so, we are inclined to care more about our own costs and benefits than about those falling upon future generations: après moi. . . .

Nonetheless, the market creates special impediments to a proper weighing of future values. Consider a forward-looking farmer in Iowa concerned about the implications of the soil washed from his land as he raises his corn. If he prices his corn to reflect the value of the soil sacrificed in its production, he will have no buyers since others will be selling for less. If he increases his costs by adopting different farming methods to preserve the soil, he will be unable to compete with farmers who stick to the less costly, more destructive methods. Either way, the market will cause him to lose money, perhaps to go bankrupt so that his farm will fall into other, less principled hands. Even if all the farmers individually wish to conserve, the market by itself offers them no way to translate that value into an economically feasible course of action. The market is a power system that, as in the parable of the tribes, can prevent individual actors from being able to survive while acting on their true values.

For such reasons, the proper provision for the future requires collective political decisions to supplant the myopic vision of the atomistic market. A multitude of autonomous actors are often powerless to make necessary decisions; if these decisions are to be made, people must be able to come together and make a treaty with one another—to conserve fuel, to restore strip-mined land, to fund research for nuclear fusion energy three generations hence. Also, the society as a whole has a deeper commitment to the future than have its individual agents. Actors in the market can move in, make the "fast buck," and leave.[18] Last century's overgrazers in Arizona and forest strippers in Minnesota could take their money elsewhere while the injured land remained. Although individuals and corporations (and their money) are mobile, societies are stationary. The future is thus better entrusted to the society as a whole, with its commitment to the flourishing of that system in that place. Finally, it is perhaps easier for a people to act wisely and unselfishly in making a few large public decisions than in making many small private decisions. Effective leadership can bring out the best, most altruistic motives of its people, and dramatize them for public display.

In all these ways, the fragmented system of the market fails to place the true values upon the transactions it oversees; and consequently synergy requires the intrusion of collective decision making into the atomistic market process.

---

18. Moreover, the problem of the market's myopia regarding the future is worse when interest rates are high, so that a dollar today is worth much more than a dollar tomorrow.

D. Moral Confusion and Choice in the Market Economy

The market is said to be a wonderful servant for meeting human needs. Its enthronement of consumer sovereignty through the free choices of the market, it is argued, dictates that what people want will rule the allocation of social resources. My discussion of market justice has modified this view. Unfortunately, it requires still further modification from another direction.

The market is a power system that rules human choices as much as it is shaped by them. This danger from the market is implied in the discussion of externalities. The market, we saw, is a selective listener. It can attend to some kinds of human needs far better than to others. The market specializes in what can be exchanged in discrete transactions. This embraces a considerable variety of goods and services. But it also excludes a great deal, including much of the flesh and blood of human social life. Money, the saying goes, cannot buy happiness, and here is the reason for it. Much of human happiness comes from experiences like human interconnectedness and communion with nature—the kinds of "public goods" with which the market cannot deal. It is as though in the orchestra of human needs, the market hears the horns and drums but is deaf to the strings.

It might seem at first that this selectivity would not be a problem. After all, needs not met in the market can be met elsewhere. Other institutions (schools, churches, government) are there listening to other sounds. So why not assume that the entire ensemble reflects the totality of human needs? This might be a valid argument were the market only a "listener" and not also a power system actively shaping the social world around it.

Even the supposedly "sovereign" consumer can be changed, to some degree, into a vassal of the ruling market system. This reversal of the ostensible relation between the human needs expressed by consumers and the system of production is at the heart of the frequent criticism of modern advertising (see Servan-Schreiber, 1970, pp. 18–19). The springs of human motivation that were supposed to drive the machine become—as with other power systems—transformed into grist for its mill. Ezra Mishan, for example, uses the fashion industry to illustrate the "myth" of consumer sovereignty: "The choice of the pace of fashion, surely a crucial choice, is not open to the individual. . . . (A)t present, it is left entirely to commercial interest to exploit to the limit of technical feasibility. The fashion industry is the prime example of an activity dedicated to using up resources, not to create satisfactions, but to create dissatisfactions with what people possess—in effect to create obsolescence in otherwise perfectly satisfactory goods" (1967, p. 114). Needs are created to serve a system the inherent purpose of which is to maximize not human fulfillment but the flow of goods. "Americans," said an advertising researcher in the 1950's, "would have to learn to live a third better if they were to keep pace with growing production . . ." (cited in Packard, 1957, p. 260).

Advertising is a form of socialization. It is like other forms in that it must begin with the organismic needs that are already there. The task of this socialization is to establish in the mind of the human being a connection between what is originally valued (the intrinsic interests of the person) and something else (determined by the interests of the socializing agent). Just as a parent may teach a connection between receiving love and behaving in an acceptable fashion, the advertiser will try to persuade the consumer that his product is somehow endowed with the values the consumer really wants. An advertising man has said, "The cosmetic manufacturers are not selling lanolin, they are selling hope. We no longer buy oranges, we buy vitality. We do not just buy an auto, we buy prestige" (quoted in Packard, 1957, p. 8). If you want to be "with it," you should drink Pepsi. If you want to be manly, you should smoke Marlboros. The market takes fundamental human needs and teaches people to attempt to fill them in ways that serve the production-maximizing market.

So what is the matter with that? Why should created needs be considered less legitimate than more original needs? If a person feels that he is buying manliness with his cigarettes, why should we object? Because, contrary to the Coca Cola advertisements, such teachings divert human attention from "the real thing." Advertising may be able to persuade mothers to give up breast-feeding for the bottle, but as the international scandal in 1981 over baby-formula marketing in poor countries brought to light, the unfortunate infants may not survive this substitution for the real thing. A person's feeling of manliness can be enhanced in ways that, although they may not enrich a corporation, have the advantage of not producing lung cancer. If it is really the "taste of love" we want to help people obtain, there are better ways of doing it than through the production and marketing of ginger ale. The connections advertising teaches are illusory, and while falsehoods can have power, that power cannot make them true. Although there is, admittedly, a placebo effect, it does not make the placebo the equivalent of real medicine.

If the capacities of the market corresponded exactly to the true needs of the human being, the market would not need to deal in placebos. But there is a gap, and where the market's needs and human needs diverge, the market—like other power systems—serves itself, even at human expense. The ultimate irrelevance of human needs to the self-serving purpose of the market system is what makes the market's form of socialization so manipulative. The salesman, says Joseph Tussman, is really the opposite of the teacher, for while the latter seeks to strengthen the human mind, the former seeks to weaken it (in Kariel, 1970, p. 21). The market's teachings are seductive, in the literal sense of leading astray.

The market persuades people to orient to its goods regardless of whether it requires turning away from the true path of fulfillment. Writes Bellah: "That happiness is to be attained through limitless material acquisition is denied by every religion and philosophy known to man but is preached incessantly by every American television set" ("The Broken Covenant," MS., p. 135).

Even as it undermines competing systems of values, the market takes the opportunity first to exploit them. This is what Jules Henry refers to as the "monetization" of values. The market's embrace of values "like love, truth, the sacredness of high office, God, the Bible, motherhood, generosity, solicitude for others," he says, is ". . . the embrace of a grizzly bear, for as it embraces the traditional values pecuniary philosophy chokes them to death" (1963, p. 62). The market, with its dynamism, tends to collapse the multidimensional language of human choice into its own two-dimensional materialistic language. Those institutions that might have filled the gap left by the market are themselves first overpowered and then transformed by the intrusive force of the market.

A couple of objections might be raised against this indictment of the market. First, the market's goods are being represented too narrowly. The market sells not only frivolities but also truly fundamental goods. Through the market one can buy a Bible as well as designer jeans, one can buy access to a good education and health care as well as gas-guzzling prestige mobiles. In other words, the market does not only deal in "the materialistic." That is true. Yet as long as there is an imperfect fit between the totality of human values and the range of goods exchangeable in the market, a real problem remains. The maximal flow of salable goods and services does not run parallel to the route to maximal human fulfillment. Thus, the market tends to elevate "materialist" values at the expense of those that mankind's greatest teachers have said are more vital.

Second, it can be objected that human needs are truly more material than these exceptional people have taught. (As Professor Yip Yat Hoong of Malaysia has said, "most important aspects of human needs are largely material or economic in nature" [*United Nations University Newsletter,* July 1977].) Witness the way the world's peoples strive for material improvement, and the way even in rich countries electoral fortunes seem to hinge more on successful economic performance than on anything else. To this argument it must be conceded that material needs are indeed important.

316

But recall the testimony of Sahlins that primitive peoples felt "affluent" in that they were content with the little they had whereas we are discontent with the much we have.

Anthropological evidence calls into question Adam Smith's presumption about the essential natural human motive, namely, that "The desire of bettering our condition comes with us from the womb and never leaves us until we go to our grave" (quoted in Weisskopf, 1971, p. 58). Again (as in chap. 5, "Under the Yoke," pp. 181–185), we confront the possibility that the preoccupation of modern peoples with material betterment is not a pure reflection of natural human priorities. But what else could be the meaning of this modern materialism? It could be that the workings of the market (and of other power systems) have taken away some older, less materialistic options.[19] As old ways of living are swept away by "progress," we are forced to find our satisfactions in the forms in which they are offered.

Another important factor is that new systems create new meanings for the various options that remain. In a world where material possessions become the criterion of personal "worth," all may strive for money not because what it buys is intrinsically so fulfilling but because the vital structure of human relationships is now determined by the materialistic language imposed by the economic system. This, I believe, is an important inference to be drawn from an international study showing that *within* a given nation the level of wealth correlates with a person's reported level of happiness, but *between* nations no such correlation is observable (reported *Christian Science Monitor*, March 1, 1978). It may be, as J. S. Mill said, that people wish not so much to be rich as to be richer than others, that is, the utility of wealth is not so much economic (material) as social (immaterial).

Here again we see the tragic condition of the civilized human being, undone by his very strength. For the same symbol-making capacity that gives mankind power at the same time makes him subject to seduction. We create symbols, and then can mistake the symbol for the object it represents. Man infuses the golden calf with numinous energy from his own being and then, in delusion, worships the golden calf. The systems that seek to use rather than serve us can persuade us to slake our inborn thirst for reality from their corrosive bottled goods.

Materialistic values, therefore, may not be an expression of human nature so much as a reflection of the way the market can shape human society and human beings.

---

19. In the liberal system, wrote Santayana, "If you refuse to move in the prescribed direction, you are not simply different, you are arrested and perverse. The savage must not remain a savage, nor the nun a nun, and China must not keep its wall" (in Cooperman and Walter, 1962, p. 138).

Where the economic system is freed from control, it becomes itself the controller. Once a society allows the market free reign, that system's control over resources, and therefore over opportunities and rewards, gives it the power to shape the other dimensions of cultural life into its own image. Of this, Polanyi has written that "Instead of economy being embedded in social relations, social relations are embedded in the economic system" (1944, p. 57). This is a principal reason why in fact no society has ever granted market forces complete autonomy, imposing instead a variety of more or less effective barriers (zoning laws, taxes and subsidies, and the like) in the way of the market's free play.

To the extent that it is set free, the market's action resembles that described by the parable of the tribes. We have seen how, in other systems, whatever has power can talk whereas the weak are compelled to listen. The market is a system that gives power to money, and thus to those whose ways are conducive to the making of money. Money talks. It is not so much that one group exploits another as that the system, by its own selective listening, determines what group will be heard. A competitive process nonrandomly selects certain actors—Standard Oil, John D. Rockefeller—to play a disproportionate role in the shaping of the system as a whole. That which determines the chooser determines the choice.[20]

Consequently, over time that music of horns and drums the market hears becomes ever more pronounced, and the instruments to which the market is deaf become inaudible to society as a whole. It has frequently been observed that the market has taught people to disregard or to view as inconsequential any values that cannot be measured in terms of prices (e.g., Cottrell, 1955, pp. 243–244; McHarg, in Helfrich, 1970, p. 23). The "externalities" of the market fall outside the ken of the members of the market society, and thus become still harder to correct by political means. We may recall,[21] as an instance of the power of the engine of productivity to select for its own message, how in the development of America the loving view of nature was overtaken by the exploitative. The horns and drums grow louder. The market's amplification of its own

20. The passing of the market system from the entrepreneurial stage to the managerial only compounds the problem of the domination of systemic logic over human choice. When the owner is also the controller of resources, he can make choices on the basis of nonmarket values as to how the resources are to be used. Today, however, the owners are stockholders (often anonymously connected through pensions, funds, and so on) who have no effective control. Even if the stockholders individually might want their steel company to sacrifice some profit for cleaner air, they have no effective way to act on that desire. Meanwhile, management declares itself responsible to its stockholders to maximize earnings. And management itself is maintained as a self-perpetuating bureaucracy in which power is given people on the basis of serving purposes and values embedded in the corporate system itself. It is exceedingly difficult for other values to interrupt the momentum of the self-governing system.

21. Chap. 7, "Man's Dominion."

music is also suggested in Bellah's description, in "The Broken Covenant," of another aspect of the evolution of American values. He describes the deep moral concerns of early American Protestants, bearers of the famous Protestant ethic, that man's selfishness and cupidity must not go unchecked. But eventually the religious opposition to the excessive love of wealth and to the ascendancy of materialistic values seems to have given ground, "for many of the most widely known of the 19th century preachers, admonitions of the dangers of wealth become ever more perfunctory. . . ." Puritans like Winthrop, Mather, and Edwards, writes Bellah, "however much they emphasized the value of hard work, were deeply sensitive to the tension between religion and the world, between God and Mammon" (pp. 75–76). These he contrasts with their successors, of whom the Episcopal Bishop of Massachusetts is typical. Wrote the bishop in 1901: "In the long run, it is only to the man of morality that wealth comes. . . . Godliness is in league with riches . . ." (quoted in ibid.). In the long run, we might say instead, it is to the force of wealth in the market system that competing morality eventually succumbs.

The market's selective attention to various values creates moral confusion among society's members. The audience, hearing only the drums and the trumpets, will tend to forget the song of the violin. Eventually, the violinist may get discouraged at the failure of the system to amplify his part and stop playing. At the least, the new generation will have little reason to take up string instruments. And of course, as the system teaches people to march to its drummer, the ability of the system to call the tune grows all the greater.

E. Conclusion

As a market society evolves, it is not only that people are making choices among the offerings of the market. At the same time, the market is making choices among the people and values offered by society. To the extent this is so, the market functions as a power system, shaping human destiny independently of human will. The truth remains that the market acts as the servant of human needs, but it is important also to recognize how it becomes their master.[22]

The way the market functions as a power system can be illuminated by analogy with the parable of the tribes. The evolution of the market

22. "The transcendant principle of progress" in liberal philosophy, complained Santayana, "requires everything to be ill at ease in its own house; no one can be really free or happy but all must be tossed, like herded emigrants, on the same compulsory voyage, to the same unhomely destination" (in Cooperman and Walter, 1962, p. 138). (In this respect, see also a criticism of Hayek's subordination of individual human factors to the ideal of "progress" [cited in Crespigny, in Crespigny et al., 1975, p. 58]).

319

society is *shaped by the powerful:* the market listens to some more than to others, and those heard are selected according to the system's own criteria. The market even fosters *cultural homogenization:* the market's forces compel conformity to what the market finds competitively successful—discarding the "mom and pop" store, forbidding the Iowa farmer to act responsibly on the problem of soil erosion, making compulsory ever-higher standards of efficiency (according to certain kinds of inputs and outputs). The market also *shapes people to serve its purposes,* as exemplified by the materialist orientation just discussed. Finally, since the needs of the market correspond imperfectly to the needs of human beings, *the power of the market to direct the internal evolution of the market society cannot be trusted to serve human welfare.*

5. House Divided Revisited

The restructuring of man by civilization was explored in depth in chapter 5. Here I briefly outline this process in terms of how the wholeness of the individual human system is subverted.

It can be debated how thoroughly integrated and harmonious man is by nature. Perhaps some of the interconnections are tenuous in the creature with the fast-flowering neocortex; perhaps the "ethical animal" inherently encompasses considerable tension. The minimal claim of this work is that by nature the human being is far more whole than we find him/her in the civilized state.

The root of this magnified disharmony, as we saw, is the conflict between the demands of civilization and the inherent needs of the human organism. Power lies at this root first in the way the selection for power shapes the requirements of civilization, and second in the power the civilized system wields to mold the developing person. Born the most helpless and dependent of creatures, the human being restructures himself to appease the powers he depends upon. To achieve peace with the world, the developing person declares war upon himself.

The internalization of the conflict between human nature and civilization entails a division of the human system into those "parts" that reflect the inborn nature and those that represent the demands of the unnatural cultural environment.

One view of this dichotomy is the duality of mind and body. On the one hand, the body comes to us from nature. The body is the unfolding of a blueprint designed by aeons of biological evolutionary processes. On the other hand, the mind is, if not a tabula rasa, an organ of relative indeterminacy and receptivity. Here civilization can inscribe its commandments. Thus if nature conflicts with culture, so too will body be at odds with mind. And one sign of the triumph of the power of civilization will be man's rejection of his own body. We note here the civilized pattern of shame and prudishness. In the words of Pope Innocent III about man: "impure conception, loathesome feeding in the mother's womb, wretchedness of physical substance, vile stench, discharge of spittle, urine and faesces." About this "catalogue of [man's] unsavoriness," Nietzsche says: "On his way to becoming an 'angel' man has acquired that chronic indigestion and coated tongue . . . so that at times he stops his nose against himself . . ." (1956, p. 199). In attempting to become what he is not, man scorns what he is. He also must learn to ignore it. Under unnatural conditions, the natural inclinations of the body may become maladaptive. J. Stephen Gartlan has described the plight of macaques living in captivity. Although their emotional/physiological responses at times of stress prepare the monkey for rapid and sustained movement away from the stress, "the particular conditions of captivity . . . ensure that escape and withdrawal from noxious stimuli is generally impossible" (in Quiatt, 1972, p. 107). David Hamberg's work on emotions shows civilized peoples to suffer from a similar mismatch between inclination and feasibility. Adaptation thus requires an ability to disregard many messages from the body, however urgent. This becomes a goal of socialization for the conditions of "captivity" civilized people live under. Herman Katchadourian writes: "A willingness and seeming ability to defy the innate rhythms of the body for social or personal ends has become one of the hallmarks of adulthood in the Western world" (1976, p. 52).

Another way of looking at the internalization of the conflict between human nature and civilization is in terms of a struggle between different elements of the mind. The mind is, after all, in part a natural expression of the body as a whole. The human psychological system is inherently complex, containing elements that reflect natural impulse as well as elements that incorporate learned controls. Every psychology connects a part of the psyche with the body, calling it the "appetitive" part, the id, or whatever. The other part is more educable, more rational, and more detached from the natural impulse. To the extent that civilization opposes impulse, socialization implies conflicts between these parts of the psyche. The tendency of traditional civilized psychologies is to advocate the dominance of the more civilized and rational part over the less. Aristotle calls for "a mutual justice between them as between ruler and ruled" (*Nicomathean Ethics* 11 1138b). (Traditional Chinese philosophy advocates a similar order.) Aquinas, too, sides with the more rational (ergo civilized and educable) part of man: "Man's good is to be in accord with reason, and his evil to be against reason." Thus spake the great synthesizer of the Western tradition's classical element with the Christian element. On the issue of the subordination of the impulsive and irrational elements of the human psyche, the two cultural currents were confluent. Yet in the Christian tradition, the struggle against the natural went further. No longer is the outcome of the conflict a structure of ruler and ruled with an appeal to some kind of "mutual justice." Now the war requires unconditional surrender. (Recall Freud's image of a garrison within a conquered city [p. 194, above].) This is manifested by a more complete rejection of the less favored part. Such rejection can be inferred from Saint Paul's sense of his will: "For the good that I would, I do not; but the evil that I would not, that I do" (Romans 7:19). Augustine adopted a similarly truncated view of what his "self" consisted. His struggle against his erotic impulses was long and hard. Impulses he could control when awake—when his "superego" was on the job—would haunt him at night, gaining expression in dreams Augustine found most troubling. "Am I not then myself, O Lord my God?" the anguished Augustine asks. Nietzsche attempts to describe the problems of creatures suffering from "Bad conscience, reduced to their weakest, most fallible organ, their consciousness!" (1956, p. 217).

As with all the other systems I have explored, the loss of wholeness entails high costs. (1) The wages of disregarding the messages of the body can be sickness or death. Gartlan's macaques undergo "degenerative phsyiological changes." So, it appears, do the inmates of the zoo of civilization. Katchadourian suggests that a partial explanation of "the current plague of psychosomatic ailments" may be that the "culturally set" requirements of life in industrialized societies is often out of phase with the body's basic rhythms (1976, p. 51). (2) Intrapsychic conflict—"The War Within"—makes man the sick animal. Where the psyche cannot achieve true justice between those parts of the mind representing the forces of nature and civilization, neurosis results. Writes Fenichel: "Neurotics are persons who are alienated from their instinctual impulses. They do not know them and they do not want to know them" (1945, p. 477). According to the psychological theory of Alexander Lowen, the connection between neurosis and the body is still more intimate. Muscular rigidity, he says in *The Language of the Body*, "is the mechanism of repression" (1958, p. 14). With controls embodied in muscular tensions, the free flow of human energies is strangled. Man is literally, in Saint Paul's words, at war with the law in his members. (3) The agony of internal warfare can give way to the emptiness of alienation, as human beings lop off their humanity to fit into the great machine of civilization. Thomas Carlyle perceived this as the Industrial Revolution emerged: "Men are grown mechanical in head and in heart, as well as in hand" (quoted in L. Marx,

1964, p. 174). More than a century later, Fromm described the "cybernetic man," a creature almost "exclusively cerebrally oriented." The excessively intellectual approach of the cybernetic man, says Fromm, "goes together with the absence of an affective response" (1973, pp. 351–352). Reason grows unreasonable. Nietzsche contemplated the condition of creatures severed from their elemental forces and the guidance they formerly offered: "I doubt there has ever been on earth such a feeling of misery, such a leaden discomfort" (1956, p. 271).

Civilization could not exist without human flexibility. This apparent human gift has proved a curse as well, making civilized human life subject to a twofold evil. First the evil that man *suffers,* caused by the distortion of our natures. Then the evil man that *does,* out of the rage and confusion that come from his unnatural predicament. Power's play molds a tormented and destructive animal.

6. The Death of the Unnatural

Death stalks civilization. Death is a fate to which flesh is inevitably heir. But the shadow that falls across our civilization is cast by death of another kind. It is death by unnatural causes, a kind of death to which only the unnatural are prey.

Leering behind the unprecedented living systems of our civilization are two specters of unnatural death. The first has revealed itself through the long course of civilized history; the second has arisen only in the twentieth century. The first is that specific civilizations have not only risen but also fallen, not only flowered but withered and died. The second is the appalling prospect that civilization may now destroy itself utterly, that our species may be on the path toward suicide, that the entire biosphere may pay the supreme penalty for nurturing so creative/destructive a form of life.

The Rise and Fall of Civilizations

The parable of the tribes implies a *linear* path for civilization's growth, a path toward ever-higher levels of power, but many of the few who ponder history's broad sweep have emphasized instead the *cyclical* rising and fall of major civilized systems. It is on this basis that Mosca challenged theories attempting to explain the evolution of civilization with a selective model. (He has in mind theories using "natural" selection, which the parable of the tribes does not, but the challenge applies anyway.) History, he says, does not show the consistently progressive movement one would expect

323

from such a theory. "What we see, instead, is a nation, or a group of people, now leaping forward with irresistible impetus, then collapsing or lagging wretchedly behind" (1939, p. 34). He says such evolutionary theories account for this falling "very badly, or rather, not at all." The time has come to incorporate into the perspective of the parable of the tribes the cyclical patterns that have impressed people from the philosophers of the classical world to Toynbee and Spengler in our own time.

To begin with, the cycles do not contradict the more linear assertions of the parable of the tribes. Rather, they are embedded in an overall linear trend toward power. For example, Adams says of the history of the early civilizations: "The rise and fall of kingdoms and imperial centers, over a three-to-four-thousand-year period in the Old World and for at least a millennium before Columbus in the New World, were oscillations that prehistorians have shown to reveal a gradual and inexorable increase of control and power" (1966, p. 298). Modern history certainly underscores this linearity, as even Mosca concedes.

The challenge, then, is to explain why systems that rise also fall. By itself, the selective model of the parable of the tribes cannot do so (except to the extent that the falling is as described below[23]). But we have now taken the original theory of selection and integrated it with a vision of the dichotomy between natural and unnatural systems, and this higher perspective gives us a glimpse of the answer: the new selective process that emerged with civilization, unlike the organic selective process from which it emerged, favors systems that ultimately are unviable.

This view obviously takes issue with those who employ organic images to describe why civilizations that flower also wither. As was said earlier, civilizations are not like organisms in the essential respect that they have no inherent blueprint that dictates the process of its development even unto its demise. Each Roman was designed to die in a way that Rome itself was not. Beyond that, if a civilization is to be compared with a natural living system, the suitable comparison would not be with a single

---

23. Often the "falling" of civilizations is like an optical illusion. When the backward leap forward, those in front appear to fall back. Thorstein Veblen wrote about the "advantage of backwardness" (cited by Service, 1971, p. 34), which is the capacity of the less formed to improve upon the model of the innovators while the leaders become trapped in the limitations of their original breakthroughs. Service, for example, cites the leap into alphabetical writing over the backs of the once advanced and suddenly relatively encumbered peoples using hieroglyphics (ibid., p. 37). Thus one can gain the impression of cycles because one's point of reference is moving along the linear progression (like watching the motion of a point on the wheel of a moving bicycle). In a later book, Service generalizes about the early civilizations that "their demise was caused by a weakness that was relative to others' new strength . . . the first classic civilizations, therefore, did not fall, they were pushed" (1975, pp. 314, 322). It is far from clear, however, that Rome was pushed by anyone who would have been its match when Roman power was at its crest.

organism. Rome is not a tree but a forest. Trees die, but a climax forest can go on forever, barring catastrophic intrusions from outside the systems of life. Rome did die, or at least "fall." And it was not only pushed: for the challenges to which it eventually succumbed would not have been sufficient to overwhelm Rome in its prime; and when Rome had fallen, that part of the world was long left with no power comparable to Rome in its glory. Rome, representing here as it so often does both the might and frailty of civilized societies, "died" of unnatural causes because civilizations are unnatural systems that fail to emulate the wholeness of other living systems.

The absence of a blueprint is illustrative of civilization's general foray into uncharted territory. In terra incognita, one can easily lose one's way. The unproved can prove unreliable. The experiment *can* fail. But civilization's problems transcend these fallbacks of what in chapter 1 I called the "commonsense" view. To survive the emergency created by the plunge of civilization into anarchy, civilized societies are compelled to adopt a modus vivendi which ultimately proves a modus morte.

The unnatural Hobbesian state allows only the powerful to survive, but the ways of power are not the ways of life. The perpetual emergency requires the adrenalin society, but unrelenting stress leads to fatigue, and disregarded injuries will at last undermine the social organism. Steward describes how the very processes of empire building in the ancient world led ultimately to internal decline, "as the standard of living decreased and the death rate increased to the point that local populations were willing to support revolutions against imperial authority" (1955, pp. 206–207). A similar view of the deterioration of the great ancient civilizations is articulated by Leslie White. The great empires arose, he says, as

> international competition and conflict intensified. . . . But the political systems in which this cultural development found expression were not suited to stability, peace, and productive industry in the long run. Directed toward subjugation and exploitation at home, and conquest and spoliation abroad, the economic bases of these great cultures were undermined one after another, until, with the collapse of the Roman state, the era of the great cultures produced by the Agricultural Revolution came to an end. (1949, pp. 352–353)

Civilized societies continue to fall into the pit between the immediate requirements for surviving the struggle for power and the long-term requirements for maintaining a healthy social organism. An especially clear and poignant example is the state of Israel which has been subject to threats of such extraordinary intensity and constancy that in a mere generation power's necessity has left a deep imprint. A state founded with the most utopian of visions has been compelled increasingly to adopt the structures and values of a garrison state.[24] Even before the 1973 war, Arieli wrote of the dilemma of his country: "The continuation of full mobilization of the country's resources for 'improving Israel's security situation' will undermine, even in the short run, the basis of her security—the stability of her society. There can be no security for Israel without social stability and a healthy community" (1972, p. 30). In this, at least, Israel is not alone. Today (1981) the administration governing the United States is stripping billions of dollars away from social programs to support a trillion-dollar buildup of armaments.

The killing fatigue of the perpetual hype applies also to the relationship between the civilized society and the natural environment it exploits. This relationship, as we saw, is corrupt (though only partly because of the necessities of competitive power). Corruption means debilitation of the whole in this sphere just as it does in a governmental system. Just as a ruler like Zaire's Mobutu drains away the vitality of the whole social organism, so also a corrupt regime between a civilized society and the ecosystem replaces life with death. Carter and Dale, in *Topsoil and Civilization*, argue that the rise and fall of specific civilizations have their roots in ecological practices. It is, they say, because man has despoiled most of the lands he has lived on for long that civilizations in older settled regions have declined while the locus of progressive civilizations has shifted from place to place (p. 7). "Most of the progressive and dynamic civilizations of mankind started on new land—on land that had not been the center of a former civilization" (p. 12). After exhausting its land, and the land it could conquer, these civilizations began to decline. "After that, a new civilization arose on new land among some of the semi-civilized barbarians. Then the pattern was repeated" (p. 15). The quick fix leads to slow death. The great fleet of Rome was built through deforestation and degradation of the region. The United States now attempts to right its worsening trade balance through agricultural exports, so straining the land that it is predicted that a mere fifty years could see a 30 percent decline in the soil's productivity. The benefits are immediate and fleeting while the costs are cumulative and eventually deadly.

And then civilization has the problem of making the human spirit into a reliable piece for its inhumane machine. The problem is twofold.

24. In my view, as I write during the 1982 siege of Beirut, prominent elements in the Israel of Begin and Sharon have carried the orientation toward power beyond the requirements of objective necessity. But even this excess appears to be the fruit of the chronic struggle. Perpetually beset by real threats to their survival, and consequently crazed by anxiety and rage, people can be in the grip of "compulsions" other than those visibly imposed from without. The struggle for power, almost from its beginning, has been able to gain in momentum from its impact with the tormented human psyche.

On the one hand, because civilization depends upon a twisting of that spirit out of its natural shape, the human being has a tendency to strain against playing the required role. On the other hand, the agony of that twisting can madden the human creature, thus introducing an additional destructive and irrational force into the system.

The ability of experience to mold character in the learning animal may seem to make human nature irrelevant to the durability of civilized systems. But it does not. Just as the bending of spring steel leads to an unstable configuration, so also does the distortion of human nature which civilization requires. There is a functional difference between motivations that are inherently fundamental to the human being and those that must be molded by a specific set of experiences: the first is automatically renewed with each generation, the second requires that each generation recapitulate the necessary experiences. But the expression of human desires upon the historical stage changes circumstances, and changed circumstances mean that the children of one group of actors will have different formative experiences from their parents. From different experience, in turn, emerges different character. The motivational foundation tends thus to be undone.

Consider the contrast between the needs for love and for power. Because love has been an essential element of the strategy of our species for survival probably back to our prehuman ancestors, the need for love is a major component of human nature. The need for power, by contrast, is the fruit of particular experiences, especially the painful experience of being a powerless victim. The need to be on top grows out of the feeling or fear of being on the bottom. The rise of Nazism in Germany, for example, is said to be in part the consequence of Germany's humiliation at Versailles. Power, unlike love, is desired (as Hobbes perceived) less as a positive good in itself than as a guarantee of avoiding its opposite.

Systems based on inherent, intrinsically satisfying human values will be more stable than those based on learned, deficiency-based values. A society based on bonds of love, such as the Tasaday of the Philippines, renews its motivational base with each generation. But a system dependent upon a motive to compensate for deprivation contains the seeds of its own undoing. For by achieving its purpose, the motivation eliminates the source of the need. The children of the powerful will tend not to match their parents' hunger for power. (The drive for power is used here as representative of a whole class of motivations essential to the workings of civilized societies.)

Power tends to go to those who crave it most, but why should those people crave it who are born to power and who experience its inability truly to scratch the itch? Ruling groups can try to repeat the deprivations necessary to replicate the character structure. The children of a ruling class, for example, may be subjected to humiliations to make them hunger for the dominant role into which they are to grow: the literature about the English schoolboy from the ruling class illustrates this. But history suggests that drives for power prove unstable in the long run, and that their half-life erodes the system's basic fuel. Warriors are the founders of aristocracies, but their descendants become dandies. Power ceases to be the object sought and becomes instead the inherited capital that purchases other goods. Eugene Rice writes: "In England, men of talent and modest origins made fortunes as clothiers or in the wholesale trade of woolen cloth. Their sons held administrative offices and began to buy up land in their home counties. The grandsons settled on these estates and founded gentry families" (1970, p. 58). Whole nations, having found their place in the sun, may get burned out. Some suggest that the drive to excel and achieve has waned in the United States, while the Japanese tell us "We are driven" even as they gain bigger pieces of the market. (Opinion polls from Japan during the 1970s suggest, however, that Japanese success is eroding its attitudinal foundations among the young of Japan, and that the Japanese climb toward being Number One may be cut short, as was the duration of "The American Century.") The instability of the appetites that fuel civilization makes its progress uneven and cyclic. The medieval Arab theorist, Khaldun, based his theory of the rise and fall of civilizations on a process of decadence of this kind. An empire, according to Khaldun, has a "natural life span" of no more than three generations. The first is the generation of conquest the strength and solidarity of which begins to disappear in the second as sedentary living and luxury take their toll. This erosion proceeds further in the third, so that the empire becomes "senile and worn out," and then faces destruction (summarized in Laurer, 1973, pp. 28–29).

Because power systems require an uphill struggle against the basic tendencies of human nature, what rises will also fall.

Civilization's struggle against human nature can lead to destruction also because bending the human spirit causes pain, and pain can be maddening. The rage of the injured animal (as argued in chap. 5, "Fighting Mad") can fuel the system, but the system's capacity to channel that rage is hardly foolproof. If irrational factors break through those channels, the fuel can cause a "meltdown" of the power generator, with deadly results to both system and people. Freud's vision did not deceive him when he saw Thanatos struggling against life in civilization, although he misinterpreted the nature of that specter. Enraged and suffering creatures have good reasons to combine with the natural love of life an impulse to embrace death. Like the maimed Samson bringing down the idolatrous temple upon himself and his foes, civilized man may find in destruction a way of achieving both vengeance and escape from agony. My experience in foreign policy circles in Washington and my more distant perceptions of the Kremlin lead me to suspect that deep beneath the surface of conscious thought some of those who think the unthinkable do not find the thought so horribly repugnant. In past centuries, human beings in their misery have prayed to God to bring apocalypse unto the earth. Now, at last, they can do it themselves.

Apocalypse Now?

In some ways, the specter of destruction that haunts today's civilization is nothing new. Particular societies still gain and lose in vigor and drive and coherence. Today's ecological destruction simply continues a process begun by shepherds' flocks and farmers' cleared fields. The eruptions of violence still spill the same blood that ancient epics tell of, and for largely the same reasons. But, of course, one thing is new: unlike our ancestors, we now have good cause to wonder whether the destructiveness of present systems may inflict irreversible damage upon human life, civilization, and the earth, ending forever the human experiment and perhaps even bursting the precious film of life enveloping our globe.

What has changed is the magnitude of civilization's destructive potential. This is an inevitable consequence of the growth of power. Four billion people armed with modern technology are simply a bigger bull in the ecological china shop than a few hundred million using the technologies of archaic civilizations. The explosion of the power of armaments has been still more dramatic. Only a generation ago a war was fought over a far larger area with far more potent weapons than any conflicts of earlier ages. As unprecedented as was the might and scope of World War II, the total destructive force unleashed then was but a minuscule fraction of what the world's two superpowers are now poised to rain down upon one another. The most destructive war the world has yet seen still killed only a small percentage of the earth's human population, and the scars it made on the biosphere were small and quickly healed. The World War III that we dread would be exponentially more devastating in both respects.[25] And finally and relatedly, the emergence of a truly global civilization makes of this planet a single basket for all our eggs. When a single system can encompass the entire earth in its grasp, there is no refuge from the destructiveness of its clumsiness or fury.

25. We live also with the image of Auschwitz and Buchenwald. That holocaust does not point the way to universal destruction, but it does show that even massacres—like these other ways that civilization delivers death—can be magnified by modern efficiency.

It is therefore evident that civilization cannot extend indefinitely the pattern it has made in the past ten thousand years. To continue the trajectory described by the parable of the tribes would be to plunge into the abyss. Power is like a cancer that now threatens to destroy the very living energies it depends upon. Its accelerating growth progresses to the point where mankind must either succumb or find a treatment. The treatment, the alternative to death, is to find a way to displace the ways of power by restoring the ways of life. If for us there is no return to the womb of nature's system, it is essential that we change the ways of our unnatural systems. Their present ways clearly carry upon their backs the plague of death.

Mankind, then, faces a life-or-death choice. More of the same means death, so the preservation of life requires transformation. Our choice is not like the coming to a crossroads, for the choice is continuous and many faceted. In a sense, the choices have been confronted by civilized peoples since this whole experiment began, and it would be unfair and inaccurate to suggest that the persistence of the problem of power is due to a failure on their part to make the right choices. The dangers they faced were less than ours, but so also were their capacities to break the grip of power over human destiny. The same geometric growth of human powers which casts a darker shadow over our times generates a brighter glow at the end of the tunnel. The same growth of knowledge that has accelerated the modern spurt of power brings into sharper focus the nature of our problems and of the solutions they require. The same globalization of civilization which brings such risks makes conceivable a genuine containment of the contaminant of power. As our power to do evil has grown, so has our ability to do good. Every day, all over the earth, millions of people struggle in countless ways to deflect the course of human destiny from the abyss. And not without effect. For the century that has brought global conflict has witnessed also the germination of the seeds of global cooperation. It has been in the era of nuclear war that the virtues of peace have come to enjoy unprecedented prestige. The century that threatens ecological disaster has seen an extraordinary emergence of new ecological consciousness. The age of Auschwitz has also made universal the concept, if not the practice, of human rights. Norman Cousins has written that any problem human beings have the power to make for themselves they also have the power to solve. This equation between human challenges and human powers does not follow logically, and the facts may prove it overly optimistic. But there are some ideas—like this one from a man who, perhaps by sheer force of positive will, overcame his own disease—that we have nothing to lose by assuming to be true.

330

Chapter Eight

Conclusion: Therefore Choose Life

I have set before you life and death, blessing and cursing; therefore choose life, that both thou and thy seed may live.—Deuteronomy 19:30

As in the first chapter, so in the concluding one: a note of hope.

The parable of the tribes is hardly gospel, in the literal sense of "good news." But neither is it prophecy, for the future remains to be written. Thus a work preoccupied with the dark side of civilized life can be dedicated to overcoming the powers of darkness. The destructive evolutionary process described here is nonteleological, but mankind whose destiny is at stake is endowed with purpose in the service of life. The question is whether we shall discover within ourselves the understanding and the will to contain the rule of power. The malady that arose as an unwanted side effect of man's inventive consciousness can conceivably be remedied by the further development of that same creative force. The parable of the tribes, then, serves not to condemn but to challenge: can we change systems that channel vital energies to serve power into systems that channel power to serve the needs of human and other life?

This book is a work of diagnosis, dwelling upon the pathological to illuminate the etiology of the problems that afflict us. Diagnosis is, however, only a first step. It is also necessary to prescribe a course of treatment, a means of achieving the wholeness civilization now lacks. My intention is to explore in future work how the ills diagnosed here may be remedied. Yet, to the extent that it succeeds in its aims, *The Parable of the Tribes* can itself be a part of the treatment of the problems it describes. Even in dwelling upon the negative, it can have a positive effect, for effective treatment requires good diagnosis. The better we understand the root cause of the defects of our systems (as was argued here in the critique of Marxism) the more likely will our good intentions lead to good results. The parable of the tribes, therefore, has implications for how our systems must be redesigned.

If redesign of the system is one side of the challenge facing us, ignition of the spirit is the other. The dulling of our feelings, Cousins believes, is why we are in danger of failing at the tasks our civilization presents us (1981, p. 34). Ten people fired with faith and dedication can better wrest civilization from its current trajectory than a thousand who are dispirited and demoralized. The experience that civilization imposes upon us can in many ways drain off the human powers that are indispensable to our success. My hope is that this work can help to replenish those springs, to make the stirrings of the human spirit a more formidable power against power. There are several ways in which the message of this book, for all its delineation of our bondage, may be a tool of liberation.

(1) The parable of the tribes leads beyond guilt. We are creatures who seem naturally to interpret our misfortunes as punishment for our sins. If it was true for the bubonic plague, how much more readily will we assume that the destruction we as a species visibly inflict upon ourselves is a manifestation of and a punishment for our depravity. But the parable of the tribes shows that we are more the victims than the villains in this crime drama. A vision of how little mankind has controlled the destiny of even its own creations may be a blow to human pride, as the first page of this book suggested. But it also offers absolution from the guilt which seethes below the surface of consciousness in our times and which debilitates our capacity for constructive work in the world. We have a long way to go, and we shall hardly be likely to get there encumbered by unnecessary burdens. We shall be better able to act responsibly to shape the future if we do not punish ourselves with guilt over our misshapen past.

(2) The perspective offered here should mitigate against enmity. If it is assumed that blame must be fixed for the evils that plague us, then the only alternative to guilt is hostility. If it is not our fault, it must be theirs. Any vision of our dilemma that lifts guilt, therefore, should also help dull the point of our intertribal animosity. The parable of the tribes encourages us to see all mankind as subject to the same distressing and

disorienting circumstance. If we can see how much we are like Zucker-man's baboons, thrown together in a frightening and anarchic situation, we are more likely to find the means to overcome our mutual fears with constructive mutual empathy. The parable of the tribes tells us the path away from enmity *must* be mutual. Yet it is also true that the expectation of enmity can be self-fulfilling. In the chronic antagonisms of our age—United States–Soviet, Arab-Israeli—each actor can be like a man before a mirror: every belligerent gesture is reflected back and promotes a further escalation of conflict. The commonness of our problems by itself provides no assurance of cooperation in action. Nonetheless, whatever increases our awareness of commonness—of the kinship implied by our shared humanity, of our being-in-the-same-boat implied by the idea of spaceship earth, of the panic we feel in the civilized zoo—increases our capacity to act for the common good.

(3) The parable of the tribes may enhance people's sense of common purpose in yet another way. Ours is an age of fragmentation in both vision and action. Our world has become so complex that we have largely lost our ability to see things whole. And so we set about our elephantine problems with the incoherence of the blind men in the fable: one feels the tail and says, "It's a rope," another the leg and says, "It's a tree." Thus, we have constructive but unconnected groups addressing specific areas of concern: one group is concerned about the environment, another about matters of war and peace, another about civil liberties, another about human potential. This work attempts to supply a unifying vision of our entire predicament, a perspective that reveals each area of our concerns to be a manifestation of a basic underlying human condition in civilization. The potential usefulness of such a perspective lies not so much in questioning the ideas or intentions of specific constructive missions as in providing a basis for the many groups to see themselves (and to act) as part of a coherent movement for the renewal of civilization. Whatever helps people of goodwill to see and to feel the connections among them potentially strengthens the force of goodness. Another of Aesop's fables tells of the farmer who demonstrates for his sons that while sticks can easily be broken one by one, they are unbreakable when tied into a bundle. The idea that "in unity is strength" is one seized upon by the selection for power, but that principle can also be employed to empower humanity to overcome its bondage to power.

(4) The parable of the tribes is a message to liberate the individual human spirit.

(*a*) It does so, if it is successful, first by *driving a wedge between us and our systems*. These powerful systems that mold us and rule our lives teach us to give them our allegiance. Dennis Wrong, in *Power* (1979), argues

333

persuasively that the oppressed have almost as big a need to believe in the legitimacy of the regime that dominates them as do their oppressors. With civilization, all of us are to some degree in that position. It is discomfiting to be out of joint with the surrounding order. There is a part of us that takes up the task as given, surrendering ourselves to it even when it only helps what seeks to destroy us, like the British colonel in the film *The Bridge over the River Kwai* who in the end fights (and dies) to save the bridge he has masterfully built for the enemy whose prisoner he is. A part of us resents those who disrupt the smooth flow of business as usual, even if that business is the digging of our own graves. In this, we are like the concentration camp inmates, about whom I read somewhere, standing in neat order awaiting the visit from Herr Commandant Oberführe: an old Jew collapses from hunger and, when punitively beaten by the SS guards, moans and groans; the feeling of his fellow inmates is, "Why does that damned Yankel make such a fuss? Why is he disrupting everything?" Evidently, it is not an unmixed blessing to be liberated from our allegiance to the surrounding order, from our displaced goals and our routines. But certainly, to the extent that this order demands that we sacrifice some sacred part of ourselves and threatens ultimately to destroy us, it is imperative that we take the leap of becoming our own men and women who go in a direction of our own envisioning even if it is against the flow. The parable of the tribes endeavors to sever the unquestioning loyalty of the Good Soldier Schweik within us, and to make visible the basis for deeper allegiances. Recognizing the dangers of anarchy, we must recognize that we need our systems and must beware of creating chaos in our efforts to divert the destructive course of power. But to utilize the channels is not to let them determine the course.

(*b*) For people to have the inner power to be self-possessed, they must own the core of themselves. For people to have the vision to chart a course against the current, they must discover the compass that lies within. The parable of the tribes provides one angle for peering into our essential natures. This perspective has spiritual implications. It points toward a sacred human nature, toward a vision of ourselves as we are at the source. In our civilized state, this picture of our essential humanity is obscured, like a great work by an Old Master that has been painted over. One must know the masterpiece is there before one can begin to retrieve it. As the picture emerges before our inner eyes, we discover in ourselves indeed something of God's image; a creative and potent force that orients toward the sacred.

In the Buddhist literature of India is a spiritual tale of a tiger cub that, because of circumstance, was brought up among goats. Seeing only the example of goathood, he became like a goat, or as much like one as a tiger could. One day, after the tiger had begun to mature, the herd was attacked by a fierce old male tiger:

> Discovering himself face to face with the terrible jungle being, [the young tiger] gazed at the apparition in amazement. The first moment passed; then he began to feel self-conscious. Uttering a forlorn bleat, he plucked a thin leaf of grass and chewed it, while the other stared.
>
> Suddenly the mighty intruder demanded: "What are you doing here among these goats? What are you chewing there?" The funny little creature bleated. The old one became really terrifying. He roared, "Why do you make this silly sound?" and before the other could respond, seized him roughly by the scruff and shook him, as though to knock him back to his senses. (Zimmer, 1951, p. 6)

Ultimately, the young tiger is led to discover his tigerhood:

> He arose and opened his mouth with a mighty yawn, just as though he were waking from a night of sleep—a night that had held him long under its spell, for years and years. Stretching his form, he arched his back, extending and spreading his paws. The tail lashed the ground, and suddenly from his throat there burst the terrifying, triumphant roar of a tiger.
>
> The grim teacher, meanwhile, had been watching closely and with increasing satisfaction. The transformation had actually taken place. When the roar was finished he demanded gruffly: "Now do you know what you really are?" (p. 7)

I hope this work conveys some of the liberating force of my own encounter with the old tiger.

(5) Yet such liberation is not enough, and by itself may indeed be dangerous. If the baboons can escape to the savanna, then setting them free is solution enough. But what if they must find a life fit for baboons within the confines of some zoo? We will never find a way toward a human world without that compass that lies within, but being lost as we are in unfamiliar territory our compass alone cannot show us the way. Throughout history the roaring of tigers, seeking to regain what an unsuitable domestication had taken from them, has been as often the occasion for destruction as for liberation. (The roar of Hitler and those for whom he was the *Führer* was an expression of both the diseased aspect of civilization and the human rebellion against it.)

We are in unnatural circumstances and are thus subject to a confusion that we cannot rely upon our natural being alone to dispel. The inescapability of this unnatural condition means that we must be more (and therefore also less) than "the natural man." The creatures that must design a zoo for themselves must necessarily forfeit some of their natural innocence. To escape from confusion, they must cultivate clarity of understanding to an unnatural degree. Strangers in a strange land need a map as well as a compass. We are thus endangered not only by "dullness of feeling" but by inadequacy of thought as well.

The challenge facing us is to bring together the primitive and the highly sophisticated. We need to discover a harmonizing integration between the sacred energies we bring with us from our Source and the indispensable tools we have developed upon our journey. The long and tortuous path we have traveled makes the building of these bridges a difficult task. This work embodies my effort at such a synthesis.

BIBLIOGRAPHY

Acherson, Neal. "Goodbye to All That," *New York Review of Books,* December 9, 1976.
Adams, George Burton. "Feudalism." In *Encyclopaedia Britannica,* 14th ed.
Adams, Richard Newbold. *Energy and Structure.* University of Texas Press, Austin, 1975.
Adams, Robert M. "Ancient Incas and Modern Revolution," *New York Review of Books,* March 18, 1976.
———— . "Anthropological Perspectives on Ancient Trade," *Current Anthropology,* September 1974.
Adams, Robert McC. *The Evolution of Urban Society: Early Mesopotamia and Prehispanic Mexico.* Aldine, Chicago, 1966.
Adler, Nathan. "The Antinomian Personality: The Hippie Character Type." Repr. from *Psychiatry,* 31, 4 (Nov. 1968), 325–338.
———— . "Ritual, Release, and Orientation: The Maintenance of the Self in the Antinomian Personality," MS., 1971.
The Advocates. "Should the Developed Nations Limit Their Growth?" Public Broadcasting System, June 13, 1972.
Aho, James A. *Religious Mythology and the Art of War: Comparative Religious Symbolisms of Military Violence.* Greenwood Press, Westport, Conn., 1981.
Aleksandar, Bozovic. *Colonialism and Neo-colonialism.* Medunarodna Politika, Belgrade, 1964.
Alfven, Hannes. *Worlds-Antiworlds: Antimatter in Cosmology.* W. H. Freeman, San Francisco, 1966.
Alinsky, Saul. "Speaking Freely," Public Broadcasting System, May 8, 1972.
Allais, Maurice. "Pareto, Vilfredo: Contributions to Economics," *International Encyclopedia of the Social Sciences,* 1968.
Alland, Alexander. *Adaptation in Cultural Evolution.* Columbia University Press, New York, 1970.
Allen, Dick, ed. *Science Fiction: The Future.* Harcourt, Brace Jovanovich, New York, 1971.
Alumni Magazine Consortium. "The Rise and Fall of Empires: An Empirical Discussion," *Johns Hopkins Magazine,* August 1982.
Andrzejewski, Stanislaus. *Military Organization and Society.* Routledge and Kegan Paul, London, 1954.
Angell, Alan. "Allende's First Year in Chile," *Current History,* February 1972.
Apter, David. *The Politics of Modernization.* University of Chicago Press, Chicago, 1965.
Aquinas, St. Thomas. "St. Thomas Aquinas on Aristotle." In Ebenstein, 1954.

Ardrey, Robert. *The Social Contract: A Personal Inquiry into the Evolutionary Sources of Order and Disorder.* Atheneum, New York, 1970.

Arendt, Hannah. *Eichmann in Jerusalem: A Report on the Banality of Evil.* Viking Press, New York, 1963.

————. *The Origins of Totalitarianism.* Harcourt Brace and World, New York, 1966.

————. *Men in Dark Times.* Harcourt Brace and World, New York, 1968.

————. "Reflections on Violence," *New York Review of Books,* February 27, 1969.

————. "Thoughts on Politics and Revolution," *New York Review of Books,* April 22, 1971.

————. "Lying in Politics: Reflections on the Pentagon Papers," *New York Review of Books,* November 18, 1971.

Arieli, Yehoshua. "The Price Israel Is Paying," *New York Review of Books,* August 31, 1972.

Arnold, Thurman W. *The Symbols of Government.* Yale University Press, New Haven, Conn., 1935.

Aron, Arthur, and Elaine Aron. *Psychology in the Light of the Science of Creative Intelligence: Unfolding Deeper Levels of the Mind.* Maharishi International University, 1973.

Aron, Raymond. *The Century of Total War.* Beacon Press, Boston, 1954.

————. *Democracy and Totalitarianism.* Weidenfield and Nicolson, London, 1965a.

————. *Main Currents in Sociological Thought,* Vol. I. Anchor Books, Garden City, N.Y. 1965b.

————. *Peace and War: A Theory of International Relations.* Doubleday, Garden City, N.Y., 1966.

————. "Richard Nixon and American Foreign Policy," *Daedalus,* Summer 1972.

Arrow, Kenneth J., and Tibor Scitovsky, eds. *Readings in Welfare Economics.* Richard D. Irwin, Inc., Homewood, Ill., 1969.

Asch, Solomon E. "Gestalt Theory," *International Encyclopedia of the Social Sciences,* 1968.

Auden, W. H. *A Certain World: A Commonplace Book.* Viking Press, New York, 1970.

Auden, W. H., and Louis Kronenberger. *The Viking Book of Aphorisms.* Penguin Books. Middlesex, England, 1966.

Aurelius, Marcus. "Meditations," *Britannica Great Books.*

Austin, Paul Britten. Review of *The New Totalitarians* by Roland Huntford, *New York Times Book Review,* February 27, 1972.

Bacon, Francis. *Novum Organum,* Edwin A. Burtt, ed. *The English Philosophers from Bacon to Mill.* Modern Library, New York, 1939.

Bagby, Philip. *Culture and History: Prolegomena to the Comparative Study of Civilizations,* University of California Press, Berkeley and Los Angeles, 1959.

Bagehot, Walter. *Physics and Politics.* Beacon Press, Boston, 1956.

Banton, Michael. "The Autonomy of Post-Darwinian Sociology." In Banton, 1961.

Banton, Michael, ed. *Darwinism and the Study of Society.* London, Tavistock, 1961.

Barbu, Zevedei. *Democracy and Dictatorship: Their Psychology and Patterns of Life.* Grove Press, New York, 1956.

————. *Society, Culture and Personality.* Schocken Books, New York, 1971.

Barkow, Jerome H. "Darwinian Psychological Anthropology," *Current Anthropology,* October 1973.

Barnes, Harry Elmer. *Historical Sociology, Its Origins and Development: Theories of Social Evolution from Cave Life to Atomic Bombing.* Philosophical Library, New York, 1948.

————. *Introduction to the History of Sociology.* University of Chicago Press, Chicago, 1948.

————. "Gumplowicz," *International Encyclopedia of the Social Sciences,* 1968.

Barnet, Richard, and Ronald Müller, "Global Reach," *The New Yorker,* December 9, 1974.

Barnett, S. A. "Communication in Animal and Human Societies." In Banton, 1961.

————. "Deus Le Volt?" *New York Review of Books,* May 21, 1970.

Barraclough, Geoffrey. "Hitler's Master Builder," *New York Review of Books,* January 7, 1971.

————. *The Crucible of Europe.* University of California Press, Berkeley and Los Angeles, 1976.

Bartholomew, George A., Jr., and Joseph B. Birdsell. "Ecology and the Protohominids," In Montague, 1962.

Barry, H., J. L. Child, and M. K. Bacon. "Relation of Child Training to Subsistence Economy," *American Anthropology,* 61 (1959), 51–63.

Bashan, A. L. *The Wonder That Was India.* Grove Press, New York, 1954.

Bates, Marston. *Man in Nature.* Prentice-Hall, Englewood Cliffs, N.J., 1961.

Bateson, Gregory. *Steps to an Ecology of Mind.* Ballantine Books, New York, 1972.

Bauer, Wolfgang and Herbert Franke. *The Golden Casket: Chinese Novellas of Two Millennia.* Harcourt Brace and World, New York, 1964.

Baumer, Franklin L. *Religion and the Rise of Scepticism.* Harcourt Brace, New York, 1960.

Beaufre, Andre. *An Introduction to Strategy.* Trans. R. H. Barry. Faber and Faber, London, 1965.

Becker, Ernest. *Escape from Evil.* Free Press, New York, 1975.

Behrendt, R. F. "The Socio-Cultural Development up to the Present Time and Our Place in It." In Eisenstadt, 1966.

Behrens, C. B. A. "Which Side Was Clausewitz on?" *New York Review of Books,* October 14, 1976.

Bellah, Robert N. *Tokugawa Religion.* Free Press, Glencoe, Ill., 1957.

————. *Beyond Belief: Essays on Religion in a Post-Traditional World.* Harper and Row, New York, 1970*a*.

————. "No Direction Home." The Dudleian Lecture, Harvard Division, November 1970*b*. MS.

————. "The Broken Covenant: American Civil Religion in Time of Trial." MS.

————. "Emile Durkheim on Morality and Society: Introduction." MS.

————. "Evil and the American Ethos." In Sanford et al., 1971.

————. "To Kill and Survive or to Die and Become: The Active Life and the Contemplative Life as Ways of Being Adult," *Daedalus,* Spring 1975.

Beloff, M. *The Age of Absolutism.* Hutchinsons University Library, London, 1954.

Bender, Lauretta. *Aggression, Hostility and Anxiety in Children.* Charles C. Thomas, Springfield, Ill., 1953.

Benedict, Burton. "Societies, Small," *International Encyclopedia of the Social Sciences,* 1968.

Bennedict, Ruth. "Patterns of the Good Culture," *Psychology Today,* June 1970.

Bennis, Warren G. "Organic Populism: A Conversation with Warren G. Bennis and T. George Harris." *Psychology Today,* March 1970.

Bereisches Genesis: A New Translation with a Commentary. Trans. and commentary by Rabbi Meir Zlotowitz. Mesorah Publications, Brooklyn, N.Y., 1980.

Berlin, Isiah. "The Question of Machiavelli," *New York Review of Books,* November 4, 1972.

Berman, Marshall. Review of *Relations in Public* by Erving Goffman, *New York Times Book Review,* February 27, 1972.

Berr, Henri. "Foreword: Rome the Organizer; the Perfecting of the State." In Homo, 1962.

Bhagwati, Jaddish. "The United States in the Nixon Era: The End of Innocence," *Daedalus,* Summer 1972.

Bibby, Geoffrey. *Four Thousand Years Ago.* Alfred A. Knopf, New York, 1961.

Bigelow, Robert. *The Dawn Warriors: Man's Evolution toward Peace.* Little Brown, Boston, 1969.

————. "The Relevance of Ethology to Human Aggressiveness," *International Social Science Journal* (UNESCO), 23, 1 (1971).

Billington, James H. "Revolution: Fire in the Minds of Men," *Wilson Quarterly,* Summer 1980.

Binford, L. R. "Post-Pleistocene Adaptations." In Binford and Binford, 1968.

Binford, Sally R., and Lewis R. Binford, eds. *New Perspectives in Archeology.* Aldine, Chicago, 1968.

Birdsell, J. B. "Some Population Problems Involving Pleistocene Man," *Cold Spring Harbor Symposia on Quantitative Biology,* Vol. XXII, Biological Laboratory, Cold Spring Harbor, Long Island, N.Y., 1957.

Bjerre, Jens. *Savage New Guinea.* Hill and Wang, New York, 1964.

Blau, Sheridan D., and John B. von Rodenbeck. *The House We Live In: An Environmental Reader.* Macmillan, New York, 1971.

Bleibtreu, John N. *The Parable of the Beast.* Macmillan, New York, 1968.

Bloch, Marc. *Feudal Society.* Vol. 2. University of Chicago Press, Chicago, 1965.

Bogardus, Emory S. *The Development of Social Thought.* Longmans, Green, New York, 1955.

Bohannan, Paul, ed. *Law and Warfare: Studies in the Anthropology of Conflict.* Natural History Press, Garden City, N.Y., 1967.

Bonner, John Tyler. *Cells and Societies.* Princeton University Press, Princeton, 1955.

Borgese, Elizabeth. "The Blue Revolution: Harvesting the Fruits of the Sea," *Center Report,* April 1975.

Boserup, E. *The Conditions of Agricultural Growth.* Aldine, New York, 1965.

Bottomore, T. B. "Marxist Sociology," *International Encyclopedia of Social Sciences,* 1968.

—————— . "Machines without a Cause," *New York Review of Books,* November 4, 1971.

Boughey, Arthur S., ed. *Readings in Man, the Environment and Human Ecology.* Macmillan, New York, 1973.

Boulding, Kenneth. *The Image.* University of Michigan Press, Ann Arbor, 1956.

—————— . "Economics as a Moral Science," *American Economic Review,* 78, 2 (February 1969).

—————— ."The Economics of the Coming Spaceship Earth." In Blau and Rodenbeck, 1971.

Boulding, Kenneth, and Tapan Murkerjee, eds. *Economic Imperialism.* University of Michigan Press, Ann Arbor, 1972.

Bousset, Jacques Benigne. "Politics Drawn from the Very Words of Holy Scripture." In Tierney et al., 1972.

Bowen, Elenore Smith (pseud. for Laura Bohannan). *Return to Laughter.* Doubleday-Anchor, Garden City, N.Y., 1954.

Bowlby, John. "Separation Anxiety," *International Journal of Psychoanalysis,* 39 (1958), 350–373.

—————— . *Attachment and Loss,* Vol. I, *Attachment.* Basic Books, New York, 1969.

—————— . *Attachment and Loss,* Vol. II, *Separation: Anxiety and Anger.* Basic Books, New York, 1973.

Boyden, Stephen. "Cultural Adaptation to Biological Maladjustment." In Boyden, 1970.

Boyden, Stephen, ed. *The Impact of Civilization on the Biology of Man,* University of Toronto Press, Toronto, 1970.

Bozeman, Adda B. *Politics and Culture in International History.* Princeton University Press, Princeton, 1960.

Braeman, John, Robert H. Bremner, and David Brody, eds. *Change and Continuity in Twentieth Century America: The 1920's.* Ohio State University Press, Columbus, 1968.

Braidwood, Robert J. *Prehistoric Men.* 7th ed. Scott, Foresman, Glenview, Ill., 1967.

Braidwood, Robert J., and Gordon R. Willey, eds. *Courses toward Urban Life: Archeological Considerations of Some Cultural Alternates.* Aldine, Chicago, 1962.

Bramson, Leon, and George W. Goethals, eds. *War: Studies from Psychology, Sociology, Anthropology.* Basic Books, New York, 1964.

Braudel, Fernand. *Capitalism and Material Life 1400–1800.* Harper and Row, New York, 1967.

Bridges, Hal. *American Mysticism: From William James to Zen.* Harper and Row, New York, 1970.

Bro, Harmon Hartzell. *High Play: Turning on without Drugs.* Coward-McCann, New York, 1970.

Bronowski, J. "The Disestablishment of Science," *Encounter,* July 1971.

Brosin, Henry W. "Evolution and Understanding Diseases of the Mind." In Tax, 1960.

Brown, Bruce. *Marx, Freud and the Critique of Everyday Life: Toward a Permanent Cultural Revolution.* Monthly Review Press, New York, 1973.

Brown, Lester. *World without Borders.* Vintage Books, New York, 1972.

Brown, Norman O. *Life against Death.* Vintage Books, New York, 1959.

————. *Love's Body.* Vintage Books, New York, 1966.

Brown, Peter. "Violence in Olympia," *New York Review of Books,* December 25, 1976.

Bruce-Briggs, B. "Against the Neo-Malthusians," *Commentary,* July 1974.

Bukharin, Nicolai. *Imperialism and World Economy.* Howard Pertig, New York, 1966.

Bukovsky, Vladimir. "A Letter from Vladimir Bukovsky," *New York Review of Books,* March 9, 1972.

Bundy, McGeorge. "The Missed Chance to Stop the H-Bomb," *New York Review of Books,* May 13, 1982.

Burke, Kenneth. *A Grammar of Motives.* George Braulter, New York, 1963.

Burland, Cottie. *North American Indian Mythology.* Paul Hamlyn, Middlesex, England, 1965.

Burtt, Edwin A., ed. *The English Philosophers from Bacon to Mill.* The Modern Library, New York, 1939.

Burrow, J. W. *Evolution and Society: A Study in Victorian Social Theory.* University Press, Cambridge, 1966.

Butterfield, Herbert. *The Origins of Modern Science.* Macmillan, New York, 1961.

Butzer, Karl W. *Environment and Archaeology: An Introduction to Pleistocene Geography.* Aldine, Chicago, 1964.

Bychowski, Gustav. "Joseph V. Stalin: Paranoia and the Dictatorship of the Proletariat." In Wolman, 1971.

Bychowski, Gustav. "Oliver Cromwell and the Puritan Revolution." In Zawodny, 1966.

Caesar, Julius. *The Gallic War and Other Writings.* Trans. and introduced by Moses Hadas. Modern Library, New York, 1957.

Campbell, Donald T. "Evolutionary Theory in Social Science: A Reappraisal," Draft of paper prepared for 1961 conference, Northwestern University, "Social Science and The Underdeveloped Areas: A Revival of Evolutionary Theory." MS.

Campbell, Joseph. *The Masks of God: Primitive Mythology,* Viking Press, New York, 1969.

Cannon, Walter B. *The Wisdom of the Body.* New York, 1932. Repr. W. W. Norton, New York, 1963.

Caplan, Frank. *The First Twelve Months of Life.* Grosset and Dunlap, New York, 1973.

Carneiro, R. "A Theory of the Origin of the State," *Science* 169 (1970), 733–738.

Carrington, Richard. *Elephants.* Basic Books, New York, 1939.

Carter, Vernon, and Tom Dale. *Topsoil and Civilization.* University of Oklahoma Press, Norman, Okla., 1974.

Cartter, Allan M. "Wages," *International Encyclopedia of Social Sciences,* 1968.

Casagrande, Joseph, ed. *In the Company of Man,* Harper and Brothers, New York, 1960.

Casson, Lionel. "Godliness and Work," *Science 81,* September 1981.

Castaneda, Carlos. *The Teachings of Don Juan.* Ballantine Books, New York, 1968.

Cattell, David T. "Dissent and Stability in the Soviet Union," *Current History,* October, 1970.

Caws, Peter. "Science and Sentiment in America: Philosophical Thought from Jonathan Edwards to John Dewey," *New York Times Book Review,* March 12, 1972.

Chagnon, Napoleon. "Yanomamo Social Organization and Warfare," In Fried et al., 1968.

Chambre, Henor. "Marxism," *Encyclopaedia Britannica,* 15th ed.

Chevalier, Michael. *Society, Manners and Politics in the United States.* Intro. by John William War. Gloucester, Mass., Peter Smith, 1967.

Childe, V. Gordon. *The Prehistory of European Society*. Penguin Books, London, 1958.

Chomsky, Noam. "The Case against B. F. Skinner," *New York Review of Books*, December 30, 1971.

Chuang Chou. *The Sayings of Chuang Chou*. James R. Ware, ed. Mentor Classics, New American Library, New York, 1963.

Clark, Grahame, and Stuart Piggott. *Prehistoric Societies*. Hutchinson, London, 1965.

Clausewitz, Carl von. *The Living Thoughts of Clausewitz*. David McKay, Philadelphia, 1943.

Cohen, Benjamin J. *The Question of Imperialism: The Political Economy of Dominance and Dependence*. Basic Books, New York, 1973.

Cohen, Mark Nathan. "Archaeological Evidence for Population Pressure in Pre-Agricultural Societies," *American Antiquity*, 40, 4 (1975).

————. *The Food Crisis in Prehistory: Overpopulation and the Crisis of Agriculture*. Yale University Press, New Haven, 1977.

Cohen, Yehudi, ed. *Man in Adaptation: The Biosocial Background*. Aldine, Chicago, 1974.

Cole, Lamont C. "Playing Russian Roulette with Biogeochemical Cycles." In Helfrich, 1970.

Coles, Robert. "Understanding White Racists," *New York Review of Books*, December 30, 1971.

Colfax, J. David, and Jack L. Roach. *Radical Sociology*. Basic Books, New York, 1971.

Comfort, Alex. *Ageing: The Biology*. Routledge and Kegan Paul, London, 1964.

Conel, J. LeRoy. *Life as Revealed by the Microscope: An Interpretation of Evolution*. Philosophical Library, New York, 1969.

Conway, Jill. "Intellectuals in America: Varieties of Accommodation and Conflict," *Daedalus*, Summer 1972.

Cook, James. "A Tiger by the Tail," *Forbes*, April 13, 1981.

Coon, Carleton S. *The Hunting Peoples*. Little, Brown, Boston, 1971.

Cooperman, David, and E. V. Walter, eds. *Power and Civilization: Political Thought in the Twentieth Century*. Thomas Y. Crowell, New York, 1962.

Cordova-Rios, Manuel, and F. Bruce Lamb. *Wizard of the Upper Amazon*. Atheneum, New York, 1971.

Cotlow, Lewis. *In Search of the Primitive*. Little, Brown, Boston, 1966.

Cottrell, Fred. *Energy and Society: The Relation between Energy, Social Change, and Economic Development*. McGraw Hill, New York, 1955.

Coulbourn, Rushton. "Toynbee's Reconsiderations: A Commentary," *Journal of World History*, 8, 1 (1964).

Cousins, Norman. *The Human Option*. W. W. Norton, New York, 1981.

Cox, C. Barry, Ian N. Healey, and Peter D. Moore. *Biogeography: An Ecological and Evolutionary Approach*. 2d ed. Blackwell Scientific Publications, Oxford, 1976.

Cox, Harvey. *The Feast of Fools*. Harvard University Press, Cambridge, Mass., 1969.

Cox, Oliver. *Capitalism as a System*. Monthly Review Press, New York, 1964.

Crespigny, Anthony de. "F. A. Hayek: Freedom for Progress." In Crespigny and Minogue, 1975.

Crespigny, Anthony de, and Kenneth Minogue, eds. *Contemporary Political Philosophers*. Dodd, Mead, New York, 1975.

Cropsey, Joseph. *Polity and Economy: An Interpretation of the Principles of Adam Smith*. Martinus Nujohh, The Hague, 1957.

Curtin, Philip D. "The Black Experience of Colonialism and Imperialism," *Daedalus*, Spring 1974.

Dalton, George. *Economic Systems and Society: Capitalism, Communism and the Third World*. Penguin, Middlesex, England, 1974.

Dalton, George. "Introduction." In Polanyi, 1968.

Dansereau, Pierre. "Ecology and the Escalation of Human Impact," in *International Social Science Journal* (UNESCO), 22 (1971).

Darlington, C. D. *The Evolution of Man and Society.* Simon and Schuster, New York, 1969.

Darwin, Charles. *The Expression of Emotions in Animals and Man.* University of Chicago Press, Chicago, 1965.

Davis, James C., ed. *Pursuit of Power: Venetian Ambassadors' Reports on Turkey, France, and Spain in the Age of Philip II, 1560–1600.* Harper and Row, New York, 1971.

Davis, Kingsley, and Wilbert E. Moore. "Some Principles of Stratification." In Laumann et al., 1970.

De Bary, Wm. Theodore, ed. *The Buddhist Tradition in India, China and Japan.* Random House, New York, 1969.

De Bary, Wm. Theodore, Wing-tsit Chan, and Chester Tan, eds. *Sources of Chinese Tradition,* Vol. II. Columbia University Press, New York, 1960.

Dennison, George. *The Lives of Children.* Vintage Books, New York, 1969.

Derathe, Robert. "Rousseau, Jean Jacques," *International Encyclopedia of Social Sciences,* 1968.

De Reuck, Anthony V., ed. *Conflict in Society.* Little Brown, Boston, 1966.

Deutsch, Karl W. *The Nerves of Government: Models of Political Communication and Control.* Free Press, New York, 1963.

————— . *The Analysis of International Relations.* Englewood Cliffs, N.J., Prentice-Hall, 1968.

Devereux, George. "The Displacement of Modesty From Pubis to Face," *Psychoanalytic Review,* Winter 1965–66.

De Vore, Irven, ed. *Primate Behavior: Field Studies of Monkeys and Apes.* Holt, Rinehart and Winston, New York, 1965.

De Vos, George. "Conflict, Dominance and Exploitation in Human Systems of Social Segregation: Some Theoretical Perspectives from the Study of Personality in Culture." Repr. from De Reuck, 1966.

Diamond, Stanley, ed. *Primitive Views of the World.* Columbia University Press, New York, 1964.

Diamond, Stanley. "Introduction: The Uses of the Primitive." In Diamond, 1964.

————— . "The Search for the Primitive." In Montagu, 1968.

Dice, Lee R. *Man's Nature and Nature's Man.* Greenwood Press, Westport, Conn., 1973.

Dobb, Maurice. "Economic Thought: Socialist Thought," *International Encyclopedia of Social Sciences,* 1968.

Dobzhansky, Theodosius. *The Biology of Ultimate Concern.* New American Library, New York, 1967.

Dole, Gertrude E., and Robert L. Carneiro, eds. *Essays in the Science of Culture,* Thomas Y. Crowell, New York, 1960.

Doob, Leonard W. *Becoming More Civilized: A Psychological Exploration.* Yale University Press, New Haven, 1960.

Dorson, Richard M. *Folk Legends of Japan,* Charles E. Tuttle, Rutland, Vt., and Tokyo, 1962.

Dostoevsky, Fyodor. *The Brothers Karamazov.*

Douglas, Mary. *Natural Symbols: Explorations in Cosmology.* Random House, New York, 1970.

————— . "Deciphering a Meal," *Daedalus,* Winter 1972.

Downs, Robert B. *Books That Changed America.* Macmillan, New York, 1970.

Doxiadis, C. A. "Three Letters to an American," *Daedalus,* Summer 1972.

Droscher, Vitus B. *The Magic of the Senses: New Discoveries in Animal Perception.* E. P. Dutton, New York, 1969.

Dubos, Rene. *The Dreams of Reason: Science and Utopias.* New York, Columbia University Press, 1961.

————— . *So Human an Animal.* Charles Scribner's Sons, New York, 1968.

————— . "Is Man Overadapting to his Environment?" *Current* 128 (April, 1971), 34–39.

Dumond, D. E. "Population Growth and Cultural Change," *Southwestern Journal of Anthropology,* 21, 4 (1965), 302–324.

Durbin, E. F. M., and John Bowlby, "Personal Aggressiveness and War." In Bramson and Goethels, 1964.

Durkheim, Emil. *The Division of Labor in Society.* Free Press, New York, 1933.

Duverger, Maurice. *Modern Democracies: Economic Power vs. Political Power.* Holt, Rinehart and Winston, New York, 1974.

Dybikowski, James C. "Freedom and Docility: The Experimental College at Berkeley," *Soundings,* 51, 1 (Spring 1971).

Easton, Stewart C. *The Rise and Fall of Western Colonialism: A Historical Survey from the Early Nineteenth Century to the Present.* Frederick A. Praeger, New York, 1964.

Ebenstein, William, ed. *Political Thought in Perspective.* McGraw-Hill, New York, 1957.

Eberstadt, Nicholas. "Hunger and Ideology," *Commentary,* July 1981.

Eccles, Henry E. *Military Concepts and Philosophy.* Rutgers University Press, New Brunswick, N.J., 1965.

Eccles, Sir John. *The Brain and The Unity of Conscious Experience.* Cambridge University Press, Cambridge, 1965.

Ehrenwald J. "Neurosis in the Family: A Study of Psychiatric Epidemiology," *Archives of General Psychiatry,* Vol. III (1960).

Ehrlich, Paul, and Anne H. Ehrlich. *Population/Resources/Environment.* W. H. Freeman, San Francisco, 1970.

Eiseley, Loren. *The Firmament of Time.* Atheneum, New York, 1960.

——— . *The Mind as Nature.* Harper and Row, New York, 1962.

——— . *The Unexpected Universe.* Harcourt, Brace and World, New York, 1969.

Eisenstadt, S. N. *The Political Systems of Empires.* Free Press, New York, 1963.

——— . *Social Differentiation and Stratification.* Scott, Foresman, Glenview, Ill., 1971.

——— . "Post-Traditional Societies and the Continuity and Reconstruction of Tradition," *Daedalus,* Winter 1973.

Eisenstadt, S. N., ed. *Readings in Social Evolution and Development.* Pergamon Press, Oxford, 1966.

Eliade, Mircea. *The Quest: History and Meaning in Religion.* University of Chicago Press, Chicago and London, 1969.

Elias, Norbert. *The Civilizing Process: A History of Manners.* Urizen Books, New York, 1978.

Ellsberg, Daniel. "Laos: What Nixon Is up to," New York Review of Books, March 11, 1971.

Emerson, Ralph Waldo. "Nature" and "The American Scholar." In *The Heart of Emerson's Essays,* ed. Bliss Perry. Houghton Mifflin, Boston, 1933.

——— . *The Selected Writings of Ralph Waldo Emerson,* ed. Brooks Atkinson. Modern Library, New York, 1950.

Emerson, Rupert. "Colonialism: Political Aspects," *International Encyclopedia of the Social Sciences,* 1968.

Endleman, Robert. "Reflections on the Human Revolution," *Psychoanalytic Review,* Summer 1966.

Engles, Friedrich. "Engels on Hegel." In Ebenstein, 1957.

——— . "Excerpt from *The Origin of the Family, Private Property and the State.*" In Feuer 1959.

——— . "On Historical Materialism." In Feuer, 1959.

Epictetus. "The Discourses of Epictetus," *Britannica Great Books.*

Erikson, Erik. *Young Man Luther.* W. W. Norton, New York, 1958, 1962.

——— . *Gandhi's Truth: On the Origins of Militant Non-Violence.* W. W. Norton, New York, 1969.

——— . "Letter to Gandhi," *New York Review of Books,* July 31, 1969.

Erikson, Kai T. *Wayward Puritans: A Study in the Sociology of Deviance.* Wiley, New York, 1966.

——— . "A Return to Zero," *American Scholar,* Winter 1966–67.

Fairbank, John K. "On the Death of Mao," *New York Review of Books,* October 14, 1976.

Falk, Richard A. *Legal Order in a Violent World.* Princeton University Press, Princeton, 1968.

―――――― . "Arms Control, Foreign Policy and Global Reform," *Daedalus,* Summer 1975.

Farber, Seymour M., and R. H. L. Wilson, eds. *Man and Civilization: Control of the Mind: A Symposium.* Vol. 2. McGraw Hill, New York, 1963*a.*

―――――― . *The Potential of Women.* McGraw-Hill, New York, 1963*b.*

Federalist, by Alexander Hamilton, James Madison, and John Jay. Jacob E. Cooke, ed. Wesleyan University Press, Middletown, Conn., 1961.

Feifer, George. "Dark Side of Solzhenitsyn," *Harpers,* May 1980.

Fenichel, Otto. *The Psychoanalytic Theory of Neurosis.* W. W. Norton, New York, 1945.

Feuer, Louis S., ed. *Marx and Engels: Basic Writings on Politics and Philosophy.* Doubleday, New York, 1959.

Fieldhouse, D. K. *The Theory of Capitalist Imperialism.* Longman's, London, 1967.

―――――― . "Colonialism: Economic Aspects," *International Encyclopedia of the Social Sciences,* 1968.

Flannery, Kent V. "Archaeological Systems Theory and Early Mesoamerica." In Streuver, 1971.

―――――― . "The Cultural Evolution of Civilization," *Annual Review of Ecology and Systematics,* 8 (1972).

Florman, Samuel C. "In Praise of Technology," *Harper's,* November 1975.

Forbes, R. J. *The Conquest of Nature: Technology and its Consequences.* New American Library, New York, 1968.

Forster, E. M. "The Machine Stops." In Allen, 1971.

Frady, Marshall. "My Dream Came True. I Was Mr. Maddox," *New York Review of Books,* April 6, 1972.

Frankfort, H. et al. *Before Philosophy: The Intellectual Adventure of Ancient Man.* Penguin Books, Baltimore, 1946.

Frankl, Viktor. *Man's Search for Meaning.* Beacon Press, Boston, 1963.

―――――― . *The Will to Meaning: Foundations and Applications of Logotherapy.* World, New York, 1969.

Franz, M. L. von. "The Process of Individuation." In Jung et al., 1964.

Freedman, Jonathan L. "The Crowd: Maybe Not So Madding after All," *Psychology Today,* September 1971.

Freeman, Derek. "The Evolutionary Theories of Charles Darwin and Herbert Spencer," *Current Anthropology,* September 1974.

Freuchen, Peter. *Book of the Eskimos.* World, Cleveland, 1961.

Freud, Sigmund. *Totem and Taboo.* Routlege and Kegan Paul, London, 1950.

―――――― . *A General Selection from the Works of Sigmund Freud,* ed. John Rickman. Doubleday Anchor, Garden City, N.Y., 1957.

―――――― . *Beyond the Pleasure Principle.* Bantam Books, New York, 1959.

―――――― . *The Ego and the Id,* W. W. Norton, New York, 1960.

―――――― . *Civilization and Its Discontents,* W. W. Norton, New York, 1961.

―――――― . *Collected Papers.* Collier Books, New York, 1963.

―――――― . "Formulations Regarding the Two Principles in Mental Functioning." In Freud, 1963, Vol. IV.

―――――― . *The Future of an Illusion.* Doubleday, Garden City, N.Y., 1964.

―――――― . *The Origin and Development of Psychoanalysis.* Henry Regnery, Chicago, 1965.

―――――― . *An Outline of Psychoanalysis.* W. W. Norton, New York, 1969.

―――――― . *Group Psychology and the Analysis of the Ego.* W. W. Norton, New York, 1975.

Fried, Morton H. "On the Evolution of Social Stratification and the State." Bobbs-Merrill reprint from *Culture in History,* S. Diamond, ed., Columbia University Press, 1960.

―――――― . "Warfare, Military Organization and the Evolution of Society," *Anthropologica,* ser. 3 (1961), 134–147.

————— . *The Evolution of Political Society.* Random House, New York, 1967.

Fried, Morton, Marvin Harris, and Robert Murphy, eds. *War: The Anthropology of Armed Conflict and Aggression.* Natural History Press, Garden City, N.Y., 1968.

Friedenberg, Edgar Z. *Coming of Age in America: Growth and Acquiescence.* Random House, New York, 1965.

————— . "National Self-Abuse," *New York Review of Books,* June 4, 1970.

————— . "Dear Mr. Rockefeller," *New York Review of Books,* February 24, 1972.

Friedman, Milton. *Capitalism and Freedom.* University of Chicago Press, Chicago, 1962.

Frisch, Karl von. *Man and the Living World.* Trans. Elsa B. Lowenstein. Harcourt, Brace and World, New York, 1962.

Fromm, Erich. *Man for Himself.* Holt, Rinehart and Winston, New York, 1947.

————— . *The Anatomy of Human Destructiveness.* Holt, Rinehart and Winston, New York, 1973.

Fuller, Buckminster. *Utopia or Oblivion: The Prospects for Humanity.* Overlook Press, New York, 1969.

Furnass, S. Bryan. "Changes in Non-Infectious Diseases Associated with the Processes of Civilization." In Boyden, 1970.

Galbraith, John Kenneth. *The Affluent Society,* 2d ed. Houghton Mifflin, Boston, 1969.

Gallagher, J. and Robinson, R. "The Imperialism of Free Trade," in *The Economic History Review,* Ser. 2, VI, 1 (1953).

Gann, L. H. and Duignan, Peter. *Burden of Empire: An Appraisal of Western Colonialism in Africa South of the Sahara,* Hoover, Stanford, 1967.

Gartlan, J. Stephen. "Structure and Function in Primate Society," in Quiatt, 1972.

Geertz, Clifford. *The Religion of Java.* Free Press, Glencoe, Ill., 1960.

————— . "The Growth of Culture and the Evolution of Mind." In Scher, 1962.

————— . "The Impact of the Concept of Culture on the Concept of Man." In Platt, 1965.

————— . *Person, Time, and Conduct in Bali: An Essay in Cultural Analysis.* Cultural Report Series 14, Southeast Asia Studies, Yale University, New Haven, 1966.

————— . "Village," *International Encyclopedia of the Social Sciences,* 1968.

————— . "The Balinese Cockfight," *Daedalus,* Winter 1972.

Gerth, Hans, and C. Wright Mills. *Character and Social Structure.* Harcourt, Brace and World, New York, 1953.

————— . *From Max Weber: Essays in Sociology.* Oxford University Press, New York, 1958.

Gibson, McGuire. "Population Shift and the Rise of Mesopotamian Civilization." In Renfrew, 1973.

Giedion, Siegfried. *Mechanization Takes Command: A Contribution to Anonymous History.* W. W. Norton, New York, 1948.

Gillespie, C. C. *The Edge of Objectivity.* Princeton University Press, Princeton, 1960.

Ginsburg, Robert, ed. *The Critique of War.* Henry Regnery, Chicago, 1969.

Glacken, Clarence J. "Man against Nature: An Outmoded Concept." In Helfrich, 1970.

Goffart, Walter. *Barbarians and Romans.* Princeton University Press, Princeton, 1980.

Goffman, Irving. *Asylums: Essays on the Social Situation of Mental Patients and Other Inmates.* Aldine, Chicago, 1962.

Goldman, Irving. "Status Rivalry and Cultural Evolution in Polynesia," *American Anthropologist,* San Francisco, 1955.

Goldsmith, M. M. *Hobbes' Science of Politics.* Columbia University Press, New York, 1966.

Goodall, Jane. *See* Lawick-Goodall, Baroness Jane.

Goodman, Paul. *The Community of Scholars.* Random House, New York, 1962.

————— . *New Reformation: Notes of a Neolithic Conservative.* Random House, New York, 1970.

Goodsell, James Nelson. "Guatemala: Edge of an Abyss," *Current History,* February 1972.

346

Gordon, Donald F. "Value, Labor Theory of," *International Encyclopedia of the Social Sciences*, 1968.

Gordon, Lillian. "Beyond the Reality Principle: Illusion or New Reality," *American Imago*, 27, 2 (1970).

Gottwald, Norman K. "Sociological Theory as Ideology and Commitment to Social Change." MS.

Gould, Stephen Jay. *The Panda's Thumb*. W. W. Norton, New York, 1981.

Goulet, Denis. *The Cruel Choice*. Atheneum, New York, 1977.

Graubard, Mark. "The Frankenstein Syndrome: Man's Ambivalent Attitude to Knowledge and Power." Repr. for private circulation from *Perspectives in Biology and Medicine*, 10, 3 (1967).

Grayson, George W. "Peru under the Generals," *Current History*, February 1972.

Greenberg, Joseph H. *Universals of Language*. 2d ed. M.I.T. Press, Cambridge, Mass., 1966.

Gregg, Richard B. *The Psychology and Strategy of Gandhi's Non-Violent Resistance*. Garland, New York, 1972.

Grenier, Richard. "The Horror! The Horror!" Review of A. V. Antonov-Ovseyenko, *The Time of Stalin: Portrait of a Tyranny, New Republic*, May 26, 1982.

Gross, Bertram M. "An All-American 'Friendly Facism,'" *Current*, February 1971, from *Social Policy*, November-December 1970.

Grousset, René. *The Empire of the Steppes*. Rutgers University Press, Brunswick, N.J., 1970.

Gumplowicz, Ludwig. *Outlines of Sociology*, edited and with intro. by Irving L. Horowitz. Paine-Whitman, New York, 1963.

Habermas, Jurgen. *Knowledge and Human Interests*. Beacon Press, Boston, 1971.

Hacker, Andrew. "Cutting Classes," *New York Review of Books*, March 18, 1976.

Haldane, J. B. S. *The Causes of Evolution*. Cornell University Press, Ithaca, N.Y., 1966.

Hall, Calvin. "Cognitive Theory of Dream Symbols," *Journal of General Psychology*, 48 (1953), 169–186.

Hallowell, A. I. *Culture and Experience*, University of Pennsylvania Press, Philadelphia, 1955.

———— . "Self, Society, and Culture in Phylogenetic Perspective." In Tax, 1960.

Hamburg, David A. "Emotions in the Perspective of Human Evolution." In Washburn and Jay, 1968.

———— . "Recent Research on Hormonal Factors Relevant to Human Aggressiveness," *International Social Science Journal*, 23, 1 (1971).

Hamilton, Alexander. See *Federalist*.

Hammel, Eugene A., and William S. Simmons, eds. *Man Makes Sense: A Reader in Modern Cultural Anthropology*. Little Brown, Boston, 1970.

Hampshire, Stuart. "A New Philosophy of the Just Society," *New York Review of Books*, February 24, 1972.

Hanna, Thomas. *Bodies in Revolt*. Holt, Rinehart and Winston, New York, 1970.

Harding, D. W. "Your Move," in *New York Review of Books*, May 21, 1970.

Hardy, Sir Alister. *The Divine Flame*. Collins, London, 1966.

Hardy, A. C. *The Living Stream*. Harper and Row, New York, 1965.

Harlan, H. C., ed. *Readings in Economics and Politics*. Oxford University Press, New York, 1961.

Harner, M. J. "Population Pressure and the Social Evolution of Agriculturalists," *Southwestern Journal of Anthropology*, 26 (1970), 67–86.

Harrington, Michael. *The Accidental Century*. Macmillan, New York, 1965.

Harris, Marvin. *The Rise of Anthropological Theory: A History of Theories of Culture*. Thomas Y. Crowell, New York, 1968.

Hartman, Ernest. *The Biology of Dreaming*. Charles C. Thomas, Springfield, Ill., 1967.

Hartmann, H. *Ego Psychology and the Problem of Adaptation*. International University Press, New York, 1958.

Harva, Urpo. "War and Human Nature." In Ginsberg, 1969.

Haverfield, Francis John. "Roman Army," *Encyclopaedia Britannica*, 14th ed.

Hayek, Friedrich August. *The Road to Serfdom*. University of Chicago Press, Chicago, 1956.

————— . "The Primacy of the Abstract." In Koestler and Smythies, 1970.

Heilbroner, Robert. *The Worldly Philosophers*. Simon and Schuster, New York, 1961.

————— . "Do Machines Make History?" *Technology and Culture*, July 1967.

————— . *The Making of Economic Society*. 2d ed. Prentice-Hall, Englewood Cliffs, N.J., 1968.

————— . *The Economic Problem*, 2d ed. Prentice-Hall, Englewood Cliffs, N.J., 1970.

————— . "The Multinational Corporations and the Nation State," *New York Review of Books*, February 11, 1971.

————— . "Radical Conservative," Review of Barrington Moore, *Reflections on the Causes of Human Misery, New York Review of Books*, October 5, 1972.

————— . "Through the Marxian Maze," *New York Review of Books*, March 9, 1972.

Helfrich, Harold W., Jr., ed. *The Environmental Crisis: Man's Struggle to Live with Himself*. Yale University Press, New Haven, 1970.

Henry, Jules. *Culture against Man*. Random House, New York, 1963.

————— . "Culture, Personality and Evolution." In Montagu, 1962.

Herodotus. *The History of Herodotus*. Trans. George Rawlinson, ed. Manuel Komroff. Tudor Publishing Company, New York, 1928.

Hicks, John. *A Theory of Economic History*. Oxford University Press, Oxford, 1969.

Hillenbrand, Martin J. *Power and Morals*. Columbia University Press, New York, 1949.

Hinde, Robert A. "The Nature and Control of Aggressive Behaviour," *International Social Science Journal* (UNESCO) 23, 1 (1971).

Hitler, Adolph. "The Führer's Words." In Cooperman and Walter, 1962.

Hobbes, Thomas. *Leviathan: On the Matter, Form and Power of a Commonwealth Ecclesiastical and Civil*. Basil Blackwell, Oxford, 1960.

Hocart, A. M. *Social Origins*. London, 1954.

Hodgkin, Thomas. "Some African and Third World Theories of Imperialism." In Owen and Sutcliffe, 1972.

Hoebel, E. Adamson. *The Law of Primitive Man*. Harvard University Press, Cambridge, Mass., 1964.

Hoffmann, Stanley. "International Relations: The Long Road to Theory." Bobbs-Merrill Reprint Series in the Social Sciences PS-130, Indianapolis, 1959.

Hofstadter, Richard. *Social Darwinism in American Thought*. Beacon Press, Boston, 1955.

Holsti, Ole R. "Crisis, Stress and Decision-making," *International Social Science Journal* (UNESCO), 23, 1 (1971).

Holt, John. *How Children Fail*. Dell, New York, 1964.

————— . *The Underachieving School*. Dell, New York, 1970.

Homer. *The Iliad*. University of Chicago Press, Chicago, 1951.

Homo, Leon. *Roman Political Institutions*. Barnes and Noble, New York, 1962.

Hook, Sidney. *Towards the Understanding of Karl Marx: A Revolutionary Interpretation*. John Day, New York, 1933.

Hopper, Stanley Romaine, ed. *Spiritual Problems in Contemporary Literature*. Institute for Religious and Social Studies, Harper, New York, 1952.

Horowitz, David, ed., *Marx and Modern Economics*. MacGibbon and Kee, London, 1969.

————— . *Radical Sociology: An Introduction*. Canfield Press, San Francisco, 1971.

Hughes, H. Donald. *Ecology in Ancient Civilizations*. University of New Mexico Press, Albuquerque, 1975.

Human Variations and Origins: An Introduction to Human Biology and Evolution, W. H. Freeman, San Francisco, 1949–1967. Readings from *Scientific American*.

Hunt, Richard N. *The Political Ideas of Marx and Engels:* Vol. I *Marxism and Totalitarian Democracy 1818–1850.* University of Pittsburgh Press, Pittsburgh, 1974.

Huxley, Francis. *The Invisibles.* Rupert Hart-Davis, London, 1966.

The I Ching. Trans. Richard Wilhelm. Princeton University Press, Princeton, 1967.

Iriye, Akira. *Power and Culture: The Japanese American War 1941–1945.* Harvard University Press, Cambridge, Mass., 1981.

Iyeengar, B. K. S. *Light on Yoga: Yoga Dipika.* Schocken Books, New York, 1966.

Jackson, George. "Soledad Brother: Two Prison Letters from George Jackson" (intro. by Greg Armstrong), *New York Review of Books,* October 8, 1970.

Jaulin, Robert. "La Paix Blanche." Interview by Francoise Morin and Jacques Mousseau, *Psycholgoy Today,* (September 1971).

Jay, John. See *Federalist.*

Jefferson, Thomas. *Thomas Jefferson on Democracy,* ed. Saul K. Padover. Mentor Books, New York, 1939.

————— . "Jefferson on Plato." In Ebenstein, 1957.

Jervis, Robert. *Perception and Misperception in International Politics.* Princeton University Press, Princeton, 1976.

Johnson, Henry. "International Trade: Theory," *International Encyclopedia of the Social Sciences,* 1968.

Jordan, Ann T. "Semi-sedentary Hunters and Gatherers and the Beginnings of Agriculture." Mimeographed.

Jouvenel, Bertrand de. *On Power: Its Nature and the History of Its Growth.* Viking, New York, 1949.

Jung, C. G. *The Archetypes and the Collective Unconscious.* Bollingen Series 20, Pantheon Books, New York, 1959.

————— . "Archetypes of the Collective Unconscious." In Jung, 1959.

————— . "Conscious, Unconscious and Individuation." In Jung, 1959.

————— . *Memories, Dreams, Reflections.* Recorded and ed. Aniela Jaffe. Pantheon Books, Random House, New York, 1963.

————— . *Psychology and Religion: East and West.* Bollingen Series 20, Princeton University Press, Princeton, 1969.

Jung, Carl G., et al. *Man and His Symbols.* Doubleday, Garden City, New York, 1964.

Kahler, Erich. *The Tower and the Abyss: An Inquiry into the Transformation of the Individual.* George Braziller, New York, 1957.

————— . *Out of the Labyrinth: Essays in Clarification.* George Braziller, New York, 1967.

Kahn, Fritz. *The Human Body in Structure and Function.* Random House, New York, 1965.

Kahn, Roger. *The Battle for Morningside Heights: Why Students Rebel.* William Morrow, New York, 1970.

Kahn, Theodore H. *An Introduction to Hominology: The Study of the Whole Man.* C. C. Thomas, Springfield, Ill., 1972.

Kaplan, David. "The Law of Cultural Dominance." In Sahlins and Service, 1960.

Kaplan, Marcos. "The Power Structure in International Relations," *International Social Science Journal* (UNESCO), 26, 1, (1974).

Kapleau, Philip, ed., *The Three Pillars of Zen: Teaching, Practice and Enlightenment.* John Weatherhill, Tokyo, 1965.

Kapp, K. William. *The Social Costs of Private Enterprise.* Harvard University Press, Cambridge, Mass., 1950.

Kariel, Henry S., ed. *Frontiers of Democratic Theory.* Random House, New York, 1970.

349

Katchadourian, Hernan A. "Medical Perspectives on Adulthood," *Daedalus,* Spring 1976.

Keene, Donald, ed. *Anthology of Japanese Literature.* UNESCO Collection, Grover Press, New York, 1955.

Keller, Albert Galloway. *Societal Evolution: A Study of the Evolutionary Basis of the Science of Society.* Macmillan, New York, 1916.

Kempton, Murray. "The Damned," *New York Review of Books,* August 13, 1970.

————. "Cops." *New York Review of Books,* November 5, 1970.

————. "Truman and the Beast," *New York Review of Books,* March 11, 1971.

Kendall, Willmoore. "Social Contract," *International Encyclopedia of Social Sciences,* 1968.

Kenyatta, Jomo. *Facing Mount Kenya,* Vintage Books, New York, 1965.

Keynes, John Maynard. *The End of Laissez-Faire,* Leonard and Virginia Woolf, London, 1927.

King, Preston. *The Ideology of Order: A Comparative Analysis of Jean Bodin and Thomas Hobbes,* Barnes and Noble, New York, 1974.

Kipling, Rudyard. *Rudyard Kipling's Verse, Inclusive Edition 1885–1926.* Doubleday, Doran and Co., Garden City, New York, 1928.

Knorr, Klaus. *Power and Wealth: The Political Economy of International Power.* Basic Books, New York, 1973.

Koestler, Arthur. *The Yogi and the Commissar and Other Essays.* Macmillan, New York, 1946.

————. *The Invisible Writing.* Macmillan, New York, 1954.

————. *The Ghost in the Machine.* Macmillan, New York, 1967.

Koestler, Arthur, and Smythies, John Raymond, eds. *Beyond Reductionism: New Perspectives in the Life Sciences.* Macmillan, New York, 1970.

Komroff, Manuel. *The Great Fables of all Nations.* Tudor, New York, 1935.

Kostelanetz, Richard, ed. *Social Speculations: Visions for Our Time.* William Morrow, New York, 1971.

Krader, L. *Formation of the State.* Prentice Hall, Englewood Cliffs, N.J., 1968.

Kroeber, Alfred L. *An Anthropologist Looks at History* (foreword by Milton Singer; ed. Theodora Kroeber). University of California Press, Berkeley and Los Angeles, 1966.

Kuhn, Thomas. *The Structure of Scientific Revolutions.* University of Chicago Press, Chicago, 1970.

Kung-sun, Yang. *The Book of Lord Shang: A Classic of the Chinese School of Law.* Trans. Dr. J. J. L. Duyvendak. University of Chicago Press, Chicago, 1928 (repr. 1963).

Kuznets, Simon. "Modern Economic Growth: Findings and Reflections," *American Economic Review,* June 1974.

La Barre, Weston. *The Peyote Cult.* Schocken Books, New York, 1969.

————. "Materials for a History of Studies of Crisis Cults: A Bibliographic Essay," *Current Anthropology,* February 1971.

Laing, R. D. *The Politics of Experience.* Ballantine Books, New York, 1967.

Lambo, T. Adeoye. "Aggressiveness in the Human Life Cycle within Different Socio-cultural Settings," *International Social Science Journal* (UNESCO), 23, 1 (1971).

Lamont, Corliss. "Will Facism Arise in America?" *Current,* September 1971.

Landtman, Gunnar. *The Origin of the Inequality of the Social Classes.* Greenwood Press, New York, 1968.

Lasch, Christopher. "The Good Old Days," Review of Oscar Handlin and Mary Handlin, *Facing Life: Youth and the Family in American History, New York Review of Books,* February 10, 1972.

Laski, Harold J. *A Grammar of Politics.* George Allen and Unwin, Ltd., London 1967.

Lathrap, Donald W. "The 'Hunting' Economies of the Tropical Forest Zone of South America: An Attempt at Historical Perspective," in Lee and DeVore.

Laumann, Edward O., Siegel, Paul M. and Hodge, Robert W., eds. *The Logic of Social Hierarchies.* Markham Publishing Company, Chicago, 1970.

350

Laurer, Robert H. *Perspectives on Social Change*. Allyn and Bacon, Boston, 1973.

Lawick-Goodall, Baroness Jane Van. *My Friends the Wild Chimpanzees*. National Geographic Society, Washington, D.C., 1967.

———. *In the Shadow of Man*. Dell, New York, 1971.

Lawrence, D. H. *Studies in Classic American Literature*. Thomas Seltzer, New York, 1923.

Laszlo, Erwin, ed. *The World System: Models Norms Variations*. George Brazillier, New York, 1973.

Leach, Edmund. "Buddhism in the Post-Colonial Order in Burma and Ceylon," *Daedalus*, Winter 1973.

Leach, E. R. *Runaway World?* British Broadcasting Corporation, London, 1967.

Leacock, E. "Social Stratification and Evolutionary Theory: Introduction," *Ethnohistory*, 5 (1958) 193–199.

Lefebvre, Henri. *The Sociology of Marx*. (Trans. from French Norbert Guterman). Pantheon Books, New York, 1968.

———. *Everyday Life in the Modern World*. Allen Lane, Penguin Press, London, 1971.

Leiss, William. "Utopia and Technology: Reflections on the Conquest of Nature," *International Social Science Journal* (UNESCO), 22 (November 4, 1971).

Leites, Nathan. *Psychopolitical Analysis: Selected Writings of Nathan Leites*. Elizabeth W. Marvick, ed. Halsted Press, New York, 1977.

Lenczowski, John. "A Foreign Policy for Reaganauts," *Policy Review*, 13 (Fall, 1981).

Lenin, V. I. "Lenin on Marx." In Ebestein, 1957.

———. "The Success of the Bolsheviks." In Cooperman and Walter, 1962.

———. *Imperialism: The Highest Stage of Capitalism*. In Fieldhouse, 1967.

Lenski, Gerhard. *Power and Privilege: A Theory of Social Stratification*. McGraw-Hill, New York, 1966.

———. *Human Societies: A Macrolevel Introduction to Sociology*. McGraw-Hill, New York, 1970.

Leon, Paolo. *Structural Change and Growth in Capitalism: A Set of Hypotheses*. Johns Hopkins University Press, Baltimore, 1967.

Leontief, Wassily. "The Significance of Marxian Economics for Present Day Economic Theory." In Horowitz, 1969.

———. "Mysterious Japan: A Diary," *New York Review of Books*, June 4, 1970.

———. "The Trouble with Cuban Socialism," *New York Review of Books*, January 7, 1971.

———. "The Limits of Economics." Review of Robert Heilbroner, *Between Capitalism and Socialism*, *New York Review of Books*, July 20, 1972.

Lerner, Max. "Visions of the Apocalypse." Review of Jonathan Schell, *The Fate of the Earth*, *New Republic*, April 28, 1982.

Lesser, Alexander. "War and the State." In Fried et al., 1968.

Lester, Julius. *Black Folktales*. Richard W. Baron, New York, 1969.

Leuba, Clarence. *The Natural Man: As Inferred Mainly from Field Studies of Men and Chimpanzees*. Doubleday, Garden City, N.Y., 1954.

Levi-Strauss, Claude. "A Conversation with Claude Levi-Strauss," by Andre Akoun, Francoise Morin, and Jacques Mousseau. *Psychology Today*, May 1972.

Lewi, Michael. "Culture and Gender Roles: There's No Unisex in the Nursery," *Psychology Today*, May 1972.

Lewis, Bernard. *The Arabs in History*. Harper and Row, New York, 1966.

Lewis, C. S. *That Hideous Strength*. Macmillan, New York, 1946.

Lewy, Guenther. *Religion and Revolution*. Oxford University Press, New York, 1974.

Lichtheim, George. "Alienation," *International Encyclopedia of Social Science*, 1968.

———. *Imperialism*. Praeger, New York, 1971.

Lienhardt, G. *Divinity and Experience: The Religion of the Dinka*. Oxford University Press, Oxford, 1961.

Lifton, Robert Jay. *History and Human Survival*. Random House, New York, 1970.

351

Lindsay, A. D. *The Modern Democratic State,* Oxford University Press, New York, 1962.

Lipset, Seymour Martin. In Michels, 1966, "Introduction."

Lipset, Seymour Martin, and Richard B. Dobson. "The Intellectual as Critic and Rebel," *Daedalus,* Summer 1972.

Livingston, Arthur. In Mosca 1939, "Introduction."

Locke, John. *An Essay Concerning the True Original, Extent and End of Civil Government.* In *The English Philosophers from Bacon to Mill,* Edwin A. Burtt, ed. Modern Library, New York, 1939.

Lorenz, Konrad. Interview by Edwin Newman. Public Broadcasting System, November 28, 1971.

Lowen, Alexander. *The Language of the Body.* Collier Books, New York, 1958.

Lowi, Theodore J. *The End of Liberalism.* W. W. Norton, New York, 1969.

Lukacs, George. *History and Class Consciousness.* MIT Press, Cambridge, Mass., 1971.

Luttwak, Edward. *The Grand Strategy of the Roman Empire.* Johns Hopkins University Press, Baltimore, 1976.

Lynn, R. "Anxiety and Economic Growth," *Nature,* 219 (1968).

MacArthur, Robert H., and Joseph H. Connell, *The Biology of Populations.* John Wiley and Sons, New York, 1966.

McClelland, David C. *The Achieving Society.* D. Van Nostrand, Princeton, 1961.

McDermott, John. "Technology: The Opiate of the Intellectuals," *New York Review of Books,* July 31, 1969.

McFarland, Gerald W. "Notes on the New Left Historians," *Soundings,* 53, 4 (Winter 1970).

McHarg, Ian L. "The Plight." In Helfrich, 1970.

Machiavelli, Niccolò. *The Discourses.* Trans. with introduction and notes by Leslie J. Walker. Routledge and Kegan Paul, London, 1950.

Machlup, Fritz. "The Best Society: Efficiency and Equality." In Tinbergen et al., 1972.

MacIntyre, Alasdair. *Herbert Marcuse: An Exposition and a Polemic.* Viking Press, New York, 1971.

McKie, Ronald. *The Company of Animals: A Naturalist's Adventures in the Jungle of Malaysia.* Harcourt, Brace and World, New York, 1965.

MacLean, Paul D. "The Paranoid Streak in Man." In Koestler and Smythies, 1970.

MacLuhan, Marshall. *From Cliche to Archetype.* With Wilfred Watson, Viking Press, New York, 1970.

McNeill, William H. *The Rise of the West: A History of the Human Community.* University of Chicago Press, Chicago, 1963.

Madison, James. See *The Federalist.*

Maharishi Mahesh Yogi. *Transcendental Meditation: Serenity without Drugs.* New American Library, New York, 1963.

Mailer, Norman. *Miami and the Siege of Chicago.* World, New York, 1968.

Mair, Lucy. *Primitive Government.* Peter Smith, Gloucester, Maine, 1962.

Manning, Bayless. "Goals, Ideology and Foreign Policy," *Foreign Affairs,* January 1976.

Manuel, Frank E., and Fritzie P. Manuel. "Sketch for a Natural History of Paradise," *Daedalus,* Winter 1972.

Mao Tse-tung. "Combat Liberalism." In De Bary et al., 1960.

———. "The Dictatorship of the People's Democracy." In De Bary et al., 1960.

———. "On New Democracy." In De Bary et al., 1960.

———. "On the Correct Handling of Contradictions among the People." In De Bary et al., 1960.

Marcuse, Herbert. *Eros and Civilization: A Philosophical Inquiry into Freud.* Beacon Press, Boston, 1966.

———. *Negations: Essays in Critical Theory.* Beacon Press, Boston, 1969.

Marek, Kurt W. *Yestermorrow: Notes on Man's Progress,* translated from German by Ralph Mannheim, Alfred A. Knopf, New York, 1961.

Margalej, Ramon. *Perspectives in Ecological Theory*. University of Chicago Press, Chicago, 1968.

Markham, Jesse "Oligopoly." In *International Encyclopedia of Social Sciences*, 1968.

Marler, Peter. "Communication in Monkeys and Apes." In De Vore, 1965.

Marx, Karl. *Capital: A Critique of Political Economy*. Modern Library, New York, 1906.

—————. "Excerpt from A Contribution to the Critique of Political Economy." In Feuer, 1959.

—————. "Excerpts from *Capital: A Critique of Political Economy*." In Feuer, 1959.

—————. *The German Ideology*. International Publishers, New York, 1970.

—————. *Grundgrisse: Foundations of the Critique of Political Economy*. Trans. and with intro. by Martin Nicolaus. Random House, New York, 1973.

Marx, Karl, and Friedrich Engels. *The Communist Manifesto*. Penguin Books, Middlesex, England, 1967.

—————. "Economy and Society." In Horowitz, 1971.

Marx, Leo. *The Machine in the Garden: Technology and the Pastoral Ideal*. Oxford University Press, New York, 1964.

Masters, R. E. L. *Eros and Evil: The Sexual Psychopathology of Witchcraft*. Julien Press, New York, 1962.

Masters, R. E. L., and Jean Houston. *The Varieties of Psychedelic Experience*. Holt, Rinehart and Winston, New York, 1967.

Matson, Floyd W. *The Broken Image*. George Braziller, New York, 1964.

May, Rollo. *Man's Search for Himself*. W. W. Norton, New York, 1953.

—————. *Love and Will*. W. W. Norton, New York, 1969.

Mayer, John Robert. "The Transformation of the Role of Authority in the Modern World," *S. J. Philosopher's Index*, 8 (Summer/Fall 1970), 171–176.

Mbiti, John S. *African Religions and Philosophy*. Frederick A. Praeger, New York, 1969.

Mead, Margaret. *Continuities in Cultural Evolution*. Yale University Press, New Haven, 1964.

Meadows, Dennis L. "What Are Man's Prospects?" *Current*, October 1971. Repr. from *The Futurist*, August 1971.

Meerloo, Joost A. M. *Suicide and Mass Suicide*. E. P. Dutton, New York, 1962.

—————. *Unobstrusive Communication: Essays in Psycholinguistics*. Van Gorcum, Assen, the Netherlands, 1964.

Meier, Norman C. *Military Psychology*, Harper, New York, 1943.

Melman, Seymour. "The Big American Machine Breaks Down," *Nation*, March 20, 1972.

Mettler, Fred A. "Culture and the Structural Evolution of the Neural System." In Montagu, 1962.

Metzner, Ralph, ed. *The Ecstatic Vision*. Macmillan, New York, 1968.

Meyer, Alfred G. "Marxism," *International Encyclopedia of Social Sciences*, 1968.

Michaelson, Michael. "The Coming Medical War," *New York Review of Books*, July 1, 1971.

Michels, Robert. *Political Parties: A Sociological Study of the Oligarchical Tendencies of Modern Democracy*. Free Press, New York, 1966.

Mill, John Stuart. *On Liberty* in Edwin A. Burtt, *The English Philosophers From Bacon to Mill*, Modern Library, New York, 1939.

—————. *Essays on Politics and Culture*, Anchor Books, Garden City, New York, 1962.

Miller, David L. *Gods and Games*. The World Publishing Company, New York, 1970.

Miller, Hugh. *Progress and Decline: The Group in Evolution*. Pergamon Press, Oxford, 1964.

Miller, Neal E., et al. "The Frustration-Aggression Hypothesis." In Zawodny, 1966.

Milosz, Czeslaw. *Native Realm: A Search for Self-Definition*. Doubleday, Garden City, New York, 1968.

Mises, Ludwig von. *Human Action: a Treatise on Economics*. Yale University Press, New Haven, 1949.

—————. *Theory And History: An Interpretation of Social and Economic Evolution*. Yale University Press, New Haven, 1957.

Mishan, Ezra J. *The Costs of Economic Growth*. Frederick A. Praeger, New York, 1967.

Mitzman, Arthur. *The Iron Cage: An Historical Interpretation of Max Weber,* Alfred A. Knopf, New York, 1970.

Modupe, Prince. *I Was a Savage.* Museum Press, London, 1958.

Montagu, Ashley. *The Direction of Human Development.* Harper, New York, 1955.

————— . *On Being Human.* Hawthorne Books, New York, 1966.

————— . *Touching: The Human Significance of the Skin.* Columbia University Press, New York, 1971.

Montagu, M. F. Ashley, ed. *Culture and the Nature of Man.* Oxford University Press (Galaxy Books), New York, 1962.

————— . *The Concept of the Primitive.* Free Press, New York, 1968.

Morgan, Edmund S. "The American Revolution: Who Were 'The People'?" *New York Review of Books,* August 5, 1976.

Morgan, George W. "Human Studies: A New Direction for Thought and Education," *Soundings,* 54, 1 (Spring 1971).

Morgenthau, Hans J. "Historical Justice and the Cold War," *New York Review of Books,* July 10, 1969.

————— . *Politics among Nations,* Alfred A. Knopf, New York, 1972.

Morley, John. "Morley on Machiavelli." In Ebenstein, 1957.

Morton, Frederic. *The Rothchilds: A Family Portrait.* Atheneum, New York, 1962.

Mosca, Gaetano. *The Ruling Class.* McGraw-Hill, New York, 1939.

Mumford, Lewis. *The Story of Utopias.* Boni and Liveright, New York, 1922.

————— . *The City in History: Its Origins, Its Transformations, and Its Prospects.* Harcourt, Brace and World, New York, 1961.

Murdick, George Peter. "Evolution in Social Organization." In *Evolution and Anthroplogy: A Centennial Appraisal.* Theo Gauss and Sons, Washington, D.C., 1959.

Murphy, E. F. *Governing Nature.* Quadrangle Books, Chicago, 1967.

Nader, Ralph. "A Citizen's Guide to the American Economy," *New York Review of Books,* September 2, 1971.

Needler, Martin C. "A Critical Time for Mexico," *Current History,* February 1972.

Nef, John U. *War and Human Progress: An Essay on The Rise of Industrial Civilization.* Harvard University Press, Cambridge, Mass., 1950.

Neill, A. S. *Summerhill: A Radical Approach to Child Rearing.* Hart, New York, 1960.

Neumann, Franz. "Totalitarian Dictatorship." In Cooperman and Walter, 1962.

Nevins, Allen. *Study in Power: John D. Rockefeller, Industrialist and Philanthropist,* Vol. I. Charles Scribner's Sons, New York, 1953.

Newcomb, W. W., Jr. "Toward an Understanding of War." In Dole and Carneiro, 1960.

Ngugi, James, "The Independence of Africa and Cultural Decolonization," *The Courier,* (UNESCO), January 1971.

Nicolaus, Martin, and Talcott Parsons, "The Professional Organization of Sociology." In Colfax and Roach, 1971.

Nietzsche, Friederich. *The Genealogy of Morals.* Doubleday, Garden City, N.Y., 1956.

————— . *The Will to Power.* Random House, New York, 1967.

————— . *Beyond Good and Evil.* In *The Basic Writings of Nietzsche.* Modern Library, New York, 1968.

Nikhilananda, Swami. *Hinduism: Its Meaning for the Liberation of the Spirit.* Harper, New York, 1958.

Nisbet, Robert A. *Social Change and History: Aspects of the Western Theory of Development.* Oxford University Press, New York, 1969.

Nizam, Al-Mulk. *The Book of Government, or Rules for Kings.* Trans. from the Persian by Hubert Drake. Routledge and Kegan Paul, London, 1960.

Northrup, F. S. C. *The Meeting of East and West.* Collier Books, New York, 1946.

————— . "Man's Relation to the Earth in Its Bearing on His Aesthetic, Ethical and Legal Values." In Thomas, 1956.

Noy, Div. *Folktales of Israel.* University of Chicago Press, Chicago, 1963.

Noy, Pichas. "Cultural Patterns of Aggression." In Winnik et al., 1973.

Nussbaum, Frederick L. *The Triumph of Power and Reason 1665–85.* Harper, New York, 1953.

Nye, Wilbur Sturtevant. *Bad Medicine and Good: Tales of the Kiowas.* University of Oklahoma Press, Norman, 1962.

Oakeshott, Michael. In Hobbes, 1960, Introduction.

Odum, Eugene P. *Fundamentals of Ecology.* W. B. Saunders, Philadelphia, 1971.

———. "The Strategy of Ecosystem Development." In Boughey, 1973.

Odum, Howard T. *Environment, Power and Society.* John Wiley and Sons, New York, 1971.

Oparin, A. I. *Life: Its Nature, Origin, and Development.* Academic Press, New York, 1964.

Opler, Marvin. "Cultural Evolution and the Psychology of Peoples." In Dole and Carneiro, 1960.

Organski, A. F. K. "Power Transition," *International Encyclopedia of the Social Sciences,* 1968.

Organski, Katherine, and A. F. K. Organski. *Population and World Power.* Alfred A. Knopf, New York, 1961.

Osgood, Robert E., and Robert W. Tucker. *Force, Order and Justice.* Johns Hopkins University Press, Baltimore, 1967.

Otterbein, Keith F. "The Evolution of Zulu Warfare." In Bohannan, 1967.

———. *The Evolution of War.* HRAF Press, 1970.

Owen, Roger, and Bob Sutcliffe, eds. *Studies in the Threory of Imperialism.* Longman, London, 1972.

Packard, Vance. *The Hidden Persuaders.* David McKay, New York, 1957.

Papandreou, Andreas. "Speaking Freely." Interview by Edward Newman. Public Broadcasting System, May 7, 1972.

Papandreou, Andreas G., and John T. Wheeler. *Competition and Its Regulation.* Prentice-Hall, New York, 1954.

Parkinson, Cyril Northcote. *The Evolution of Political Thought.* Viking Press, New York, 1960.

Parsons, Talcott. "Certain Primary Sources and Patterns of Aggression in the Social Structure of the Western World." In Zawodny, 1966.

———. *Societies: Evolutionary and Comparative Perspectives.* Prentice-Hall, Englewood Cliffs, N.J., 1966.

———. "The Impact of Technology on Culture and Emerging New Modes of Behaviour," *International Social Science Journal* (UNESCO), 22 (November 4, 1971).

———. *The System of Modern Societies.* Prentice-Hall, Englewood Cliffs, N.J., 1971.

Paton, Alan. *Towards the Mountain: An Autobiography.* Scribner, New York, 1980.

Patinkin, Don. "Interest," *International Encyclopedia of the Social Sciences,* 1968.

Pepper, Stephen C. *World Hypotheses: A Study in Evidence.* University of California Press, Berkeley and Los Angeles, 1961.

Perls, Fritz, Ralph F. Hefferline, and Paul Goodman. *Gestalt Therapy: Excitement and Growth in the Human Personality.* Dell, New York, 1951.

Pettitt, George A. *Prisoners of Culture.* Charles Scribner's Sons, New York, 1970.

Pfeiffer, John E. *The Emergence of Man.* Harper and Row, New York, 1969.

———. "The First Food Crisis," *Horizon,* Autumn, 1975.

Phillips, A. P. "The Evolutionary Model of Human Society and Its Application to Certain Early Farming Populations of Western Europe." In Renfrew, 1973.

Piazzini, Guy. *The Children of Lilith.* Trans. from French by Peter Green. E. P. Dutton, New York, 1960.

Pigou, A. C. *The Economics of Welfare,* 4th ed. Macmillan, London, 1962.

Pilbeam, David, *The Evolution of Man.* Funk and Wagnalls, New York, 1970.

_____ . "The Fashionable View of Man as a Naked Ape Is: 1) An Insult to Apes; 2) Simplistic; 3) Male-oriented; 4) Rubbish," *New York Times Magazine*, September 3, 1972.

Platt, John R., ed. *New Views of the Nature of Man*. University of Chicago Press, Chicago, 1965.

Plumb, J. H. In Clark and Piggott, 1965, "Introduction."

Poppino, Rollie E. "Brazil: New Model for National Development?" *Current History*, February 1972.

Polanyi, Karl. *The Great Transformation*. Beacon Press, Boston, 1944.

_____ . *Primitive, Archaic and Modern Economies*, ed. George Dalton. Anchor Books, Garden City, N.Y., 1968.

Polanyi, Michael. *Personal Knowledge: Toward A Post-Critical Philosophy*. University of Chicago Press, Chicago, 1958.

Pollock, Francis. "Toward Protecting Consumers," *Columbia Journalism Review*, March/April 1974.

Price, A. Grenfell. *The Western Invasions of the Pacific and Its Continents*. Oxford, Clarendon Press, 1963.

Price, David. "Earth People," *Parabola*, Spring 1981

Pruitt, Dean G., and Richard C. Snyder, eds. *Theory and Research on the Causes of War*. Prentice-Hall, Englewood Cliffs, N.J., 1969.

Pulliam, H. Ronald, and Christopher Dunford. *Programmed to Learn: An Essay on the Evolution of Culture*. Columbia University Press, New York, 1980.

Quiatt, Duane D., ed. *Primates on Primates: Approaches to the Analysis of Nonhuman Primate Behavior*. Burgess, Minneapolis, 1972.

Radin, Paul. *Primitive Man as Philosopher*. Dover, New York, 1957.

Radinsky, Leonard. "Cerebral Clues," *Natural History*, May 1976.

Radomysler, A. "Welfare Economics and Economic Policy." In Arrow and Scitovsky, 1969.

Randal, Judith. "The Orphan Drug Games," *Science 82*, September 1982.

Ranke, Leopold. "The Great Powers." In Von Laue, *The Formative Years*, Princeton University Press, Princeton, N.J., 1950.

Rawls, John. *A Theory of Justice*. Belknap Press of Harvard University Press, Cambridge, Mass., 1971.

Redfield, Robert. *The Folk Culture of Yucatan*. University of Chicago Press, Chicago, 1941.

_____ . *The Primitive World and its Transformations*. Cornell University Press, Ithaca, N.Y., 1953.

Redl, Fritz. "The Superego in Uniform." In Sanford and Comstock, 1972.

Reich, Charles. *The Greening of America*. Excerpts in *The New Yorker*, September 26, 1970.

Reich, Wilhelm. *The Mass Psychology of Fascism*. Farrar, Straus and Giroux, New York, 1970.

Reiche, Reimut. *Sexuality and Class Struggle*. NLB, London, 1970.

Reischauer, Edwin O. and John K. Fairbank. *East Asia: The Great Tradition*. Houghton Mifflin, Boston, 1960.

Renault, Mary. *The King Must Die*, Pantheon, New York, 1958.

_____ . *Bull From the Sea*. Pantheon, New York, 1962.

Renfrew, Colin. *The Emergence of Civilization: The Cyclades and the Aegean in the Third Millennium B.C.*. Methuen, London, 1972.

Renfrew, Colin, ed. *The Explanation of Culture Change: Models in Prehistory*. Duckworth, London, 1973.

Renouvin, Pierre, and Jean-Baptiste Duroselle. *Introduction to the History of International Relations*. Praeger, New York, 1964.

Rensch, Bernhard. *Homo Sapiens: From Man to Demigod.* Columbia University Press, New York, 1972.

Reuck, A. V. S. de and Ruth Porter, eds. *Ciba Foundation Symposium: Transcultural Psychiatry.* Little Brown, Boston, 1965.

Rice, Eugene F., Jr. *The Foundations of Early Modern Europe, 1460–1559.* W. W. Norton, New York, 1970.

Ricoeur, Paul. "The Control of Power." In Cooperman and Walter, 1962.

Ridgeway, James. *The Closed Corporation.* Random House, New York, 1968.

Rieff, Philip. *The Triumph of the Therapeutic: Uses of Faith After Freud.* Harper and Row, New York, 1966.

Rifkin, Jerome. *Entropy.* Viking Press, New York, 1980.

Robinson, Joan. *An Essay on Marxian Economics.* St. Martin's Press, New York, 1966.

Roddam, John. *The Changing Mind.* Jonathan Cape, London, 1966.

Roe, Anne, and George Gaylor Simpson, eds. *Behavior and Evolution.* Yale University Press, New Haven, 1958.

Roe, Derek. *Prehistory: An Introduction.* University of California Press, Berkeley and Los Angeles, 1970.

Rogin, Michael Paul. "Liberal Society and the Indian Question," *Politics and Society,* May 1971a.

———. "Max Weber and Woodrow Wilson: The Iron Cage in Germany and America," reprinted from *Polity,* 3, 4 (1971b).

———. *Fathers and Children: Andrew Jackson and the Subjugation of the American Indian.* Random House, New York, 1976.

Roheim, Geza. *The Origin and Function of Culture,* Nervous and Mental Disease Monographs. New York, 1943; (repr. Johnson Reprint, 1968).

Robartz, Phillipe. "Aggressive Behaviour and Social Behaviour in Animals," *International Social Science Journal* (UNESCO), 23, 1, 1971.

Röpke, Wilhelm. "Collectivism and the Human Spirit." In Cooperman and Walter, 1962.

Rosen, Kurth, ed. *Testing Theories of Economic Imperialism.* Lexington Books, Lexington, Mass., 1974.

Rosenberg, Charles E. *The Family in History.* University of Pennsylvania Press, Philadelphia, 1975.

Roslansky, John D., ed. *The Uniqueness of Man.* North-Holland Publishing, Amsterdam and London, 1969.

Ross, Leonard. "The Myth that Things Are Getting Better," *New York Review of Books,* August 12, 1972.

Rostow, Eugene V. "America, Europe and the Middle East," *Commentary,* February 1974.

Rostow, W. W. *Politics and the Stages of Growth.* Cambridge University Press, Cambridge 1971.

Roszak, Theodore. *The Making of a Counter-Culture,* Doubleday, New York, 1969.

———. "In Search of the Miraculous," *Harpers,* January 1980.

Rothblatt, Ben, ed. *Changing Perspectives on Man.* University of Chicago Press, Chicago, 1968.

Rothman, Stanley, and Phillip Isenberg. "Freud and Jewish Marginality," *Encounter,* December 1974.

Rothmyer, Karen. "Citizen Scaife," *Columbia Journalism Review,* August/September, 1981.

Rothschild, Emma. "GM in More Trouble," *New York Review of Books,* March 23, 1972.

Rougemont, Denis de. *Man's Western Quest.* Harper, New York, 1957.

Rousseau, Jean Jacques. *A Discourse on the Origin of Inequality.* In *The Social Contract and the Discourses.* E. P. Dutton and Company, New York, 1950.

Rowe, John Howland. "A Social Theory of Cultural Change," *Kroeber Anthropological Society Papers,* 26 (1962), 75–80.

Rubel, Maximilian. "Marx, Karl," *International Encyclopedia of Social Sciences,* 1968.

Ruckelshaus, William. "Yes—The Environment Can Be Saved," *Saturday Review World*, December 14, 1974.

Russell, W. M. S. and C. Russell. *Violence, Monkeys and Man*. Macmillan, London, 1968.

Sagan, Eli. *The Lust to Annhilate: A Psychoanalytic Study of Violence in Ancient Greek Culture*. Psychohistory Press, New York, 1979.

Sahlins, Marshall D. *Social Stratification in Polynesia*. University of Washington Press, Seattle, 1958.

———. "The Social Life of Monkeys, Apes and Primitive Man." In Quiatt, 1972.

———. *Stone Age Economics*. Aldine Atherton, Chicago, 1972.

Sahlins, Marshall D., and Elman R. Service, eds. *Evolution and Culture*, University of Michigan Press, Ann Arbor, 1960.

Sampson, Ronald. *The Psychology of Power*. Pantheon, New York, 1966.

Sanday, Peggy Reeves. "The Sociocultural Context of Rape," *Journal of Social Issues*, 3, 4 (1981).

Sanford, Nevitt. "Authoritarianism and Social Destructiveness." In Sanford et al., 1971.

Sanford, Nevitt, Craig Comstock, et al. *Sanctions for Evil*. Jossey-Bass, San Francisco, 1971.

Santayana, George. "The Irony of Liberalism." In Cooperman and Walter, 1962.

Schachter, Rabbi Zalman M. "The Conscious Ascent of the Soul." In Metzner, 1968.

Schaller, George B. *The Year of the Gorilla*. Ballantine Books, New York, 1964.

Schapiro, Leonard. "Russia: The Pursuit of the Extreme," *New York Review of Books*, November 25, 1976.

Schelling, Thomas. *The Strategy of Conflict*. Galaxy, New York, 1963.

Scher, Jordan M. *Theories of the Mind*. Free Press, New York, 1962.

Schiller, Herbert I. *Mass Communications and American Empire*, Augustus M. Kelley, New York, 1969.

Schmookler, Andrew. "The Parable of the Tribes: The Problem of Power in Social Evolution." Ph.D. diss., University of California, Berkeley, 1977.

Schmookler, Jacob. *Invention and Economic Growth*. Harvard University Press, Cambridge, Mass., 1967.

Schorske, Carl E. "Weimar and the Intellectuals I," *New York Review of Books*, May 7, 1971.

Schultz, Adolph H. *The Life of Primates*. Universe Books, 1969, New York.

Schumpeter, Joseph. "Capitalism." In *Encyclopaedia Britannica*, 14th ed.

Schumpeter, Joseph. "On Imperialism." In Boulding and Murkerjee, 1972.

Schweitzer, Albert. *On the Edge of the Primeval Forest*. A & C Black, London, 1928.

———. *The Philosophy of Civilization*. Macmillan, New York, 1960.

Schweitzer, Arthur. "Economic Systems and Economic History," *Journal of Economic History*, 25, (4) (1965), 660–679.

Scitovsky, Tibor, "Two Concepts of External Economies." In Arrow and Scitovsky, 1969.

Scott, Mary. "Axles, Time, and the Pineal Gland," *Theoria to Theory*, 4, 1 (1970).

Seligman, Ben B. *Permanent Poverty*. Quadrangle Books, Chicago, 1968.

———. "The State of Social Science," *Commentary*, October 1968, pp. 76–79.

Semmel, Bernard. *The Rise of Free Trade Imperialism*, Cambridge University Press, Cambridge, 1970.

Sennett, Richard. "Survival of the Fattest," in *New York Review of Books*, August 13, 1970.

Sennett, Richard, and Jonathan Cobb. "Betrayed American Workers," in *New York Review of Books*, October 5, 1972.

Servan-Schreiber, Jean-Jacques. *The Radical Alternative*. Macdonald, London, 1970.

Service, Elman R. *A Profile of Primitive Culture*. Harper, New York, 1958.

———. *Primitive Social Organization: An Evolutionary Perspective*. Random House, New York, 1962.

———. *The Hunters*, Prentice-Hall, Englewood Cliffs, N.J., 1966.

————. *Cultural Evolutionism: Theory in Practice.* Holt, Rinehart and Winston, New York, 1971.

————. *Origins of the State and Civilization: The Process of Cultural Evolution.* W. W. Norton, New York, 1975.

Seward, Desmond. *The Monks of War.* Paladin, Suffolk, 1972.

Shah, Indries. *Tales of the Dervishes.* E. P. Dutton, New York, 1967.

————. *Caravan of Dreams.* Octagon Press, London, 1968.

————. *Wisdom of the Idiots.* Octagon Press, London, 1969.

Shapiro, Samuel. "Uruguay's Lost Paradise," *Current History,* February 1972.

Shaw, George Bernard. *Seven Plays.* Dodd, Mead, New York, 1951.

Sheehan, Neil. Review of Gen. Maxwell Taylor, *Swords and Plowshares, New York Review of Books,* April 9, 1972.

Shils, Edward. "Charisma," *International Encyclopedia of Social Sciences,* 1968.

Silber, John R. "The Population of Time," *Center Magazine,* September/October 1971.

Silberg, Richard. *The Devolution of the People.* Harcourt, Brace and World, New York, 1967.

Sills, Yole G. "Social Science Fiction," *International Encyclopedia of Social Sciences,* 1968.

Simeons, Albert T. *Man's Presumptuous Brain: An Evolutionary Interpretation of Psychosomatic Diseases.* E. P. Dutton, New York, 1961.

Simpson, Dwight, J. "Turkey: A Time of Troubles," *Current History,* January 1972.

Simpson, George Gaylord. "The Biological Nature of Man." In Washburn and Jay, 1968.

Sinari, Ramakant. "The Problem of Human Alienation," *Philosophy and Phenomenological Research,* 31 (September 1970), 123–130.

Singer, Peter. "Bioethics: The Case of the Fetus," *New York Review of Books,* August 5, 1976.

Sinnott, E. W. *Cell and Psyche: The Biology of Purpose.* University of North Carolina Press, Chapel Hill, 1950.

————. *The Problem of Organic Form.* Yale University Press, New Haven, 1963.

Slater, Philip E. "Cultures in Collision," *Psychology Today,* July 1970.

————. *The Pursuit of Loneliness: American Culture at the Breaking Point.* Beacon Press, Boston, 1970.

Smelser, Neil J., and William T. Smelser, eds. *Personality and Social Systems.* John Wiley and Sons, New York, 1963.

Smith Adam. *The Wealth of Nations.* Modern Library, New York, 1937.

Smith, David E. "Symposium: Psychedelic Drugs and Religion," *Journal of Psychedelic Drugs,* I, 2, (1967–1968), 45–71.

Smith, Gaddis. Review of Joyce and Gabriel Kolko, *The Limits of Power: The World and United States Foreign Policy, 1945–1954, New York Times Book Review,* February 27, 1972.

Smith, Hedrick. *The Russians.* Quadrangle, New York, 1976.

Snow, Alpheus Henry. *The Question of Aborigines: In the Law and Practice of Nations.* G. P. Putnam's Sons, New York, 1921.

Snow, C. P. "C. P. Snow: How the Bomb Was Born," *Discover,* August 1981.

Solovyov, Vladimir, and Elena Klepikova. "Dual Power in the Kremlin: Pragmatists and Princes," *Antioch Review,* Summer 1982.

Sorokin, Pitirim A. *Social and Cultural Dynamics: Basic Problems, Principles and Methods,* Vol. IV. American Book, New York, 1941.

Spain, James W. *The Way of the Pathans.* Robert Hale, London, 1962.

Spengler, Oswald. *The Decline of the West.* Abridged ed. Alfred A. Knopf, New York, 1962.

Sprout, Harold H. *The Ecological Perspective on Human Affairs, with Special Reference to International Politics.* Princeton University Press, Princeton, 1965.

Sprout, Harold, and Margaret Sprout. "Rising Demands and Insufficient Resources." In Boulding and Murkerjee, 1972.

Spuhler, J. N., ed. *The Evolution of Man's Capacity for Culture.* Wayne State University Press, Detroit, 1959.

Stalin, Joseph. "Foundations of Leninism." In Cooperman and Walter, 1962.

Stark, W. "Natural and Social Selection." In Banton, 1961.

Starr, Roger. "Mumford's Utopia," *Commentary,* June 1976.

Steel, Ronald. "Did Anyone Start the Cold War?" *New York Review of Books,* September 27, 1971.

————. Review of Richard J. Barnet, *The Roots of War, New York Times Book Review,* June 11, 1972.

Stein, Maurice R., Arthus J. Vidich, and David Manning White, eds. *Identity and Anxiety: Survival of the Person in Mass Society.* Free Press, Glencoe, Ill., 1960.

Steward, Julian H. *Theory of Culture Change: The Methodology of Multilinear Evolution.* University of Illinois Press, Urbana, 1955.

Stewart, Douglas J. "Morality, Mortality and the Public Life: Aeneas the Politician," *The Antioch Review,* 32, 4 (1973).

Stigler, George J. "Competition," *International Encyclopedia of Social Sciences,* 1968.

Stone, I. F. "The Test Ban Comedy," *New York Review of Books,* May 7, 1970.

————. "In the Bowels of Behemoth," *New York Review of Books,* March 11, 1971.

————. "Can Russia Change," *New York Review of Books,* February 24, 1972.

Stone, Lawrence. "The Disenchantment of the World," *New York Review of Books,* December 2, 1971.

Strauss, Leo. *Natural Right and History.* University of Chicago Press, Chicago, 1953.

————. *What Is Political Philosophy.* Free Press, Glencoe, Ill., 1959.

Strayer, Joseph Reese, ed. *The Interpretation of History.* Princeton University Press, Princeton, 1943.

Streuver, Stuart P., ed. *Prehistoric Agriculture.* American Museum Sourcebooks in Anthropology. Natural History Press, Garden City, N.Y., 1971.

Sullivan, J. W. N. *The Limitations of Science.* Mentor Book, New York, 1933; repr. (1959).

Sullivan, Richard E. *Heirs of the Roman Empire.* Cornell University Press, Ithaca, N.Y. 1960.

Sumner, William Graham. *Social Darwinism: Selected Essays.* Prentice-Hall, Englewood Cliffs, N.J., 1963.

Suttles, Wayne. "Subhuman and Human Fighting," *Anthropologica,* 3, 2 (1969), 148–163.

Sweezy, Paul M. *Theory of Capitalist Development: Principles of Marxian Political Economy.* Monthly Review Press, New York, 1956.

————. "Growing Wealth, Declining Power," *Monthly Review,* March 1974.

Sypher, Wylie. *Loss of the Self in Modern Literature and Art.* Random House, New York, 1962.

Szasz, Thomas S. *The Manufacture of Madness: A Comparative Study of the Inquisition and the Mental Health Movement.* Harper and Row, New York, 1970.

Talmon, J. L. *The Origins of Totalitarian Democracy.* Frederick A. Praeger, New York, 1960.

Tarrant, John J. *Drucker: The Man Who Invented the Corporate Society.* Cahners Books, Boston, 1976.

Tatu, Michel. "The Devolution of Power," *Foreign Affairs,* July 1975.

Tawney, R. H. *The Acquisitive Society.* Harcourt, Brace and World, New York, 1948.

————. In Weber, 1958, Foreword.

Tax, Sol, ed. *Evolution after Darwin,* Vol. II, *The Evolution of Man: Man, Culture and Society.* University of Chicago Press, Chicago, 1960.

Taylor, A. J. P. "Rational Wars," *New York Review of Books,* November 4, 1971.

Terkel, Studs. "Servants of the State," *Harpers,* February 1972. Conversations with Daniel Ellsberg and Tony Russo.

The Texts of Taoism. Trans. James Legge, introduction by D. T. Suzuki. Julian Press, New York, 1959.

Theobald, Robert. *An Alternative Future for America.* Swallow Press, Chicago, 1968.

Thieme, Frederick P. "The Biological Consequences of War." In Fried et al., 1968.

Thoman, Roy E. "Iraq under Baathist Rule," *Current History,* January 1972.

Thomas, Lewis. *Lives of a Cell.* Bantam Books, New York, 1974.

————— . "Debating the Unknowable," *Atlantic Monthly,* July, 1981.

Thomas, William L., Jr., ed., *Man's Role in Changing the Face of the Earth.* University of Chicago Press, Chicago, 1956.

Thompson, William Irwin. "Alternative Realities," *New York Times Book Review,* February 13, 1972.

Thoreau, Henry David. "Economy." In Harlan, 1961.

Thorpe, W. H. *Learning and Instinct of Animals.* Harvard University Press, Cambridge, Mass., 1963.

————— . *Science, Man and Morals.* Metheuen, London, 1965.

————— . "Vitalism and Organicism." In Roslansky, 1969.

Thucydides. *The Peloponnesian War.* Trans. Richard Crawley. Modern Library, New York, 1951.

Tierney, Brian, Donald Kagan, and L. Pearce Williams, eds. *Great Issues in Western Civilization.* Vol. 2. Random House, New York, 1972.

Tiger, Lionel. "Understanding Aggression," *International Social Science Journal* (UNESCO) 23, 1, (1971), Introduction.

Tiger, Lionel, and Robin Fox. *The Imperial Animal.* McClelland and Stewart, Toronto, 1971.

————— . "The Primate Pilgrimage: From Bananas to Ballots," *Psychology Today,* February 1972.

Tillich, Paul. "You Are Accepted." Mimeograph.

Tinbergen, Jan. "Some Features of the Optimum Regime." In Tinbergen et al, 1972.

Tinbergen, Jan, et al. *Optimum Social Welfare and Productivity.* New York University Press, New York, 1972.

Tocqueville, Alexis de. *Democracy in America.* Vintage Books, Random House, New York, 1945.

Townsend, Robert. Review of Robert Heilbroner et al., *In the Name of Profit, New York Times Book Review,* April 30, 1972.

Toynbee, Arnold. *A Study of History,* Vol. II, *Pre-Genesis of Civilization.* Oxford University Press, Oxford, 1963.

————— . "Technical Advance and the Morality of Power." In Urban, 1971.

Trevor-Roper, H. R. *The Crisis of the Seventeenth Century: Religion, the Reformation and Social Change.* Harper and Row, New York, 1967.

Trewartha, Glenn T. *A Geography of Population: World Patterns.* John Wiley and Sons, New York, 1969.

Trotsky, Leon. "Their Morals and Ours." In Cooperman and Walter, 1962.

Tucker, Robert W. "Professor Morgenthau's Theory of Political Realism." Bobbs-Merrill reprint series in the Social Sciences, PS–287, 1952 (from *American Political Science Review*).

————— . "Equalitarianism and International Politics," *Commentary,* September 1975.

————— . "Swollen State, Spent Society: Stalin's Legacy to Brezhnev's Russia," *Foreign Affairs,* Winter 1981–82.

Turnbull, Colin M. *The Forest People.* Simon and Schuster, New York, 1962.

————— . "The Lesson of the Pygmies," *Human Variations,* 1947–67 (1963).

————— . "Human Nature and Primal Man," *Social Research,* Autumn 1973.

Tyson, Alan. "Homage to Catatonia," *New York Review of Books,* February 11, 1971.

UNESCO. *Human Rights: Comments and Interpretations.* Columbia University Press, New York, 1949.

United Nations University Newsletter. July 1977.

Urban, G. R., ed. *Can We Survive Our Future? A Symposium.* St. Martin's Press, New York, 1971.

Vagts, Alfred. *The History of Militarism.* W. W. Norton, New York, 1937.

Van Doren, Carl C. *Benjamin Franklin.* Greenwood, New York, 1938.

Vayda, Andrew P. "Expansion and Warfare among Swidden Agriculturalists," *American Anthropologist* (n.s.), 63, (2), pt. 1, (1961), 346–358.

_____ . "War, Primitive," *International Encyclopedia of the Social Sciences,* 1968.

Verlinden, Charles. *The Beginnings of Modern Colonization.* Cornell University Press, Ithaca, N.Y., 1970.

Vogel, Ezra. *Japan as Number One.* Harvard University Press, Cambridge, Mass. 1979.

Vogel, E. F., and N. W. Bell. "The Emotionally Disturbed Child as a Family Scapegoat," *Psychoanalysis and the Psychoanalytic Review,* 47 (1960).

Von Laue, Theodore H. *Leopold Ranke: The Formative Years.* Princeton University Press, Princeton, 1950.

Waddington, C. H. *The Ethical Animal.* George Allen and Unwin, London, 1960.

_____ . "The Human Evolutionary System." In Banton, 1961.

Wagner, Richard H. *Environment and Man.* W. W. Norton, New York, 1971.

Waite, Robert G. L. *The Psychopathic God: Adolph Hitler.* Basic Books, New York, 1977.

Wallace, Anthony F. C. "Dreams and the Wishes of the Soul: A Type of Psychoanalysis Theory among the Seventeenth-Century Iroquois." Repr. from *American Anthropologist,* 60 (April 1958).

_____ . "Religious Revitalization: A Function of Religion in Human History and Evolution." In Hammel and Simmons, 1970.

Wallerstein, Immanuel. *The Modern World System: Capitalist Agriculture and the Origin of the European World Economy in the Sixteenth Century.* Academic Press, New York, 1974.

Waltz, Kenneth N. *Man, the State and War: A Theoretical Analysis.* Columbia University Press, New York, 1959.

Walzer, Michael. "Regicide and Revolution," *Social Research,* Winter 1973.

Ward, Barbara, and Rene Dubos. *Only One Earth.* W. W. Norton, New York, 1972.

Ward, John William. "Violence, Anarchy, and Alexander Berkman," *New York Review of Books,* November 5, 1970.

Washburn, Sherwood L. "Behaviour and the Origin of Man." The Huxley Memorial Lecture, 1967. Repr.

_____ . "The Study of Human Evolution." *Condon Lectures.* Oregon State System of Higher Education, Eugene, Oreg., 1968.

_____ . "Human Evolution." Talk given on Voice of America, March 1972. Mimeograph.

Washburn, S. L., and Phyllis C. Jay, eds. *Perspectives on Human Evolution.* Holt, Rinehart and Winston, New York, 1968.

Watson, Burton. *Han Fei Tzu: Basic Writings.* Columbia University Press, New York, 1964.

Watt, Kenneth E. F. *Principles of Environmental Science.* McGraw-Hill, New York, 1973.

Webb, Lee. "Computerized Police Systems in the U.S.?" *Current,* September 1972.

Weber, Max. "The Social Causes of the Decay of Ancient Civilization," *Journal of General Education,* October 1950.

_____ . *The Protestant Ethic and the Spirit of Capitalism.* Charles Scribner's Sons, New York, 1958.

Webster, David. "Warfare and the Evolution of the State: A Reconsideration," *American Antiquity* 40, 4 (1975).

Weil, Andrew. *The Natural Mind.* Houghton and Mifflin, Boston, 1972.

Weiner, Herbert. *9½ Mystics: The Kabala Today.* Holt, Rinehart and Winston, New York, 1969.

Weiss, Paul A. "The Living System: Determinism Stratified." In Koestler and Smythies, 1970.

Weisskopf, Walter A. *The Psychology of Economics.* University of Chicago Press, Chicago, 1955.

———. *Alienation and Economics.* E. P. Dutton, New York, 1971.

———. "The Image of Man in Economics," *Social Research,* Autumn 1973.

Wendt, Herbert. *In Search of Adam: The Story of Man's Search for Truth About his Earliest Ancestors.* Houghton Mifflin, Boston, 1956.

West, Raynard. *Conscience and Society: A Study of the Psychological Prerequisites of Law and Order.* Emerson Books, New York, 1945.

Wheelis, Allen. *The End of the Modern Age.* Basic Books, New York, 1971.

———. "In the Reign of the King of Whirl: The Conditions of Morality," *Antioch Review* 22, 4 (1974).

Whitcomb, David K. *Externalities and Welfare.* Columbia University Press, New York, 1972.

White, K. Geoffrey, Joseph B. Juhasz, and Peter J. Wilson. "Is Man No More than This? Evaluative Bias in Interspecies Comparison," *Journal of the History of the Behavioral Sciences* (July 1973), 203–212.

White, Leslie. *The Science of Culture: A Study of Man and Civilization.* Grove Press, New York, 1949.

———. *The Evolution of Culture: The Development of Civilization to the Fall of Rome.* Grove Press, New York, 1959.

White, Lynn. "The Historical Roots of our Ecological Crisis," *Science,* March 10, 1967.

Whitehead, Alfred North. *Nature and Life.* University of Chicago Press, Chicago, 1934.

Whitehead, Lawrence. "Bolivia Swings Right," *Current History,* February 1972.

Whitney, Thomas P. "Russian Imperialism Today." In Boulding and Murkerjee, 1972.

Whole Earth Catalogue. Portola Institute, Santa Barbara, Calif., 1969.

Whorf, Benjamin Lee. *Language, Thought, and Reality: Selected Writing of Benjamin Lee Whorf.* J. B. Carroll, ed. Technology Press of the Massachusetts Institute of Technology, Cambridge, Mass., 1956.

Whyte, William H., Jr. *The Organization Man.* Simon and Schuster, New York, 1956.

Wicker, Tom. "The Politics Before Us," *New York Review of Books,* February 11, 1971.

Wiener, Norbert. *The Human Use of Human Beings.* Doubleday, Garden City, N.Y., 1954.

Williams, William Appleman. "Ol' Lyndon," *New York Review of Books,* December 16, 1971.

Winnik, Heinrich Z., Raphael Moses, and Mortimer Ostow, eds., *Psychological Bases of War.* Quadrangle, New York, 1973.

Winslow, Earle M. *The Pattern of Imperialism: A Study in the Theories of Power.* Columbia University Press, New York, 1948.

Wittfogel, Karl A. "Developmental Aspects of Hydraulic Societies." In Streuver, 1971.

Wolff, H. G., et al. *Stress and Disease.* Charles C. Thomas, Springfield, Ill., 1968.

Wolman, Benjamin, ed. *The Psychoanalytic Interpretation of History.* Basic Books, New York, 1971.

Woodhouse, Edward J. "Re-Visioning the Future of the Third World: An Ecological Perspective on Development," *World Politics,* 25, 1 (October 1972).

Woodruff, William. *The Impact of Western Man: A Study of Europe's Role in the World Economy 1750–1960.* St. Martin's Press, New York, 1966.

Woodward, C. Vann. "Our Own Herrenvolk," *New York Review of Books,* August 12, 1972.

Woolf, Leonard. *Imperialism and Civilization.* Harcourt Brace, New York, 1928.

Wooldridge, Dean E. *The Machinery of the Brain.* McGraw Hill, New York, 1963.

———. *Mechanical Man: The Physical Basis of Intelligent Life.* McGraw Hill, New York, 1968.

Wright, Benjamin Fletcher. Introduction to *The Federalist,* by Hamilton, Madison and Jay. Belknap Press, Harvard University Press, Cambridge, Mass., 1966.

Wright, Henry T., and Gregory A. Johnson. "Population, Exchange and Early State Formation in Southwestern Iran," *American Anthropologist,* 77, 2 (1975).

Wright, Quincy. *A Study of War.* 2d ed. University of Chicago Press, Chicago, 1965.

Wrong, Dennis. "The Oversocialized Conception of Man in Modern Sociology." In Smelser and Smelser, 1963.

———. "The Functional Theory of Stratification: Some Neglected Considerations." In Laumann et al., 1970.

———. *Power: Its Forms, Bases, and Uses.* Harper and Row, New York, 1979.

Wylie, J. C. *Military Strategy: A General Theory of Power Control.* Rutgers University Press, New Brunswick, N.J., 1967.

Zartmann, I. William. "Europe and Africa: Decolonization or Dependency?" *Foreign Affairs,* January 1976.

Zawodny, J. K. ed. *Man and International Relations: Contributions of the Social Sciences to the Study of Conflict and Integration,* Vol. I, *Conflict.* Chandler, San Francisco, 1966.

Zimmer, Heinrich. *Philosophies of India.* Pantheon, New York, 1951.

Zorza, Victor. "Computerizing Soviet Society," *Current,* September 1971.

Zuckerman, Michael. "Dr. Spock: The Confidence Man." In Rosenberg, 1975.

Zürcher, Erich. "China: History of," *Encyclopaedia Britannica,* 15th ed.

ACKNOWLEDGMENTS

The path that has led me at last to the publication of *The Parable of the Tribes* has been consistently arduous and at times frighteningly lonely. That strain evokes in me a voice that wants to say, "I wish there had been more help and comfort along the way!" But after giving that voice its say, I am led to recollect that this was a path I freely chose—or one that I willingly accepted when it was laid before me by One greater than myself—and that whatever its hardships I never wanted another.

Having acknowledged that to myself, the voice of complaint is dispelled, making way for me to feel my gratitude.

I am grateful first of all to two good women without the support of whose love I would never have been able at two crucial junctures to climb the mountain to see what was there for my seeing: M. R. in 1970, and G. H. in 1975.

Then there are the institutions and people who helped clear out a sufficient niche in the world for me that I could come in out of the cold as I pursued this work.

I am grateful to the Danforth Foundation for supporting my studies from 1970 to 1973. I give thanks also to the Graduate Theological Union in Berkeley, California, for being willing to see whether, with freedom, I might be able to achieve the purpose I had set before myself, rather than assuming that I could not or dismissing that purpose as irrelevant because it had arisen from within me.

The men who comprised my doctoral committee deserve my gratitude for that same willingness. I know they are rare because it took over a year of constant searching to find five like them. Professor David Steward, of the Pacific School of Religion, was kind and supportive to me as the chairman of the committee. It is difficult for me to overstate how deeply I appreciate the encouragement I received from the late Professor Jeffrey Smith, from our meeting at a Danforth interview in 1970 until the completion of my doctoral work seven years later. My thanks also to Dr. Robert Somers, then of the Institute for Research in Social Policy in Berkeley, California; to Professor Michael Rogin, of the University of California, Berkeley; to Professor Norman Gottwald, of the Graduate Theological Union; and to Professor John Dillenberger, then also of GTU, who joined the committee at the end.

My gratitude to the Ford Foundation, and particularly to Richard Sharpe, who was then a Program Officer there, for the two-year grant that enabled me to transform my 1600-page doctoral dissertation into the present book. I would also like to thank Professor Marvin Bressler, of Princeton University, and Dr. Robert Fuller, then of Worldwatch Institute, for their support along the way.

I am grateful to the people at the University of California Press for bringing the book out, and for joining me in caring about it. In particular, my thanks to my editor, John R. Miles, who believed in this book early on.

Finally, I want to thank the many people in my life, friends and family, whose caring for me warmed me in the wilderness.

INDEX

Absolute monarchies, role of warfare in creation of, 98

Absolute rule, trend away from, 93–94

Absorption and transformation, 21–22

Acheson, Dean, 70n

Acquired characteristics, transmission of, through learning, 15–16

Actaeon, myth of, 263–264

Adams, Richard N., 85, 255

Adams, Robert: on history of early civilizations, 324; on religious imagery of Meso-American Indian, 80

Ad Beatissimi (Benedict XV), 106

Adrenalin society, modern civilization as, 111–114, 325

Advertising, modern, 314; as form of socialization, 315–316

Affluence: in primitive societies, 182; and satisfaction of human needs, 182; and surcease from toil, 176

Afghanistan, 127; as Soviet Vietnam, 124

Africa, 127; cultural boundaries vs. national borders in, 40; cultural transformation of, 52; destruction in, of last primeval ecosystems, 248; destruction of native cultures in, 45; southern, 84; survival of primitive societies in, 43

African(s), psychological alteration of, with modernization, 178

Age of Absolutism, The (Beloff), 94

Aggression, 186; channeling, 163–165; in children, 160–162, 163; and chronic emergency in modern societies, 111–

112; defensive, and escalation of conflict, 70; Freud's theory of, 161–162, 193, 194; and modern warfare, 166–167; primate, in captivity, 135–136; in primitives, 160

Aggression, collective, 31, 162n; channeling individual aggression into, 164–165; displacement and, 164; social requirement for, 164; and warfare, 163–164, 166–167

Agrarian societies: attitude toward nature, 258; exploitation by ruling class in, 274–275; and greater potential for development of power, 58; planning in, 177; and predations of nomadic "barbarians," 57; size of, 81–82. *See also* Agricultural revolution; Agriculture

Agricultural revolution, 252; and civilizing of primitive world, 38; labor required by, 91, 176; and need for planning, 177

Agricultural societies. *See* Agrarian societies; Horticultural societies

Agriculture, emergence and development of: and advantages over hunting and gathering, 68; and emergence of civilization, 17–18; population pressures as cause of, 66–68; and restructuring of human social life, 68; and rise of warfare, 77, 79; why adopted by primitive societies, 64–68. *See also* Agrarian societies; Agricultural revolution

Aho, 187n

Prussia, 99–100, 113, 288; role of force in unification of, 85, 98
Psychoanalysis, 3, 36; Western cultural environment and, 191–192. *See also* Freud, Sigmund
Psychoanalytic Theory of Neurosis, The (Fenichel), 191–192
Psychological Care of Infant and Child (Watson), 158
Psychological evolution, rise of civilization and, 155–211. *See also* Freud, Sigmund; Reason, rationality
Psychology: as biology, 36; and development of capitalism/democracy, 188–189
Psychopathology, sadism and lust for power, 169
Psychosomatic ailments, 322
Psychotherapy, humanistic, 231
Pulliam, H. Ronald, 220
Punishment, for expressing anger, 162–163
Puritan ethic, erosion of, 179
Puritanism, contrasted with Confucianism, 259–260
Puritans, attitude toward nature, 260
Pursuit of Loneliness, The (Slater), 185
Pygmies, Ituri forest, 80

Quiatt, Duane D., 76, 321
Quintana Roo, survival of, by withdrawal, 43

Radical individualism, 205
Radical theory: danger of, 285; and perpetuation of injustice, 228
Radomysler, A., 303
Rage: channeling, 193; disciplining, 186
Raglan, Lord, on hunter vs. headsman, 176
Randal, Judith, 303n
Ranke, Leopold, on formation of French state, 99
Rationalism: as characteristic of Western civilization, 196–197; Confucian vs. Puritan, 260; and loss of meaning and value, 200–204. *See also* Reason, rational thinking
Rationality, functional, 197, 198, 200, 208; and evil, 203; and means and ends, 202
Rational man of economics. *See* Economic man

Rawls, John, on just society, 240
Reagan, Ronald: awareness of necessity and overeager embrace of struggle for power, 127–128; and nuclear arms race, 128–129; simpleminded view of world, 129
Reality principle, 183; vs. pleasure principle, 152, 174–175
Reason, rational thinking, 194–208, 273n; and alienation, 201, 205–208; definition, 195; dominance of, in modern psyche, 207; and human nature, 196; as instrument of violence, 205n; objective validation of, 195–196; and power, 197, 202; powers of, 194–196, 198, 202; and progress, 196–200; and rationalism, 200–204; and subordination of natural impulse, 321–322; and severance from basic values, 197. *See also* Rationalism; Rationality
Receptive character, Fromm's, 171, 172
Redfield, Robert, 43, 52n, 92, 258; and stoic peasant, 171, 172
Redistribution of wealth, 69, 304–306
Reductionism, 254; applied to evolution of civilization, 36; in heroic view of history, 62; parable of tribes vs., 24–25; and Western scientific tradition, 35
Reiche, Reimut, on anal character type, 177
Relationships, human, effect of alienation on, 205–208
Religion: civilized, moral anguish expressed in, 154; and discipline, 187n; and displacement of present by future, 178–180; and materialism, 319; teachings of, to support work ethic, 176n, 185; use of, to motivate human will, 106
Religious imagery, changing, with emerging civilizations, 80
Renfrew, Colin, 53
Renunciation, ethic of, 178
Repression: of instinctual drives, 152–153; and internalization of conflict and social order, 191–192
Republic (Plato), 239, 262
Resistance, meaningful, to intersocietal threat, 52–53
Resource exhaustion, 225n
Resources, control of: and disregard for human welfare, 101–103; for economic growth, 177–178; and mobilization for

Designer: Kitty Maryatt
Compositor: Publisher's Typography
Printer: Vail-Ballou
Binder: Vail-Ballou
Text: 11 pt. Baskerville
Display: Baskerville
Indexer: Kathryn M. Tidyman